INNER EXPLORATIONS
VOLUME IV

EAST-WEST CONTEMPLATIVE
DIALOGUE

Inner Explorations: Collected Works

Most of these books are online at http://www.innerexplorations.com, and they are also available in print.

Volume I: Christian Mysticism:
From St. John of the Cross to Us: The Story of a 400 Year Long Misunderstanding and What it Means for the Future of Christian Mysticism

Volume II: Christian Theology:
Mind Aflame: The Theological Vision of One of the World's Great Theologians: Emile Mersch

The Inner Nature of Faith: A Mysterious Knowledge Coming Through the Heart

Is There a Solution to the Catholic Debate on Contraception?

Volume III: Christian Philosophy:
Mysticism, Metaphysics & Maritain: On the Road to the Spiritual Unconscious

The Mystery of Matter: Nonlocality, Morphic Resonance, Synchronicity and the Philosophy of Nature of Thomas Aquinas

Volume IV: East-West Contemplative Dialogue:
God, Zen and the Intuition of Being

Christianity in the Crucible of East-West Dialogue: A Critical Look at Catholic Participation

Volume V: Jungian Psychology:
Tracking the Elusive Human, Vol. 1: A Practical Guide to C.G. Jung's Psychological Types, W.H. Sheldon's Body and Temperament Types, and Their Integration

Tracking the Elusive Human, Vol. 2: An Advanced Guide to the Typologcial Worlds of C.G. Jung, W.H. Sheldon, Their Integration, and the Biochemical Typology of the Future

Volume VI: Jungian-Christian Dialogue:
Jungian & Catholic? The Promises and Problems of the Jungian-Christian Dialogue

St. John of the Cross & Dr. C.G. Jung: Christian Mysticism in the Light of Jungian Psychology

Volume VII: Simple and Sustainable Living:
The Treasures of Simple Living: A Family's Search for a Simpler and More Meaningful Life in the Middle of a Forest

Christianity in the Crucible of East-West Dialogue
A Critical Look at Catholic Participation

and

God, Zen and the Intuition of Being

James Arraj

Inner Growth Books

Copyright © 2001 by James Arraj.

All rights reserved.

Printed in the United States of America.

This is the first edition of *Christianity in the Crucible of East-West Dialogue*, and the second edition of *God, Zen and the Intuition of Being*, which first appeared in 1988.

ISBN 0-914073-03-6

To Philip St. Romain

Christianity in the Crucible of East-West Dialogue

A Critical Look at Catholic Participation

Table of Contents

A Short Orientation 11

Introduction 13
   Enlightenment Experiences 14
   Metaphysical Experiences 15
   Christian Mystical Experiences 15
   The Structure of This Book 17

Part I: A Pilgrimage Through East-West Dialogue 19

Chapter 1: Buddhist-Christian Dialogue 19
   The Sanbo Kyodan 20
   David Loy's Questionnaire 21
   An Informal Survey 22
   Koun Yamada's Questions to Christians 22
   Ruben Habito 23
   Hugo Enomiya Lassalle 27
   Willigis Jäger 29
   Elaine MacInnes 32
   Patrick Hawk 34
   Chwen Jiuan Agnes Lee and Thomas Hand 35
   Robert Kennedy 37
   Roger Corless 40
   Maria Reis Habito 40
   A Closer Look at the Sanbo Kyodan 42
   Thomas Merton 45
   Donald Mitchell, Robert Jonas, James Grob 49
   Heinrich Dumoulin 51
   Hans Waldenfels 53
   Ichiro Okumura 53

Kakichi Kadowaki 54
A Buddhist-Christian Dialogue at Naropa Institute 55
The Ground We Share 56
David Hackett 57
Modern Attempts to Renew the Christian Contemplative Life 59
Centering Prayer 59
John Main 61
Vipassana Meditation and John of the Cross 61
Hans Küng 62

Chapter 2: Hindu-Christian Dialogue 67
Modern Hindu-Christian Dialogue 67
The Current State of the Hindu-Christian Dialogue in India 68
Abhishiktananda 69
Jacques Dupuis on Abhishiktananda 73
Bettina Bäumer 75
Sara Grant 77
Abhishiktananda Through Advaitan Eyes 78
Anthony de Mello 79
Bede Griffiths 80
Wayne Teasdale 85
Kundalini Yoga 87
Philip St. Romain 89
The Personal and the Impersonal 90
Duality and Nonduality 91
Concepts Eastern and Christian 92
Core Experiences and the Culturally Conditioned Nature of Language 92
The Christian Life of Prayer and Eastern Ways of Meditation 93

Part II: A Crisis in Catholic Theology 96

Chapter 3: Theology Without a Net 96
Christian Mysticism 96
Christian Metaphysics 97
Christian Theology 98
Theology Without a Net 101
Ivone Gebara 102

Tissa Balasuriya 105
Michael Morwood 107
Diarmuid O'Murchu 110
Daniel Maguire 111
John Dourley 113
Conclusion 117

Chapter 4: Religious Pluralism 121
Salvation Outside the Church 121
Anonymous Christians 123
Jacques Maritain and the First Act of Freedom 124
Two Fundamental Principles 126
Paul Knitter 130
Joseph O'Leary 137
John Keenan 144
Jacques Dupuis 147
Dominus Iesus 149

Chapter 5: What Kind of Dialogue? 156
Catholic Pluralism 157
Christian Philosophy 159
The Nature of Theology 162
Two Kinds of Mysticism 165
Louis Gardet 166
R.C. Zaehner 167
Jan van Ruusbroec 168

Part III: A Metaphysical Dialogue 172

Chapter 6: Islamic Metaphysics 172
Hadi ibn Mahdi Sabzawari 173
Toshihiko Izutsu 173
Historical Background 174
Mulla Sadra 175
Fazlur Rahman 180
Creator and Creation 182

Chapter 7: A Dialogue with Nonduality? 187
Ippolito Desideri 187
Geshe Rabten 188

Dzogchen 190
A Dialogue with Nonduality 191
Toshihiko Izutsu 192
Ibn 'Arabi 193
Chuang-tzu 194
David Loy 196

Chapter 8: The Metaphysics of St. Thomas and Enlightenment 203
Zen Enlightenment and the Intuition of Being 205
A Christian View of Enlightenment 209
The Loss of the Affective Ego 210
Philosophical Language vs. Liberation Language 211
Western No-Self Experiences 212
The Loss of the Affective Ego and Individuation 215
The Loss of the Affective Ego and Christian Mystical Experience 215
Philip St. Romain 216
Bernadette Roberts 218
St. John of the Cross and the Loss of the Affective Ego 220
On the Nature of the Loss of the Affective Ego 225
The Spiritual Unconscious 226
Enlightenment and the Experience of No-Self 227

Summary and Conclusions 229
Christian Mysticism and Metaphysics 229
Catholic Theology 230
Christian Enlightenment? 232

Bibliography 235

Index 247

A SHORT ORIENTATION

In my earlier *God, Zen and the Intuition of Being*, which is included in this volume, and in part of *Mysticism, Metaphysics and Maritain*, I had sketched out the possibility of a dialogue between the metaphysics of Thomas Aquinas and Zen, and tried to show that there could be a Christian metaphysical explanation of enlightenment. In this book I wanted to explore that path further, and that is what I have done, especially in *Part III*.

But as I wandered through the worlds of Buddhist-Christian and Hindu-Christian dialogue, I began to realize there was a whole dimension to these dialogues that I had not really paid much attention to. I had imagined that the heart of these dialogues was about trying to fathom the luminous wisdom found in the East, and bringing it into relationship with Christianity's own deep metaphysical, theological and mystical traditions, and I still believe that to be the case. But I had not realized how estranged some Catholics were from these traditions.

The result is that they see the beauty of the East, but instead of being stimulated by it to bring forth the treasures of Christianity so that deep can speak to deep, they don't see these treasures, and end up trying to enrich Christianity by reinterpreting it in Buddhist or Hindu categories, and by doing so, impoverish it. So this book is going to alternate between what I see as the deficiencies of some of the Catholic participants in East-West dialogue, and the dialogue that could take place between enlightenment and the metaphysics of St. Thomas, and it is going to try to accomplish both these goals by asking whether Eastern enlightenment is the same as Christian contemplation, or Christian metaphysical insight.

A Note on Terminology

I will use the words *advaita*, or nonduality, natural mysticism, and mysticism of the self, as equivalent ways to refer to the central core experience of enlightenment to be found in the different religions of the East.

INTRODUCTION

MYSTICS, METAPHYSICIANS AND MEDITATION MASTERS

All too often the world has ridden to war under the banners of religion. But in sharp contrast to this terrible fact is the growing dialogue between Christianity and Eastern religions that is spreading around the globe and entering deep into the hearts of its participants. Part of this dialogue has been highly visible: the Assisi meeting of world religious leaders, the Universal Declaration of Nonviolence, the World Parliament of Religions in Chicago, the UNESCO meeting in Barcelona on the contribution of religion to the culture of peace, etc.

But there is another dimension of dialogue which is no less promising, the dawning encounter of the contemplatives of each tradition. A Japanese Zen master staying at the 1,000 year old monastery of Montserrat in Catalonia makes his way up the mountain side to the hut of a Benedictine hermit, and finds a scroll of the Heart Sutra on his wall. The Bhagavad-Gita is sung on the banks of the Kaveri River in Tamil Nadu in southern India, as it has been for ages past, but this time it comes from the lips of a Christian guru in the robes of a Hindu sannyasi at the ashram of Shantivanam. An American Zen master in the lineage of Koun Yamada Roshi begins a sesshin, or Zen retreat, but he is also a Catholic priest, and most of the participants are Christians.

What would a Tibetan monk or a wandering Hindu holy man have to say to a Christian contemplative in the tradition of John of the Cross? Or what would a Zen master say to a Christian metaphysician who is following in the footsteps of Thomas Aquinas? In such dialogues each would have to try to articulate the inner experience at the heart of his or her own spiritual tradition. Let's try to get a glimpse of what these experiences are like.

Enlightenment Experiences

In 1953, Koun Yamada was a 47-year-old Japanese businessman and a Zen student under the direction of Yasutani Roshi when he had an enlightenment experience that transformed his life. His account of this experience is all the more fascinating because it was Yamada's own Catholic students who were to play a major role in bringing Zen into the Catholic Church. One day Yamada was riding home on a train when he read the traditional Zen saying that goes: "I came to realize clearly that Mind is no other than mountains and rivers and the great wide earth, the sun and the moon and the stars." And he felt that he had finally realized what this statement meant, and tears began to come to his eyes. He went home with a feeling of great expectancy. "At midnight I abruptly awakened. At first my mind was foggy, then suddenly that quotation flashed into my consciousness: "I came to realize clearly that Mind is no other than mountains and rivers, and the great wide earth, the sun and the moon and the stars." And I repeated it. Then all at once I was struck as though by lightning, and the next instant heaven and earth crumbled and disappeared. Instantaneously, like surging waves, a tremendous delight welled up in me, a veritable hurricane of delight, as I laughed loudly and wildly: "Ha, ha, ha, ha, ha, ha! There's no reasoning here, no reasoning at all! Ha, ha, ha!" The empty sky split in two, then opened its enormous mouth and began to laugh uproariously: "Ha, ha, ha!"[1] That morning his teacher told him that he had reached a wonderful degree of insight called "Attainment of the emptiness of Mind." [2]

A woman described a similar experience like this: "While I gaze at 'nothingness,' I perceive the sound of raindrops and the wind rustling through the trees, and steps in the night. From afar the clear voice of a bird is heard. Already it is dawn and in the morning sun the dew sparkles on the tips of leaves. It is as if the whole sun came pouring down drop by drop. Oh, what glory! Oh this splendor, this vastness is nothingness; like the great ocean, all is nothingness. From the depths of my body tears gush forth in solitude."[3]

This is the kind of experience that the Zen master Fumon wrote about in his death poem:[4]

Magnificent! Magnificent!
No-one knows the final word.
The ocean bed's aflame,
Out of the void leap wooden lambs.

Metaphysical Experiences

There are also metaphysical experiences that are at the heart of the Christian metaphysical tradition, and which seem to have a deep analogy with enlightenment. Raissa Maritain talks of one that happened to her in 1905 soon after visiting the cathedral at Chartre. She was "on a journey and watching the forests glide by" her car window. "I was looking out of the window and thinking of nothing in particular. Suddenly a great change took place in me, as if from the perception of the senses I had passed over to an entirely inward perception. The passing trees suddenly had become much larger than themselves, they assumed a dimension prodigious for its depth. The whole forest seemed to be speaking and to speak of Another, became a forest of symbols, and seemed to have no other function than to *signify* the Creator."[5]

Another woman told me of a similar experience:" One afternoon I was sitting in my kitchen. As the sun went down it came through the window and struck a single yellow daffodil. The sun illuminated it to such a degree that the light seemed to come from within it, and I was overwhelmed by the isness of the flower, its very act of existence. Breathlessly I stared at the wonder of it all, and felt drawn to the Creator of this isness, this miracle of being."

Christian Mystical Experiences

There are also Christian contemplative experiences like those at the heart of the writings of Teresa of Avila and John of the Cross. These kinds of experiences still take place today.

A father of six children and a lay Carmelite describes the mystical experience that came to him many years before and led to his conversion to Catholicism. After a car crash he was reading Paramahansa Yogananda's *Autobiography of a Yogi*, and began to interiorly to reach out to the God described there: "In this act of believing I was giving my heart and mind to this living God whose name I did not know other than he was the only one, true living God, and He was the God of love, and He was honest, truthful. I was giving my heart to Him in trust, in belief, and He was giving Himself back to strengthen that, or affirm that that act is true, is acceptable... It was a reciprocal ongoing thing. That's how I would describe it. It wasn't just me making acts as I think most humans conceive of the acts of religion that we make. We just make them, but we never get anything back. There is no conscious existential reciprocity. What I went through at that time was a living experience. So exciting."[6]

A married American business woman describes this kind of contemplation like this: "What I experience as infused contemplation is an awareness of something from God coming down into me, and it is tangible. It is not physical, but it is just as tangible as touching something that is physical. And I also experience that a part of me is drawn up into God and held in God, and it feels like my attention is held in God. The amount of my attention that is held in God varies. There are times when my attention is held in God, and my mind can in a way wander at the same time, but this sense of being held remains. That's kind of hard to describe, but there are degrees of how much I feel absorbed into it."[7]

John of the Cross expresses this relational love mysticism in one of his greatest poems, "The Spiritual Canticle" where he writes:

Where can your hiding be,
Beloved, that you left me thus to moan
While like the stag you flee
Leaving the wound with me?
I followed calling loud, but you had flown.[8]

It is the relationships among these three kinds of experiences that we are going to explore. Are they simply the same? It is hard to imagine that Fumon and John of the Cross had the same kind of experience, and then wrote the radically different poems that they did. At the same time, all three experiences seek to somehow know and experience the absolute, the ultimate ground of things.

Is the deepest wisdom of the East, the very experience of enlightenment, the same as what happens in Christian metaphysical or mystical experience? This is the primordial question that is at the heart of the East-West dialogue. If up until now this question has often been in the background, in the future I believe it will become more and more visible and unavoidable. It is a question that radiates tremendous energy that influences all we say and do. This is a question that is surrounded with such difficulties that some would consider it unanswerable, or even unaskable. But I think it is inevitable. The more the East-West dialogue spreads, and the deeper it goes, the more it will become clear that this question lies at the heart of it.

It is our task to try to make this question more explicit, even to insist on it over and over again, first from one direction, and then another, so it begins to emerge from its obscurity. Once this begins to happen we can address it more directly and begin to try to answer it.

The Structure of This Book

In *Part I, Chapter 1* we look at the fascinating dialogue between Christianity and Zen Buddhism, especially on the part of the Catholic Zen students of the Sanbo Kyodan School.

Chapter 2 focuses on the Hindu-Christian dialogue, especially the interior dialogue that the Benedictine monk, Henri Le Saux called Abhishiktananda, carried on between his Christian faith and the path of advaitan, or nondual, Vedanta he tried to live out in India. These two chapters alert us to the serious challenges that East-West dialogue pose for Christian belief, for we see tendencies on the part of Christians to refashion Christianity in the light of the Eastern forms of meditation they are practicing.

Part II, Chapter 3 looks at the historical and psychological dynamics of contemporary Catholic theology that underlie, in part, these tendencies towards the reformulation of Christianity.

And *Chapter 4* examines how these same dynamics play a role in the current formulations concerning the central theological questions of God's universal salvific will and the role of Jesus in the salvation of all people.

Chapter 5 states that there are, in fact, two fundamental kinds of mysticism, and thus, two kinds of East-West dialogue. In one, Christian love mysticism looks for partners in the deep devotional currents of Hinduism and Buddhism – which is a dialogue we are not going to pursue here – and in the other, Eastern enlightenment needs to find the most suitable Christian partner.

Part III hopefully demonstrates that this partner is Christian metaphysics. *Chapter 6* introduces Christian metaphysics indirectly by way of Islamic metaphysics.

Chapter 7 touches on the metaphysical dimension that exists in Tibetan Buddhism, and goes on to ask whether there could be a dialogue between Eastern nonduality and Christian metaphysics.

Chapter 8 looks at a Christian metaphysical explanation of enlightenment, and explores how the question of the existence of a self can allow us to put this East-West metaphysical dialogue into a wider context. By way of conclusion, we look at the question of whether it is advisable, and in what fashion, for Christians to practice Eastern forms of meditation.

Notes

1. Kapleau, Philip. *The Three Pillars of Zen*, p. 205.
2. Ibid., p. 206.
3. Dumoulin, Heinrich. *Zen Enlightenment.* p. 146.
4. Takahashi, Shinkichi. *Afterimages.* p. 38.
5. Maritain, Raissa, *We Have Been Friends Together.* P. 115-116.
6. Patchett, Joseph. *A Contemplative Journey: Video.*
7. *A Visit with a Contemplative: Video.*
8. John of the Cross, *Poems,* "The Spiritual Canticle" p. 31. Translated by Roy Campbell.

PART I

A PILGRIMAGE THROUGH EAST-WEST DIALOGUE

CHAPTER 1

BUDDHIST-CHRISTIAN DIALOGUE

Is the Christian life of prayer and contemplation the same as the Zen-Buddhist life of meditation leading to enlightenment? Is there a role that Christian metaphysics could play in such a dialogue? These are questions that inexorably are addressing themselves, whether consciously or not, to the Catholic participants of the Buddhist-Christian dialogue, and are questions which have tremendous theological ramifications which concern the very identity of Christianity, itself. What I want to do here is to set the stage to begin to answer them by seeing what these Catholic participants have had to say about them.

Two points, however, should be kept in mind. There is much more to Buddhism than the expression it finds in the nondual doctrine of Zen that has so attracted Christians. Buddhism possesses deep devotional currents. Secondly, in our search we are going to take a brief look at what many leading Catholic figures in the Buddhist-Christian dialogue have said about our subject. This will sometimes show them at a disadvantage, for it is not a question that they have often addressed directly, and that impression should be balanced by the realization that there is much more to their work than what we are focusing on here.

The Zen-Christian dialogue is perhaps the most intensive and extensive dialogue that Christians have been carrying out with the East. Nowhere has the impact of East-West dialogue on Christians been greater. Many Christians have taken up the practice of Zen meditation, and some have even become Zen teachers and are spreading this practice of meditation around the whole Christian world. This makes our questions even more pressing.

The Sanbo Kyodan

The Sanbo Kyodan, or the Three Treasures Teaching Association of Kamakura, Japan, was created in 1954 by Yasutani Hakuun Ryoko (1885-1973) who was a student of Harada Daiun Sogaku (1871-1961) both of whom drew on Soto and Rinzai Zen. Yasutani's successor was Yamada Koun Zenshin (1907-1989). He was succeeded as the head of the Sanbo Kyodan by Kubota Akira (1932-) and Kubota's dharma successor Yamada Masamichi (1940 -) who is Yamada Koun's son.[1]

Yamada Koun was particularly open to Catholic priests and sisters, and it is from this lineage that many of the Catholic Zen masters who are at the forefront of the Zen-Christian dialogue have come, directly or indirectly. Among them we can mention Niklaus Brantschen, Pia Gyger, Ruben Habito, Thomas Hand, Patrick Hawk, Willigis Jäger, Robert Kennedy, Hugo Lassalle, Elaine MacInnes, Kathleen Reiley, AMA Samy, Ana Maria Schlütter, and others.[2]

These students have created centers around the world, and they, in their turn, are training their own students and granting them permission to teach. Therefore, the Zen-Christian dialogue is not only a theoretical question for Catholic theology and spirituality. Zen is entering deeply into the Catholic Church, and it cannot help but raise difficult questions. Our question here is how Zen enlightenment relates to Christian contemplation and metaphysics, and it brings in its wake many other questions. When, for example, the Catholic Zen teachers give a Zen-Christian retreat, are they doing Zen, or Christian prayer? Or do they believe that they are the same? Or when, for example, they are training their own students, are they training them in Zen, or Zen and Christianity, so that as a result their students are rooted in both traditions? If they are training them only in Zen, what does this say about their understanding of the relationship between Zen and Christianity?

Yamada Roshi once asked one of his students who was a Catholic sister, ""What is the relation between Emptiness and God?" Without the least sign of trepidation she answered, "Emptiness is God. God cannot be thought of as other than emptiness.""[3] This answer could be taken as a symbol of both the great potential that exists in East-West dialogue, and yet, at the same time the problematical response of Catholics to this dialogue. There is a very profound way in which it can be said that emptiness is God, but this entails the Christians not only saying this from a Zen point of view, but fathoming this statement from a Christian metaphysical point of view. The second statement, "God cannot be thought of as other than emptiness," raises questions not only about the relationship between this Zen insight and the Christian metaphysical tradition, but with how we can understand it in the light of Christian faith and the Christian mysteries, themselves.

David Loy's Questionnaire

There is, perhaps, no better symbol of the kind of questions we are going to try to address in this chapter, and the difficulty in answering them, than the story of David Loy's questionnaire on the relationship between Zen and Christian practice. Loy, an American Buddhist living in Japan, and himself a student of Yamada Roshi, as part of his preparation for an article called "A Zen Cloud? Comparing Zen *Koan* Practice with *The Cloud of Unknowing,*" sent a questionnaire to the Christian students of Yamada which, in 1987, consisted of twelve priests, ten sisters, and one Protestant minister. But, he tells us, "the results were disappointing. Only four responded, plus one non-Christian Zen teacher. Of those, the replies were roughly divided between those who had found it a good introduction to Zen practice and those who found *The Cloud* opaque and not very satisfying. But everyone emphasized the importance of keeping the two paths separate in order not to confuse them, and the general sentiment was that a path as well developed as Zen has no need for such supplementation. The most interesting result of my inquiries was a division among Christian Zen teachers (most of them in Europe), between those who want to maintain a strong distinction between Zen practice and Christian practice, and those who see them as aiming at the same thing and therefore to be eventually united – which seems to mean using mostly Zen practice with Christian terminology. But evidently *The Cloud* has not figured in this debate."[4]

An Informal Survey

I did my own informal survey when preparing for the initial meeting of the working group of the Society of Buddhist-Christian Studies of people practicing in both traditions, which my wife and I helped create with the Zen teacher, Susan Postal, and which was held in Boston in 1992. I wrote to Catholics deeply involved in the Buddhist-Christian dialogue, and asked them what they thought about the relationship between enlightenment and contemplation. Their answers covered a wide spectrum: I can't see the point of the question; I don't think it can be answered; They are essentially the same; They are different; The essential difference comes from Christ. And the responses included a penetrating meditation on the *I AM* in Exodus in relationship to Zen, as well as pointing out Thomas Merton's ideas on the subject. The actual meeting of the working group turned out to be very dynamic with fascinating stories by people deeply involved in both traditions, but it did not directly deal with this fundamental question about enlightenment and contemplation. What did appear very clearly was how many Buddhists with Christian roots felt wounded by their former connections with Christian churches.

It would be rash to base too much on such small responses, but the division among the Christian Zen teachers ought to stay in the forefront's of our minds as we proceed to look at what various Catholics deeply involved in Zen have to say. If they cannot agree among themselves, then we are faced with serious questions with important ramifications for Christianity. Our efforts to address this issue are going to be something like forcing them to answer Loy's survey, perhaps almost against their will, since for the most part they don't deal directly with this issue. However, I think we will find that in final analysis they express themselves strongly in one way or another.

Koun Yamada's Questions to Christians

We might ask why Koun Yamada was so open to having priests

and religious as Zen students. Such openness was certainly not a universal quality among Japanese Zen teachers, but Koun Yamada was a married layman, the administrator of a hospital, married to a doctor, and a student of Yasutani who, in his own way, had broken with the Soto and Rinzai lineages of his time, and criticized them for not focusing on the central importance of attaining *kensho*, or awakening. But if the key in Yasutani's mind was the attainment of enlightenment, and this represents a kind of core experience that transcends the various schools of Zen, then perhaps Yamada was in a special privileged place to carry this idea one step further. If the heart of Zen is the experience of enlightenment, could not Christians attain to this experience while remaining Christians and not becoming Buddhists?

Ruben Habito

The fact of having Christians as students and seeing them advance in their Zen practice could not help but raise questions in Koun Yamada's mind. For a long time he restrained himself from asking these questions lest he confuse his Christian students, but finally, he addressed them to two of his advanced students, Hugo Lassalle and Ruben Habito: "First, why did you not just continue meditational practices following your own Christian tradition instead of coming to Zen? Was there something lacking in Christianity that led you to seek something in Zen, or did you have some dissatisfaction with Christianity that led you to Zen? And also a question to Christians who have had the Zen experience through the *mu koan*: How would you express this experience in your own Christian terms? And a third question: For those who have had the *mu* experience there is given the *koan* about the origin (*kongen*) of *mu*. How would you answer a question about the origin of God?"[5]

Fr. Lassalle answered the first question by explaining that his initial motivation to practice Zen was his desire to enter more deeply into the inner life of the Japanese people, and Zen had enabled him to understand the Christian mystical tradition better.

Ruben Habito's answers went deeper. The practice of Zen had been preceded by his struggle to find meaning in life, and to face the question of God, both before and after he had joined the Jesuits. This search reached a certain culmination in his first breakthrough in Zen:

"... For me the *mu*-experience, triggered by my working on the *koan* of Joshu's dog, literally shook me inside out, and kept me laughing and even crying for about three days, as I remember. People around me must have thought I was going crazy then. I can only say at this point that the experience enabled me to see the truth, the forcefulness, the real reality of what Paul wanted to express in Galatians 2:20 - "It is no longer I that live, but Christ in me!"

"So to answer Yamada Roshi's first and second question in the same breath, I came to Zen in the search for my True Self, and the *mu*-experience was its discovery, the discovery of my total nothingness. And yet this total nothingness is also total everythingness, the discovery of an exhilarating world of the fullness of grace surpassing all expectations, active even before the beginning of the world (Eph. 1:1-11), and one can only exclaim again with Paul, Who can fathom "the breadth and length and height and depth," and Who can "know the love of Christ which surpasses all knowledge"? (Eph. 3:18-19).

"And if you ask the origin of all this, I can only admit I don't know. One can only humbly receive, from moment to moment, the fullness of grace."[6]

It is interesting to note how seamless this integration of Zen is with his prior Christian training, as shown by the natural way in which he has recourse to the Scriptures and the use of the term grace. In the face of such dynamic experience, our question of the relationship between contemplation and enlightenment, still less metaphysics, could easily appear to be the ingrained theological resistance of a Christian mentality dominated by concepts and bereft of experience. Yet, is it possible to see in this passage hints of a unification of Zen and Christianity in which the spiritual practices of both would be identified? Or is there something more nuanced or subtle going on here where it would be possible to say that contemplation and enlightenment are not different, but they are not the same – not one, not two?

In a videotaped interview he describes how he became the first Catholic religious in the circle of Yamada's students to attain *kensho* or enlightenment in November, 1971. Reflecting on whether the Christian experience of contemplation is the same as enlightenment, he tells us that in reading the profound insights to be found in the letters of St. Paul, he found that they "pointed to the same dimension that I somehow felt overwhelmed by in that Zen experience, and so now, reading those passages, became triggers for me to reenter that same experience, and so I boldly say *same* because for me it is the same."[7]

It is important to note that the answer that Ruben Habito gives to Yamada, and probably Yamada's questions, themselves, are cast in the pattern of the classical Zen dialogue. In fact, Habito's answer to Yamada was in the form of the demonstration of a koan, and that was probably what Yamada was asking for.[8] But is it possible to ask these questions from another perspective from the point of view of our pilgrimage through East-West dialogue in order to concretely situate our question?

Why did Christians come to Zen? Did they feel a dissatisfaction with Christianity? It seems that this was often the case, and why wouldn't it be? The Christian mystical tradition had entered into a long, dark night at the end of the 17th century that it was just beginning to recover from at the time of the Second Vatican Council. And the Christian metaphysical tradition of St. Thomas had been handed on in a rather lifeless, conceptual way rather than in the form of an initiation into the mystery of being. As a consequence even candidates for the priesthood were poorly instructed in it. Instead, they were often force-fed an over-conceptualized philosophy and theology – unfortunately, in the name of Thomas Aquinas – that did little to nourish them philosophically and theologically, and still less spiritually. Further, at a certain critical juncture of the life of prayer, which could be called the dark night of the senses in the wide sense of the term, ordinary discursive forms of prayer begin to fail. This failure makes itself felt in the diminishment of consolation and gratification that prayer used to bring, and practical help in resolving this crisis was lacking. Zen, therefore, represented, and still represents, an attractive choice in the face of these deficiencies in Christian philosophy, theology and spirituality. Zen aims at direct experience, and so is a powerful antidote to over-conceptualization.

How can we express the new experience in Christian terms? We can read this question in different ways. One would be to answer it as a koan, as Habito did, and that is probably the way it was meant by Yamada. But there is another way to look at it. We could rephrase the question in terms of what the Christian mystical and metaphysical tradition had to say about the mu experience, or the nature of enlightenment. Unfortunately, it appears that many Christian Zen students, to one degree or another, are unacquainted with or estranged from these mystical and metaphysical traditions. Their over-conceptual presentation has caused them to be held in contempt. Christian Zen students, having tasted the new freedom of Zen experience, can hardly be expected to look kindly on these old conceptual prisons, but the result is that they are unable to answer Yamada's questions in a distinctively Christian way. They are unable to believe that Christian mysticism and metaphysics have the resources to tackle such a difficult issue. Thus, they can tacitly act as if Zen meditation and the Christian life of prayer are the same thing, or they can keep them in separate compartments, but rarely can they find the enthusiasm for dealing with Yamada's questions from a distinctively Christian point of view.

It is much the same case with Yamada's third question about the origin of God. A question about the origin and nature of God is central to any Buddhist-Christian dialogue. Later in this same interview Yamada remarks: "Recently one of my disciples, who is a Benedictine nun, presented to me a book written by a German Catholic priest, subtitled *Foundations for Buddhist-Christian Dialogue*. It was written by Hans Waldenfels, S.J., and the title of the English translation is *Absolute Nothingness*. I was very much impressed with the contents of the book, and it led me to see that what you Christians call God may not be too different from what we are concerned with in Zen. Just the other day I had a meeting with four Catholic priests who have finished the Zen *koan* training, and during our free discussion I asked them about this, and all of them seemed to agree on the common ground of what you call God and what we are concerned with in Zen. Fr. Lassalle came later, and he also shared the same view."[9]

In a very profound way it is possible to say that Zen is about God, or more precisely, it is, indeed, a mystical experience of God, and this is saying a great deal, for then it becomes clear why Christians can and have embraced Zen so deeply. It is rather ironic and sad that Christians who thirst for God fail to find God amidst constant talk about God in Christian theology, and constant prayer exercises and go on to find a certain assuagement of that thirst for God in Zen Buddhism which refuses to talk about God. But as important as it is to recognize that Zen enlightenment can be an experience of God from a

Christian perspective, this does not lead to the conclusion that Zen meditation is the same as the Christian life of prayer, or that their goals are the same. The same God can be approached from different directions and under different formalities.

Hugo Enomiya Lassalle

Hugo Lassalle (1898-1990) was a German Jesuit who was in Hiroshima at the time the atomic bomb was dropped on the city. Later he collected funds to build a cathedral dedicated to world peace, and he was to create a Catholic zendo called *Shinmeikutsu*, or the Cave of Divine Darkness, west of Tokyo. He was one of the first serious Catholic practitioners of Zen in Japan, and he completed his study under Yamada Roshi after many years, and was given permission to teach.

In his *Living in the New Consciousness* he writes about the content of enlightenment that it is the "experience of undivided, absolute reality. This reality can be experienced either as personal or impersonal…

"Hardly anyone today would question whether Zen enlightenment and similar experiences in other non-Christian religions are genuine experiences of the Absolute, even though they are impersonal in nature. Were they personal in nature, they would be the same as an experience of God in the Christian sense… Genuine mystical experience resists all attempts at conceptual expression. This means that anyone who attempts to do so will utilize the categories available, although this, by its very nature, can easily lead to misunderstandings.

"In enlightenment, the Buddhist experiences his deepest self as one with absolute existence, and is strengthened as a result in his faith in the nonduality of all existence. The Christian and anyone who believes in a personal God experiences the self not only in himself, but also in his relationship to an absolute personal reality."[10]

This leaves us a bit with the impression that the underlying experience is the same, but is experienced differently by different people because of their expectations and religious conditioning. But in other places he is more nuanced and states that in both Zen and Christianity "absolute and undivided being is experienced… The distinction resides in the fact that the Zen experience is an apersonal one, while the Christian experience is a personal apprehension of the absolute. The responsive feeling of the recipient is so different that there must also be some essential distinction in the phenomenon, itself."[11]

He also writes, "... if God did not exist there would be no creatures, but the converse does not hold: In the case that not a single atom of the entire universe existed, God would not on that account be less by a single hair than he now is with the whole universe. Hence the Christian, as long as he retains his belief in God, will not be persuaded to relinquish this view even by an experience of satori. To the contrary, he will live this experience as a being-one with God and thus will rather be strengthened in his faith in God."[12] This is a truly Christian sentiment and it would be hard to imagine saying the same thing from a Buddhist perspective.

But we read in his *Zen Meditation for Christians* that the prayer of supernatural recollection is considered a gratuitous gift of God (*gratia gratis data*) by Christians, and in Zen we "see that the same breakthrough is much more probable, and practically a certainty for anyone who practices with fervor and perseverance. It is certainly plausible that many Christian mystics were aided by a special grace from God. But that is not proof that there is no way to achieve the necessary breakthrough by purely natural means."[13] This statement is quite problematical from the point of view of Christian mysticism. If Fr. Lassalle means by supernatural recollection the beginning of infused contemplation according to Teresa of Avila, it would not be correct to say that this supernatural recollection is a *gratia gratis data*, that is, a grace freely given but accidental to the substance of the life of prayer, for contemplation is an integral part of this life. Further, and more importantly, if this gift is a supernatural grace in the sense that it is a free gift of sharing in God's own life in a special way, it cannot be attained by purely natural means, and there is no way to lay siege to heaven to acquire it in the form of some sort of intensive meditation retreat.

It appears that there are two currents in Lassalle's thought about the relationship between Zen enlightenment and Christian prayer and contemplation, and they are not fully integrated. But if there are some important tensions in his thought that need to be resolved, these tensions, and the questions they represent, seem unfortunately to disappear when we look at some of the other Catholic members of the Sanbo Kyodan.

Willigis Jäger

Willigis Jäger is a Benedictine monk, and another student of Yamada Roshi, who when he returned home to Germany after his training he created a Zen-Christian center at Würzburg. We are left in little doubt about his own views about our questions which we find in his *The Way to Contemplation*, and the effects his answer will have on Christian doctrine. He looks at the practice of Zen meditation as a form of contemplation akin to what is found in Teresa of Avila: "Some may ask whether this form of contemplation is really prayer. But those who reach it know for sure that they are praying. It is of secondary importance whether these individuals then use familiar religious formulas to express themselves or – as very often happens – use, instead the general knowledge of profound experience."[14]

He equates Zen's "awareness of one's own being" to the "prayer of quiet" and tells us that this awareness, as well as the words of God and Jesus, must be transcended. "In the end there is not even a person."[15] Unsurprisingly, he shows a predilection for Meister Eckhart and informs us that "God is one and manifold. This is probably a key to an understanding of the Creation story. Creator and creature are one in essence."[16] "... (D)ogmas are simply formulations based on the experiences of profoundly religious human beings. God reveals Himself to them, and their experience finds expressions in myths, rituals and symbols which are culturally conditioned."[17] The formulas of faith are like shells that must be broken to reach the kernel inside. "When all is said and done, the issue for believers is not to discover the life of God in the form of an indwelling. Rather, they must realize that they themselves, as they are, are expressions of the divine."[18] Mystical experience for Jäger seems identical with Zen awakening, and in the process of reaching it all religions become culturally conditioned gropings towards one summit. This, of course, is a radical transformation of Christianity in which it is reinterpreted in Buddhist categories and its own distinctive love mysticism is seen as a lower stage of Zen enlightenment.

In *Contemplation: A Christian Path* Jäger wants to understand mystical experience in the light of Ken Wilber's transpersonal psychology. Wilber describes a prepersonal level, a rational or personal level, and a transpersonal one. The transpersonal, itself, is divided into the subtle – visions and prophesies, for example, – the causal where one experiences union with a personal God, and "the level of pure consciousness, referred to as "the void," "Godhead," "sunyata," "Tathagata," or simply "the ground," "in which" one experiences pure being. At this level, "pure being" is nothing other than that which emerges from it: "form is emptiness, emptiness is form."[19]

Naturally, Wilber's schema suits Jäger quite well, but Jäger does not address the underlying question of whether it is actually correct. The identification of the highest states in all religions is assumed, and most of Jäger's book is a tissue of quotes from Meister Eckhart, *The Cloud of Unknowing,* and John of the Cross, all interpreted in the light of this assumption.

Later we are told that Christian dogma is based on an outmoded model of the universe in which "God is the creator of the universe, and the center of the universe is the earth."[20] But since the cosmology is wrong, then the dogma must be wrong, as well, and we ought to replace it with a *philosophia perennis* which is that highest level of insight to be found in both East and West. Once again, the assumption that Christian dogma is intrinsically dependent on the cosmology of the time in which it was written is not really examined, still less demonstrated. What we have, in essence, is a kind of sleight of hand in which Christianity as it has been traditionally understood vanishes, and then reappears, made over into Eastern categories.

In *Search for the Meaning of Life: Essays and Reflections on the Mystical Experience* Jäger follows the same path we have been tracing. It could certainly be called a mystical path, but it is one cut out of a particular kind of cloth. Peter Heinegg, the translator, calls Jäger a mystical theologian, and tells us that even people well versed in Catholic spirituality might be surprised at what they will find in this collection of lectures. A way of translating that is to say that he realizes that Jäger departs significantly from traditional Christian doctrine and spirituality. And he does. But it doesn't seem to cause him any hesitation. He will tell us: "In the final analysis, how I formulate my experience of Ultimate Reality depends upon whether my understanding of the self and the world is anthropological or cosmic,"[21] which is a sentiment we are going to hear echoed over and over again. For cosmic we should read impersonal, and for anthropological we should read people who still live in the pre-Copernican era and interpret things in terms of a "preeminently personal structure."[22] Christians have redogmatized and repersonalized the fundamental mystical experience that all religions are meant to lead to. "But against the background of continual advances in the sciences and especially psychology, this personalistic bias is looking increasingly problematic. Interpretation of Jesus' life and teaching has not kept pace with scientific findings. Ultimate Reality is transpersonal and beyond the concept of God, cherished by the traditional theistic religions, which lack the cosmic and holistic perspective."[23] We need to overcome the "so-called ontological dualism between God and creation..."[24] And that is what Jesus did.

Mysticism, both East and West, points to the same reality. "The wave *is* the sea, but then again, it *is not* the sea."[25] This is what Christian mysticism is when it "has not been pressed through the sieve of dogmatic theology..."[26] This one mysticism is what we find in Eckhart's godhead, or Teresa's interior castle, or Zen's essential nature. "They all come from the same experience of Being, but because of the differences of time, culture, education, and religious allegiance, they articulated the experience quite differently."[27] But what does this kind of nondualist imperialism do to Christianity? It eliminates its distinctive nature. Let me be clear about this. Used in this way, Zen awakening, which could be a wonderful gift for Christians, becomes destructive to Christianity.

In the West, God and man are essentially separate, we are told. In the East, however, they are of the same essence. If we look at God as a Father who watches over us and of whom we ask for things, we remain "mere beggars."[28] Jäger believes that he is expounding an esoteric school of nondual mysticism. Theology for the most part remains locked up in its archaic ideas. God must be seen as "the totality of everything that exists."[29] "God reveals himself as mind and matter"[30] and can only be really grasped in transcendent experience. "Part of the tragedy of theistic religions is that they overstress history. The truth of a religion, however, lies concealed in its symbols, images, and myths."[31]

The difference that matters between religions can be defined, according to Jäger, in terms of esotericism vs. exotericism. Esotericism is oriented towards inner experience, while exotericism is "based exclusively on scriptures, dogmas, ritual, or symbolism."[32] But the only value in these things is that they point to the one, universal mystical experience, or ultimate reality. Many Christians remain in an infantile state of oral or meditative prayer. They need to learn a more grown-up form of contemplative prayer, and "contemplation is something one can be trained to do."[33] And this, I imagine, is what Jäger sees as what he is doing when he gives a retreat. And he is entirely comfortable in interpreting John of the Cross in the light of this nondual mystical experience that we can be trained to do.

But what is particularly disturbing in all this is his deep separation, even alienation, from traditional Christian faith. "What would happen," he asks, "if we could prove historically that Jesus' bones had been recovered? Would Christianity then be just a bad joke?"[34] He interprets the resurrection in the way we would expect. It has nothing to do with whether Jesus rose or not. "It is an experience that we can have: that our deepest essence is divine, and hence cannot die."[35] Therefore, "If the bones of Jesus were to be found today and it could be proven that he had rotted in his grave, my faith in Jesus would not change in the least."[36] But, of course, we need to ask just what kind of faith in Jesus does he have, and what is sad about all this is that he really doesn't think that he has lost anything.

Elaine MacInnes

Elaine MacInnes, a Catholic nun, went to Japan in 1961 as a missionary, and eight years later became a disciple of Yamada Koun Roshi. In 1976 she set up a Zen center in the Philippines. In her book, *Light Sitting in Light: A Christian's Experience in Zen*, we have another valuable opportunity to see our fundamental question appear through the sincere comments of a Zen-Christian practitioner. She tells us, for example, that she has found "Eastern and Western meditation practices to be quite different, and I use both daily."[37] Later she highlights this difference by saying that Christianity creates a relationship to the transcendental God, "a relationship that implies "the other."[38]

But what is the relationship between them? "I used to feel the word 'communion' was apt in describing Zen prayer, but now I feel perhaps 'participation' is closer to what's happening, where one's whole being is unimpededly as it were, infused with the Divine.

"However, when I entered the convent in 1953, it was almost impossible to find a teacher for guidance in contemplation. At best, one is told that mystical prayer is God's gift and one can only ask for it. I was fortunate enough to find a book which kept me on the path. I had to come to the Orient to learn that there are teachers in this Way and there is a practice, which will lead to mystical experience, although the experience itself is 'a gift from beyond' as Dogen Zenji implied."[39]

We are left with the impression that relational prayer is to be completed by contemplative prayer, and it is here where the East excels. Yamada Roshi, for example, wanted his Catholic students "to give the Church a shot in the arm, as far as contemplative prayer in concerned."[40] She asks whether Zen meditation is really prayer, and why would Christians need it since they have all different kinds of prayer? And she answers, "My Zen spirituality has been grounded in a specific experience which has led me to appreciate 'Unknowable' and 'Unnameable' as appropriate synonyms for the intimate God of my childhood."[41]

But this still leaves unresolved the basic question of the relationship between these two ways of approaching God. And we can wonder what Buddhists might make of such an explanation, and especially what they would make out of her phrase "Zen prayer." What she seems to be saying is that Christians know discursive ways of praying, but for the deeper ways of silent contemplative prayer it was necessary for her to go to the Orient in order to find a teacher. Christians, too, have this tradition of contemplative prayer, she tells us, and it can be found in John of the Cross, Meister Eckhart, Tauler and many others.[42] And she will associate the breathing of the air of John of the Cross, by which he tries to describe the heights of transforming union, with the emphasis on breathing in Zen meditation.[43] And it came natural for her when summing up her Zen training, to quote Dogen: "I came to realize clearly that Mind is no other than mountains, and rivers, and the great wide earth, the sun and the moon and the stars."[44] And then to immediately cite a passage that she felt was parallel to it from John of the Cross: "My beloved is the mountains and lonely wooded valleys..."[45] And when someone asked her, "Did any of the Christian mystics have a kensho, do you think?" she answered, "The articulation of some of our mystics leads me to think they had that same experience – John of the Cross, Meister Eckhart and Tauler, for example. I often tell Christians that a Buddhist taught me what John of the Cross means by his frequent use of nada, the Spanish word for 'nothing'."[46]

How do we reconcile, then, Sister Elaine's statement that there is a difference between meditation East and West, and the comments we have just seen? Perhaps the only way to do that is to identify Christian contemplation and Zen enlightenment, and have them represent the upper reaches of the life of prayer, while Christian prayer, or relational prayer, represents the lower slopes of the mountain.

Patrick Hawk

Patrick Hawk is a Redemptorist priest and a Zen master in the lineage of Robert Aitkin and Willigis Jäger. In "The Pathless Path," a brief article that appeared in *The Catholic World* in May-June 1989, he describes his early spirituality as following the way of devotion and piety, which way eventually came to a dead-end. "Then one cannot practice as one did before. It is a bewildering time. There is no more consolation; all is dry and seemingly unprofitable."[47] This sounds much like St. John of the Cross' dark night of sense in the wide sense of the term in which the gratification that often comes at the beginning of the life of prayer through spiritual practices fades away. Gradually he found his way out of this impasse by means of Zen. "Somehow Christianity and Zen did not seem to be two ways to me. A pathless path beyond the forms and words of each tradition emerged from within."[48] He studied with Willigis Jäger and tells us: "This was a year of intense practice both of Christian contemplation and Zen."

But given his previous remarks and Jäger's own comments it would not be unfair to ask whether both of them considered Christian contemplation and Zen enlightenment to be the same thing. Later, Fr. Hawk will say, "Training in Contemplation or Zen is done face-to-face. One does the practice year after year, face to face with one's teacher hundreds of times year after year. One personalizes the insight gained through practice in daily life year after year. How does one become a master of Contemplation or Zen?"[49] Does this "or" refer to two different things, or two names for the same thing? The latter choice is not a bad bet, but whether this is explicit with Patrick Hawk is another matter: "How to live in the tension of East and West is similar to how a person lives with the tension of having two arms. With practice one becomes ambidextrous. It is just a matter of doing. Let not your right hand know what your left hand is doing and it is done."[50] But not letting your right hand know what your left hand is doing does not further a dialogue about our central question about whether Christian contemplation is the same as Zen enlightenment, and what relationship it might have with Christian metaphysics.

Chwen Jiuan Agnes Lee and Thomas Hand

Chwen Jiuan Agnes Lee, a member of the Missionary Sisters of the Immaculate Conception, and the American Jesuit, Thomas Hand, who spent 29 years in Japan and was part of the circle of Catholic Zen students around Yamada Roshi, collaborated in writing *A Taste of Water: Christianity Through Taoist-Buddhist Eyes.*

And this subtitle is a rather exact description of what this book is about: "We want to be very clear about what we have attempted to do. From our own study and experience we have tried to look at Jesus of Nazareth and the Christian path through Taoist/Buddhist eyes... One point to be emphasized is that we realize perfectly well that some of our formulations about God, Jesus and human life do differ from conventional Christian teaching, including that of the Catholic Church. We have consistently presented these interpretations not as our fixed positions, but as what we feel the great Taoist and Buddhist masters might say from their enlightened viewpoint. We offer them not as dogmas, but only as options as to how the original Christian teachings may well be interpreted and understood under the impact of contact with the light of eastern philosophies of life. Both of us, as Catholics, are quite happy to ultimately follow the directives of the church community."[51]

Fair enough. But the authors go on to make it clear that their own personal perspectives coincide with that of the great Taoist and Buddhist masters. They ask themselves: "Is there such a thing as a fixed, unchanging tradition or culture or religious consciousness? What does it really mean to be faithful and loyal to tradition?" And they answer: "These questions force us to turn to inner experience as the only foundation for advancement and expansion of consciousness."[52] And they take as their patron Henri Le Saux, Abhishiktananda, who they feel has done from the advaitan, or nondual, point of view what they would like to do from a Taoist and Buddhist one. Let's see what kind of language this perspective gives rise to. While we make clear distinctions, for example, between creatures and God, the human and the divine, nature and grace, and so forth, we need to realize that: "the real God is different from all such categorization. In the final experience of God there is no question of separation, distinction or relationship."[53]

The experience of Ignatius of Loyola as he walked along the banks of the Cardoner River ought to be understood as an experience of enlightenment. "Certainly St. Ignatius of Loyola here joined innumerable men and women of both east and west in the one, simple, basic reality-experience. He has no words like emptiness, *sunyata*, thusness, or tao with which to express the event… More and more we feel that through the impact of far eastern enlightenment, Judeo-Christians can find within their own heritage these very same insights."[54]

Once the perspective is taken in which nonduality is seen as the highest spiritual goal, then conceiving God as a person is seen as an attachment to a human way of understanding God. "Remember that personal always means relational, and relation always means separation. The east says that although it is a helpful approach, personal relationship with God is not the reality we call transpersonal oneness."[55] Then it is only one small step to reinterpreting the doctrine of the Trinity where the word persons is taken "not as indicating three distinct and subsistent relations, but simple convenient, existential terms to express the inexpressible."[56] Once this is done, then we find that there are many insights in the East that can be labeled trinitarian in this sense.

Inspired by Ken Wilber, they find that an evolutionary view of consciousness fits in with this eastern perspective. The traditional Christian understanding of paradise and original sin needs to be revised so that we can now, with Wilber, see "that this paradise was not that of fully realized human beings, but rather a very primitive, infant-like state of awareness which knew nothing of the complexity and fears of modern consciousness."[57] In this way a new understanding of these Christian doctrines emerges: "for centuries the Christian interpretation has to some degree confused this pre-personal security and bliss with that trans-personal union which human nature is oriented toward. The fall from Eden is not really a fall but a rising to a higher level of individuated consciousness!"[58]

Our traditional understanding of Jesus also has to undergo a similar transformation. "Simply put, we would like to say that salvation is not so much a matter of redemption, as en*light*enment."[59] Moses in the Old Testament brought the Jewish people to a personal God, but here there is "still subject-object dualism and always at least a subtle distinction between creature and creator. Jesus, too, maintains this worshipping awareness when he teaches his disciples to pray, "Our Father in heaven." But in the end Jesus himself moves beyond all subject-object dualism. Both his soul and the personal God are dissolved in the void he entered through his radical disidentification, his *kenosis*."[60]

We need to "discover the original inner experience of Jesus and his disciples."[61] But what is this experience but enlightenment, itself? Everything else, "scriptures, dogmas, sacraments, liturgies, etc. – are only skillful means to this end."[62] What Christianity has had up until now are "credal formulas carefully worked out mainly during the first five centuries of church history" which are "basically western expressions of the Christ experience."[63] What we really need, however, are insights from the East to help us rediscover this original inner experience of Jesus. But, of course, just what would be left of traditional Christianity if we did this?

In a videotaped interview Fr. Hand recounts how he went down the hill from the Jesuit Language House in Kamakura to the zendo of Koun Yamada in November, 1967, to become the first priest to sit there. He went on to introduce other religious to this group, like Kathleen Reiley, and later Ruben Habito. In this interview, since he is not taking up a more formal Taoist-Buddhist perspective, he frames what he sees as the principal unresolved problems in the Buddhist-Christian dialogue without formulating answers to them.[64]

Robert Kennedy

Robert Kennedy grew up in the Irish Catholic world of Brooklyn, New York, joined the Jesuits and was ordained in Tokyo in 1965. In the upheavals of the Second Vatican Council he tells us his own religious certitudes were swept away and "most painfully, I lost my way in prayer. The precious words and images and the stately liturgy that sustained me for so long suddenly froze on my lips and in my heart. What a grace that was, though I didn't know it then."[65] This sounds much like the experience of Patrick Hawk. He eventually took up Zen practice with Yamada Roshi and finished his training under Tetsugen Glassman in New York. "Since my installation as a Zen teacher in New York in December 1991, I have been asked by Zen practitioners if I had lost my Catholic faith and didn't know it, or if I had lost it and didn't have the courage to admit it. As far as anyone can answer a question like that, I never have thought of myself as anything but Catholic and I certainly never have thought of myself as a Buddhist. What I lost was a Catholic culture that has now all but disappeared from the American scene. I learned painfully that faith is never to be identified with the cultural forms of any given age, and especially so when that cultural form is taken for granted and deeply loved. While this simple truth may be obvious to the reader, in my experience it was a truth burned into my soul.

"What I looked for in Zen was not a new faith, but a new way of being Catholic that grew out of my own lived experience and would not be blown away again by authority or by changing theological fashion."[66]

He notes that when the Dalai Lama spoke at the John Main seminar in London in 1994 on Christianity, he "resisted all suggestion that Buddhism and Christianity are different languages for the same essential beliefs and said that the two faiths are so different that those who call themselves "Buddhist-Christians" are trying "to put a yak's head on a sheep's body." Behind the enlightening teaching and wise caution of the Dalai Lama, I heard again the words of Yamada Roshi to me: "I am not trying to make you a Buddhist, but to empty you in imitation of your Lord Jesus Christ."[67]

What would Fr. Kennedy say in response to our questions? There is a rich Christian mystical tradition that "parallels Zen meditation."[68] "Zen reminds us, as do Eckhart, Merton, and many other contemplatives, that the highest point of our Christian mysticism is reached not in the experience that I know God or that I love God – not in any I-Thou experience – but in the experience that God lives in us.

"It is most especially in this immanent aspect of contemplative prayer that Zen can confirm and assist the contemplative. Zen gives us a method to put contemplation into practice. The Zen training *sesshin* does not allow the student to analyze or theorize about prayer. Instead it plunges him at the outset into the contemplative act in which there is no subject or object. The koan *mu* in not an object of meditation. Rather, by becoming *mu* in unthinking concentration, the retreatant is no longer aware of an "I" standing against a "Thou." He is aware only of *mu*. Comparing Christianity and Zen mysticism on this point Yamada Roshi gave us a Christian Japanese translation of Paul's letter to the Philippians. The phrase "Jesus emptied himself" reads "Jesus became *mu*." The roshi urged us to become not good Buddhists but good Christians, to become *mu* in imitation of Christ. A Zen *sesshin*, directed by an accomplished master, can help the Christian to achieve precisely this goal."[69]

It must be noted that a transcendence of an I-Thou relationship is problematical even at the deepest levels of Christian mysticism. A John of the Cross or other great Christian mystics, however far they may have traveled by way of via negativa, did not find it necessary to leave the I-Thou relationship aside, and to say that Zen gives us a method to put contemplation into practice, or that the sesshin does not allow the student to theorize about prayer, appears to have already transformed Christian mysticism into Buddhist categories under the guise of freeing it from its limitations. It is already assumed that zazen is prayer, and is contemplation in action, when that is not clear from the Christian point of view at all. Nor is it clear that the kenosis of the *Letter to the Phillipians* is the emptying that Zen promises.

In *Zen Gifts to Christians* Kennedy follows the path of his earlier book. It is mostly a rather lyric appreciation of Zen and what it could do for Christianity, and he rarely deals with the more pointed issues of East-West dialogue that flow beneath the surface of what he is saying. Nor, it might be noted, does he speak about Christian gifts to Zen Buddhists.

He addresses, for example, the issue of the relationship between the creator and creatures, but smoothes away the differences between a Buddhist nonduality, and what could be called a Christian one.[70] When it is a question of emptiness, he asks: "How can the Zen "view" of emptiness – the presence of co-arising "beings" whose selfhood has been hollowed out – ever be a gift for Christians who have been taught to believe in an immutable divine essence?"[71] And he answers: "From so many faiths we come together to sit and meditate in the *zendo*, not to solve a philosophical problem but to experience the emptiness of all our ideas about God and no God, self and no self. Together we enter into the presence of mystery and mutual service."[72] He immediately qualifies this answer, and adds: "However, by no means am I saying this is the only way to practice interfaith dialogue. Indeed some interfaith dialogue takes place precisely to confront philosophical problems."[73] But this is something that he clearly does not want to concern himself with. And while it is true that we may all experience the emptiness of our ideas in zazen, we are still confronted, whether on the meditation cushion or off of it, with whether the experience that Zen leads to is identical to what the life of Christian prayer and contemplation is meant to lead to.

He writes later: "Zen teaches that the absolute simply is unknowable and cannot be known or described through reason. For this reason Zen categorically rejects the various essentialist philosophies that are based on reason and that flourish in both Buddhist and non-Buddhist cultures."[74] And even if we try to balance this by saying, "Zen is not disparaging human reason or philosophical thinking,"[75] we are left with the same kind of question we just saw. If we take the negative Zen view of concepts as normative, where does that leave Christianity and its long-held belief that concepts, whatever their limitations, can say something about the divine mysteries themselves?

The real issue here is not whether Zen has great gifts to give Christianity. It does. But these Zen gifts are wrapped up in a particular way, and need to be unwrapped before they can be truly understood and used in a Christian context.

Roger Corless
Maria Reis Habito

In an incisive but unpublished essay called, "Dual Practice With Form and Without Form: The Doctrinal Consequences," Roger Corless speaks of dual practice, or practice across traditions, by which he means the authentic practice in two traditions where the same person functions as two independent practitioners. From this perspective he criticizes the dual practice of Catholics in the Sanbo Kyodan School of Zen, and suggests that they extract satori, or kensho, from the fullness of Buddhist theory and practice and regard it as the essence of a supposed universal mysticism. To illustrate this process of extraction he looks at a paper, itself unpublished, on Hugo Enomiya Lassalle given by Maria Reis Habito at the 1987 meeting of the Society for Buddhist-Christian Studies where she writes: "Satori as the experience of the absolute occurs in the West as well as in the East, and its interpretation depends on the respective religious background."

Corless comments: "There is assumed to be a common, universal, trans-historical, non-doctrinal, intuitively attained *Urgnosis* which is documented as having been experienced identically by some Roman Catholics and by some East Asian Mahayanists, especially those identified as belonging to a Ch'an or Zen lineage, and this is, we are implicitly assured, also the heart of the experience of other Christians, other Buddhists, and, indeed, all spiritually aware humans in all times and places. When expressed in language, however, this experience degrades into talk of doctrinally limited categories such as Dharmadhatu, Trinity, Tao, Brahman, etc."

While Corless' concern is the failure to have a genuinely dual practice, his remarks shed light on our own preoccupation with the fundamental relationship between enlightenment and contemplation, and metaphysical experience. To the degree that the Catholic members of the Sanbo Kyodan believe that there is a common core doctrine to be found in both Buddhism and Christianity, to that degree they will tend to identify enlightenment with contemplation, and as a secondary effect of that identification, the doctrinal formulations of Christianity will, themselves, become quite secondary if not irrelevant. But it would certainly be premature to ascribe to someone like Maria Reis Habito this kind of facile identification of contemplation with enlightenment for I have heard her speak in a moving way of her own Christian life. She grew up in a deeply Catholic family, and she recounts that once, when she was practicing Zen meditation, and pondering the difficulty in believing that God was love, she had a deep experience of that love flooding the zendo and all the people in it.[76]

This brings us to an important point. In certain cases we have been seeing Catholics whose theological formuations about the relationship between enlightenment and the Christian life could be judged deficient, but as important as this theological level is, it cannot be equated with the inner life of these people. God works in mysterious ways in the depths of our hearts, and we can barely glimpse what is happening there in ourselves, still less in other people.

It is worth commenting for a moment on the phrase dual practice which, itself, causes difficulties similar to our fundamental questions. When it was used at the first meeting of the ongoing working group of practitioners in both traditions at the Boston meeting of the Society of Buddhist-Christian Studies, several people objected strongly to it because they felt that their practice was one thing and not two. But is this not another way of indicating an answer to our question? In a similar way, to use the phrase dual practice could easily be an indication of an inclination to answer the question in the opposite way. Even the similar phrase "practice across traditions" is not without its problems, for it can indicate a practice that somehow transcends the tradition it is rooted in. "Dual practice" in the sense that Roger Corless uses it, in which he practices his Christianity on alternate days with his Tibetan Buddhism, and is a rather dramatic symbol of his openness to our fundamental questions and could be taken as an answer to our question, i.e., the practice is dual because Zen meditation and the life of prayer are two different things.[77] All this illustrates once again how beneath the surface of the current Buddhist-Christian dialogue powerful currents exist generated by our basic issues.

A Closer Look at the Sanbo Kyodan

One of the best accounts of the Sanbo Kyodan is Robert Sharf's "Sanbokyodan: Zen and the Way of the New Religions."[78] Sharf had read Philip Kapleau's *The Three Pillars of Zen* as a teenager, and, like many other people, found it a pleasant contrast to the more theoretical Zen, like that of D.T. Suzuki, that was known in the West before this book's appearance. The heart of the book is the teaching of Yasutani and accounts of his interviews with his students, as well as their descriptions of their kensho, or enlightenment, experiences.

Through the work of Philip Kapleau, Robert Aitken, Maezumi Taizan and others, the teaching of the Sanbo Kyodan has played a major role in shaping American Zen, which stands in contrast to its somewhat marginal status in Japan. Both Harada and Yasutani, although formed in traditional Rinzai and Soto Zen, broke with it and radically criticized these traditions as having become overly institutionalized and letting the intuitive fires of kensho become extinguished. They, in contrast, created a school directly oriented to the attainment of enlightenment, especially though the mu koan. All the rest of Buddhism, that is, Buddhism as a religion with its scriptures, religious ceremonies, cultural forms, doctrines like reincarnation, and the role of study, was given secondary status. The whole enterprise was made to hinge on the attainment of enlightenment through intensive Zen retreats, or sesshins, in which the students were urged to do their utmost to achieve this breakthrough, and many did. And with it came new status within the organization.

Zen masters traditionally have warned against an over conceptual approach to Zen, but as Sharf puts it: "... there is a world of difference between issuing such warnings in a monastic environment where ritual and doctrinal study are *de rigueur*, and issuing such warnings to laypersons with little or no competence in such areas. In short, the Sanbokyodan has taken the antinomian and iconoclastic rhetoric of Zen literally, doing away with much of the disciplined ceremonial, liturgical, and intellectual culture of the monastery in favor of the single-minded emphasis on *zazen* and a simplified form of koan study."[79] The Sanbo Kyodan became a training school of koan study aimed at enlightenment. One student went so far as to call it a "kensho machine." "The published testimonials of sect members vividly attest to the fact that ardent practice can lead to kensho in the space of a year, a month, or even a single sesshin. Indeed, it was the rule, rather than the exception, to find one or two students experiencing their first kensho during each sesshin conducted by Yasutani and Yamada."[80] Once the first breakthrough had been made, progress in dealing with 600 or 700 subsequent koans often went quickly, even at the pace of one koan per interview with the master, and the whole koan course could be done in six years.[81] Another way to put this might be to say that the students were intensively schooled in how to attain enlightenment and then how to express this attainment in the unique "language" of koans.

Stuart Lachs in his online article, "Coming Down from the Zen Clouds: A Critique of the Current State of American Zen,"[82] covers some of the same ground as Robert Sharf, but does so from the point of view of how the emphasis on enlightenment may have caused a certain abstraction in American Zen from the moral dimension of Buddhism.

But we have to ask what effect this departure from traditional monastic Zen has had on the Sanbo Kyodan's Catholic students. Actually, I think these departures and innovations of the Sanbo Kyodan school suited them quite well. They would have had difficulties if they were required to participate in Buddhist religious ceremonies, like the taking of the lay precepts. But their instinctive sympathy went much deeper. Catholic priests and religious in the late 1960s and early 70s were on the rebound from an over-institutionalized Church and an over-conceptualized philosophy and theology. They, like many of their counterparts in the West, craved a more experiential approach to spirituality which, for the most part, they had not found in their Christian spiritual traditions. Therefore, the emphatic statements of the leaders of the Sanbo Kyodan that Zen was not a religion, but a deep and direct experience of reality beyond the words and ceremonies and doctrines of the different Buddhist traditions could only resonate with them because it opened the door to their own participation in Zen practice.

But this whole core doctrine idea found in the Sanbo Kyodan acts like a two-edged sword. While it opens the door for Christian participants, it also tends to carry with it a distinctive view of Christianity in which Christianity, itself, is another embodiment of this same core doctrine that is found in Zen. "Sanbokyodan leaders would not place Christianity and Zen on an equal footing; as mentioned above, they claim rather that Zen is the experiential truth lying behind all religious traditions, Christianity included."[83] Or as Sharf also indicates a little later, following the work of Gavin D'Costa, "Christianity is ultimately explained in terms of Zen."[84] Yamada Koun, himself, put the matter this way: "Almost all Buddhist sects can be called religions. Zazen, however, is quite different in this respect. Quite simply, it is the core of all Buddhist sects. As you know, there are many sects in Buddhism, but the core or essence of them all is the experience called satori or self-realization. The theories and philosophies of all the sects are but the clothing covering the core. These outer wrappings are of various shapes and colors, but what is inside remains the same. And the core, this experience, is not adorned with any thought or philosophy. It is merely a fact, an experienced fact, in the same way that the taste of tea is a fact. A cup of tea has no thought, no idea, no philosophy. It tastes the same to Buddhists as it does to Christians. There is no difference at all."[85]

It would be easy for the Catholic students of Yamada to move, even perhaps unconsciously, from the initial position which says that Zen is an intuitive experience of the essence of Buddhism, and therefore they can practice it as Christians, to the next position which says that what is experienced in Zen is also the essence of Christianity. Then Christianity would, indeed, be interpreted in Buddhist categories, and there would be what could be called a *koanization, or kenshoization,* of Christianity.

It is worthwhile exploring Buddhist-Christian dialogue beyond the circle of the Sanbo Kyodan, for it will give us a better idea of the problems involved and some indications of ways to resolve them.

Thomas Merton

"John of the Cross, who never left 16th century Spain, experienced satori," so writes Christopher Nugent at the beginning of his essay, "Satori in St. John of the Cross" in which he hopes to illuminate the remarks of John Wu, who in 1937, in his book *Beyond East and West* wrote: "…When I read… John of the Cross: "to possess nothing; to be all things, be willing to be nothing" – I understood… and added a word on the margin: "Taoistic"." John Wu's good friend, Thomas Merton, is also quoted as being in agreement with this bold assertion about John of the Cross. "Frankly, I would say that Zen is nothing but John of the Cross without the Christian vocabulary."[86] But as enjoyable as this essay is from a literary point of view, it does not convince us of its principal point. It takes more than St. John's *nada, nada, nada* and emptiness, for beyond certain similarities of language the real issue is what this nothingness gives birth to. For John of the Cross it is the means by which we are transformed by love into God. This language of nothingness is at its deepest level the language of love and an interpersonal mysticism. As far as Thomas Merton's assertion here, we will have to look at that in more detail.

Merton's "Zen is nothing but John of the Cross" was not something that he pondered and then carefully wrote down. Rather, it came at the beginning of a talk he gave to a group of contemplative sisters when he directed a retreat for them at his Abbey of Gethsemani. These talks were transcribed and published in 1992 as *The Springs of Contemplation*, and were sometimes given while he sat with the sisters on the bank of a pond or lake. So what we have here is not a carefully weighed judgment on Merton's part, but more of a spontaneous remark made to a sympathetic audience he felt at ease with, and perhaps would not have minded dazzling a bit.

The whole passage reads: "I'm going to talk about Zen for a while. I've brought with me a book by a German-Japanese Jesuit, Heinrich Dumoulin. I know at least three Japanese Jesuits who are quite interested in Zen. This is a worthwhile book, not the last word by any means, but good. This man has actually been in a Zen monastery and gone through the training. Now instead of the *Spiritual Exercises*, he gives his fellow Jesuits Zen retreats. They're as close to Saint John of the Cross as anything can be. Frankly, I would say that Zen is nothing but John of the Cross without the Christian theology. As far as the psychological aspect is concerned, that is, the complete emptying of self, it's the same thing and the same approach.."[87]

We need to take these words in the same off-hand and casual way that he uses later in the same talk: "Fromm got interested in Zen through his contact with Suzuki, whom he knew quite well. I knew Suzuki, too. At first, we had a long written dialogue. Then we met. In a certain sense, he is my Zen master; he authenticated my understanding of Zen so that I could speak about it with a certain confidence."[88]

Merton was more nuanced in his written works. He distinguished, for example, between natural and supernatural mystical experience. He wrote to Aldous Huxley in 1958: "I would call aesthetic and natural an experience which would be an intuitive "tasting" of the inner spirituality of our own being... or an intuition of being as such arrived at through an intuitive awareness of our innermost reality." In contrast, "a fully mystical experience has in its very essence some note of a direct spiritual *contact of two liberties*, a kind of a flash or spark which ignites an intuition of all that has been said above, *plus* something much more which I can only describe as "personal," in which God is known not as an "object" or as "Him up there" or "Him in everything" nor as "the All" but as – the biblical expression – I AM, or simply AM. But what I mean is that this is not the kind of intuition that smacks of anything procurable because it is a presence of a Person and *depends on the liberty of that Person*."[89] He ends this long letter: "May I add that I am interested in yoga and above all in Zen, which I find to be the finest example of a teaching leading to the highest natural perfection of man's contemplative liberty."[90]

In a 1965 letter to Philip Griggs, a member of the Rama Krishna Mission in California, Merton lays out some basic Christian principles that should shape interreligious dialogue from a Christian point of view. A fervent sadhu could be closer to God than a superficial Christian. At the same time, this does not prevent a Christian from believing that the Church possesses a more perfect doctrine and sacramental system.[91]

Merton goes on to point to one of the key principles of any dialogue between Hindu Vedanta and Christianity: "It cannot be said that a Christian (or at least a Catholic) believes that man is divine by nature. If he did the whole point of Christian teaching would be lost. The Christian belief is, let me state it clearly and without ambiguity, that man is divine *not by nature but by grace*, that is to say that his union with God is not an ontological union in one nature, but a personal nature in love…"[92]

But in 1968, shortly before his death, we have Merton saying, as we have just seen, "Frankly, I would say that Zen is nothing but John of the Cross without the Christian vocabulary." Does this mean that Merton suddenly changed his mind about the principles that he thought governed East-West dialogue? That is not very likely. In an uncompleted manuscript called, *The Inner Experience: Notes on Contemplation*, which Merton may have planned to revise after his Asian journey, and which the Merton Legacy Trust would only allow to be published as a series of articles, he writes: "Satori allows us to observe "the natural working of the inner self"."[93] "For us, there is an infinite metaphysical gulf between the being of God and the being of the soul, between the "I" of the Almighty and our own inner "I". Yet paradoxically our inmost "I" exists in God and God dwells in it. But it is nevertheless necessary to distinguish between the experience of one's own inmost being and the awareness that God has revealed Himself to us in and through our inner self. We must know that the mirror is distinct from the image reflected in it. The difference rests on theological *faith*."[94]

Further, in his 1968 *Zen and the Birds of Appetite* he comments that D.T. Suzuki's *Mysticism: Christian and Buddhist* is, in fact, a comparison between Meister Eckhart and Zen. This kind of comparison has remained popular in Zen circles over the intervening years, but Merton continues, "to take Meister Eckhart as representative of Christian mysticism is hazardous."[95] He is certainly not denying the very Zen-like qualities to be found in Eckhart, but only indicating that Eckhart can hardly be taken as an entirely unambiguous exponent of the Christian mystical tradition. He goes on to indicate his reservations, as well, about a certain kind of thought which takes for granted that all religions meet at the top: "This has never been demonstrated with any kind of rigor..."[96] Later he says, "The basic insights of Buddhism are philosophical and metaphysical," and continues, "Obviously the best way to open a serious dialogue between Christian and Buddhist thought would be to discuss something of the nature of Buddhist enlightenment and to see whether some analogy to it could be found in Christian thought."[97] While there is some merit in comparing Buddhist enlightenment to Christian mysticism and ethics, the most promising meeting-point, in his mind, is metaphysics. This preference for metaphysics is perhaps a reflection, in part, of Merton's intimate knowledge of the Thomist metaphysical tradition, especially as represented by Jacques Maritain. They had corresponded and become friends after the publication of Merton's *Seven Story Mountain*, and several of their letters deal with Maritain's ideas on natural mysticism, or mysticism of the Self, by which he tries to understand enlightenment from a Christian metaphysical point of view, and which we will look at later.

Merton, then, who was well-read in the best of the traditional Thomist philosophy and theology, was well aware that it was possible to speak of both a natural and a supernatural contemplation, and he did so. Supernatural contemplation was the same as the infused contemplation of the Christian mystical tradition, while one of the major forms of natural contemplation was a metaphysical intuition. And when he began to dialogue with Zen, he associated this metaphysical intuition with Zen enlightenment. He writes: "... all the reality that exists, and all the goodness of everything that exists and is good, can be spiritually tasted and enjoyed in a single metaphysical intuition of being..."[98]

If there are two kinds of contemplation, there can be two distinct kinds of knowledge of God. In one, "God is known as "present in the metaphysical depths of everything that is," but he is not known "in His infinite transcendence"."[99]

As Merton entered more deeply in East-West dialogue, he saw the value of applying these fundamental distinctions. As Thomas King puts it in his *Merton, Mystic at the Heart of America*, "The metaphysical intuition provides a better basis for a dialogue with Eastern monks than a contemplation entirely centered on the Judeo-Christian revelation." And King cites Merton to the effect that "... the supernatural Kerygma and the metaphysical intuition of the ground of being are far from being incompatible. One may be said to prepare the way for the other. They can well complement each other, and for this reason Zen is perfectly compatible with Christian belief and indeed with Christian mysticism, if we understand Zen in its pure state, as metaphysical intuition."[100] The night before Merton died in Bangkok, he said: "Zen and Christianity are the future."[101] But it does not look like he saw that future in terms of a realization that both Christianity and Buddhism are saying the same thing in different terms.

Donald Mitchell, Robert Jonas, James Grob

Donald Mitchell's *Spirituality and Emptiness* broadens the discussion that had sprung up around Masao Abe's comparison of Buddhist emptiness with Christian kenosis, or emptying. He does so by including more of the Kyoto School of Buddhist philosophical reflection to which Abe belonged, and looking at the issue not only theologically, but from the point of view of Christian spirituality.

What is particularly important and interesting for the theme we have been pursuing here is the nuanced way in which he avoids reducing Christian mystical experience to Zen experience. Members of the Kyoto School like Nishitani and Abe feel "that Absolute Nothingness entails the *total* emptying of any far-side reality apart from the near side of our world."[102] For them there can be no dualism between God and creatures. But Mitchell feels that Christianity should not be treated this way. The far-side reality of God cannot be collapsed into the near side reality of creatures. To do so is to "lose the richness of the Christian vision of God" and "empty out Christian hope of eternal life in the heart of this trinitarian mystery."[103] God cannot be identified with the forms of creation. "…the radical dependence of creation on God is not matched with a radical dependence of God on creation which would be called for by the Buddhist logic that identifies Emptiness and forms."[104]

The same issue can be looked at from the perspective of mystical experience. "Is the Void something that is "prior" to God? Is it an Absolute Nothingness out of which even God arises?"[105] Mitchell realizes that Christians who practice Zen might be tempted to answer these questions affirmatively, but he believes that it is incorrect to do so: "… a Christian mystic finds that through the grace of Christ indwelling within, he or she is given a "spiritual eye," as it were, to see into the mystery of the Void. And he or she finds therein a far-side dimension that is *not* absolutely identified with the near side of creation, and is *not* formless and impersonal."[106]

In short, while not at all denying the importance and reality of the Zen experience, or what is being called here, "the near side of mystical experience," our perspective cannot be limited to this. "If, on the other hand, one turns one's attention into the heart of the Void, then that Void becomes, unlike Buddhist Absolute Nothingness, an onto-theological category of experience. And if that attention is graced in a particular way by God, one can discover therein that the Void has a personal trinitarian far-side dimension."[107] Mitchell concludes: "…the Buddhist experience of Absolute Nothingness is an experience of God, of God as the kenotic ground of existence. But this Emptiness is not prior to God, it is the depth of the kenotic dynamic of the triune and personal God that is the other side…"[108]

In a videotaped interview he tells us contemplation is not something we can produce, but ultimately something God grants, and he goes on to describe how the Zen experience can bring someone to a deep sense of God's presence in and through the world, and Christian contemplation moves through that experience so that we realize that there is another side, that there is a transcendent dimension. Zen gives us an indication of the silent mystical horizon as it is played out in the interrelatedness of life, and the infinite is encountered in this experience so that it looks like that is it. But through the grace of God one realizes that that infinite opens up on the other side into the life we will share with God when we die, that paradise we call the Trinity. The Zen experience is absolutely authentic, and the Christian contemplative experience does not contradict it, but complements it.[109]

Robert Jonas, director of the Empty Bell Retreat Center dedicated to Buddhist-Christian dialogue, has come to a similar conclusion. Both Buddhists and Christians can come in silence to a precious moment of pure presence. But for Christians, there is another one there, a holy one, so Christians will say that Jesus lives in us. There is always an interpersonal dimension in the spiritual practice, an inner voice, a sense of inner presence that leads one to make contact with an other in an ultimate way. The ground of what is ultimately so is relational. Then when I stand up from prayer, I am still in the presence of that relational sense. It is a relational universe.[110]

James Grob, a Christian contemplative deeply versed in Eastern forms of meditation, after graphically describing both his Christian and Eastern experiences, arrives at an analogous perspective. He once saw himself being created and held into existence by Christ, by the Word, which was like a fountain flowing into him. His human self appeared as a thin membrane supported by the flowing out of the fountain, and he could see himself as a distinct creature. Suddenly the entire context was transformed as if by an immense electrical charge, and the membrane was participating in and part of, totally by gift, the entirety of what God is.[111]

What is fascinating about these Christian contemplative accounts is that in actual experience there is no conflict between enlightenment and contemplation, and there is certainly no feeling given from these people of any hostility, or even bias, against enlightenment, but rather, they show a deep openness to it that is born of experience. But it is an experience that has been transformed from within by the interpersonal mystery of God's love. From a Christian perspective, therefore, there is no need either to deny the authenticity and great beauty of enlightenment, or to try to transform Christian contemplation into another experience of it.

Heinrich Dumoulin

Attempts to take a look at Zen from a Christian metaphysical point of view have not been completely lacking. Heinrich Dumoulin (1905-

1995), the Jesuit historian of Zen Buddhism, for example, in his *A History of Zen Buddhism*, devotes a section to natural mysticism by which he means: "an immediate religious experience of reality or a psychic contact with the absolute being, and distinguishes Zen from the supernatural mysticism of grace as well as from the manifold phenomena of magic in the history of religion."[112] He goes on a little later: "The mystical experience which, as in the case of Zen, occurs outside the intimate I-thou communion of the soul with its Maker, belongs by contrast to natural mysticism, a concept generally recognized today by Christian theologians."[113] And he touches on the work of Mager, August Brunner, Gardet and Merton. At the heart of natural mysticism the soul "becomes aware, at the foundation of its own spiritual substance, of God's eternal creative spirit."[114] But this enlightenment experience, while it has a spiritual and absolute character, is understood in a monist way. "If, therefore, Zen presents itself as a kind of natural mysticism, it must be emphasized that the pantheistic strain in its teaching stems, not from experience, but from the philosophy of the Zen mystics. Experience itself can only permit the consciousness of contact between the spiritual self and the realm of the Absolute, and thus it is basically open to the theistic possibility. Indeed, one finds among the Zen mystics an oscillation between a faith which reaches out to a transcendent Other and the absolutizing of the ego believed to be identical with the All. In intimate contact with adherents of Zen, one finds inescapably a certain contradiction in the religious attitude of many a zealous Zen disciple."[115] Interestingly enough, this section on natural mysticism seems to have disappeared from his expanded *Zen Buddhism: A History*. Perhaps the dropping of the section was the result of Dumoulin's growing understanding of Zen, and the decline of the traditional neo-scholastic philosophy at the time of the Second Vatican Council which went together with a reevaluation of the traditional use of the terms natural and supernatural, and the rise of a new awareness of God's universal salvific will. These are issues we will look at in more detail a little later.

If we have been seeing examples of how Christians have adopted Zen Buddhism, Dumoulin in this new edition provides us with some very interesting historical examples of Buddhists who embraced Christianity with equal enthusiasm. It tells us, for example, of the Japanese tea masters of the 16th century who were Christians like

Takayama Ukon, who was part of Rikyu's tea circle,[1116] and the Zen master Kesshu who became a Christian.[117]

Hans Waldenfels

Much the same distinction between Zen and Christian mysticism that we have been seeing is made by Hans Waldenfels in his *Absolute Nothingness*: "In Pseudo-Dionysius, identification or union with God is for man to enter the Godhead by getting rid of what is man – a process called *theosis*, i.e., deification. This position of Pseudo-Dionysius became the basis of subsequent Christian mysticism. It may not be wrong to say that for him, the Godhead in which one is united is the "Emptiness" of the indefinable One. The words "nothing, nothing, nothing" fill the pages of *The Dark Night of the Soul*, written by St. John of the Cross. For him nothingness meant "sweeping away of images and thoughts of God to meet Him in the darkness and obscurity of pure faith which is above all concepts"."

But Waldenfels goes on: "Despite the great similarity between Zen and Christian mysticism we should not overlook an essential difference between them. In the above quoted passage, Pseudo-Dionysius calls that which is beyond all affirmation and all negation by the term "Him." Many Christian mystics call God "Thou." In Zen, however, what is beyond all affirmation and all negation – that is, Ultimate Reality – should not be "Him" or "Thou" but "Self" or one's "True Self." I am not concerned here with verbal expressions, but the reality behind the words. If Ultimate Reality, while being taken as Nothingness or Emptiness, should be called "Him" or "Thou," it is, from the Zen point of view, no longer ultimate."[118]

Ichiro Okumura

Ichiro Okumura in his "Zen and Christianity – Memories of My Conversion," tells us that as a young student at Tokyo University he was a German major, and through this means gained some idea of Christianity, but he was enamored of Zen and despised Catholicism as a distorted fairy tale and actively struggled against it. "After an oppressive darkness of almost three years, a sharp light seemed to sear my brain, as if I had somehow been struck by lightning. Immediately, it became clear to me that what was distorted was not the Bible, but my own mind! My strong resistance to "Incarnation", which I considered to be the basic doctrine of Christianity, and my desire to demythologize the Bible had changed into an insatiable thirst for the true image of Christ. I had been captured by Christ in my very struggle against him. It was the summer of my twenty-sixth year."[119]

He became a Carmelite and later looked at Zen from the point of view of Christian spirituality and John of the Cross. His conversion gave him a distinctive perspective on this Zen-Christian dialogue. "But my experience in my youth, when I was seized by Christ in my very struggle against Him, led me to feel a quiet but firm resistance at the "Zen-Christian Colloquium", when the other participants were tempted to agree that "all religions are in fact reducible to one".

"I still feel great pleasure when I come in contact with brave Zen Masters and good books on Zen, savoring as I do the breadth of the Zen mind and a sort of relief from some of the stiltedness of Western thinking prevalent in Christian theology. But I must say that I can find in Christ alone the deep human mystery that cannot be reached through any other religion, including Zen-Buddhism. Perhaps this will seem to our non-Christian friends to be only my own prejudice!"[120]

Kakichi Kadowaki

The Jesuit Kakichi Kadowaki, in a 1966 article called, "Ways of Knowing: a Buddhist-Thomist Dialogue," argues for the astute conclusion that there is "a genuine analogy between the Buddhist theory of knowing and the Thomistic notion of connatural knowledge."[121] Later, in his *Zen and the Bible*, he explores reading both the Bible and koans with what he calls the whole body, and compares St. Ignatius' spiritual exercises with a Zen sesshin. It was at a sesshin at Fr. Lassalle's zendo *Shinmeikutsu* that he met a man whom he calls Mr. S, who told him with great earnestness that many Catholics come there for sesshins, and he thought that their zeal indicated "that they have at last found in Zen something which they had given up hope of finding anywhere else." But beyond that, Mr. S felt that there was "something deep in the soul of Catholics that harmonizes perfectly with Zen

CHRISTIANITY IN THE CRUCIBLE

meditation, and that something too deep to fathom came out of this."[122]

Kadowaki feels that Zen and Christianity "differ in a fine point regarding their ultimate aims, but that in regard to their overall frame work and structure they are very similar."[123] But this was something he wanted to leave for further examination. He also feels that a new scriptural hermeneutic could come out of approaching the Bible in the spirit of Zen.

A Buddhist-Christian Dialogue at Naropa Institute

If our question often emerges from the writings of the people most involved in Zen-Christian dialogue from a Christian point of view, it also constantly struggles to surface whenever there are intensive conversations between Buddhists and Christians.

At a Zen-Christian meeting at Naropa Institute, recounted in *Speaking of Silence*, a person listening to the panel of Christians and Buddhists asked: "When I listen to both the Buddhists and the Christians, I hear that basically there is no difference."[124] Brother David Steindl-Rast, a Camaldolese monk, answered, "...in my mind there cannot be conceived of two ways that are lived out more differently than Buddhism and Christianity... But they come from the same experience and by very different routes, lead to the same experience."[125]

In another exchange, Fr. Thomas Keating, one of the founders of the Centering Prayer movement, whose purpose is to renew the Christian mystical tradition, asked: "..when one has shed this ego-centeredness with its aggression and selfish self-seeking, is there not still an identity left, which may actually be very good?" The Tibetan monk Trungpa Rinpoche responded: "Well, I think now we have reached the key point. Egolessness means that there is no ego – at all."

Fr. Keating: "That's what I thought it meant..."

Trungpa Rinpoche: "Union with God cannot take place when there is any form of ego. Any whatsoever. In order to be one with God, one has to become formless. Then you will see God."

Fr. Keating: "This is the point I was trying to make for Christians by quoting the agonizing words of Christ on the cross. He cried out, "My God, my God, why hast thou forsaken me?" (Mark 15:34) It seems that his sense of personal relationship with God, as God's son, had disappeared. Many interpreters say that this was only a temporary experience. But I am inclined to think, in light of the Buddhist description of no-self, that he was passing into a stage beyond the personal self, however holy and beautiful that self had been. That final stage would then also have to be defined as the primary Christian experience. Christ has called us Christians not just so that so that we will accept him as savior, but so that we will follow the same process that brought him to his final stage of consciousness."[126]

Certainly as we become sensitized to our question, we can see the ambiguity running through these kinds of exchanges. Is the no ego that Trungpa Rinpoche talking about actually a no ego in the Christian metaphysical or mystical sense? Certainly Christian spirituality knows a great deal about the loss of self, but can we really identify that loss of self with what Buddhists are talking about? Can Fr. Keating's reflections really be squared with our traditional understanding of the Christian mysteries?

The Ground We Share

In another dialogue between Robert Aitken, a Zen master in the tradition of Yasutani, and Brother David Steindl-Rast, recounted in *The Ground We Share*, Aitken asked whether Brother David believed in Aldous Huxley's perennial experience underlying the great religious traditions. Brother David responded: "Although some people I highly respect hold that the religious traditions can't be traced back to one universal experience, my conviction that they can has grown over the years."[127] Later Aitken Roshi says: "A Buddhist cannot take metaphysics seriously because he or she knows that the truth of metaphysics is only as true as the truth of no metaphysics, while Christians, I think, tend to take metaphysics seriously. In other words, a Christian can never say there's no such thing as Christ."[128] And Brother David responds: "I'm convinced, since both traditions come from the same experiential awareness, that it must be possible for me to find this point expressed somewhere in Christianity."[129] And he goes on to find an example of the negation of Christ in the idea that the cosmic Christ "will hand over the kingdom to the Father, and God, who is the silence out of which the Word came in the beginning, will be all in all. At that point, the Word returns to the Silence."[130] I will leave it to the reader to determine how convincing this parallel is.

One more exchange comes close to expressing an answer to our question. Aitken Roshi: "...When Brother Peter, novice master at Our Lady of Guadalupe described his meditation to me, it sounded exactly the same as shikantaza. In fact, it is exactly the same." Brother David responds: "And that's not an individual case. For centuries, the Church has had what we call Prayer of Silence or Prayer of Union. It's widely practiced, especially these days. Existentially and experientially, as you rightly say, it's the apophatic, experiential aspect of Christianity."[131] Here Christian mystical experience is being identified with shikantaza or Zen's silent sitting.

But even with these rather forthright statements, neither dialogue partner seems fully comfortable with an out and out identification between Zen and Christianity. They both realize that there is a personal dimension in Christianity that does not exist in the same way in Zen. Brother David, for example, will say: "This sense of a personal relatedness with the Ultimate is expressed in Christian terminology calling the Silence, the altogether Other, father or mother or friend or spouse or lover."[132] And Aitken Roshi: "...in Christianity there's a much warmer, personal feeling of relationship to the Ultimate than in Buddhism... The other side of the coin is the more metaphysical side – the cool side, if you will – which has been strongly developed in Buddhism and not so strongly in Christianity."[133]

David Hackett

This same kind of exchange, complete with the same kind of ambiguities and uncertainties, can be found in the letters of David Hackett to Thomas Keating. They were written when Hackett was a young man visiting Japan and other parts of Asia in the early 1970s. Hackett went to visit Hirata Roshi, for example, who was not enthusiastic about what he saw happening in the Zen-Christian dialogue. "Rather than deepen Christian faith, the Roshi argued, zazen may well threaten it. He was especially worried about Christian monks doing zazen and went so far as to call Father Lassalle's Zen retreat house a "great adventure" in a negative sense." When Hackett recounted this to Heinrich Dumoulin, Dumoulin was both surprised and amused because Hirata was a friend of his, and though he respected what

Hirata had to say, he thought it somewhat naïve: "Christians are now doing zazen and getting results that do not threaten but rather deepen their faith."

When Hackett visited Fr. Oshida, a Dominican who had a community in rural Japan that practiced zazen, Fr. Oshida thought that there were Christians who "have gone too far into Zen, so that there is a sterile feel to them. They are highly disciplined and no doubt well along on their paths, yet this closed focus on Zen – while not denying Christianity – makes them seem less joyful."[134]

Hackett wrote to Phra Khantipalo, an Englishman who was a Hinayana Buddhist monk in Sri Lanka, and who was decidedly negative about Buddhist-Christian dialogue. "You mentioned about meditation – and I have met both with Dom Aelred and Father Merton in this connection. However, it does not seem to have been realized by these good teachers that components of one religion cannot be borrowed and grafted onto another."[135] And talking about the Buddhist practice of cutting off all views, he goes on to say: "… it would mean for a Roman Catholic ceasing to believe in God, the Trinity, the Virgin Mary, the Saints, and so on, all the dogmas on which that religion is founded… I cannot see many Christians being prepared to go so far, for if they do they can no longer be Christians."[136]

Later Hackett, a Catholic convert, was considering joining the Trappists and discussed his life of prayer with one of the monks: "I told Raphael that zazen was my prayer life. I did go to daily Mass and read the Gospels but practiced no other forms of prayer. Raphael asked what I did to reach God in the time between meditations. To this I admitted that I had rarely spoken to God in prayer. Rather I have trusted my meditation efforts to bring me closer to him than words might allow."[137] Hackett understands Brother Raphael to be telling him he still has need of discursive forms of prayer. "Still I argued vehemently with Raphael. Why should I engage in discursive prayer if I can readily leap this initial stage and enter into the intimacy of zazen? Talking to God and doing such things as the rosary now seem so silly if I can have a far deeper experience through meditation. In a stunning reply, Raphael noted that discursive prayer must be part of the contemplative process."[138]

This exchange stands in contrast to an earlier passage where Hackett writes: "My hunch is that Christianity and zazen should work toge-

CHRISTIANITY IN THE CRUCIBLE

ther much like positive and negative theology. They are like a two-stage rocket. Zen meditation is not the same as silent prayer, the infused contemplation of Christianity, if it is not driven to its heights by Christian positive theology. Christians who deny this and place extra emphasis on their zazen at the expense of scripture study and discursive prayer are perhaps not well-grounded in an open-ended positive theology or are in rebellion against a too thorough indoctrination in a narrow-minded positive theology. I imagine that it is possible for people in either instance to lose their Christian roots."[139]

The real issue is not how discursive forms of Christian prayer are necessary preparations for the more contemplative prayer that is done in zazen, but rather, whether zazen really should be called contemplative prayer at all, as Hackett points out. Further, infused contemplation as it has been understood in the Christian mystical tradition, is not the result of intensive meditation efforts like Zen sesshins, but rather, is a free and loving gift from God.

Modern Attempts to Renew the Christian Contemplative Life

For the most part we have been encountering Catholics who have taken up Eastern forms of meditation and brought them back to often predominately Christian audiences. But there is another dimension to this story. Some of the people deeply involved in modern attempts to renew the Christian contemplative life have been strongly influenced by Eastern forms of meditation.

Centering Prayer

In the late 1960s and early 1970s the monks of the Trappist monastery of St. Joseph in Spencer, Massachusetts, whose abbot then was Thomas Keating, were seeing young people, often Christians, who had a thirst for a deeper spiritual life that was not being satisfied within the Christian churches. And so they looked to the East. The monks, themselves, had a Zen meditation master give retreats at the Abbey, and we have seen Thomas Keating dialoguing at Naropa, exchanging letters with David Hackett, and he wrote a laudatory preface to Bernadette Roberts' problematical attempt to extend the Christian mystical path in the direction of nonduality in her book, *The*

Experience of No-Self, an attempt we will look at later. Keating, together with Basil Pennington, who was seriously interested in transcendental meditation, and William Messenger who had an interest in *The Cloud of Unknowing,* collaborated in developing what they called centering prayer, which was an attempt to reconnect with the Christian mystical tradition of not out the *Cloud,* but John Cassian and the desert fathers, the Cistercian tradition of prayer, as well as John of the Cross. Centering prayer, itself, was quite straight-forward. A prayer word was chosen which symbolized an inner receptivity to God's presence and action, and the word was repeated whenever the person praying found him or herself distracted from this receptivity, and waiting upon God. Eventually centering prayer retreats developed that seemed reminiscent of Zen sesshins, or intensive Zen meditation retreats in which someone would practice centering prayer four to six hours a day.

While centering prayer is an attempt to renew the Christian mystical tradition, it is legitimate to ask not only how well it reconnects with that tradition, but more to the point here, what role Eastern forms of meditation have played in how contemplation is understood.

Keating, for example, in his response to a question about centering prayer: "Sometimes there are no thoughts. There is only my self-awareness. I don't know whether to let go of it or be aware of it," writes: "That is a crucial question. If you are aware of no thoughts, you are aware of something and that is a thought. If at that point you can lose the awareness that you are aware of no thoughts, you will move into *pure consciousness.* In that state there is no consciousness of self. When your ordinary faculties come back together again, there may be a sense of peaceful delight, a good sign that you were not asleep. It is important to realize that the place to which we are going is one in which the knower, the knowing, and that which is known are all one. Awareness alone remains. The one who is aware disappears along with whatever was the object of consciousness. This is what divine union is. There is no reflection of self. The experience is temporary, but it orients you toward the contemplative state. So long as you *feel* united with God, it cannot be full union."[140]

Does this represent the authentic Christian mystical tradition? Or are we seeing a transformation in the understanding of Christian contemplation that would make it equivalent to enlightenment?[141]

John Main

Another modern attempt to renew the Christian contemplative life was carried out by the Benedictine monk, John Main. In his form of Christian meditation a person chooses a prayer word, and faithfully uses that word like a Christian mantra. But where did this practice come from? John Main, before he became a monk, met a Hindu guru called Swami Satyananda who taught him to use a mantra, and explained to him that in this way he could come to awareness of the Spirit of the universe that dwells in our hearts.

His Benedictine novice master told him not to use this form of meditation, but later he felt he discovered, like the advocates of centering prayer, that this practice was to be found in John Cassian and *The Cloud of Unknowing*. This led him to develop a Christian mantra-type meditation.

It is fair to ask, however, in what way this Eastern background has influenced how Christian contemplation is conceived. Is it enough, for example, to have a Christian intent in practicing this kind of mantra prayer, to turn it into a Christian contemplation? Or does the very method used tend to direct the meditation towards the goal of enlightenment? Is an assumption being made that these two goals are the same? In this particular case answering these questions is made more complex by the fact that Swami Satyananda had attended Roman Catholic schools, and had considered becoming a Christian, and so we might be dealing with a more theistic kind of Hinduism than the advaitan Vedanta we have been seeing.[142]

Vipassana Meditation and John of the Cross

Mary Jo Meadow and the Discalced Carmelite Kevin Culligan find that "the actual experienced practice" of John of the Cross' Christian contemplation and the Theravadan Buddhist Vipassana meditation are "amazingly alike."[143] In "Congruent Spiritual Paths" they proceed to draw out these similarities. The Buddhist insight that mental and material phenomena are void of self, or ego, is equated with John of the Cross' first sign that is meant to mark the transition from meditation to contemplation, that is, that one cannot meditate like before. There are, indeed, certain similarities to be found here, as will become more evident when we look at the question of the loss of the affective ego, but in John of the Cross this inability to use the faculties in the best of circumstances is meant to lead to the experience of infused contemplation, which is an experience of union with God. Unfortunately, our authors do not ever really compare this kind of contemplation with Eastern enlightenment, but instead leave us with the impression that these two spiritual paths lead to the same goal.

Springs Steele in an article called "Christian Insight Meditation: A Test Case on Interreligious Spirituality"[144] shows how Meadow and Culligan in their *Purifying the Heart* continue to identify "the endpoint of Theravadan Buddhist *vipassana* meditation (*nibbana*) and the endpoint or ultimate goal of John's spirituality (union with God, spiritual marriage),"[145] and look at the *vipassana* method as "ultimately neutral and thus transferable to any spiritual tradition,"[146] and comments: "the ultimate consequence of the position that *vipassana* meditation is a non-tradition-dependent method leading to the ultimate religious end of all spiritual traditions is to render all such traditions irrelevant. If such is in fact the case, why bother trying to assimilate *vipassana* to John of the Cross anyway?"[147]

Hans Küng

The dialogue between Christianity and Eastern religions demands that we ask difficult questions. They cannot be avoided, and we cannot avoid formulating these questions under the mistaken guise that to do so is somehow undiplomatic or against the spirit of true dialogue. Hans Küng in his *Christianity and World Religions* does not let his deep commitment to dialogue stand in his way of raising some pointed issues. He cites Winston King: "There is, in fact, an unacknowledged but functionally real "implicit self" of decidedly significant proportions right in the center of the Theravada not-self, which gives this doctrine its redeeming and enlightening meaning…"[148] Küng points out that not all Buddhists have held extreme interpretations of the no-self doctrine, and "emptiness" has received a variety of interpretations.

A case can be made, as well, for giving a positive meaning to "nothingness." Küng asks: "Would it not be less misleading to say that the absolute is *also* absolute being, or Being Itself, that "emptiness" is *also* "fullness," "shunyata" is also "pleroma"?[149] Later he writes, "Would it then be wholly impermissible to conclude that what Christians call "God" is present, under very different names, in Buddhism, insofar as Buddhists do not refuse on principle, to admit any positive statements?"[150] And he goes further and points out that the distinctive character of the monotheistic religions is that God is a "partner who grounds and embraces human interpersonality."[151] "Where others only heard an endless silence, the Jewish, Christian, and Islamic scriptures tell of a people being addressed and claimed by its God. Where others experienced unechoing space and the void, this people was allowed to discover for itself and others that the Absolute can be heard and spoken to, that it is a mysteriously communicative and responsive *Thou*."[152]

Our questions have now taken a concrete form, and in doing so answers begin to emerge. Yet so extensive is the Buddhist-Christian dialogue that our wanderings have only taken us through a part of it. We could have looked, for example, at the work of the Irish Jesuit, William Johnston, whose long sojourn in Japan has given us a stream of books on Christian mysticism, as well as its interface with Zen Buddhism like his *Mystical Theology, Letters to Contemplatives*, "All and Nothing: St. John of the Cross and the Christian-Buddhist Dialogue," etc., or the work of AMA Samy, the Indian Jesuit born in Burma, whose *Why did Bodhidharma Come to the West?: On the Transmission of Zen to the West* which has been published in German and Dutch, but not yet in English. But we have gained enough of a sense of this dialogue, and so let's continue this process by looking at the Hindu-Christian dialogue.

Notes

1. Cf. T. Matthew Ciolek web pages.
2. Cf. Habito, Rueben, "*In Memoriam:* A Tribute to Yamada Koun Roshi."
3. Loy, David. "A Zen Cloud?" p. 57.
4. Ibid., p. 58-59.
5. Habito, Ruben. *Total Liberation: Zen Spirituality and the Social Dimension.* p. 87.

6. Ibid., p. 88-89.
7. Habito, Ruben. *Profiles in Buddhist-Christian Dialogue.* Cf. his presentations in the three videos called *Buddhist-Christian Dialogue in Action*: 1992, 1996 and 2000.
8. Ibid.
9. Habito, Ruben, *Total Liberation*, p. 89-90.
10. Lassalle, Hugo Enomiya. *Living in the New Consciousness.* p. 121-122.
11. As cited in Dumoulin, *Zen in the Twentieth Century*, p. 136-137.
12. Ibid., p. 137.
13. Lassalle, Hugo Enomiya. *Zen Meditation for Christians.* p. 44.
14. Jäger, Willigis. *The Way to Contemplation.* p. 24.
15. Ibid., p. 25.   16. Ibid., p. 38.   17. Ibid., p. 67.
18. Ibid., p. 70.
19. Jäger, Willigis, *Contemplation: A Christian Path.* p. 3.
20. Ibid., p. 92.
21. Jäger, Willigis. *Search for the Meaning of Life*, p. 5.
22. Ibid.   27. Ibid., p. 32.   32. Ibid., p. 73.
23. Ibid., p. 6.   28. Ibid., p. 43.   33. Ibid., p. 84.
24. Ibid.   29. Ibid., p. 57.   34. Ibid., p. 240.
25. Ibid., p. 14.   30. Ibid.   35. Ibid., p. 241.
26. Ibid.   31. Ibid., p. 62.   36. Ibid.
37. MacInnes, Elaine. *Light Sitting in Light: A Christian's Experience in Zen.*, p. xiii.
38. Ibid., p. 25.   41. Ibid., p. 77.   44. Ibid., p. 105.
39. Ibid., p. 15.   42. Ibid., p. 15.   45. Ibid.
40. Ibid., p. 41.   43. Ibid., p. 24.   46. Ibid., p. 113.
47. Hawk, Patrick, "The Pathless Path," p. 129.
48. Ibid.   49. Ibid., p. 131.   50. Ibid.
51. Chwen Jiuan Agnes Lee and Thomas Hand, *A Taste of Water: Christianity Through Taoist-Buddhist Eyes*, p. 2-3.
52. Ibid., p. 3.   56. Ibid., p. 63.   60. Ibid., p. 98.
53. Ibid., p. 12.   57. Ibid., p. 72.   61. Ibid., p. 149.
54. Ibid., p. 41-42.   58. Ibid., p. 74.   62. Ibid., p. 148-149.
55. Ibid., p. 54.   59. Ibid., p. 86.   63. Ibid., p. 149.
64. Hand, Thomas. *Profiles in Buddhist-Christian Dialogue.* Cf. the presentations of both Thomas Hand and Chwen Jiuan Agnes Lee in *Buddhist-Christian Dialogue in Action*: Boston 1992.
65. Kennedy, Robert E. *Zen Spirit, Christian Spirit: The Place of Zen in Christian Life*, p. 11. Cf. also his presentation in

Buddhist-Christian Dialogue in Action: Boston 1992.

66. Ibid., p. 13.
67. Ibid., p. 16.
68. Ibid., p. 39.
69. Ibid., p. 36-37.
70. Ibid., p. 68-71.
71. Ibid., p. 86.
72. Ibid., p. 86-87.
73. Ibid., p. 87.
74. Ibid., p. 95.
75. Ibid.
76. Habito, Maria Reis. *Buddhist-Christian Dialogue in Action: Tacoma, 2000.*
77. Corless, Roger. *Profiles in Buddhist-Christian Dialogue.*
78. Sharf, Robert. "Sanbokyodan: Zen and the Way of the New Religions."
79. Ibid., p. 427-428.
80. Ibid., p. 436.
81. Ibid., p. 437.
82. Lachs, Stuart. "Coming Down From the Zen Clouds."
83. Sharf, Robert. "Sanbokyodan: Zen and the Way of the New Religions," p. 440.
84. Ibid.
85. Yamada, Koun. "Zazen and Christianity."
86. Nugent, Christopher. (May 1993) "Satori in St. John of the Cross."
87. Merton, Thomas. *Springs of Contemplation*, p. 177.
88. Ibid, p. 183.
89. *The Hidden Ground of Love: Letters of Thomas Merton*, p. 438.
90. Ibid., p. 439.
91. Ibid., p. 438-439.
92. Ibid., p. 439.
93. Merton, Thomas. "The Inner Experience. Notes on Contemplation" in three parts, in *Cistercian Studies*, p. 7.
94. Ibid., p. 9-10.
95. Merton, Thomas. (1968) *Zen and the Birds of Appetite*, p. 42.
96. Ibid., p. 43.
97. Ibid., p. 80.
98. King, Thomas. *Merton, Mystic at the Heart of America*, p. 42.
99. Ibid.
100. Ibid., p. 44.
101. Ibid., p. 45.
102. Mitchell, Donald. *Spirituality and Emptiness*, p. 61.
103. Ibid., p. 62.
104. Ibid., p. 66.
105. Ibid., p. 24.
106. Ibid., p. 25.
107. Ibid.
108. Ibid., p. 26.
109. Mitchell, Donald. *Profiles in Buddhist-Christian Dialogue..*
110. Jonas, Robert. *Profiles in Buddhist-Christian Dialogue.* Cf. his presentation in *Buddhist-Christian Dialogue in Action: Tacoma 2000.*
111. Grob, James. *Blossoms of Silence.*
112. Dumoulin, Heinrich. *A History of Zen Buddhism*, p. 282.
113. Ibid., p. 284.
114. Ibid., p. 287.
115. Ibid., p. 288.

116. Dumoulin, Heinrich. *Zen Buddhism: A History*. Vol. 2, p. 244.
117. Ibid., p. 245.
118. Waldenfels, Hans. *Absolute Nothingness: Foundations for a Buddhist-Christian Dialogue*, p. 141.
119. Okumura, Ichiro. "Zen and Christianity: Memories of My Conversion", p. 98.
120. Ibid., p. 100. Cf. Okumura's *Awakening to Prayer*.
121. Kadowaki, Kakichi, S.J. "Ways of Knowing: A Buddhist-Thomist Dialogue," pp. 574-595.
122. Kadowaki, Kakichi, S.J. *Zen and the Bible: A Priest's Experience*, p. 9.
123. Ibid., p. 89.
124. Walker, Susan, editor. *Speaking of Silence: Christians and Buddhists on the Contemplative Way*, p. 147.
125. Ibid., p. 148.
126. Ibid., p. 168-169.
127. Aitken, Robert and David Steindl-Rast. *The Ground We share: Everyday Practice, Buddhist and Christian*, p. 3-4.
128. Ibid., p. 20.
129. Ibid.
130. Ibid.
131. Ibid., p. 23-24.
132. Ibid., p. 36.
133. Ibid., p. 37.
134. Hackett, David. G. *The Silent Dialogue: Zen Letters to a Trappist Abbot*, p. 74.
135. Ibid., p. 105.
136. Ibid., p. 105-106.
137. Ibid., p. 151-152.
138. Ibid., p. 152.
139. Ibid., p. 91.
140. Keating, Thomas. *Open Mind, Open Heart*, p. 73-74.
141. See the discussion in *From St. John of the Cross to Us*, pp. 205-211, and also the web discussion on centering prayer at http://www.innerexplorations.com/chmystext/cm1.htm
142. See the web discussion on John Main's Christian meditation at http://www.innerexplorations.com/chmystext/john.htm
143. Meadow, Mary Jo. "Congruent Spiritual Paths" p. 181.
144. Steele, Springs. "Christian Insight Meditation: A Test Case on Interreligious Spirituality," pp. 217-229.
145. Ibid., p. 219.
146. Ibid., p. 226.
147. Ibid.
148. Küng, Hans. *Christianity and the World Religions: Paths of Dialogue with Islam, Hinduism and Buddhism*, p. 383.
149. Ibid., p. 389.
150. Ibid., p. 392.
151. Ibid., p. 398.
152. Ibid.

CHAPTER 2

HINDU-CHRISTIAN DIALOGUE

Our long pilgrimage through Buddhist-Christian dialogue will allow us to examine the Hindu-Christian dialogue at less length, yet see the same kinds of issues emerge. The roots of Hindu-Christian dialogue can be traced back as far as the Jesuit missionary Roberto de Nobili in the 17th century. He realized that he needed to enter deeply into Indian religious thought and religious customs in order to really make contact with the people to whom he wanted to bring the message of Christianity.

Modern Hindu-Christian Dialogue

The modern phase of the Hindu-Christian dialogue can be found in the work of the Bengali Brahmin convert Brahmabandhab Upadhyaya who founded the journal *Sophia* and tried to create a Hindu-Christian ashram, and in the work of the Belgian priests C. Dandoy and P. Johanns who created the review *The Light of the East* in the 1920s and 30s in collaboration with Swami Animananda who was a disciple of Upadhyaya. Other contributors to this modern dialogue with Hinduism include Olivier Lacombe, Jacques-Albert Cuttat, and R. C. Zaehner.

An interesting example of this earlier dialogue from the Hindu side can be found in Swami Siddheswarananda's *Hindu Thought & Carmelite Mysticism,* which was the result of a series of lectures given at the Sorbonne between 1949 and 1953. There he addressed the question of the parallels between Hindu thought and the Carmelite mysticism he had been studying. This reading must have been penetrating enough because it gave him a sense of the difference between the two traditions. He realized that someone who had read the descriptions of spiritual experience in Teresa of Avila, and then got to know Ramakrishna, would try to find parallels. But he concludes that: "This way of thinking prevents us from realizing perfectly the different positions of these mystics. To reduce these different positions to unity is to create artificially a universal which crumbles under the slightest critique."[1]

Later he asks himself whether the thought of John of the Cross is really pure jnana, or union by knowledge by which the soul is united with the Absolute, and he says it is impossible to say. But he goes on and comments: "Insofar as St. John of the Cross is a seeker of the Supreme Cause, one cannot say of him that he is a pure jnanin. For him God remains the Father of creatures, the Supreme Cause to which the world is subordinated. When the soul is united with Him, it remains despite that union, different from the Spirit which illuminates it. Certainly, "The soul is transformed; it participates in that which is God, it appears to be God rather than the soul; it is God by participation (but) it conserves its natural being, as distinct from God as before, despite its transformation, as the window is distinct from the ray which shines through it"."[2]

But it is with the founding of the first Catholic ashram Saccidananda, or Shantivanam, on the banks of the Cavery River at Kulittalai in Tamil Nadu by the French priests Jules Monchanin and Henri Le Saux in 1950 that the Hindu-Christian dialogue attained a new level of intensity. Saccidananda Ashram was followed in 1955 by the creation of Kurisumala Ashram in Kerala by Bede Griffiths and Francis Mahieu. Jules Monchanin died in 1957, and Le Saux felt called to a solitary life and left Saccidananda for the Himalayas in 1968. The ashram was then taken over by Bede Griffiths. Other well-known Hindu-Christian ashrams include Jeevan Dhara founded by Vandana Mataji in the Himalayas and Christa Prema Seva Ashram in Pune, refounded by Sara Grant in 1972, and Anjali Ashram in Mysore founded in 1979 by D.S. Amalorpavadass.[3]

The Current State of the Hindu-Christian Dialogue in India

Deep interest on the part of Christians – perhaps mostly Westerners – in the Christian-Hindu dialogue should not blind us to the lack of enthusiasm that Hindus might have for it. Richard Taylor, assessing the current state of Hindu-Christian dialogue in a study published in 1989, reports how an Anglican missionary, deeply involved in this dialogue, told him "that there are very few Hindus really interested in dialogue."[4] Along the same lines, Bede Griffiths stated: "Hindus as a whole are not much interested in dialogue. They tend to think that all differences in religions are unimportant."[5] And conservative Hindus in North America feel that even progressive ashrams like Shantivanam and Jeevan Dhara are "misappropriating Hindu style and contents in order to mislead Hindus and to engage in illicit religious conversions..."[6] Certainly, the current resurgence of Hindu nationalism in India and the many acts of violence against Christians would make us believe that this climate has not changed for the better.

Abhishiktananda

Abhishiktananda (Henri Le Saux) (1910-1973) was a French Benedictine monk who went to India in 1948 and, together with Jules Monchanin, helped found the Hindu-Christian ashram, Shantivanam. It is perhaps indicative of the course that his life in India took that he is usually referred to by his Hindu name, while this is not the case with Jules Monchanin or their successor at Shantivanam, Bede Griffiths. It was in the life of Abhishiktananda that the interior drama of the Hindu-Christian dialogue made itself felt most poignantly. He felt a deep call within himself to follow the advaitan or nondual path as far as he could into the depths of his soul, but at the same time he felt tormented by the feeling that such a calling was irreconcilable to the Christian faith to which he was so deeply attached. This conflict was to continue in varying ways for most of his life in India.

His letters and journals from those years reveal three broad stages in his journey. In his first few years in India he expressed the desire to bring Christ to the people of India, and he saw Christianity as the fulfillment and culmination of Hinduism. This attitude changed under the impact of deeper and deeper advaitan experiences brought about by his meeting with Sri Ramana Maharshi and his long retreats on the sacred mountain of Arunachala. The growing advaitan life within him precipitated a long struggle to reconcile it with his Christianity. In his final years when he finally had found a true disciple in the French theological student Marc Chaduc, it appears as if that struggle resolved itself in favor of advaita.

We are left at once admiring his spiritual courage to plunge into the depths of the advaitan experience, while at the same time regretting the limits of his theological formation that made this such a torment, and in final analysis, not being able to embrace the advaitan formulations of Christianity that he set forth in order to resolve the conflict.

In the early stages of his stay at Arunachala he realized that his life as a Hindu sannyasi, that is, as a wandering Hindu monk given over to the contemplative life, had been in his mind a means of an apostolate to bring Christ to India, and not seen so much for itself. Now he begins to contemplate that goal in a more radical way.[7] Yet, at this early stage, he still will say, "I dream of a Christian India because I think that then only will India find its spiritual fulfillment."[8]

But with his deepening experience of advaita comes the growing tendency to look at Christianity with advaitan eyes. "Descend to the greatest depth of myself, into the divine Self, ground of my own self, and embrace all beings in nonduality." And in a moment he will write about this kind of deep knowledge, "Is that not in any case the essence of eternal life defined by Christianity…?"[9]

Or more pointedly, "And the Spirit in his own time will cause to arise in the dawning of my soul, the Supreme Ego, the "I am Brahma," (*Brahma aham asmi*) the true I (*aham*)." But then he will immediately say something that is very difficult to reconcile with the inner spirit of Christianity, "It is a mistake to say THOU to the Spirit, for the Spirit is not other than myself."[10]

He writes profoundly of the advaitan experience: "One simply IS. And this fundamental experience is at the same time that of the unique and single EXISTENCE."[11] And he goes on to say how this existence, or BEING, embraces what one used to call one's self, or others, or God. But he is unable to look at this experience from the perspective of his own Christian faith and the resources of the Christian mystical and metaphysical traditions.

He will write, "Dare to make the final leap into pure *advaita* – so the voice continually whispers to me…"[12] But the way he is doing this is going to make his Christianity seem more and more problematical, and this growing difficulty is symbolized by his great reluctance to be at Shantivanam. Yet, at the same time, his Christianity which has such deep roots inside him fights back. "What gnaws at my body as well as my mind is this: after having found in *advaita* a peace and a bliss never experienced before, to live with the dread that perhaps, that most probably, all that my latent Christianity suggests to me is nonetheless true, and that therefore *advaita* must be sacrificed to it... In committing myself totally to *advaita*, if Christianity is true, I risk committing myself to a false path for eternity..."[13] Unfortunately, it does not seem to occur to him that there could be a way to live out both the deep advaitan experience and his deep commitment to the Christian faith.

It is worth looking at in more detail – but still very briefly considering the hundreds of pages that Abhishiktananda's letters and journals cover- first at these interior conflicts and then how he seemed to resolve it in favor of an advaitan perspective. He writes in his journal for Christmas, 1953: "Christmas in the depths of the heart, at the heart of Arunachala. But can an advaitan Christmas be felt? Whatever is felt is not of the truth. Whatever is thought is not of the truth..." But in a moment he goes on: "And even so I let myself be caught up in singing First Vespers and Matins. And I was tormented while remembering the joys of the past."[14] He sums up this trial: "From now on I have tasted too much of *advaita* to be able to recover the "Gregorian" peace of a Christian monk. Long ago I tasted too much of that "Gregorian" peace not to be anguished in the midst of my *advaita*."[15]

A little later he will write: "The West has never really accepted that there is anything beyond understanding. In fact, the concept of understanding has taken precedence over the concept of being." In a similar vein, "every Thou addressed to God is a lie, or rather an error."[16] It is as if he takes the valid idea that the divine reality transcends our thoughts and feelings, but unduly extends it under the influence of advaita so that it becomes a principle that can only be destructive of Christianity. Then he is led to say: "The mystery of the living God is no other than the mystery of the *atman*."[17] Or, "Christianity can only be advaitan."[18] And yet, with all this, he writes on Dec. 26th, 1954: "Christmas eve full of anguish. Very different from last year. A deeper fall into the abyss. Walking on a knife-edge. Unable to decide for one side or the other. What a torment."[19]

As late as 1970 we find traces of this same conflict. One day he will write: "Christianity has been ossified into a religion." And the next, "The fundamental anguish of no longer being able to find one's "bearings" in a faith that is woven into one's guts!" And yet, a few days later, "...the whole long history of salvation boils down to the blinking of an eye – a flash of lightning – an awakening. It has its conceptual, mythical and sociological form only for one who is not awakened..."[20]

But towards the end of his life, probably under the influence of having the experience of a disciple who seemed to whole-heartedly give himself to the advaitan experience, the conflict seems to lessen and be resolved from an advaitan perspective. "The saving name of Jesus is Brahman, it is *atman*. He saves by revealing the *atman-brahman*... Nothing that is on the conceptual level has absolute value. Now, Christian dogmas are conceptual-mythical expressions of the "mystery". "Christ's *namarupa* (names and forms) necessarily explodes, but the Church wants to keep us virtually at the level of the *namarupa*."[21] Later he will continue that thought: "Christ is not a *namarupa*. His true name is I AM."[22] What he is saying is that Christianity, and Hinduism as well, as religions are the conceptual expression of the fundamental experience of advaita, and as such they must be transcended. "Christian experience is really the experience of *advaita* lived out in human communion. And that is what the Trinity is. But we have sought to escape this fire by deifying formulas and institutions."[23] Or, "Do I call him Christ? Yes, within one tradition, but his name is just as much Emmanuel-Purusha. Can he be Krishna? Rama? Shiva? Why not, if Shiva is in Tamulnadu the form of that archetype which seeks to become explicit at the greatest depth of the human heart?"[24]

With this kind of approach not only the whole effort to theologically understand the mystery of Jesus that appears in the Gospel dissolves, but the Incarnation, itself, becomes a manifestation of the advaitan experience. "The Jewish-Greek effort to give an absolute character to the Incarnation is the effort of someone who has not been blinded by the Divine Light."[25] Christianity as it has been traditionally understood in the Church and how Abhishiktananda, himself, understood it as a Benedictine monk, recedes away. Advaita moves to the center of the stage and everything is interpreted in the light of his profound experience of it. "The trinitarian mystery is the revelation of my own depth... The Trinity can only be understood in the experience of *advaita*."[26]

Jacques Dupuis on Abhishiktananda

Jacques Dupuis, a Belgian Jesuit, spent many years in India where he had known Abhishiktananda. In recent years he taught at the Gregorian University in Rome, and edited its review *Gregorianum*. His deep theological interest in interreligious dialogue, together with a personal sympathy for Abhishiktananda and his interior journey, make his evaluation of Abhishiktananda's work all the more interesting.

He begins his study of Abhishiktananda in his *Jesus Christ at the Encounter of World Religions* by pointing out that Abhishiktananda's encounter with Hinduism was more difficult than that of the native Indian convert to Catholicism Brahmabandhab Upadhyaya who at the beginning of the century had also wished to live as a Hindu-Christian monk. For Upadhyaya Hinduism was a cultural and social reality while, as we have seen for Abhishiktananda, it meant a terrible struggle in order to live out what he conceived as the implications of advaita. Dupuis summarizes the kinds of questions that he faced: "Is this the experience of which the Christian mystics have spoken and written? It is at least akin to it: Both are in themselves ineffable, beyond words and concepts. However, is not the experience of advaita still more radical than its Christian counterpart, if it is really the awareness of the Absolute itself translated into a poor, reflected gleam in the ephemeral consciousness of my phenomenal self – a reflection that denies itself in the very act of self-expression, in the awakening of authentic awareness?"[27]

Advaita seemed to demand of Abhishiktananda "the supreme renouncement of himself, and over and above that, the still more radical renouncement of the Divine "You" encountered in prayer."[28] If advaita appeared to Abhishiktananda to require this, it is little wonder that this struggle would last "almost to the end. It is not an exaggeration or derogatory to say that his whole life was marked by the quest for a synthesis – ever elusive, never accomplished – save in the "discovery of the Grail" that swept him off."[29]

Dupuis believes that Abhishiktananda found a certain serenity at the end of his life in accepting "a life of irresoluble tension transcending theoretical reconciliations. Abhishiktananda writes: "It is still best, I think, to hold, even in extreme tension, these two forms of a single 'faith,' until the dawn appears."[30] Dupuis also feels that Abhishiktananda came upon an answer after his heart attack in 1973, and expressed it as follows: "After several days, it finally came to me, like the marvelous solution of an equation: I have found the Grail. And I say this, I write it, to anyone who can grasp the image. At bottom, the quest for the Grail is but the quest for Self. It is a unique quest, signified by all the myths and symbols."[31]

But certainly we can ask, as we have asked before, whether this Grail is not, in fact, Abhishiktananda's acceptance of the ultimacy of the experience of advaita from which he will now serenely judge all things, Christianity included. How else are we supposed to think when Abhishiktananda insists that Christianity is a realm of words and forms, while advaita, in itself, is an existential experience? Given this perspective, he will write: "The awakening to mystery has nothing to do with the dogmas of the Trinity, the Incarnation, the Redemption... The whole Trinitarian edifice collapses."[32]

Statements such as this lead Dupuis to point out their problematical theological character. Is it really possible, for example, to draw such sharp distinctions between concepts and experience, and the Jesus of history and the Christ of faith? "Are we then to say that the *advaita* experience, in its ineffability, ultimately transcends the Trinitarian experience, which depends on concepts...?"[33] "Should we, and can we... identify the consciousness of Jesus with the *advaita* experience...?"[34] And Dupuis concludes: "We have seen that Abhishiktananda's experience poses more problems than it solves. The way in which he experienced the encounter between Hindu *advaita* and Christian doctrine seems to pose more than one dilemma: between mystical apophaticism and theological cataphaticism; between a unity that abolishes distinctions and an interpersonal communion that deepens in direct proportion to the distinctions themselves; between history conceived as an epiphenomenon of relative value and history invested with ontological density."[35]

The issues that Dupuis raises have a single root. Abhishiktananda has taken the perspective of advaitan experience and views everything from there. The non-conceptual nature of that experience, for example, leads him to question the validity of concepts in general, as well as the value of history. Christianity and its most intimate mysteries of the Trinity and the Incarnation – however much Abhishiktananda was attached to them – become mythic formulations pointing to the advaitan experience that transcends these names and forms like it does all names. Little wonder that Abhishiktananda felt that he was being torn in two because such an interpretation leaves little of authentic Christianity intact. Did he arrive at a true synthesis of Christianity and advaita in the closing moments of his life? It seems unlikely. Rather, it is more probable that he accepted the advaitan perspective that he had been moving towards for so long.

It is important to realize that Abhishiktananda's dilemma, and particularly his answer to it is not intrinsic to the Hindu-Christian dialogue itself. Dupuis indicates that it was not present in the same way in the life of Upadhyaya, nor does it appear in the same way in the life of Jules Monchanin with whom he founded Shantivanam, or that of Bede Griffiths who followed him there.

Bettina Bäumer

Bettina Bäumer, who could be called a disciple of Abhishiktananda, describes him as someone who "underwent this excruciating and blissful experience, remaining faithful to both traditions and he found freedom by transcending both."[36] This idea of transcending both is amplified when she writes: "A Christian may reach a point in his or her experiences where the externals of religion are transcended, and thus touch also upon the experience of other traditions. This has been called "transcending religions" in a mystical experience, where the labels do not matter any longer."[37]

How does this work out in practice? "If somebody asks (or I ask myself): how can you believe in Christ and Shiva at the same time? My answer will be a further question: who is Christ? Who is Shiva? And, who am I? Shiva is not a name or any mythological personality, he is the "gracious one", the great Lord (*Parameshvara*), the ultimate Reality (*anuttara*), the most intimate I-consciousness of every conscious being. Christ is not merely the historical personality, otherwise I would not have cared to follow him. He is "the Way, the Life and the Truth" – but not in an exclusive sense; on the contrary. Even beyond that he is essentially the "I am": "Then you will know that 'I am'." How can one limit the "I am" to only one person? Here I learn from Kashmir Shaivism or Ramana Maharshi that the ultimate "I" of every conscious being is the divine "I". The ultimate realization is not of some "objective" truth: "This is He", but the personal discovery: "I am He". In this way every spiritual practice in the inter-religious context leads to a kind of purification from mere conceptions."[38]

But in this passage it is not both traditions that are transcended – which, in itself would pose all sorts of problems for Christianity – but rather, Christianity is transformed into Hindu categories.

In an article called "Abhishiktananda and the Challenge of Hindu-Christian Experience" she develops these ideas more at length. She feels that there are four stages in Abhishiktananda's evolution in which he goes "from the convinced missionary with a certain fulfillment theology to the stage of one who was shaken by a real encounter with Hindu spirituality and torn apart by two experiences, two 'ultimates', two identities, two worlds of religious expression, and, in his own words, 'two loves'; from there to a third stage of relativizing all formulations, all 'names-and-forms', all concretizations of the one, unspeakable, inexpressible Mystery, and, finally, to a stage of reidentifying the 'correspondences' which he discovered at both ends of his experience in the light of an 'explosion' of all previous concepts."[39]

It is this last stage that most interests us because where I am seeing a certain acceptance by Abhishiktananda of his advaitan perspective, and thus, a lessening of tension because of this, Bettina Bäumer is finding a more positive meaning, "which amounts to a liberation, which did not destroy his faith in Jesus but transformed it."[40] Let's look at several of the passages in Abhishiktananda she brings forth to demonstrate this. "Moreover I recognize this mystery, which I have always adored under the symbol of Christ, in the myths of Narayana, Prajapati, Shiva, Purusha, Krishna, Rama, etc. as the same mystery. But for me, Jesus is my *sadguru*. It is in him that God has appeared to me; it is in his mirror that I have recognized myself, in adoring him, loving him, consecrating myself to him."

"Christ is the total transparency of this *aham asmi* (I AM) to which I awaken at the source of my consciousness. Christ – if he has any value for me – is the very mystery of this awakening to myself."[41]

Unfortunately, these kinds of passages seem to emphasize the basic problem rather than resolve it. Abhishiktananda seems to be saying that he has a special relationship to Christ because that is how he enters into the advaitan experience. But it is this experience, itself, which is firmly in the center of his spiritual universe, and Krishna, Rama, or Buddha, can all be ways to transcend the world of names and forms, and enter into advaita. It is precisely the centrality given to the advaitan experience which is at issue. Once it is put in the center of things in this way Christianity, as it has been historically understood, is transformed in a way which appears incompatible with Christian faith.

Sara Grant

Sara Grant, a Catholic sister and a member of the Hindu-Christian ashram Christa Prema Seva, made a detailed study of Sankara, the 9th century Hindu sage, and she came to the conclusion that Sankara and Thomas Aquinas agree on the kind of relationship that exists between creator and creation. They find a relationship in which the creation is dependent on the cause "for its very existence as a subsistent entity, whereas the cause is in no way dependent on the effect for its subsistence."[42]

This is certainly promising for the Hindu-Christian dialogue, but how does it fit in with the doctrine of nonduality that is expressed by the great Hindu sages when they utter words like *tattvamasi*, that art thou, or *aham brahmasmi*, I am Brahman? Sara Grant writes: "…even today it remains an open question whether Sankara personally believes in this ultimate survival of the individual as such. Most commentators would probably say he did not."[43] But this does not seem to give her much pause in subtitling her book: "Confessions of a Christian Non-Dualist." She goes on to say: "that the Gospel lived radically leads straight to advaita." And "the perfect practical handbook for living out advaita is the Gospel."[44] This, she feels, would have all sorts of theological repercussions for we would have to look at: "our dualistic way of thinking and speaking about God as somehow "over against" us, as an ultimate Object, or even "Thou"."[45]

Abhishiktananda Through Advaitan Eyes

Whatever the difficulties we might have in deciding just where Abhishiktananda stood, he can appear quite straight-forward to an advaitan Hindu, as witnessed by Swami Nityananda Giri's article, "Sadguru Sri Gnananda" who was Abhishiktananda's guru. There Swami Nityananda tells the story of how Sri Gnananda met a Jesuit priest from Tamil Nadu who was drawn to advaita, and who Abhishiktananda had advised to see him. The Jesuit "asked the sage whether he should become a Hindu to pursue his advaitic Vedantic *sadhana*. Sri Gnanananda told him that there was no need to change his religion. Vedanta is the transcendent element in all great religions. He should go deep into his own religion and would discover it there. Advaita would make a Christian, a true Christian. Later the priest became an internationally known teacher of Zen meditation."[46]

This sounds much like the kind of advice that Yamada Roshi would give to his Christian students, and we need not take this story as an indication that the Jesuit accepted it without qualification, but simply as a typical Eastern attitude towards Christianity. Nityananda gives us a straight-forward vedantan view of Christianity. Christ is an avatar, and God appears at a certain stage as the Lord of creation and the cause of it. But at a higher stage we have to go beyond God to the Godhead, or Brahman. "God and Godhead are to be understood as two states of the One Reality: the Relative and the Absolute, the Becoming and the Being. The Godhead is the *plenum* of undifferentiated Existence beyond time, space and causation, which is called *sat*."[47]

All this is very beautiful and of great metaphysical depth, but from a Christian perspective does not embrace the whole essence of Christianity. And what conclusion does Swami Nityananda come to about Abhishiktananda? "When we read Swami Abhishiktananda's description of his experience of 'I AM', it is clear that he left far behind all his theological attempts to get the advaitic experience into a Trinitarian framework."[48] And he has plenty of ammunition to draw on for this conclusion, including a letter that Abhishiktananda wrote to Murray Rogers: "The more I go (on), the less able I would be to present Christ in a way which could still be considered as Christian..."[49]

Once again, the point here is not to denigrate in the least the essential advaitan experience, which I believe to be a profound mystical experience of God, but because it is so powerful it needs to be handled by Christians with great delicacy.

Naturally there is much more to the Christian-Hindu dialogue than the role played by Abhishiktananda, but he illustrates in a profound and interior way the same kind of issues we have seen in regard to the Sanbo Kyodan school.

Anthony de Mello

Anthony de Mello in his book *Sadhana: A Way to God* suggests doing various exercises like becoming aware of one's breath. He warns people, however, not to overdo it lest they produce hallucinations or, "draw out material from the unconscious that you may not be able to control."[50] He goes on to deal with an objection sometimes raised in his contemplation groups that such an exercise in awareness has nothing to do with Christian prayer and contemplation. In response he tells us that such an exercise is contemplation like that found in the *Cloud of Unknowing*, or in John of the Cross' "dark night of the senses."[51] We have a mystical faculty of the heart which would spring into action if we would quiet the dross of words, thoughts and images that cover it. It is a loving, silent gaze at God, but since God is formless, we are gazing at a blank. "Now that is just what is demanded of some people if they would go deep into communion with the Infinite, with God: gaze for hours at a blank."[52] If they persevere they will little by little discover there is a glow in that darkness, that their idleness is filled with God's activity.

This is where exercises in awareness come in. We must silence the mind, and this is what we do with exercises like observing our breathing. Thus, such an exercise is contemplation in the strict sense of the word.[53] Indeed, the results are identical with religious exercises and with what people experience while practicing "the prayer of faith or the prayer of quiet."[54]

What are we to think of this? At the least, it is oversimplified and misleading. Christian contemplation, strictly speaking, or its initial stages in the prayer of quiet is not the result of anything we can do. Nor does someone like John of the Cross advise us to deliberately silence our discursive activity. While the terminology here may be Christian, the structure is borrowed from Eastern thought and imposed on a Christian situation. Therefore, those in his contemplative groups who questioned de Mello were raising important issues that his answers do not adequately deal with.

After I wrote these lines about de Mello, the Congregation for the Doctrine of the Faith issued a warning letter about the dangers they felt existed in de Mello's writings. This set off an uproar by evoking all sorts of emotions that have polarized the Church since the time of the Second Vatican Council, and it brought forth criticisms of Rome's insensitivity to the concrete demands of interreligious dialogue. But two points need to be made about this. First, we need to look at the dynamics that underlie these kinds of conflicts, which we will do when we look at the state of contemporary Catholic theology. This is a question we will turn to in *Chapter 3*. But there is another issue, as well. Are there, in fact, theological deficiencies in de Mello's writings that ought to be examined?

Bede Griffiths

Wayne Teasdale's *Toward a Christian Vedanta* which appeared in 1987 was one of the first major studies of Bede Griffiths, and it directly addresses an issue that is closely allied to the questions we have been pursuing. "Can there be a Christian advaita?" it asks, a Christian form of Vedanta?[55] And Teasdale tries to answer these questions by looking closely at Bede Griffith's understanding of the relationship between the Trinity and Saccidananda, or Hinduism's being, knowledge and bliss, which represents the fullest experience of advaita. He sets this question in its context by looking at the history of Christian sannyasa, that is, attempts by Christians, starting with Roberto de Nobili and later Brahmabandhap Upadhyaya, to live out the Hindu monastic quest for the absolute as Christians.

Bede's attempt to create a Christian sannyasa embraces not only a similar lifestyle at the ashram of Shantivanam, but a theology and contemplative spirituality, as well. Bede writes: "We seek to express our Christian faith in the language of the Vedanta as the Greek Fathers expressed it in the language of Plato and Aristotle."[56] And the heart of this attempt is the relationship between Saccidananda and the Trinity. Here we return to the issue that we saw tormenting Abhishiktananda. Abhishiktananda was an important influence on Bede as one of the founders of Shantivanam, and as a radical pioneer on the path of trying to create a Christian sannyasa. If we put the whole question in another way we can ask how we should interpret the language that stems from the Upanishads, the "thou art that." "I am Brahman." Do we see it as a testimony to ontological identification, or do we take them as mystical utterances pointing to the transformation of the soul in God by knowledge and love?

Bede comments on these statements: "In the depth of your own consciousness you are one with that power which creates the tree. You are one with the Brahman. So in the depth of our own being each one of us can experience this reality of Brahman, the source, the ground of all existence and of all consciousness. That is the Hindu mystical experience."[57] But he understands them in the sense of a transformation by knowledge and love. He does not accept the assertion that the individual person is "finally lost in the ultimate state of unity." Bede "maintains that the person only loses his or her separate existence, not identity, for that remains. The person is transfused with the Divine light, "and participates in the very being and consciousness of God.""[58]

Bede also emphasizes the role of the Purusha, or Lord of Creation, or Supreme Person in Hindu thought, which he sees as an expression of the personal aspect of the supreme reality, and one with Atman or Brahman, and thus bringing out the role of a personal God in Hinduism. In this way "the ultimate reality, the Brahman, is conceived as a personal being, the object of worship and adoration."[59] It is already possible to notice a difference in tone that is emerging between Bede and the Abhishiktananda we saw in his journals. Bede also distinguishes advaita as a state of mystical consciousness from advaita as expounded by Sankara. "...that kind of advaita which denies any reality to this world and says that God alone is real is only one form of Vedanta, and one which I certainly would never accept."[60]

Abhishiktananda will say, "Engulfed in the abyss, he (man) has disappeared to his own eyes, to his own consciousness. The proximity of that mystery which the prophetic traditions name God has burnt him so completely that there is no longer any question of discovering it in the depths of himself, or himself in the depths of it. In the very engulfing, the gulf itself has vanished. If a cry were still possible – at the moment perhaps of disappearing into the abyss – it would be paradoxically: 'But there is no abyss, no gulf, no distance.' There is no face-to-face, for there is only That-which-Is and no other to name It. 'Advaita!' "[61]

Teasdale comments that the line "God has burnt him so completely" indicates "not identity, but suggests an intimate union that obscures distinction. The rest would seem to imply a kind of identity, but it can also mean that the experience of unity with the Absolute is so deep and intense, that it is *as if* only the Absolute really is. It seems to me – drawing on the Christian tradition of mysticism – that union can be so far-reaching with God, and the soul so dominated by His glory and His act of being, that the person seems to be God. But it is not so in the ultimate sense."[62] A little later he writes, "*Sat* is actually the pure intuition and experience of one's own being in God's, or the experiential intuition of the Divine's being, the Brahman's, at the center of one's own existential act."[63]

Bede takes the relationship of Jesus with the Father as the ultimate model for a Christian advaita. There is unity, yet distinction, and he stresses the relational aspect. He carries the same perspective into his view of the Trinity. "In the Godhead itself, in the Ultimate Reality there is unity-in-distinction... It is all interpersonal relationship."[64] Elsewhere he writes, "The Ultimate Reality is love, and love *is* relationship."[65]

Teasdale clearly sees that Abhishiktananda's views on the relationship between Saccidananda and the Trinity need to be distinguished from the positions taken by Jules Monchanin and Bede. Abhishiktananda identifies the two while Bede is much more circumspect. Bede is really asking whether the doctrine of the Trinity can be expressed not only in Western theological language, too dominated in his mind by Greek thought, but in the sat, cit, ananda language of India. That is a properly Christian theological question, however difficult it is to answer. It must be realized, for example, that the baptism of Plato and Aristotle meant a transformation of their philosophies, and not a simple acceptance of them as a whole, still less a subordination of the mysteries of Christian faith to them. The insight that gave birth to Saccidananda is a kind of deep intuition of being, and therefore a very good candidate as an instrument to help create a Christian theology cast in Hindu terminology, but it is also an intuition that took place in India not in a philosophical or speculative way, but rather, in a mystical manner as the goal that the seer sought to unite himself to. Abhishiktananda, as we saw, tended to identify this goal with the goal of the Christian life of prayer and contemplation, but even if we reject this identification, we can still accept the authenticity of the Saccidananda experience and use it as a way to create an Indian theology.

While here and there Teasdale seems to express some hesitation about the relationship between Bede and Abhishiktananda in regard to this identification of Saccidananda and the Trinity, i.e., Bede "does not reduce the two experiences to each other,"[66] and says, "although an identity between Saccidananda and Trinity is not claimed by Bede, it is perhaps implied,"[67] it is because he is struggling, as Bede did, to be faithful to the Christian mystical tradition and Christian theology, and yet be fully opened to the beauty and truth to be found in the experience of Saccidananda. Teasdale suggests that there is an existential convergence between the two, but ultimately he concludes:

"In the light of Bede's understanding of a Christian advaita as it has been presented above, I think it is not inappropriate to say that the Trinitarian intuition represents a deeper experience on this ultimate continuum of realization, because of its dimension of personalism which is lacking in Hindu advaita, at least insofar as this has been represented in the mainline literature of Hindu philosophy and spirituality, particularly in the interpretation of the Sankara school of advaitism. Because interpersonal relationship is the essential characteristic of the Trinity, and since this relationship is one of communion in knowledge and love, it is thus a fair assumption to suggest, on the basis of Bede's statements, that the Trinitarian doctrine/intuition is actually a deeper, more ultimate experience of the Ultimate Reality and Mystery than the advaitic/Saccidanandan doctrine/intuition and experience. And this is as it should be, for a Christian can never accept a doctrine as more ultimate than the revelation of the *personal* nature of Divine being that has come to us in Jesus Christ."[68]

There is another perspective in which to look at this issue, and that is to say that in the experience of Saccidananda there is an actual mystical experience of God, but one that rather easily lends itself to being interpreted in nondual terms, while in the experience of the Trinity it is this very same God who is experienced, but now according to a certain inwardness where it is seen that God is a mystery of interpersonal love.

Judson B. Trapnell in *Bede Griffiths: A Life in Dialogue* describes Bede's conversion as a young man and how, in its aftermath, he developed his ideas on faith and religious experience in part by reading Jacques and Raissa Maritain on knowledge by connaturality. It would not be surprising if Bede's conversion experience played an important role in the kinds of distinctions he was to draw later between the Christian life centered on the Trinity, and advaita.

Under the heading of Christian advaita, Trapnell traces Bede's ideas on this theme, and the picture that emerges is similar to the one painted by Wayne Teasdale's study. But Trapnell in a series of articles that appeared in the Indian theological journal *Vidyajhoti* focuses on the differences between this approach of Bede, and that of Abhishiktananda. Bede, he tells us, late in his life became more sensitive to how his own approach differed from Abhishiktananda, a process that was aided by his reading of James Stuart's biography of Abhishiktananda written. "In a 1991 lecture Griffiths remarked that his predecessor at Shantivanam had gone too far in plunging into the experience of advaita and had thereby lost an important measure to balance in his theology."[69]

While Abhishiktananda could exclaim: ""what Christ is, I AM!" and, "I feel too much, more and more, the blazing fire of this I AM, in which all notions about Christ's personality, ontology, history, etc., have disappeared. And I find his real mystery shining in every awakening man, in every mythos,"[70] Bede would comment: "This 'I AM' experience is not my experience. I want to get free of the 'I' and bring it into the ultimate. I find the same (problem) with Ramana Maharshi. It's extremely difficult for me; I feel… it's a language which doesn't resonate with me. With him it seemed to, but it doesn't work with me at all. It confuses, I feel, if you say, 'I AM' is the ultimate. I think the 'I AM' was a preliminary; it was Yahweh who is the 'I AM'. But I think Jesus had gone beyond. Jesus always related to the Father; it's not simply 'I AM'. So that's where I differ."[71] Bede was not going to follow Abhishiktananda in his plunge into advaita "…I think he went too far in that direction," Bede stated.[72]

In a videotaped interview Bede remarks that Abhishiktananda came nearer and nearer to resolving the tension between advaita and his Christianity, but he never really resolved it. He goes on to say that personally he had not the same tension: "I believe that advaita is not one, is not two. It is really relationship. The Trinity is the perfect example of nondual relationship." He goes on and comments that the Hindu name for God is Saccidananda, and the Hindu aims at becoming one with the supreme being, the supreme reality in pure consciousness, and that produces a state of bliss. But it is not exactly love. There is no relationship in it.[73]

In a sympathetic, yet critical article, "Enveloped by Mystery," James Wiseman looked at Abhishiktananda's thought and concluded: "When critiqued in the light of traditional Christian thought, some prominent features of Abhishiktananda's theology are heterodox." And placing it against the background of contemporary discussions about religious pluralism, he comments: "Abhishiktananda's manner of not merely distinguishing between the cosmic Christ and Jesus of Nazareth but sharply dichotomizing them (with Jesus being but one of many authentic manifestations of the ineffable divine reality) cannot be expected to find acceptance in mainstream Catholic or Christian thought.

"Moreover, those who hold that the formulations of traditional Western theology, however ultimately inadequate, nevertheless do provide a genuine access to truth will be uncomfortable with the very sharp dichotomy Abhishiktananda drew between experience and conceptualization..."[74]

Wayne Teasdale

Wayne Teasdale is a Christian sannyasi, that is, a follower of both the Christian and Hindu contemplative paths, and a disciple of Bede Griffiths whose nuanced study of Bede we have just seen. In "Christianity and the Eastern Religions," he puts forward a model of interreligious dialogue that he calls complementarity: "Each tradition has evolved a unique perspective on the one ultimate reality, and each has a contribution to make to the whole picture."[75] And the contribution of each religion is to be sought more on the level of contemplative practice than the conceptual formulation of doctrine.

Hinduism, Buddhism and Christianity, for example, each highlight in different degrees the three fundamental forms of revelation: the cosmic, the mystical, and the historical, and thus lend themselves to the approach of complementarity. When Teasdale looks at the dialogue between Christianity and Hinduism, however, in more detail, the difficulties in carrying out such a program begin to emerge. Abhishiktananda "said that Uphanishadic mysticism brings us to the depths of the Spirit, the same Spirit at the heart of the trinitarian Godhead,"[76] and thus he felt there was "a real ontological continuity between Saccidananda and the Trinity." Teasdale sums up Abhishiktananda's position by saying, "He possessed a certitude that both advaita and Trinity were absolute; he also knew that they were somehow one, but he didn't quite know how this was so."[77]

When it is a question of the dialogue between Buddhism and Christianity, Teasdale tries to show how the Buddhist doctrine of no-self and the Christian doctrine of the Trinity are not as far apart as first may be imagined. God is not a self "in the richest sense of the substance doctrine of Greek essentialistic metaphysics."[78] God is a dynamic interrelationship, an inner communion of being, a Presence. "Ultimately, enlightenment is the awareness of and participation in this interrelationship in communion, in Presence, at the very heart of God: *that* is transcendent consciousness."[79] It, of course, remains a question whether such a formulation really overcomes the difference between self and no-self, and whether Buddhists, themselves, would find it acceptable.

In *The Mystic Heart: Discovering a Universal Spirituality in the World's Religions,* Teasdale eloquently argues for what he calls an interspirituality in which this kind of complementarity among the world's religions will hopefully lead some day, in some form as yet indiscernible in detail, to a universal spirituality. But such a visionary program does not prevent him from asking whether they are all pursuing the same spiritual goal, and in pursuit of an answer, he gives the reader short but incisive summaries of the contemplative paths of Hinduism, Buddhism and monotheistic mysticism. And while his reflections that we have seen in the previous article could be called theoretical, although still dealing with the contemplative path, here in trying to grope towards an answer he seems to rely more on his personal experience: "I have had many Advaitic experiences, and ones that might be regarded as Buddhist in nature. But my primary and enduring understanding is informed by an intimate and personal relationship with God."[80]

This leads him to conclude: "The unitive experience of the God-centered traditions of mysticism points to a strong sense of the person's distinct identity in relation to the divine. This experience is thus vastly different from the Hindu and Buddhist, although in all three of these approaches there is an awakening and enlargement of one's consciousness, identity, and potential. It is really a difference of emphasis, as Bede Griffiths wrote: "Perhaps the fundamental difference is this: that the heart of Christian mysticism is a mystery of love, whereas both in Hinduism and in Buddhism it is primarily a transformation of consciousness." Although the ultimate goals are not identical, they are complementary. The religions need one another precisely because they complete one another! Together, they enlarge our understanding of the ultimate. This is what animates and characterizes interspirituality."[81]

In the videotaped interview *The Heart of the Christian-Hindu Dialogue*, Teasdale gives a richly detailed account of the history of the Hindu-Christian dialogue, and goes on to describe the relationship between advaita and Christian contemplation: "When you experience pure unity with God, there is the temptation to feel that the identity of the person is obliterated, or that the experience of being overshadowed by God, overwhelmed by the divine, so invades the identity of the person that the person's identity is submerged and becomes so totally passive and experientially like a shadow identity; it is like a phantom identity. So one can jump to the conclusion that one's identity is not real because it is overshadowed; it is overwhelmed and invaded. I feel much of the language of pure unity… derives from a misunderstanding of the experience of unity… There is the personal. God is both personal and impersonal. In the whole Buddhist nirvanic consciousness there is a dimension of God, of the Godhead. Pure advaita is a dimension of it, but the personal is also a dimension of it… There is a dynamic communion going on within God."[82]

Kundalini Yoga

There is a dialogue between Christianity and Yoga, as witnessed to by books like Thomas Matus' *Yoga and the Jesus Prayer Tradition* and Thomas Ryan's *Prayer of Heart & Body*, but at first glance there is nothing in the religions of the East that seems stranger and more alien to Christian spirituality than kundalini yoga. There the latent energies of the body that the ancient Hindus conceived in the form of a serpent coiled around the base of the spine could be awakened by breathing exercises and meditation, and made to ascend the psychic nerve channel associated with the spine, awakening the various energy centers, or chakras leading to a transformation of both body and mind. The first chakra at the base of the spine is called the *muladhara*. It is said to have four petals, be yellow in color and is associated with the element earth. The next psychic center is in the area of the reproductive organs. This is the *svadhishthana* with six petals. It is white and associated with water. Next, at the navel, comes the *manipura* chakra with ten red petals symbolizing the element of fire. It is followed by the heart, or *anahata*, chakra with twelve petals. This chakra is smoky and is associated with air. At the base of the throat we find the *visuddha* chakra of sixteen petals. It is blue, and connected with ether. Between the eyebrows is the *ajna* chakra with two petals and associated with mind, and according to Swami Sivananda, visions of a personal god.[83] The final chakra and the goal which the energy has been seeking is the *sahasrara* with 1,000 petals. It is here that the yogi "loses his individuality in the ocean of sat-chit-ananda, or existence-knowledge-bliss" and becomes one with the lord or supreme soul.[84] This kundalini energy is awakened by pranayama, or breathing exercises, asanas or yoga postures, mudras, or special yogic gestures, concentration and devotion.

Kundalini was cultivated not only in ancient Hindu India, but in early Buddhism, as well, from whence it traveled to Tibet and survived until the present, and is to be found in Taoist literature, as well. During the 20th century it became known to the West through such works as *The Serpent Power: The Secrets of Tantric and Shaktic Yoga* by Sir John Woodroffe, *Tibetan Yoga and Secret Doctrines* edited by W.Y. Evans-Wentz, *Taoist Yoga: Alchemy and Immortality* by Lu K'uan Yü, and more recently, through Gopi Krisna's *Kundalini: The Evolutionary Energy in Man*, and through exiled Tibetan meditation masters, for example in Geshe Kelsang Gyatso's *Clear Light of Bliss*. Through these kinds of works we enter into the strange but fascinating world in which it appears that the body, itself, and its deepest energies become the instruments by which enlightenment is achieved.

CHRISTIANITY IN THE CRUCIBLE 89

We might be tempted to write all this off as of no relevance to Christian spirituality, but it is important to note that kundalini-like phenomena have appeared in other times and places with no direct connection with Eastern religions. Among the !Kung Bushmen of the Kalahari Desert in Botswana, for example, it is called *!kia* and is connected with healing and religious functions and is found among many men and women. !Kia is exercised during an all-night dance and is due to an activation of an energy called *n/um* which resides in the pit of the stomach. As the dance progresses the bushmen describe the n/um as something hot that rises up the spine to the base of the skull. It causes the person to shiver and tremble, and rapid shallow breathing draws it up. "You feel it as a pointed something which is in your backbone, and the base of your spine tingles. And then it makes your thoughts nothing in your head."[85]

Further, there has been a contemporary explosion of interest in kundalini in the West with more and more accounts of Westerners who believe they have experienced awakenings of kundalini-like energy. These things can be taken as indications that beneath the rich weight of the esoteric symbolism in traditional Eastern kundalini descriptions there may be a core experience of great power and significance.

Philip St. Romain

It was the publication of Philip St. Romain's *Kundalini Energy and Christian Spirituality* in 1991 that opened the door to the encounter of kundalini yoga and the Christian spiritual path. St. Romain was a Catholic devoted to the Christian life of prayer and contemplation when he underwent an unexpected spontaneous kundalini awakening that threw his life into turmoil. He had at that point no idea of the long traditions of kundalini yoga that existed in the East, and looked in vain in the Christian mystical literature to discover what had happened to him. He struggled to deal with the kundalini experience, itself, with its brightly colored lights, and movements of energy in various parts of the body, as well as to understand it in the light of his own training in biology and psychology, and to bring it into relationship with his own Christian faith.

Gradually he came to the conclusion that the purpose of kundalini was not to gain some sort of higher powers, but to lead to a kind of cosmic consciousness that was close to or identical with the kind of enlightenment found in Zen or other Eastern traditions: "No longer do sense perceptions feed through the intellect; no longer are there "thoughts in my eyeballs," interfering with my perceptions, as of old. Now there is just-seeing, just-smelling, just-tasting – and all this intelligently, with a silent mind.

How sweet it is – this enlightenment experience! How joyful! How freeing! No longer is there any sense of alienation, for the Ground that flows throughout my being is identical with the Reality of all creation."[86]

He eventually saw that it would not do to simply identify kundalini with Christian contemplation, or the working of the Holy Spirit, despite the analogies that exist between the two. He finally arrived at a hard-won sense that the way of kundalini energy and the undeniable beauty of enlightenment complemented but did not replace the Christian spiritual path. He expresses this sense of harmony between the deep experience of Eastern forms of meditation and the Christian life of prayer and contemplation elsewhere,[87] and thus he joins the people we saw in *Chapter 1* who have found no conflict between contemplation and enlightenment at the level of experience. When we look at the question of the affective ego later, we will return to Philip St. Romain's remarkable story.

Our pilgrimage through the writings of Catholic participants in East-West dialogue allows us to see that these dialogues raise any number of important questions. We can summarize some of these issues in a series of interconnected and overlapping points.

The Personal and the Impersonal

Whether ultimate reality is personal or impersonal goes to the very heart of the Buddhist-Christian or Hindu-Christian dialogue. Christianity is fundamentally and intrinsically personal. There is certainly a whole nuanced tradition which tries to explain how God is beyond all the names that are applied to God. But in final analysis, God is affirmed as a person, even a communion of persons, and the Incarnation is supremely personal. To imagine that this I-Thou relationship which is so rooted in Christian thought and which is expressed throughout the

Christian life of prayer and contemplation must, in some way, yield to a higher impersonal stage is, I fear, to seriously misread both the Christian mystical and theological traditions. Even a John of the Cross who is so insistent on us leaving all things behind will sing in his *Spiritual Canticle*, as we saw, "Where have you hidden yourself, my Beloved?" In short, while there is a very strong Christian apophatic tradition that cannot be neglected, it is hard to see how the personal nature of Christianity can give way to some impersonal absolute without Christianity losing its identity. Another way of putting it is that a relational love mysticism is at the very center of Christianity.

Duality and Nonduality

It would be misleading to call Zen Buddhists, and advaitan Hindus nondualists and Christians dualists. It would be better to say that for Christians God is intimately present to all things by giving them the gift of existence moment by moment, and God is even more intimately present by calling all people to share in God's love. There is, then, a certain Christian nondualism, if you will, in which we are called to become God by knowledge and love. But this cannot be given an ontological meaning so that I could say in a metaphysical way, "I am God."

It would probably by wrong, as well, to imagine that Zen Buddhism, or even the advaitan Vedanta is making any kind of ontological nondualist claims. Rather, they are trying to take into account a nondual experience, and sometimes their post-experience reflections can leave the impression that they are creating a nondual ontology. But they are not interested in philosophy in the Western sense, but rather, leading people to the experience, itself. The real question, which we will pursue later, is whether enlightenment is nondual in itself, or is presented in a nondual way because of the very means by which the enlightenment experience is attained. There should be no rush to judgment on the part of Christians as if they need to express Christianity in some nondual ontological fashion. This is not precisely what Zen Buddhists, and advaitan Hindus are doing.

Concepts, Eastern and Christian

A certain insistence in Catholic theology today on the relative and limited nature of concepts is understandable given its over-conceptual past, as well as the impact of post-modern philosophies and deepening dialogues with Eastern religions. But Christian revelation carries with it a healthy respect for conceptual statements. It is implicit in Christian revelation that these statements tell us something about the Christian mysteries, themselves. The webs of concepts, woven by Christian theology, are, of course, limited and inadequate and can be progressively improved. But that is a far different matter than to imagine we can create entirely new webs of concepts, and even webs that are contradictory to each other, and suppose that there is no way to truly judge them against the Christian mysteries, themselves. A Zen Buddhist view of concepts, for example, in which they appear as skillful means, or pointers to the ineffable reality, cannot immediately be assumed to be an adequate model for how concepts are to be used within Christianity.

Core Experiences and the Culturally Conditioned Nature of Language

It has become almost axiomatic that all religions lead to the same summit, and differ only because of the language and culture they express this journey in. But it is a quite different matter to actually prove this. Even from a phenomenological point of view it hardly seems warranted to say that Christianity and Zen Buddhism are simply two paths leading to an identical goal, and that John of the Cross', "Where have you hidden yourself, my Beloved?" is identical to Master Fumon's, "The ocean bed's aflame, and out of the void leap wooden lambs."

We have seen how the Sanbo Kyodan appears to have attempted to isolate a certain core experience of enlightenment and identify it with the heart of Buddhism, and how it is but one more step for the Christian members of the Sanbo Kyodan to imagine that this core experience is at the heart of Christianity, as well. But this is exactly what needs to be demonstrated. If, on the other hand, at the heart of Zen

Buddhism, or advaitan Hinduism is a nondual experience of the ultimate ground of things, and at the heart of Christianity a relational love mysticism, then while they are both dealing with the Absolute, they are doing so under different formalities, and to translate Christianity into nondual Buddhist, or Hindu categories is to alter its fundamental nature.

The Christian Life of Prayer and Eastern Ways of Meditation

The practice of discursive and affective forms of Christian prayer will, according to John of the Cross, lead to the dark night of the senses in the wide sense of that phrase, that is, to a certain interior crisis in which the more palpable and affectively satisfying ways of praying begin to fail. It may well be that Zen or Hindu meditation could play a role in helping Christians to deal with this difficult time of transition, but that is very different from erecting these meditations as a second and completing stage of the Christian life of prayer. Then the problem posed by the dark night of the senses is solved not in confronting the question of Christian contemplation, but by supposing that eastern meditation can take the place of the Christian contemplation that is absent. It has yet to be shown that the experience of enlightenment is equivalent to what happens in the Christian path of contemplation, so such a substitution is unwarranted.

With these issues in mind, let's go on and examine the theological background to this tendency of some Catholics engaged in Eastern forms of meditation to reinterpret Christianity as another example of nonduality.

Notes

1. Siddheswarananda, Swami. *Hindu Thought & Carmelite Mysticism*, p. 14.
2. Ibid., p. 50.
3. Cf. Ralston, Helen, *Christian Ashrams*
4. Coward, Harold. *Hindu-Christian Dialogue*. p. 123
5. Ibid.   6. Ibid., p. 125.
7. Abhishiktananda, *Ascent to the Depth of the Heart*, p. 25
8. Ibid., p. 29.   9. Ibid., p. 35.   10. Ibid., p. 39.

11. Ibid., p. 52.
12. Ibid., p. 66.
13. Ibid., p. 73.
14. Ibid., p. 82.
15. Ibid., p. 74.
16. Ibid., p. 92.
17. Ibid., p. 93.
18. Ibid., p. 94.
19. Ibid., p. 97.
20. Ibid., p. 319.
21. Ibid., p. 346.
22. Ibid., p. 357.
23. Ibid., p. 358.
24. Ibid., p. 360.
25. Ibid., p. 363.
26. Ibid., p. 388.
27. Dupuis, Jacques. *Jesus Christ at the Encounter of World Religions.* p. 71.
28. Ibid., p. 73.
29. Ibid., pp. 73-74.
30. Ibid., p. 75.
31. Ibid., p. 76.
32. Ibid., p. 78.
33. Ibid., p. 83-84.
34. Ibid., p. 84.
35. Ibid., p. 90.
36. Bäumer, Bettina. "A Journey with the Unknown" p. 38.
37. Ibid., p. 41.
38. Ibid., p. 39.
39. Bäumer, Bettina. "Abhishiktananda and the Challenge of Hindu-Christian Experience." p. 34.
40. Ibid., p. 37.
41. Ibid., p. 38.
42. Grant, Sara. *Towards an Alternative Theology.* p. 36
43. Ibid., p. 49.
44. Ibid.
45. Ibid., p. 50.
46. Nityananda, Swami. "Sadguru Sri Gnananda" p. 30.
47. Ibid., p. 31.
48. Ibid., p. 33.
49. Ibid.
50. De Mello. *Sadhana.* p. 24.
51. Ibid., p. 25.
52. Ibid., p. 26.
53. Ibid., p. 30.
54. Ibid., p. 30.
55. Teasdale, Wayne. *Toward a Christian Vedanta*, p. 4.
56. Ibid., p. 66.
57. Ibid., p. 96.
58. Ibid., p. 97.
59. Ibid., p. 100.
60. Ibid., p. 104.
61. Ibid., p. 107-108.
62. Ibid., p. 108.
63. Ibid., p. 109.
64. Ibid., p. 115.
65. Ibid., p. 117.
66. Ibid., p. 127.
67. Ibid., p. 127-128.
68. Ibid., p. 129. Cf. the similar ideas of Jacques Dupuis in *Toward a Christian Theology of Religious Pluralism*, p. 268-279.
69. Trapnell, Judson. "Two Models of Christian Dialogue with Hinduism," p. 102.
70. Ibid., p. 189-190.
71. Ibid., footnote, p. 190.
72. Ibid., p. 244, note 62.
73. Griffiths, Bede. *Exploring the Christian Hindu-Dialogue: Video.*
74. Wiseman, James. "Enveloped by Mystery," p. 256.
75. Teasdale, Wayne. "Christianity and the Eastern Religions." p. 131.
76. Ibid., p. 142.
77. Ibid., p. 144.
78. Ibid., p. 155.

79. Ibid., p. 155.
80. Teasdale, Wayne. *The Mystic Heart*. p. 224-225.
81. Ibid., p. 226-227.
82. Teasdale, Wayne. *The Heart of the Christian-Hindu Dialogue: Video*.
83. Sivananda. *Kundalini Yoga*, p. xxix, p. 256.
84. Ibid., xxix.
85. Katz, Richard. "Education for Transcendence," p. 287.
86. St. Romain, Philip. *Kundalini Energy and Christian Spirituality*, p. 107.
87. St. Romain, Philip. *Christian Prayer & Kundalini:Video* and *Kundalini Energy and Christian Spirituality:Video.* See also the online study on kundalini energy, Christian philosophy and Jungian psychology at http://www.innerexplorations.com/ewtext/ke.htm

PART II

A CRISIS IN CATHOLIC THEOLOGY

CHAPTER 3

THEOLOGY WITHOUT A NET

In *Part I* we saw a tendency among some of the Catholic participants in the East-West dialogue to reinterpret Christianity in Buddhist or Hindu categories. It is worthwhile to try to see where this tendency might be coming from. It arises, I think, from the failure of Christian mysticism, metaphysics and theology to provide them with more adequate tools with which to meet the challenge of dialogue.

Christian Mysticism

Logically we would expect that the Catholic participants in this dialogue would draw heavily on the Christian mystical tradition when confronted with Eastern forms of mysticism. With some notable exceptions, they have not, or when they have, it has often been in a problematical way. In fact, we could say that Eastern enlightenment has tended to fill the vacuum left by their lack of living contact with the Christian mystical tradition, not that they could be held personally responsible for this lack since it is very long-standing and widespread.

It would take us too far afield to explore in detail the historical circumstances in the modern history of Catholic mysticism that have given rise to this situation. I have tried to do this in *From St. John of the Cross to Us: The Story of a 400-year-old Misunderstanding and What it Means for Christian Mysticism,* but in summary this story goes like this: In the aftermath of the diffusion of the writings of the Carmelite mystics Teresa of Avila and John of the Cross in the 17th century, Christians all over Europe and beyond began to ask themselves whether they, too, in any real and practical manner could become contemplatives. This desire fueled an enthusiasm for the contemplative life that was sometimes met with over-simplified and inadequate answers. These answers and the practices they inspired, as well as a deep distrust of mysticism in general on the part of some theologians and some Church authorities, led to the crisis of Quietism at the end of the century. The condemnation of the Quietists and the fear it inspired throughout the Church was sufficient to suppress overt practical interest in Christian mysticism until the beginning of the 20th century, and in some ways, even until after the Second Vatican Council.

It was after the Council that some of the contemporary attempts to renew the contemplative life like the centering prayer movement, or the Christian meditation of John Main, began to spread widely. But these attempts often display a curious myopia about this modern history of Catholic mysticism and are they, themselves, sometimes rather strongly influenced by Eastern forms of meditation. The upshot of all this is what we have been seeing in *Part I*. Catholic priests and religious have discovered in a deeply personal way Eastern forms of meditation, but this has not inspired them to bring these kinds of mysticism into relationship with the Christian mystical tradition because that tradition had vanished from sight long ago.

Christian Metaphysics

Much the same could be said about the Christian metaphysical tradition, but for different historical reasons. There is a Christian metaphysical tradition that we saw surfacing in someone like Thomas Merton, and as we will see later, it is a prime candidate for dialogue with Eastern forms of enlightenment. But it can scarcely be said to have been brought forth by the Christian participants in the East-West dialogue because for the most part it appears not to have been known by them in any efficacious way. To be sure, they were often well acquainted with the traditional neo-scholastic philosophy and theology derived from Thomas Aquinas, but in a manner that left much to be desired, as we will see in a moment. But they were rarely brought into contact with the intuitive heart of St. Thomas' metaphysics, an intuition of being, an intuition into the primary role of the act of existence in regard to essence.

The historical reasons for this are as obscure and yet as important as those we saw in regard to Christian mysticism. Thomas Aquinas in the 13th century made a revolutionary metaphysical discovery which transformed the Greek philosophy he had received from Plato and Aristotle. He saw that existence, and not essence, was the ultimate principle of being. The history of Thomism was to become the history of the loss and rediscovery of this insight. The greatest rediscovery took place in the middle of the 20th century and was brought about by people like Jacques Maritain, Joseph de Finance, Etienne Gilson and others. But for the most part, with the exception of Maritain, they gave little thought to the subjective conditions that played a vital role in achieving this insight in the first place. Students subjected to the neo-scholasticism of the manuals rarely had any sense that beneath these ashes burned a living flame of metaphysical insight, at least in some of the followers of St. Thomas. I have tried to tell something of that story in *God, Zen and the Intuition of Being* and in *Mysticism, Metaphysics and Maritain*.

Therefore, when the Catholic participants in the East-West dialogue encountered Eastern forms of enlightenment which are deeply metaphysical in their own distinctive non-conceptual way, it rarely occurred to them to compare enlightenment with the metaphysical intuition of being because this Christian metaphysical tradition had never made itself known to them.

Christian Theology

The history of modern Catholic neoscholastic philosophy and theology has a similar tale to tell. The story starts in 1893 when Pope Leo XIII issued his encyclical letter *Aeterni Patris*, which made the doctrine of St. Thomas Aquinas normative for the Church. This was a strong impetus for the renewal of Thomist studies that had already been going on. Thomism went on to spread throughout the Church, and was revitalized by a great deal of fine scholarship, and so this turn to St. Thomas could be read as a progressive attempt to renew philosophy and theology.

But soon a dark side to this renewal began to show itself. As an official doctrine, Thomism began to take on the color of the Church's institutional structures; it became both authoritative and defensive, both traits that were not intrinsic to Thomism, itself, or to St. Thomas. These two attitudes, mixed with the need to teach large numbers of students, led to the neo-scholasticism of the manuals. The result at its worst was a Christian doctrine shattered into a thousand pieces and welded back together in the form of syllogisms. The correct expression of verbal formulas gained the upper hand in the classroom and stifled insight and creativity. It was a conceptualism which had no use for the modern world and its ideas, which were reduced to straw men and destroyed in a few lines at the end of an article. This defensiveness did not end with the world outside the Church, but extended itself to pioneers within the Church who wished to make a greater use of modern philosophy or science, or non-Catholic biblical methods and scholarship, or even other traditional schools of philosophy and theology within the Church.

This narrow neo-scholasticism waged a campaign of denunciation and condemnation at the beginning of the 20th century against what became known as modernism. Undoubtedly some of the ideas of the so-called modernists were incomplete, or even incorrect, but they were not met with calm and open, still less charitable, discussion. After World War II it came in conflict again with scholars in the Church who were following other philosophical and theological paths, for example, the transcendental Thomism opened up by Marechal, or those who were finding new theological riches in the Fathers of the Church. A common thread of many of these new developments was the desire for a more positive relationship to the world outside the Church. These attempts loosely labeled *la nouvelle théologie* were not always as philosophically and theologically precise as one would wish – how could such pioneer efforts be born completely formed? – but the response on the part of the Church authorities and the prevailing neo-scholasticism was again not one of open discussion and conciliation, but the same kind of tactics used during the time of the modernists: silencings, denunciations from

Rome, and so forth.

This struggle lasted until the Second Vatican Council and played itself out in the tension between the original schemas, which were written in the old scholastic style, and the desires for reform and openness that had been growing in the Church. But finally the forces of renewal were heard, and scored what appeared to be a decisive victory.

This led to an almost immediate collapse in large parts of the Catholic world of the old neo-scholasticism of the philosophical and theological manuals. Indeed, the speed of this collapse showed that it was propelled by the built-up pressure born of previous repressions. It also showed how little genuine Thomism had entered into the minds and hearts of its students. Authoritarianism, defensiveness and pitiful pedagogy had done their work all too well.

The theology that was born out of the Vatican II era was a more open theology in dialogue with the world outside the Catholic Church. But it was, and is, also what could be called a reaction theology. By a reaction theology I mean an aspect of contemporary Catholic theology which, while it is going about its concerns, is colored by a certain polarization that is the result of its century-long conflict with this prevailing neo-scholasticism.

If this neo-scholasticism was a conceptualism, this new reaction theology tries to see the limits of concepts, but sometimes propelled by its own past, it takes on an anti-conceptual character which begins to deny the validity of concepts as ways to know the Christian mysteries. If neo-scholasticism pretended to be ahistorical, modern Catholic theology has developed a deep and valuable sense of history, but once again at times it moves beyond this legitimate zone of compensation and verges on historicism, that is, a tendency to limit what theology can know to what history can determine. And at the heart of this reaction theology can appear a genuine tragedy. If the old neo-scholasticism acted as if its formulations were equivalent to faith itself, then contemporary theology sometimes not only sees the limitations of these formulations, but tends to overreact and reject both the formulations and the faith they were meant to express. So injured have the emotions of people become by various ecclesiastical insults that these emotions drive this reaction theology into a rejection not only of the theological deficiencies of the past, but to a rejection of

Christian faith, itself.

Theology Without a Net

Robert Frost once said that poetry without rhyme is like playing tennis without a net. The question here is whether contemporary Catholic theology is sometimes playing without a net, that is, without carefully considering the essential link between theological reflection and faith. Without faith, by which I mean an inner assent to the essential Christian mysteries like the Trinity, the Incarnation of the Word, the resurrection of Jesus, and so forth, our theological activity does not rise from its necessary foundation, and thus can drift into a form of personal religious speculation which, however pleasing and clever it may be, is really not the same as theology.

Let me be clear about what I am not trying to do here. I am not talking about the vital theological task of reformulating the traditional theological language in which the Christian mysteries have been expressed in the past. Even though I will look at possible concrete examples of this theology without a net, I am not talking about the personal faith, or lack of it, of this or that particular theologian, still less about their goodness or holiness. I am talking about their published, public theological statements. Nor am I aligning myself with an inquisitorial mentality driven by a narrow theology which stifles genuine theological creativity and is long on the exercise of ecclesiastical power, and short on due process. What I am proposing is a theological conversation in which theology looks at the vital issue of its relationship to faith, and the need of Catholic theology to actually scrutinize what can be said, and what would be in opposition to Christian faith.

A moment ago I called faith an internal assent to the essential Christian mysteries. What does that mean? It rests on an understanding of faith in which it is not simply the use of human reason about religious topics. It is an interior assent that works through love, and brings us into a living contact with God and what God has revealed, that is, the central Christian mysteries which are, in final analysis, persons rather than doctrines. This is a faith that binds the Church together, and is shared by all its members from the Pope and Bishops down to the proverbial little old lady praying the rosary in some tiny village. I would like to think that this is a common faith that is held not only by Catholics around the world, but one which they share with John the Evangelist, and Thomas who doubted, with Ignatius of Antioch, with Augustine and Thomas Aquinas, and Karl Rahner.

This is the faith that has a content, and this content has been expressed by the Apostle's Creed, and the Nicene Creed, and could be expressed in some new way, but with its substance remaining the same. If I decide that I no longer believe, for example, that Jesus died for my redemption and actually rose from the dead, or that God is like a loving mother or father who hears my prayers, and who calls me to eternal life, then I should ask myself whether my reflections about these things are really theology, or whether, in fact, I am proposing my own alternative to the Catholic faith. If it is the latter that I am doing, then I should be clear about it to myself and to the people I am addressing.

I hope the following examples of reaction theology represent a certain extreme, or even fringe, of Catholic theology, but they let us situate the tendencies to reinterpret Christianity that we saw in *Chapters 1* and *2* against the wider background of the current crisis in Catholic theology. In the next chapter we will look at the question of religious pluralism against this same background.

Ivone Gebara

Ivone Gebara is a Brazilian Sister of Our Lady who is well versed in traditional theology and philosophy. In her *Longing for Running Water: Ecofeminism and Liberation* she gives us the example of a contemporary theology trying to be more relevant to modern needs. This is a theology which reacts against the old tradition of conceptualism, but in doing so, puts itself in a problematic relationship with essential Christian doctrines.

She contrasts a patriarchal epistemology that informed the traditional theology with an ecofeminist epistemology that she wants to infuse the new theology. The old was based on an ahistorical metaphysics that put the center of life outside the cares of struggles of daily existence, and outside of history, itself. It focused on immutable doctrine and eternal truths at the price of human beings and their concrete needs. These revealed truths took on a life of their own, and could not be questioned in the light of the "Christian communities' history and lived experience. This situation also leads to teachings that sanction the power invested in male Church authorities to act as the guardians of fidelity to these doctrines. These authorities exercise control over what the faithful can and should believe, claiming that their power comes from Jesus Christ..."[1]

Read as a sociological critique of the old theology and its attendant power structures, this kind of analysis has much to recommend it. We may say that it gives us another valuable perspective on the old conceptualism and the uses and abuses of power that often went with it.

Her remedy is to propose an ecofeminist epistemology more in line with the meaningful experiences of our lives. Here the duality of the old theology between body and mind will be overcome, and we will "live the oneness of the matter and energy that are our very makeup without knowing what that oneness really is... We will welcome the transformation of our individual bodies into the mystery of our Sacred Body."[2] If we take these sentiments as expressions of a desire for a more holistic spirituality, conscious of its feminine and ecological nature, all well and good. But Sr. Gebara is led to create a new theology that not only reacts against the ills of the old, but seems to empty out the faith of its distinctive Christian content.

In it, relatedness is seen as the most basic characteristic of the human person. "(R)elatedness is the primary and ultimate ground of all that exists."[3] God is relatedness, we are told, but we are also told that "relatedness is not an entity apart from other beings; rather, it is a mystery that is associated with all that exists. Relatedness is *utterance, word, attraction, flux, energy* and *passion*... We are all both created within and creators of this relatedness."[4]

In this way she hopes to overcome the dualism of the old theology which treated the material and spiritual as if they were separate substances. "...God is not a pure essence existing in itself; rather, God is *relationship*."[5] "...We no longer speak of God existing before creation, but, in a way, as concomitant with it."[6] It is easy to sympathize with the feelings that drive this project which embrace a compassion for the poor and marginalized and a keen sense of the limitations of the old theology. But we have to ask whether we are seeing the beginnings of a new philosophy and theology, or the loss of the distinctive nature of the Catholic faith.

Sr. Gebara goes on to say things like: "prayer has to be rediscovered as a human need."[7] "We pray because we need contact with ourselves, with our community, and with the entire universe."[8] And she feels that we must ask about the concrete human needs that lead us to talk about the Trinity. "To what human experience is the Trinity related?"[9] She answers that the experience is one of human multiplicity and fragility. "This multiple divergence is Trinity."[10] ""Trinity" is the name we give ourselves..."[11]

The old theology "petrified language" and went on "to condemn or declare among the saved those who are unfaithful or faithful to their formal institutions and their discourse..."[12] This is a good point, but is the proper response to it what we have been seeing? She states the problem: "The Trinity has been presented as the absolute, the totally different, the altogether superior, independent, and perfect Being."[13] But her response is: "The Father, Son and Holy Spirit are not of divine stuff as opposed to our human stuff; rather, they are relationships – relationships we human beings experience and express in metaphorical rather than metaphysical terms."[14]

Her treatment of Jesus is much the same. While Jesus still enjoys a special place, He is "no longer the absolute reference in a dogmatic sense, that is, in the way it was presented in the metaphysical Christology..." She honors Jesus, but free of dogmatic refinements because "the christological dogmatics that has come down to us from Nicaea and Chalcedon, along with their later "refinements," took away the good flavor of the Jesus-words..."[15]

Sr. Gebara calls herself not a post-Christian, but a "post-dogmatic and post-patriarchal" Christian. Even the most solemn dogmatic formulas of the Church councils no longer speak to her. Rather, we must "dare to free Jesus from the hierarchical and dogmatic apparel in which the church has clothed him for so long."[16]

She also makes some reflections on the role that Jesus plays in the salvation of the human race. "...If we no longer speak of the salvific uniqueness of Jesus, the Christ, many feel we give up the power and uniqueness of our faith... I believe that to affirm the incarnation, or the bodiliness, of the divine does not necessarily require that Jesus have some unique metaphysical character."[17] Do we really need to say, though, that Jesus "is not the savior of all humanity" or "not the powerful son of God," but rather the "symbol of the vulnerability of love" and who "as an individual person is not superior to any other human being?"[18]

Tissa Balasuriya

Tissa Balasuriya is a Sri Lankan theologian and member of the Oblates of Mary Immaculate who rocketed to notice in the world of theology when he was excommunicated for the views presented in his *Mary and Human Liberation*. He can be said to be well versed in traditional theology in virtue of his training, i.e., licentiates in both philosophy and theology from the Gregorian University in Rome, and in contemporary theology in virtue of his interest in Asian liberation and feminist theology. The controversy that surrounded his book after his condemnation illustrates two of the prevailing themes in today's theological activity. Progressives around the world rallied to his defense, but what motivated them was their outrage at the Roman procedures which led to his excommunication and which seemed to them to be grossly deficient in terms of due process. What didn't seem to get the same attention was his theology, itself, and whether he was or was not saying things that conflicted with fundamental teachings of the Church. The lack of due process is certainly a vital issue, but it is worth examining Balasuriya's theological thought, for it brings out some of the disturbing aspects of this contemporary Catholic theology of reaction.

Edmund Hill sums up Balasuriya's position in his introduction to the book and the ensuing controversy. Balasuriya's general argument runs like this: the old classical theology is "patriarchal, male dominated, and governed by Western, Greco-Roman cultural presuppositions." And so we ought to turn to a "new feminist, liberation, inculturation dialogue theologies."[19] There is certainly a sense in which it is easy to agree with this, but of course, the issue is to determine just what that sense is. Balasuriya eloquently argues that Mary needs to be seen in solidarity with the human race, to be seen as a real woman, a woman of the Gospels, and not just raised above everyone else. But the road he takes to do this is fraught with difficulties. He argues that at the heart of devotion to Mary are qualities attributed to her, like the Immaculate Conception, but these qualities are, in turn, based on the qualities we attribute to Christ, especially in terms of redeeming us from sin, and in this way he is led to deal with the question of original sin.

This is a doctrine that he thinks lacks internal coherence, and "is based on unproved and unprovable assumptions."[20] But such a comment immediately raises a theological red flag. In just what way can we expect the Christian mysteries to be provable? Are they provable in some historically verifiable way? Or are they provable because they are found in full form in the Scriptures? Or are they provable because they psychologically resonate with us, or say something about how we should treat each other?

There is no doubt that the question of original sin poses a great challenge for contemporary theology, and Balasuriya touches on some of the elements of this question that need to be examined: the traditional link between original sin and sexuality, the injustice of punishing all people for the sins of our first parents, the apparent injustice of God towards the unbaptized, and so forth. But he doesn't really deal with them. Instead he will say: "the whole doctrine of original sin is built on the assumptions of a particular medieval Western European philosophical understanding of the human person, nature and the supernatural, which is not necessarily valid for all times and places."[21] If he had said that the Church's teaching on original sin was heavily conditioned by the historical circumstances within it arose, one could only agree with him, but there is an overemphasis here that is disturbing.

The question of original sin becomes a springboard to the issue of the role of Jesus in the salvation of the human race. "Such dogma of original sin implied that Jesus, the universal savior, conferred the graces merited by him, through the Church which he founded."[22] But Balasuriya, apparently motivated by a desire to enter more deeply into dialogue with other religions, questions this. Even if salvation came through Christ, he tells us, that does not mean "...Jesus Christ wanted a Church – say the Catholic Church – to be the mediator of that salvation."[23] This, to his mind, reduces the chance for salvation of people of other religions, or no religion at all, and is therefore unacceptable. What he is going to do is remove this problem by transforming basic Christian doctrine. It is as if he does not see the basic Christian mysteries as the foundation for all theological activity, but rather, as humanly conceived doctrines that can be altered. He will write: "Traditional theology has defined Jesus as one person having two natures: the divine and the human. This is the teaching of the Council of Chalcedon."[24] But then he comments: "Yet, who is able to know these things with any degree of acceptable certitude?"[25]

A final example highlights this misunderstanding of the nature of theology. "If the doctrine of original sin and its consequences are questioned, then the concept of redemption is also questioned. If we do not understand human nature as essentially fallen, then there is no need of an ontological redemption by Jesus Christ…"[26] And Balasuriya appears not to shrink from accepting such a line of reasoning under the guise that it is necessary for interreligious dialogue: "The traditional understanding of redemption, in which Jesus Christ is considered the unique, universal and necessary redeemer in an ontological sense which transforms fallen human nature, is one which it is not possible to use in our multi-faith context, as well as among secular people."[27]

What is taking place here is that a genuine desire for openness in dialogue is obscuring the true nature of theology and leading to unacceptable transformations of the Christian mysteries. Do we really need to do this? Even more critical is the question of whether faith itself is being lost in various instances of this kind of reaction theology.

Michael Morwood

Michael Morwood was a priest of the Missionaries of the Sacred Heart involved in adult religious education in Australia when he wrote *Tomorrow's Catholic: Understanding God and Jesus in a New Millennium*. He believes that our theological understanding of Christianity is only as good as the cosmology that shaped it. In the past we believed that God was a male person, up in the sky somewhere who looked down on us and took care of us, and that human beings started in paradise, but lost that initial state through sin. But now we have the new cosmology, and so it is clear that traditional Church teaching on paradise and original sin, for example, is "nonsense."[28]

When it comes to Jesus, in the past we believed that He was the second person of the Blessed Trinity "sent down from Heaven by the Father to redress the wrong human beings had done and to win back God's friendship."[29] But now we know better because we realize that such a religious world view is no longer relevant because it is based "on an outdated cosmology which presumes that God is up or out there somewhere and sends His Son down to this planet."[30] This is a theology that "constantly underlines the belief that Jesus is radically different from us."[31]

What Morwood is doing is setting up theological straw men, and then demolishing them. But in this straw are elements of genuine Christian doctrine which are being discarded, as well. The new cosmology really has little to do with the matter. If Morwood wants to make the point that Christian doctrine has often been presented in a deficient manner, that is fine, and it is easy to do. But he has a much more audacious agenda: a thorough-going transformation of basic Catholic doctrine.

Morwood covers much of the same ground in his later *Is Jesus God?* which appeared after his resignation from the priesthood. What was implied earlier becomes more explicit. We are faced with an "inevitable collapse of a theological system of belief dependent on Jesus being a special incarnation of God for us to be (saved)."[32] In the past things looked like this: "The Genesis stories of creation and a fall; God prepares the way for a Savior; Jesus restores what was lost; The church is the medium for "salvation"; Our particular church is the only one free from error; We engage the world around us shaped in our Christian religious convictions."[33] But now, given the new cosmology, we see things differently: "Contemporary scientific understanding of the universe and the development of life on earth; God present and active in all places at all times; *The Spirit of God working in and becoming visible through*: The material universe; The development of life; The development of human culture; The human attributes of love, generosity, caring, compassion, forgiveness."[34]

Despite how much this new story of the universe is in the news today, "it is striking how few theologians have put into writing the implications for Christian theology."[35] They undoubtedly know the implications "but there appears to be an air of intellectual dishonesty created by authoritarian insistence on fidelity to "Tradition"."[36]

The doctrine of original sin, and Jesus as our Savior, was greatly influenced by brilliant thinkers who didn't have at their disposal the knowledge of the universe we have today.[37] But now, since we know how our planet had been bombarded by asteroids, and how dinosaurs disappeared, we no longer have to think in those old ways. So, with a wave of the cosmological wand, original sin and most of the mystery of moral evil disappears. It is only because Christians have been indoctrinated in the old stories of paradise and original sin that we feel guilty about the imperfection of the current state of our evolution. And so while Morwood will not completely deny the reality of sin, we can certainly wonder what his understanding of the origin of the enormous suffering and pain we see around us is.

The resurrection of Jesus undergoes a similar process of reduction. It is a huge step, Morwood tells us, to say about the traditional understanding of the resurrection of Jesus and his sending of the Spirit, "I just don't believe it anymore."[38] But this is what Morwood has done, yet he immediately hastens to reassure us that this "is not a rejection of Christianity, but simply a rescuing of Jesus from that old world view."[39] Jesus didn't regain eternal life for us because it was never lost, and so forth and so on. "This understanding is radically different from the understanding that permeates the New Testament Scriptures and the tradition of the Christian church. Christianity is indeed at a crossroads at this point of history. Will it keep walking down the dualistic road with the images we saw above from the *Catechism of the Catholic Church?* Or will it step into the twenty-first century and begin the massive task of reformulating its understanding of the life, death, and rising of Jesus within the framework of contemporary knowledge?"[40] It is this kind of program that led to his first book being banned from sale by the Archbishop of Melbourne for serious doctrinal errors, and Morwood being accused of crudely misrepresenting Catholic teaching. Another bishop asked him if he believed Jesus was God, and his answer is what we might by now expect. This classical view of Jesus depends on its "intrinsic link" to an outmoded world view. The church should take people "through whatever data it has step by step to convince them." But that data doesn't appear to include the early Christian witness to Jesus, for that, too, is contaminated with the old world view. The data is presumably modern cosmology. "Faith must build on reason. That has always been a strong principle of Christian theology."[41] But the way Morwood seems to understand these statements is that faith is somehow subordinated and judged by reason, in this case what modern scientific cosmology has to say.

It is fascinating to hear this kind of talk about the new cosmology, which seems to be cropping up in many places. Let's get another view of looking at it from someone who proposes we need a quantum theology.

Diarmuid O'Murchu

The fundamental issue is whether, in these kinds of cosmologically inspired spiritualities, we are being presented with a way to renew or even expand our Christian vision, or a replacement for it. Let's look at another egregious example. In the past, "only those who believed in God (as described by formal religion) could be theologians. Quantum theology seeks to dismantle this exclusivity and open up the theological exploration to everybody, to all who are prepared to engage with their lived experience of the universe as a quantum reality," writes Diarmuid O'Murchu in his *Quantum Theology*[42] "God is first and foremost a propensity and power for relatedness, and the divine imprint is nowhere more apparent than in nature's own fundamental desire (exemplified in the quarks) to relate – interdependently and interconnectedly... Questions arise which become immensely disturbing for orthodox theologians. "Does God, then, have no independent existence?" "Is God somehow dependent on evolution?" These questions... arise from a certain mode of patriarchal consciousness, characteristic of our mechanistic age, needing certainty, precision, and authoritative clarity. They are valid questions, but of no real interest to a quantum theologian."[43]

Once God has disappeared into some evolutionary process, then historical Christianity is bound to soon follow. The story, we are told, is more important than the facts: "Whether or not there was an empty tomb, whether or not anybody actually saw the Risen Jesus, is not of primary significance. If through modern archaeological research we were to rediscover the remains of Jesus, thus establishing that he never rose physically from the grave, that discovery would not undermine the faith of a genuine believer. It would create immense doubt and confusion for millions who follow a dogmatic creed rather than a spirituality of the heart. (It could also be a catalyst for a profound conversion experience.)

Theologians in general and guardians of orthodox religion will find the above comments quite disturbing; some will consider them to be blatantly heretical."[44] Frankly, I do find them "quite disturbing." This kind of Quantum theology and whatever kind of Quantum spirituality that could be erected on it has lost its moorings in genuine Christian spirituality. Further, they have little to do with the actual scientific world of modern cosmology and quantum physics, which is a cauldron of competing scientific hypotheses and deadlocked philosophical debates. What these kinds of superficial spiritualities, inspired by the new cosmology, do are invoke the natural sciences for a demolition of Catholic theology that has very little to do with what the sciences are saying.[45]

Daniel Maguire

Daniel Maguire, Professor of Religion at Marquette University, in *The Moral Core of Judaism and Christianity* argues that "at their moral core the major religions of the world are not all that distant. It is at this core, too, that these classics reach deep into our common humanity and offer a universalizable trove of moral ideals, principles, and visions. Though these religions appear in separate cultures, arising from unique challenges, they are all rooted in awe and reverence for the stunning gift of life and being."[46] Pointing out the importance of this moral core is certainly a noble endeavor because it could foster cooperation between religions and men of good will on the many urgent issues that confront the human race. But Maguire, like the proponents of the reaction theology we have been seeing, cannot seem to carry out this task without putting it into opposition to Christian belief.

If some have excluded morality from the core of religion in their search for a common essence, he will reverse the perspective: "Morality is primary; religion, God-talk, and theology derive from and explain this foundational moral reverence."[47] Morality then becomes the common essence, and the world's religions including agnostic, or atheistic humanism, the many paths to that summit, or center. They all touch at their moral-mystical roots. Even this would work as a program of pluralistic cooperation, but it soon becomes elevated into a deconstruction of traditional Christian belief. The sound idea that theists and atheists, and all men of good will can cooperate, becomes a program for the relativization of Christian belief, and indeed, of all belief systems under the heading of intellectual modesty.

There is an important truth in Maguire's perception of how religions can ossify and lose their vital moral thrust. "Commitment to disengaged dogmatic formulae can easily replace morality as the sacrament of encounter with the holy."[48] But this is linked, in Maguire's mind, with the need to attack traditional Christianity. Christianity "shows the impact of its mythogenetic Hellenic sojourn... Its dogmatic structure has more than a passing similarity to religious doctrines of Greece and elsewhere."[49] There is certainly a measure of truth in this, but for Maguire it becomes a platform from which he can demolish traditional Christian understanding. Paul becomes an eclectic and creative borrower, and "an outstanding witness to the imaginative syncretism of early Christianity."[50] "The borrowing affected the very structure of what would be later called dogma. Early Christian dogmas were not very distinctive in their contemporary world. (What was distinctive was the moral vision begun in Judaism and planted in Christianity.)"[51] In short, the fundamental Christian mysteries are nothing but reflections of the Mediterranean world of virgin births, healing miracles, incarnational deifications, dying and rising gods, to be found all over the place. The theology of Jesus as the divine wisdom, put to such good effect in the Gospel of St. John, depends primarily on the myth of Isis-Osiris.

And while Maguire will say there has to be a discussion "on how the etiology of these myths relates to the essential meaning of Christianity,"[52] he has already made it clear that the essential doctrinal meaning of Christianity is of little importance as long as we preserve its moral core. The issue here is not that there are not various fascinating questions involved, which to unravel would demand a sensitive comparative history of religions, as well as a grasp of archetypal psychology; it is not even that from this historical and psychological point of view Maguire's comments are unconvincing. The real issue is the use to which he is putting these questions, which is to use them as a way to level Christian doctrine. We are left with the impression that it is only the naïve, or fundamentalist Christians who can still believe in Christian doctrines when their mythological character is evident to anyone who has the courage to look history in the face. We must leave them to their childishness and get on with the important business of genuine cooperation on pressing moral and social issues. All the wrangling about the Jesus of history and the Christ of faith, will not lead us to any conclusion, and doesn't really matter, anyway. We still have the moral core. Was Jesus divine? That is the "wrong question. Symbols are not true or false. They are meaningful or not meaningful. Like works of art or poems..."[53] The efforts of the Church Councils, as well as the Fathers and theologians, are futile and unnecessary, at least from the perspective that they were trying to do something that simply could not be done.

But once again, what drives this kind of project? We can only surmise that the life-deadening conceptualism and legalism of the institutional Church almost compels people to react against it, and attack not only these faults, but Christian belief, itself.

John Dourley

In the work of John Dourley, a Catholic priest and Jungian analyst, we are faced with not simply a Jungian analyst trying to understand Christianity from his own perspective, or even a Christian who somewhat naively uses Jung's psychology to put meaning back into Christianity, but with a more conscious and deliberate taking of position. This can be seen in Dourley's *The Illness That We Are: A Jungian Critique of Christianity.* If Jung places the "location of the genesis of religious experience" within the human psyche, then Dourley sees this kind of religious epistemology as a challenge to Christianity.[54]

"The possibility of a deity-engendering faculty within the psyche is understandably a threat to a Christianity still largely committed to living under the burden of its religious projections understood for the most part literally and historically."[55]

If gods and goddesses must spring from the fecundity of the psyche, then does this not relativize the whole idea of Christian revelation?

"The idea that the experience of the divine is due to archetypal activity native to the psyche certainly modifies, if it does not render entirely premature and adolescent, claims to absolute and exhaustive revelations which have somehow drained the consciousness of its ability to express its religious energies in future revelations. Such a final Word would seem to block rather than stimulate further and fuller statements from the unconscious."[56]

This kind of epistemology leads to the conclusion that Christianity and other religions are but partial and complete reflections of what Jung's psychology knows more directly and completely. In fact, they are not only incomplete but dangerous, for they take their revelation as some sort of absolute and impose it, often by force, on others, or enshrine this revelation in an institution that then lords it over believers.

"Rather than seeing the institutions they serve as necessarily diverse representatives of unconscious energies seeking to express themselves more fully through religious diversity, institutional theologies either deny this myth-making capacity of humanity or exempt their genesis from it in favor of a purely transcendental and supernatural ancestry."[57]

It is Jung's psychology which becomes the means by which we can uncover in various philosophies and theologies the extent in which they embody archetypal realities. Then they can be understood "as ancillae psychologiae", the handmaids of theology, "as mutually mitigating and complementary aspects of an unconscious wealth seeking fuller expression than is yet possible through any one particular system.

"From this position Jung's thought has within it the norm for differentiating between philosophical and theological standpoints that would be helpful to conscious human development, and those that would be helpful or even entail ultimately the negation of any development, through the destruction of humanity itself. The norm would be based on the question of whether or not the patterns of thought in question, be they religious, philosophical or social, lead consciousness beyond itself to the energies within the psyche that work toward its balanced revitalization and emphatic extension."[58]

Dourley is aware that he is pioneering a new religious epistemology that entails a radical critique of Christianity, and in doing so he sees himself following in Jung's footsteps, especially as Jung shows himself in his correspondence where he "gives some of the strongest indications that he was fully aware of the profound philosophical and metaphysical implications in his understanding of the psyche, a side of his thought he tends to disclaim in his published work – perhaps to avoid offending the "scientific community, as well as the more perceptive among the theologians"[59]

John Dourley shows little of this reticence. God becomes "a psychic resource in which the opposites remain undifferentiated,"[60] and theologians should "cease battling for the perseverance of their lesser faiths" and work for a "more encompassing faith."[61]

In this encompassing faith the two natures and one person of Christ become an understanding that "psychic maturity resides in the discovery of one's native divinity."[62] And if we admitted that psychological, spiritual and revelatory experiences come from a common source we would be "comfortable with the idea that religious and psychological experience are organically one."[63] If theology doesn't admit this it "should not pretend, in their dialogue with developmental psychology, that they have anything to contribute to or derive from various movements concerned with human potential."[64] In short, individuation is identical to growth in the experience of God. Revelation would not be closed but each of us would have our own personal covenant and a "new testament would be struck every time the individual was led by the Self into dialogue with it, in the interests of its (the Self's) more conscious incarnation."[65]

The resurrection "would be nothing less than the transformation of consciousness that attaches to the process of becoming whole in the here and now of everyday life,"[66] rather than something in the "realm of extraordinary geriatrics."[67]

In *Love, Celibacy and the Inner Marriage*, Dourley takes up these themes, again insisting that Jung, despite his disclaimers, had a metaphysical agenda.

"He certainly seems to enter the field of epistemology and ontology when he claims so repeatedly that all that one can know must be known through the psyche, including the reality of God."[68] And Jung's remarks about the sacrosanct unintelligibility of dogma and following Nietzsche that philosophy and theology are the "ancillae psychologiae" stir Dourley to bring this metaphysics out in the open. The voice of the unconscious becomes the voice of God,[69] and psychological maturity must be called mysticism. Dourley cites Jung to the effect that the mystic has had "a particularly vivid experience of the processes of the collective unconscious."[70] A "latent" or "surreptitious" metaphysics in Jung must attain its full stature and its implications for Christianity realized, even though it undermines "current religious configurations of transcendental monotheisms."[71] Jung's psychology really is a "metapsychology."[72] In it the old religious language must be recast. Following Jung's *Answer to Job*, Dourley formulates it: "In the beginning God had a nervous breakdown."[73] Its cause was due to God's inability to hold together the opposites of his "profoundly unconscious life." Therefore human consciousness had to be created to solve the divine problem.

He will recognize this "surreptitious" metaphysics and give it full rights as a genuine philosophy. This "Jungian philosophy" becomes the instrument by which the deficiencies of Christianity can be exposed and remedied. As a philosophy, Jung's psychology is no longer one distinctive way of knowing man and his relationship to God, but acts as if it is the only way to know these realities. Once Jung's empirical method is erected into an epistemology, then from this epistemology inexorably flows the radical reinterpretation of Christianity that Dourley proposes. Then it is presumptuous for Christianity to lay claim to a distinctive revelation. Instead it has gropingly grasped the archetypes and the process of individuation, but mistakenly elevated these insights into metaphysical entities. The point is not that God is better described as a quaternity than a trinity. No. To call God a quaternity in this fashion is to say that a revelation of God as Trinity or anything else is not possible at all, and what the Christians call God is no more that a deficient experience of the totality of the psyche that is explained more adequately by Jung's psychology. Dourley wants to create a Jungian philosophy and destroy Christianity with it. But he misunderstands the fundamental fact that an empirical psychology is one thing and philosophy is quite another.

John Dourley has something important to say. Terrible crimes are committed in the name of religion and Jung's psychology can be a great help in reducing sectarian strife. It can help us see a whole infrastructure of poorly integrated elements of the psyche which instead of being dealt with directly and in a psychological way are projected outward and fuel religious hatred. But this does not mean that religion in itself is the cause of this hatred. Nor will the creation of a Jungian philosophy or religion ever be successful because it will either violate Jung's empirical method or it will cling to this empirical method and deny that any other way of knowing is possible and therefore refashion philosophy and religion after the pattern of analytical psychology. In short, it will be a pseudo-philosophy or theology.

Conclusion

In *Part I* we saw how Christians in various ways and in various degrees under the impact of intimate contact with Eastern meditation practices have moved in the direction of replacing traditional Christian understanding with some sort of nonduality.

Now we have seen a similar process taking place across the spectrum of theology without a net. Here traditional understanding of the Christian mysteries is replaced by the new cosmology, or a certain moral core, or a standard of ecology and social justice, and so forth. It would be hard to be against the positive values that are being advocated, but there is no reason that I can see why they need to be presented as intrinsically opposed to the central Christian mysteries.

What drives these projects, then? I don't think it is an accident that we are often dealing with priests or ex-priests from religious orders. It is precisely these people who know most intimately the institutional Church, and have often suffered at its hands, and are as well in a position to write about it. They have borne the brunt of the old legalism and conceptualism, and have seen what it does to people, and I wonder if, in their minds, these failures of the institution are indelibly associated with Christian doctrine, itself. They have suffered, and seen others suffer, at the hands of people who are continually talking about the Trinity and the Incarnation, and the death and resurrection of Jesus.

If this is the case, then their attempts to liberate themselves from these oppressive structures becomes simultaneously an attempt to sweep away the theology that is so intimately connected, in their minds, with this oppressive behavior. Is it so hard to imagine that beneath the kinds of theological analyses we have been seeing are wounded feelings? If this is true, it is quite unfortunate. Then some of the impetus for reform so needed in the Church gets subverted into an attack on fundamental Christian doctrine. It is not that these doctrines do not need a careful reexamination and reformulation, and cannot be presented in a more adequate manner, but this is not what we are seeing here. What we are seeing is Christianity's fundamental identity being swept aside.

In this kind of process the Vatican reactionaries and the ultra liberal reformulators become fixated on each other. Then both the conceptualists and the anti-conceptualists have consumed a great deal of energy which could have gone into the contemplation of the great Christian mysteries, and attempts to express them more clearly.

It is certainly possible that someone might come to the conclusion that Christianity is fundamentally and irrevocably wrong, that Christians from the beginning have misunderstood and mythologically projected various archetypes on Jesus. But that is an enormous step for Christians to take, and ought to be preceded by a very clear awareness of what is at stake. Such a step means the end of Christianity, for if Christians have gotten it wrong from the beginning, there is no substance to Christianity left worth arguing about, and there is no reason not to replace Christianity with something else. And if we take such a step, we should not pretend we are representing Christianity at the table of East-West dialogue, or anywhere else.

In my reaction to this reaction theology, I am not without sympathy for Catholics who find it difficult to embrace the faith they grew up with, and need to critically examine it in order to come to a more adult one. But I am concerned when it is carried out as if what is at stake is a purely human political struggle between the theological progressives and the reactionaries. Then what can get lost are important elements of the faith, itself. Let's look at one final example of the underlying dynamics that are often involved here. It is a review of Morwood's *Is Jesus God?* by Judith Bromberg, one of the *National Catholic Reporter's* regular reviewers under the heading, "Book about God is for grownups." She tells us that this is the book she has been waiting for, but unfortunately Morwood had to resign from the priesthood to write it. And she has only one quibble with it. The title is sensationalistic because this is only part of what Morwood is saying. She does not seem to find any of the theological problems we have been looking at, but tells us, "Everyone I know who has read this book appreciates its premise and applauds its author." In her estimation the real problem is not Morwood, but the Church. She read the book with a group of friends and "all, *all* (are) still fully committed, church-going, church-serving Catholics who love the church but increasingly resist its preachments and heavy-handed dictatorialism."[74]

This attitude is wide-spread, and it is certainly fed by the maladroit conduct of the institutional Church. *The National Catholic Reporter*, itself, which has the merit of actually reporting the news, and on occasion doing some serious investigative reporting, sometimes falls itself into this kind of reaction theology. It is enough for someone to be the object of Rome's negative attentions for the reflexes of reaction, honed by many past incidents, to go into high gear, but what gets lost is what this or that theologian is actually saying. And so this kind of reaction is not a genuinely thoughtful and critical response to it.

Notes

1. Gebara, Ivone. *Longing for Running Water*. p. 43.
2. Ibid., p. 57.
3. Ibid., p. 103.
4. Ibid.
5. Ibid., p. 104.
6. Ibid., p. 105.
7. Ibid., p. 119.
8. Ibid.
9. Ibid., p. 146.
10. Ibid., p. 147.
11. Ibid., p. 148.
12. Ibid., p. 151.
13. Ibid., p. 152.
14. Ibid., p. 153.
15. Ibid., p. 178.
16. Ibid., p. 183.
17. Ibid., p. 184.
18. Ibid., p. 190.
19. Balasuriya, Tissa. *Mary and Human Liberation*. p. 6.
20. Ibid., p. 140.
21. Ibid., p. 140-141.
22. Ibid., p. 142.
23. Ibid., p. 143.
24. Ibid., p. 158.
25. Ibid.
26. Ibid., p. 159.
27. Ibid., p. 160.
28. Morwood, Michael. *Tomorrow's Catholic*, p. 31
29. Ibid., p. 53.
30. Ibid., p. 54.
31. Ibid., p. 63.
32. Morwood, Michael. *Is Jesus God?* p. 8.
33. Ibid., p. 33.
34. Ibid., p. 36.
35. Ibid., p. 40.
36. Ibid.
37. Ibid., p. 52.
38. Ibid., p. 84.
39. Ibid., p. 85.
40. Ibid., p. 86.
41. Ibid., p. 98.
42. O'Murchu, Diarmiud. *Quantum Theology*, note 2, p. 49.
43. Ibid., p. 83.
44. Ibid., p. 114.
45. This section on O'Murchu is taken from my web essay, "Can There be a Quantum Spirituality?" at http://www.innerexplorations.com/philtext/qu.htm For the

interaction between quantum physics and Christian thought, see my *Mystery of Matter*.
46. Maguire, Daniel. *The Moral Core of Judaism and Christianity*, p. 37.
47. Ibid., p. 39.
48. Ibid., p. 92.
49. Ibid., p. 92-93.
50. Ibid., p. 95.
51. Ibid.
52. Ibid., p. 97.
53. Ibid.
54. This section on John Dourley has been taken from my *Jungian and Catholic?* in Chapter 1.
55. Dourley, John. *The Illness That We Are*, p. 9.
56. Ibid., p. 10.
57. Ibid., p. 24-25.
58. Ibid., p. 38-39.
59. Ibid., p. 45.
60. Ibid., p. 55.
61. Ibid., p. 80.
62. Ibid.
63. Ibid., p. 85.
64. Ibid., p. 86.
65. Ibid., p. 96.
66. Ibid., p. 98.
67. Ibid.
68. Dourley, John. *Love, Celibacy and the Inner Marriage*, p. 19.
69. Ibid., p. 21.
70. Ibid., p. 45.
71. Ibid., p. 58.
72. Ibid., p. 94.
73. Ibid., p. 96.
74. *The National Catholic Reporter*. August 10, 2001, p. 18.

CHAPTER 4

RELIGIOUS PLURALISM

The last chapter has provided us with a glimpse of a crisis in Catholic theology which forms the background to what we saw in *Part I.* Now it can help us understand the contentious Catholic debate on religious pluralism. One of the greatest changes that took place at the time of the Second Vatican Council caused little reaction then, but now has moved to the center of the theological stage. It is a question of God's universal will that all people be saved, or in its old negative form: outside of the Church there is no salvation.

Salvation Outside the Church

The doctrine of no salvation outside the Church has a history as long as the Church, itself, and this history has been ably surveyed by Francis Sullivan in his *Salvation Outside the Church? Tracing the History of the Catholic Response.* What started out as a judgment applied by early Church leaders to those who had separated themselves from the Church by schism and heresy, later, once the Church became the official religion of the Roman empire, was applied to pagans and Jews. The whole world was seen as coextensive with the Roman world, and therefore all people must have heard the message of Christ, and if they didn't accept it, then they were culpable of rejecting it, and therefore were condemning themselves to hell.

This mentality endured for a thousand years with various degrees of severity until the age of exploration when it became apparent that the world was a lot bigger than Christians had formerly realized, and it was necessary to address the question of the salvation of those people who had never heard the Gospel. Not only had geographic awareness expanded, but a new psychological awareness began to emerge, as well, and some theologians began to realize that there was a difference between living in a society where Christianity was present, and really hearing the message of the Gospel. Theological thinking began to shift, and this shifting reached a certain definitive stage at the time of the Second Vatican Council, and afterwards in the actions and statements of the Popes which clearly state that God calls all people to salvation no matter what their religion or their lack of it.

Karl Rahner called this newly found sense of God's universal salvific will one of the most noteworthy results of the Second Vatican Council, and remarks on how little controversy it stirred.[1] He writes that this development is "one of the most astonishing phenomena in the development of the Church's conscious awareness of her faith, in this development as it applies to the secular and non-Christian world, the awareness of the difference between saving history as a whole and the history of explicit Christianity and of the Church."[2]

The old attitude that had existed in the Church up until the Second Vatican Council that those outside it were in peril of their salvation can be likened to a fog that had been thinning, but still chilled the relationship of the Church to those outside it and discomfited many people inside the Church. At the time of the Council it finally burned away, and many people in the Church saw that these old attitudes were untenable. In the preconciliar Catholic world, despite the more progressive statements by some theologians since the 16th century, the general feeling that percolated down to the local churches and the priests, religious and lay people was that all those who did not belong formally to the Catholic Church were in danger of being lost. This was one of the most pernicious effects of the old theology, and so it was hardly surprising that the new theology of openness and dialogue would react against it.

But it was so deep a change that time was necessary for the theological tremors which are now surfacing to become visible. Indeed, we are faced with the question of Catholic identity that we were looking at in the last chapter in another form. If the old neo-scholastic mentality tried to pin down this identity in a thousand details that were not essentially connected to the faith, theology today has been exploring just how much this old identity can be abandoned.

Anonymous Christians

In bare outline what Rahner had to say was this: God wills all people to be saved, and thus, people outside of the Church stand in a salvific relationship to God, but all grace comes through Jesus Christ, and must be received by an act of faith. Therefore, even non-Christians, without an explicit knowledge of Christ, are justified by the grace of Christ which they receive by faith, and therefore could be called anonymous Christians. Just how does this faith come about? The call to grace on God's part is not just external, but is interior, as well, built in, as it were, in the very way God has created all people to share in divine love. Rahner calls it a "supernatural existential," an interior dynamism at the heart of our being drawing us to God, and this operates in our awareness and actions, but not necessarily in the form of explicit concepts and discernible historical events.

It is here that the idea of anonymous Christians begins to join the mainstream of Rahner's transcendental theology, and through it some of the basic principles of Thomist theology find a new approach. Grace brings with it a new formal object, a transformation of human nature, fitting it for the supernatural goal of union with God. Rahner's supernatural existential cannot be limited, as the old theology tended to do, to particular events and circumstances linked with the visible Church, but must be seen as a much deeper and universal transformation of human nature which brings about a change in awareness and the ability to respond to this offer of grace even when there is no explicit awareness of the Christian message. There is a crucial distinction, therefore, between this universal offer of salvation "taking place at a preconceptual level in the roots of man's spiritual faculties," and the "objectification at the historical and conceptual level of the revelatory self-communication of God."[3]

In the past theology conceived of grace extrinsically as a discreet reality that could be completely lacking in an unbeliever, but Rahner wants to see it "as the innermost core of human existence in decision and freedom, always and above all given in the form of an offer that is either accepted or rejected, that the human being cannot step out of this transcendental particularity of his being at all."[4] In contrast to the attitude of past theology, Rahner holds "that right from the beginning the history of revelation runs parallel with grace and salvation history." And "there has never been a time or place that was not part of the history of revelation."[5] For a sense of just how this "preconceptual" offer can be responded to could be pursued and developed by examining Rahner's ideas on concrete individual knowledge in Ignatius Loyola, which he considered among his most important theological ideas.[6]

Jacques Maritain and the First Act of Freedom

In 1945, an essay by Jacques Maritain entitled "La dialectique immanente du premier acte de liberté," (The immanent dialectic of the first act of freedom), appeared in *Nova et Vetera* and later appeared in his book *Raisons et raisons* in 1947. This virtually uncommented-upon essay is one of Maritain's finest works, and it provides us with a way with which to delve deeper into what Rahner called a preconceptual offer.

Maritain takes as his starting point "any free act through which a new basic direction is imposed upon my life,"[7] but for simplicity's sake restricts himself to the first free act of a child which is not necessarily remembered or even concerned with an important matter, but nevertheless expresses a deep commitment. But what is the inner dynamism of this act? In it the good is chosen (or not chosen) precisely because it is good. Therefore, this choice transcends the whole order of empirical existence and it demands the existence of a separate good. The act of choosing the good "tends all at once, beyond its immediate object, toward God as the Separate Good in which the human person in the process of acting, whether he is aware of it or not, places his happiness and his end."[8]

Thus, the child in "virtue of the internal dynamism of his choice of the good... wills and loves the Separate Good as the ultimate end of his existence" and "his intellect has of God a vital non-conceptual knowledge which is involved both in the practical notion... of the moral good as formal motive of his first act of freedom, and in the movement of the will toward this good and, all at once, toward the Good."[9] The will is going beyond this or that particular good to the ground of all good things "and it carries with itself, down to that beyond, the intellect, which at this point no longer enjoys the use of its regular instruments, and, as a result, is only actualized below the threshold of reflective consciousness, in a night without concept and without utterable knowledge."[10]

Further, if such a fundamental exercise of freedom is to be efficacious and love God above all things, it must be transformed and elevated by grace and charity. This is due not only to the wounded condition of human nature resulting from original sin, but due, as well, to the fact that the good which is the ultimate goal of all good acts, "the only true end existentially" of human life, is "God as the ultimate supernatural end," that is, God in His very own life. So the whole order of good, since it deals with what actually is, is concerned by that very fact with men and women in a fallen and redeemed state called to share in God's own life. Grace is always present to envelop and attract" us, and "our fallen nature is exposed to grace as our tired bodies to the rays of the sun."[11]

This kind of reasoning faces Maritain with a serious dilemma. If such a first act of freedom is a supernatural act that leads to a relationship of friendship with God, then it must somehow involve faith, for as St. Paul says: "Without faith it is impossible to please God; for he that approaches God must believe that He exists, and is the rewarder of those who seek Him." So Maritain's dilemma reads: This faith, according to St. Paul's words, cannot be implicit faith, but how can it be explicit in the case of a child who "does not even know that he believes in God?"[12] He resolves this impasse by avoiding the implicit-explicit dichotomy which deals only with conscious conceptual knowledge, and by invoking a knowledge that "reaches its object within the unconscious recesses of the spirit's activity" in which "the intellect knows in a practical manner the Separate Good *per conformitatem ad appetitum rectum* (through conformity to the right appetite) and as the actual terminus of the will's movement."[13] Under the light of grace, the good chosen becomes the good by which I shall be saved and the separate good becomes God as savior. In short, the natural dynamism of the first act of freedom is transformed into a supernatural act and "under the light of faith, the right appetite then passes *in conditionem objecti* (into the sphere of objective actualization) and becomes, in the stead of any concept, the means of a knowledge which is speculative though escaping formulation and reflective consciousness... It is the movement of the will which, reaching beyond this good to the mysterious Existent it implies, makes this Existent become an object of the speculative intellect."[14]

This process reveals in a very striking way the kind of knowledge through connaturality that flourishes in supernatural contemplation. This knowledge coming through the first act of freedom "remains preconscious, or else hardly reaches the most obscure limits of consciousness, because, for one thing, it possesses no conceptual sign, and, for another, the movement of the will which brings it about is itself neither felt nor experienced, nor illumined and highly conscious as is love in the exercise of the gift of wisdom."[15] The knowledge coming through the gift of wisdom becomes conscious and experimental without being conceptual.

What we are seeing here is much more than the first free act of the child, for this first act of freedom is at once a supernatural act of faith and the beginning of the mystical life that is rooted in faith. The difficult theological issues that surround the nature of the act of faith can be best approached when we look at them from the perspective of knowledge through connaturality which links together this first act with its higher and more developed expressions. So while this knowledge coming through the choice of the good is not in itself mystical knowledge, it "appears as an obscure preparation for and call to that experimental knowledge of God which is supernatural in its very mode of operation, and which reaches its highest degree in mystical contemplation."[16]

These remarks of Maritain were written in a different context from the one that faces us here, but it would not be difficult to transpose them into a nuanced explanation of how, from a Christian perspective, we might imagine God's universal salvation operating in people's hearts and minds.

Two Fundamental Principles

Neither Karl Rahner nor Jacques Maritain, despite their differences in approach, felt it necessary to alter the central Christian truth of the universal salvific role of Jesus in order to develop an understanding of God's universal call to salvation, and how it might actually operate outside the Church. Building on what they have said, it is possible to begin to enunciate two fundamental principles. One has to do with God's universal salvific will, which could be called an existential principle, and the other with how Christians perceive this universal salvific will which works itself out through Jesus Christ. This could be called an essentialistic principle.

The first principle says that God wishes to draw all women and men to share in the divine life of grace. Our hearts are made for this goal, and ceaselessly long for it and try to achieve it. Naturally this is a Christian belief, which our dialogue partners might not explicitly share. But it is a vital principle from the Christian side because it asserts the fundamental equality of the people on both sides of the dialogue. Christians must presume that their dialogue partners share in the life of grace and grow in it by their good actions. They cannot imagine that they, themselves, are actually closer to God, or somehow more pleasing in God's sight because of their explicit profession of Christian beliefs.

The logic of this position, I think, is quite unassailable. God from the beginning has destined the human race to a supernatural goal, which is to share in God's own life. This divine intention still exists in a very real and concrete way, and is rooted in the heart of every person. It flowers in grace which grows through all good actions. Thus, there is an intrinsic unity and equality between all men and women, irregardless of their formal beliefs. Our Buddhist and Hindu dialogue partners, for example, are thus our brothers and sisters, children like us of the one God. Let us say that the human race possesses a concrete or existential unity in regard to the life of grace, and our dialogue partners may be more advanced in that life than we are, even if, according to their own belief system, they do not formally admit the existence of God. There is an actual existential pluralism in which people take widely divergent and even conceptually incompatible paths, and arrive at this final goal of union with God.

To say this is not a form of Christian religious imperialism as if this principle was something that Christians were compelled to impose on non-Christians, but rather, it is something that Christians, themselves, need to believe because a contrary formulation is unacceptable. In such a contrary statement, God would be creating people made for a share in God's life, and then willing that they don't reach that goal. And this would, in essence, be to will a contradiction. In short, this first principle flows from a belief in God's essential goodness.

Let's turn for a moment to the objective means God can use to draw us to our final goal. There is no reason why the universal salvific action of God which touches every heart cannot work through the people and things of this world. It is entirely in accord with the social dimension of our human nature that this would happen. Therefore, our daily lives can be said to be filled with situations which mediate God's loving presence to us. Our daily acts of kindness and love in regard to our family and friends and the people in our communities all can be means of grace. Further, the religious ceremonies and sacred writings that make up our religion, no matter what it is, can also be used by God to draw us to our final destiny. Even if we have no religious beliefs whatsoever, those acts by which we help those around us can become means of grace for us.

What emerges, then, from our first principle is a view of a truly loving and compassionate God who intends to draw all people to their final destiny and works both in the depths of their hearts and through all the peoples and structures that surround them in order to accomplish this end. Therefore, if we apply this perspective to our partners in interreligious dialogue, we have to approach them with the firm belief that they may, indeed, be closer to God than we are, for they may have responded better to the offers of God's grace than we have.

We have called this first principle a concrete, or existential, principle. And it cannot be taken out of this concrete existential realm, and be given what can be called an essentialistic meaning. Here we arrive at the second principle. Even though all women and men are destined to the same goal and are concretely achieving that goal according to the means they have available to them, this does not mean that all doctrinal systems or spiritual paths are equivalent. A doctrine of the non-existence of the personal self, or the non-existence of God, is not automatically equivalent to a doctrine of the existence of the self and God. The two may be equivalent if we dig deep enough, but we have to dig in order to find out. Or they may point to different experiences based on different facets of reality, or one or both of them may be partially wrong or poorly formulated. What we believe and how we articulate those beliefs is important.

If the first principle is about God's goodness, the second is about a quest for understanding. It asks about the nature of the salvation that God wills for all people. How does God desire to bring it about? Traditionally Catholics have held that this salvation is bound up with Jesus. This belief is woven into the very texture of faith which sees Jesus as the Incarnate Word of God who suffered, died and rose again for the salvation of all people. For a long time this understanding of the role of Jesus and the Church was set up against God's universal salvific will in the form of an "outside of the Church there is no salvation" theology. Therefore, it is not surprising that by way of reaction contemporary theology has insisted on God's universal salvific will, and sometimes it insists on it in a unilateral way that obscures the role of Jesus in that salvation. The first step in the direction of a solution I believe to be the realization that the two principles don't contradict each other because they are not the same kind of principle.

The first principle tells us that the humanity of Jesus is not universal in the sense that all people must explicitly acknowledge the role of Jesus in order to come to salvation. But this doesn't mean that the humanity of Jesus cannot be universal in the essentialistic sense that God wills grace to flow through it so that it is not a contradiction for Catholics to hold to God's universal salvific will at the same time they believe that salvation comes through Jesus. Obviously, the universal role of Jesus and the Church is not a proposition that Catholics can expect others to believe. My point here is simply that Catholics need not disbelieve it in order to hold to God's universal salvific will.

This being said, it is important for theology to try to understand just what this universal role of Jesus means. In a certain obvious way, the humanity of Jesus is limited because Jesus was born and lived in a particular time and place, but if the humanity of Jesus is, indeed, the humanity of the very Word of God, then our perspective changes and deepens. This humanity is then no longer one human nature among many, but it is a humanity transformed from within by its assumption by the Word. It becomes a divinized humanity that stands at the very center of the human race, and incorporates into itself all people. It is here we join the traditional theological theme of the mystical body of Christ, and it would be possible to develop this view of the humanity of Jesus at length, as did one of the 20th century's great theologians, Emile Mersch. I have examined his theology in *Mind Aflame*. Here it is enough to say that the divinized humanity of Jesus is conceived of as the instrument of all grace and salvation that draws all people to share in God's own life. This is where dialogue gets difficult. But because Catholics believe in the central role of Jesus in salvation should not in itself be offensive to their dialogue partners as long as it is clear to them that Catholics hold equally firmly to the first principle of God's universal salvific will. Just about anything Catholics believe is not believed by one or other of their dialogue partners including the existence of God and the notion of salvation itself. Dialogue is not an automatic process of discarding the beliefs that separate us from others, but going on a common search for truth in a spirit of charity. But in Catholic theology we are faced with attempts to wrestle with these kinds of issues that come to very different conclusions. Let's look at some of them, and then return to these two principles.

Paul Knitter

Paul Knitter, a former Divine Word missionary, has been an important voice in the debate about religious pluralism starting with his *No Other Name? A Critical Survey of Christian Attitudes Toward the World Religions* which appeared in 1985. He felt that his own life was a microcosm of the developments that gave birth to modern Catholic religious pluralism: his membership in his missionary order, his life as a student in Rome at the time of the Council, his study of the theology of Karl Rahner, and at the Protestant Theological Faculty at the University of Marburg, and his later activities in interreligious dialogue and social justice. He has moved from an ecclesiocentrism, or exclusivism that we saw under the heading of no salvation outside the Church, to a Christocentrism, or inclusivism embodied in Rahner's anonymous Christian, to a theocentrism that tried to find a common basis for dialogue among the world's religions in the idea of the kingdom of God, and finally to a soteriocentrism, or salvation-centeredness born out of his contact with liberation theology that sees the purpose and foundation of dialogue in a preferential option for the poor.

From this perspective Knitter would see our presentation of the old exclusivism being answered by the inclusivism of Rahner and Maritain as seriously incomplete. We need, he would say, to go beyond Rahner and create a genuine religious pluralism. Let's see how his thought unfolds in his *No Other Name?* Knitter first sketches the general contemporary attitudes that favor the creation of a religious pluralism like modern ideas on world citizenship and process philo-

CHRISTIANITY IN THE CRUCIBLE

sophy, and then he focuses on Ernst Troeltsch's relativism, Toynbee's views on a common essence to religion, and Jung's ideas on how all religions emerge out of the unconscious. Next he takes us on a methodical survey of Christian attitudes towards religious pluralism in the evangelical mainline Protestant and Catholic worlds.

He provides a more detailed view of the development of Catholic theology that we have been seeing: the slow and often one-sided historical development of the two basic themes of God's universal salvific will and the role played by Jesus and the Church, the work of Karl Rahner and the Vatican Council, and so forth. But he wants to go beyond Rahner even though he makes it clear the Rahner's position has not only been widely accepted in Catholic circles, but has influenced mainline Protestant thinkers, as well. He finds that even those who disagree with Rahner's terminology and what they imagine to be its implications often advance similar positions because they see that the role of Christ in the economy of salvation has always been put forth by Christians as somehow unique, or normative. In short, Knitter wants, as the title of his book clearly states, to address whether there is any other name in which people can be saved. He feels that the traditional emphasis on the uniqueness of Jesus in the form of the old exclusivism, or even the inclusive uniqueness like that advanced by Rahner, contradicts our contemporary awareness of the relativity of history, and impedes authentic dialogue. Instead, we have to turn to a theocentrism inspired by people like John Hick, or Raimundo Panikkar, and a relational uniqueness of Jesus. This is going to be a uniqueness "defined by its ability to relate to – that is, to include and be included by – other unique religious figures."[17]

This, he admits, is a very new way of looking at Christ, but he feels it is justified by the fact that today we have a new historical consciousness of "the relativity of all cultures and historical achievements..."[18] And it is with this instrument that he seems to want to forge a new understanding of Christianity, and while he will turn to contemporary New Testament studies to bolster his position, it is this principle that really governs the development of what he is going to say. Under its impact the Incarnation becomes a myth to be taken seriously, but not literally, and it is an expression of the "*non-dualistic* unity between divinity and humanity."[19] This means that there can be "*other incarnations*."[20] This begins to sound like some of the things we have already been seeing in which the traditional understanding of the Incarnation as happening ontologically in Jesus, and in us by grace, has been altered. We no longer look to the uniqueness of the person of Jesus for fear that would impede dialogue.

For Knitter, the old Christologies developed within a classicist culture which people took for granted. For something to be true, it had to be certain and unchanging. But for our modern historical culture this no longer holds. Aristotle believed in first principles of the mind, chief of which was the principle of contradiction. "In its logical form it states that "of two propositions, one of which affirms something and the other denies the same thing, one must be true and the other false." In other words, a thing cannot be and not be at the same time, in the same way. Truth, therefore, is essentially a matter of either-or. It is either this or not this; it cannot be both."[21]

But now there must be a new understanding of truth. "Truth will no longer be identified by its ability to exclude or absorb others."[22] Rather, it has to include them, and instead of being either/or becomes a both/and kind of truth. The classical culture of the past, a culture in which Christianity lived out its life, is irretrievably gone. Now we have a historical culture. Truth is no longer Aristotle's idea of science as certain knowledge through causes. We need to follow the model of the modern sciences, for it is better to say not that something is true, but that it is on the way toward truth. True understanding is subject to revision and change. We need to recognize the reality of historical relativity which is at the heart of our modern consciousness unless we have succumbed to fundamentalism, or nationalism. While Knitter has some questions about this kind of program, he seems to embrace most of it. Aristotle's principle of non-contradiction is part of this old classical mentality, so it must go, as well. We need a new kind of telescope that will allow us to see the ongoing pluralistic nature of truth.

If we take the "ongoing pluralistic nature of truth" in a concrete sense, we can understand what Knitter is saying. We grope towards the truth in a multitude of ways which are conditioned by the limits of our particular language and culture. The existential quality of this language is brought out when he continues: "More and more Catholics have come to realize that such insistence on truth-through-exclusion easily atrophies personal faith and reduces faith to doctrine, morality to legalism, ritual to superstition. Catholics have also seen how such concern for absolute truth denigrates the value of other religious traditions."[23] But Knitter leaves us with the impression that this concrete sense is somehow opposed to what could be called an essentialistic one, as expressed in Aristotle's principle of non-contradiction, and we need to choose between the two. But we can't really dispense with the principle of non-contradiction without destroying the very language we are using, and our contact with reality along with it.

Given this model of truth, Knitter tells us theology can no longer be done within any one religious tradition. Theologians need to pursue the truths that include, and not exclude, others. Christian fundamental theology must be done in a similar fashion. The old theology born of the classical era "asserts that human nature is radically historical, and that in this historicity persons can experience an I-Thou relationship with divinity."[24] But this might have to be rethought because of the many people in the world who don't believe in a personal God. Instead, we might want to create a global fundamental theology around some kind of religious or mystical experience that embraces a reality that can be symbolized as both personal and transpersonal. "All religions, I suggest, could recognize such mystical experience (grace, enlightenment, *samadi, satori*) as the bedrock for all religion and for all reflection on religion."[25] But once you have made the assumption that Christian mystical experience is identical to satori, etc., then you are well on your way, as we have seen over and over again, to a view of the Incarnation in which the "old myth" is replaced by the universal experience of nonduality.

If we then go on to create a global systematic theology on this basis, it will not only understand Christianity better by understanding other religions, but "the cognitive claims of Christian tradition must somehow be true also for those of other religions if these claims are genuinely to be true for Christians!"[26] This is to once again confuse the essential and the existential, in this case an acceptance of God's universal salvific will with the cognitive claims every religion has, and collapse these claims to find a unity upon which dialogue can be built. But this is to eliminate genuine dialogue, which implies different viewpoints, before the dialogue even begins.

By the time Knitter edited *The Myth of Christian Uniqueness* with John Hick in 1987 he was already shifting away from this position. Just as Hick had moved from a theocentrism to a more general reality-centeredness that he hoped all religions could agree upon, Knitter was moving from his own theocentrism to a soteriocentrism inspired by liberation theology in which a *"preferential option for the poor and the nonperson* constitutes both the *necessity* and the *primary purpose* of interreligious dialogue."[27]

It is another version of the search for a common essence to religions, but this time not driven by some kind of ontological quest, but by the supposed demands of dialogue, itself, but still a search for the most common denominator in order that dialogue can take place. He wants to use the preferential option for the poor to clear away some of what he sees as some of the thorny obstacles to dialogue.

But there is a continuation here of the same kind of philosophical background music we heard before in terms of historical relativism. Contemporary philosophers have argued against any sort of foundationalism and objectivism. So there is no common essence, no way to assess the tradition from the outside and examine its truth claims, and what we are left with are different religious traditions which are ultimately incommensurable. Raimundo Panikkar, we are told, echoes these philosophers: "Pluralism does not allow for a universal system. A pluralist system would be a contradiction in terms. The incommensurability of ultimate systems is unbridgeable."[28] Yet the critics of any search for a common essence, or foundation, will warn against the dangers of radical scepticism.

Knitter, rightly uneasy about how these claims can be reconciled, sums it up as follows: "The philosophers and theologians mentioned above are all, paradoxically, firm believers in the possibility and the value of communication and dialogue between apparently "incommensurable" traditions. They seek a difficult, paradoxical path between foundationalism and relativism; even though there are no pre-established common foundations, we can still talk to and understand each other."[29] But he adds, "Just how this works out is not clear."[30] And he tries to find a solution with the help of liberation theology. He believes he can do this because of its epistemological claim that without a commitment to the oppressed, our knowledge of self and other and the ultimate is deficient. The struggle for liberation becomes the shared locus of religious experience which allows people of different traditions to speak to one another.

But we are looking at the same kind of problem in another form that we have been seeing. The serious philosophical issues about our ability to know are pushed into the background by being subordinated to a kind of orthopraxis. The question of foundationalism is overshadowed by a confusion between the essential and the existential. The concrete fact of religious pluralism cannot be erected into a philosophical principle of the incommensurability of traditions without once again destroying language and reason. The quest for a common essence, however often it may be used to ignore actually existing diversity, is a reflection of our desire to truly know, and cannot be written off as futile.

If I overemphasize the visible role of Jesus and the Church in salvation, then I end up insisting that all salvation demands a visible connection with the Church. But if, on the other hand, I unilaterally insist on God's universal salvific will, then I conceive of the process of dialogue as one in which I level all the differences between the dialogue partners before the dialogue has even commenced, and before I truly know what they have to say. I end up saying, in essence, the Incarnation of Jesus cannot be true because God wills all people to be saved, and the majority of people has never known Jesus in any efficacious way. But this is just as one-sided as the old no salvation outside the Church. The new religious pluralism ends up appearing like another kind of reaction theology that is trying to compensate for the deficiencies of the old exclusivism. It is as if it is saying Christians must put into brackets, or put under a methodological doubt, their belief in Christ in order to make dialogue possible. The absolute insistence that salvation demands a visible connection to Christ in the Church is replaced by the relativization of the role of Christ.

Later Knitter, in his *Jesus and the Other Names* which appeared in 1996, reviewed the objections of his critics and tried to respond to them. At the heart of the problem with Knitter's kind of pluralism is the fact that the uniqueness of Jesus as the universal savior is rooted in the New Testament, and in the centuries since in the understanding of the Christian community. Therefore, if we substantially alter it, aren't we tampering with the very identity of Christianity, itself? Can we really separate Christianity from the person of Jesus, and who we say he is? Christianity is not just some core of moral principles, or some universal truths to be found in other religions, as well, but it is about particular historical events given a universal salvific significance. It is hard to imagine how we can put aside what Christians from the beginning have always said because we now say we have a new historical view of language and culture, or a new model of truth. Is it really possible to understand the Incarnation of Jesus in a radically new way by reducing it to a meeting of the divine and the human that happens to everyone everywhere without any real or intrinsic reference to Him?

When Knitter replies to these kinds of problems, at first glance he seems to be conceding some ground to his critics. He hopes to find a way to understand the uniqueness of Jesus that does not impede dialogue. What the New Testament says about Jesus, he tells us, must be held by Christians to be truly said about Him, but not solely said about Him. So as a Christian, I can say that God truly acts through Jesus for me, and Jesus is therefore my savior. But this does not mean that Jesus is the only savior. Christians don't know if He is the only savior, but they don't have to know it in order for Jesus to be a savior for them.

But what Knitter is conceding with one hand, he appears to be taking back with the other. Jesus can no longer be called the *"full, definitive,* and *unsurpassable"* [31] revelation of God, and he cannot be the full revelation because he cannot contain the fullness of divinity in his humanity. Nor can Christians boast of a definitive word of God in Jesus, for that would be to deposit wisdom in a container and say that nothing else can be added to it. Nor can it be held that God cannot provide a greater fullness of revelation, for that would be to "hold up a package of divine truth" as unsurpassable.

But this kind of characterization of Jesus either states the obvious, i.e., the humanity of Jesus is not the divinity, or views revelation as a static collection of truths. The distinction between truly and only does not really address the fundamental problem of just who Jesus is. If Jesus is, indeed, the Word of the Father, the Incarnate Wisdom, then in a certain way we are dealing with a full, definitive and unsurpassable revelation, as Christians have always believed. But the reason why this revelation is unsurpassable is not because it is not an unsurpassable collection of conceptual statements locked away once and for all, but rather, because Jesus is the very Word of the Father. And because He is the Word, His humanity is flooded with a fullness of grace which constitutes it as a living center of humanity, the principle, as it were, of our divinization.

Knitter will go on with an enumeration of various terms to try to resolve the underlying question. He will say, for example, that Jesus is "God's *universal, decisive,* and *indispensable* manifestation of saving truth and grace."[32] He is universal as a call for all people, decisive and even normative for what we should do, but not, Knitter says, final or unsurpassable. He is indispensable so that someone who does not have Jesus in his life is missing something, and in a qualified but real way, is unfulfilled without Christ. But once all this terminological dust settles, we find him saying that Jesus brings *a* universal decisive and unsurpassable message, but not *the* message, for there are other messages. Jesus has a relational uniqueness. He does not stand by Himself, but with others. "Jesus is a Word that can be understood only in conversations with other Words."[33] It is not hard to imagine that such a program will neither appease his critics nor please the people he is trying to dialogue with. Knitter goes on to ask why Jesus is unique. What is the content of His uniqueness? And he answers: "Ultimate Reality experienced as the God of Jesus is a God who is *known in history*, who seeks the *well-being of the oppressed*, and who is *faithful* to those who work for God's Reign on Earth."[34]

Knitter's work, as well as that of the other religious pluralists, were subjected to telling criticisms in *Christian Uniqueness Reconsidered*, especially in articles by Wolfhart Pannenberg and Paul Griffiths, and more recently in James Fredericks' *Faith among Faiths*.

Joseph O'Leary

We saw how in Paul Knitter's theological reflections on religious pluralism the question of historical relativism played an important role. But there it was in the background. With Joseph O'Leary, who teaches English literature at Sophia University, these kinds of issues take the center stage.

In *Questioning Back,* the first book in a proposed trilogy, in a chapter called "Is It Possible to Overcome Metaphysics?" we are faced with not only the failure of metaphysics that we called conceptualism, but with the charge that metaphysics is no longer possible. We are told that despite the central role it played in the West for 2,500 years, it no longer truly speaks to us, and we need to see its limits in a new way, and in this sense overcome it. We also need to overcome the classical theology that made use of metaphysics, even such a venerable use as found in the Councils of Nicaea and Chalcedon... "I hold that there is no irenic translation of classical Christian language into contemporary terms. Whatever is metaphysical in that language must pass through the crucible of the critique of metaphysics."[35]

This kind of overcoming will proceed under the banner of Heidegger with some help from Derrida. O'Leary will admit that St. Thomas gave "an unprecedented metaphysical depth to the notion of "being"..."[36] But both his metaphysics and the theology that employed it are "impositions of an extrinsic paradigm on the phenomena themselves."[37] Whatever metaphysical and theological depths Thomas glimpsed seven hundred years ago, we can hardly expect them to still speak to us. "Faith and philosophy converged luminously in the thirteenth century, and seemed to have been moving apart again every since."[38]

O'Leary's critique of metaphysics and a theology that makes use of it does not attempt to overcome the limits of Thomas' metaphysics by going back to his primordial insights, and then working forward to see if they could be reformulated more adequately. Instead, he is talking about "a more radical apprehension of the phenomenality of being"[39] under the guidance of Heidegger, which is a "phenomenological return to the things themselves, but one mediated by history. We have no experience of things themselves that is not already an interpretation of them."[40] It would take us too far afield to pursue the implications of this approach in detail, but this is a view of metaphysics that is at variance with the whole philosophical tradition that leads to St. Thomas because it sees a gap between our experience of things and our deepest philosophical insights about them, a gap into which we are to insert a critique of metaphysics, and thus stand outside the whole of metaphysics and overcome it.

Heidegger, for example, was once asked, "Can God and being be identified?" And he replied, "I have asked a Jesuit who is kindly disposed to me to show me the places in Thomas Aquinas where we are told what "*esse*" really signifies and what is to be understood by the proposition: "*Deus est suum esse*."... Being and God are not identical, and I would never attempt to think the essence of God by means of being."[41] For Heidegger, Thomas' ideas on being had lost the phenomenological import they had had in Aristotle, and now he is asking this Jesuit to restore it.

O'Leary suggests that he might have been speaking to Johannes Baptist Lotz who later ventured an answer: "For Aristotle being is still veiled in beings, so that even the divine appears only as the most excellent kind of entity; Thomas Aquinas accomplished within Western philosophizing the hitherto greatest and as yet unparalleled unveiling of being (*Enthüllung*), whereby he also breaks through to the idea of God as subsistent being... In Aristotle (the ontological difference) is still quite hidden, does not yet really open up; Thomas Aquinas lives in its unfolding (*Aufbrechen*), thinks fully from the difference and in it... (Nor does) the difference as such remain unthought... In his own way Aquinas *really thought* the ontological difference itself and so wrested it from forgottenness. Yes, we dare to say that in the thinking of this difference he advanced farther than anyone else."[42]

But this doesn't satisfy O'Leary. "I would say rather that, insofar as the truth of being is accessible within metaphysics, Aquinas may have given the most perfect articulation of it possible, but that because he remained within metaphysics he had no access to the *phenomenological* apprehension of being and beings in their difference. In his system everything centers on the act of being, and this gives it a transparency and a dynamic cast not to be found in the other scholastics, who are generally more oriented to form and essence than to act and being. But does Thomas's metaphysical lucidity about the nature of being amount to a phenomenological apprehension of the presence of being? In my opinion it does not, though like all great metaphysicians he offers material for such a phenomenology."[43]

There is a certain fear and loathing of metaphysics here, and perhaps a well-earned one. The metaphysics of St. Thomas was often presented poorly and glibly so that one could hardly be expected to be captivated by its beauty. The result was a reaction against it, and against even the possibility of metaphysics. There needs to be a return to the roots of metaphysics, that is, to the primordial experiences from which it arises, to the things themselves. In this regard, however, I am not sure how much help Heidegger would be. This return is not by some sort of critique of metaphysics that must take place before reason can be employed, but it is a return to the intuitive sources of reason where it encounters actually existing things, where it comes into intimate contact with this oak tree in the garden, or that pail of water, or loaf of bread. This intuitive encounter, however it may come about, is what Maritain called the intuition of being. At these depths we are no longer dealing with an academic philosophy which, even when it is correct in its employment of concepts, is content to let these concepts be in the forefront, and the intuitive insights that gave birth to them remain hidden in the depths of the unconscious. Instead, we are moving towards a practitioner's metaphysics where there is a conscious desire to contemplate being, and to do metaphysics in the midst of the marketplace of concrete things. We certainly need an overcoming of metaphysics in this sense, but not one that throws doubt on the very possibility of metaphysics, and on the value of concepts in giving us genuine knowledge of things themselves, still less one that puts the phenomenality of things on one side and our deepest insights into being on the other.

There is, however, another very intriguing possibility. What if, in Heidegger's experience of being, there is a strong element of what in the East would be called enlightenment? Louis Gardet, in *L'experience du soi*, points to such a possibility: "Is it illusory to suggest that it is a question here of a transcription, in a language informed by the Kantian critique and the phenomenological reductions, of the experience of the Self, of the fruitful grasping (and negatively achieved) of the substantial *esse* of the soul as spirit in its first act of existence?"[44] If this is true, then it would explain the close link between these reflections on Heidegger and O'Leary's attraction to Buddhism, which we will turn to in a moment. Then what we are faced with under these hermenutical veils is the same issue we have been seeing over and over again. The experience of enlightenment is being held up as the normative way to judge both metaphysics and Christian faith.

In *Religious Pluralism and Christian Truth* O'Leary uses deconstruction and Buddhism to examine how religious language functions in regard to God and Christ. Given his ideas about metaphysics, we already have an inkling of how things will turn out. The "contemporary epistemological context" "has rendered some forms of faith and religious knowledge obsolete." But all is not lost. New possibilities open up. If only we can tread the narrow way between fixation on the old and modern temptations to dissolve faith away completely, then we can let orthodoxy emerge in a new form.[45] If the traditional metaphysics was no longer viable because it didn't speak to us, in a similar way traditional theology, even the creeds and the Christological Councils no longer speak to us, either. Under these guiding lights of deconstruction and Buddhism we can discover that religious language, even dogmatic language, is *upaya*, or skillful means. This language is like a finger pointing at the moon, but just for a moment before it is replaced by another finger. Upaya tells us "the language of faith, and the coherent logic of doctrinal reflection, have only an oblique and opaque relation to the noumenal thing-in-itself."[46]

Not only skillful means, but Buddhist emptiness, can help us deconstruct the old religious language and let orthodoxy reemerge. "The serenity of Buddhist non-theism throws an unflattering light on the rhetoric of monotheism, which is seen as pervaded by illusion. But this does not condemn us to agnostic fumblings, for Buddhism offers a spiritual horizon in which we may be able to convert our language of God into one more adequate to the phenomenality of transcendence."[47] While O'Leary is not unaware of the difficulties of using Buddhist ideas that were born in such a different historical context, he perhaps does not appreciate the magnitude of the project he is suggesting. The project of using Buddhist emptiness in a genuine Christian theology probably dwarfs that of using Heidegger's views on being to create a metaphysics compatible with Christianity. Further, to criticize the relationship between concepts and things because it does not conform to the patterns found in Zen Buddhism is to already make an implicit judgment about the normative nature of enlightenment in regard to Christian theology and mysticism. Concepts in Zen are upaya because of the distinctive kind of nonconceptual experience that is trying to be attained in enlightenment. This kind of skillful means says little about concepts themselves and their ability to know from a philosophical perspective. The upaya of Zen is not the same as the transcendence of concepts found in St. Thomas' doctrine on the names of God because for St. Thomas the concepts continue to signify, even as their limits are exposed and they are swallowed up by what they are pointing to.

O'Leary insists, along with some Buddhist scholars, that it is wrong to treat emptiness as something having a metaphysical nature, and he takes people like Masao Abe to task for it. "The notion of emptiness serves at the phenomenological level as a therapy against metaphysical delusions. But in Abe's hands it becomes itself a metaphysical absolute. This leads to a speculative engagement between this absolutised emptiness and metaphysical versions of Christian theology, which themselves need to be overcome by being recalled to their biblical roots."[48]

But there is something a little too convenient in all this. Despite the validity of the point he is making, these strictures on metaphysics rendered in the style of Nagarjuna fall a bit too readily into the preexisting modern deconstruction mentalities of both certain Christian and Buddhist scholars, and in doing so we can miss a golden opportunity. Once again, it takes the nonconceptual experience of enlightenment and the nonconceptual means by which it must be reached as normative, not only in the time of meditation, but as a critique on all our ways of knowing. Once this is done, then Christians can't reflect on their own metaphysical past because it has receded into an impenetrable hermeneutic fog. And Buddhists cannot attempt to grapple in a metaphysical way with the wonderfully rich metaphysical insights that have emerged in Buddhism over the centuries.

Masao Abe suggests that: "Most Buddhist thinkers have rather strong convictions that Buddhism is deeper than Christianity as a religion, both spiritually and intellectually."[49] It is hard to see how this impression will be overcome if Christians are not bringing their deepest metaphysical, theological and mystical traditions to the table of dialogue, but rather, are confirming this impression by coming to the conclusion that Christianity, itself, is at heart another example of Buddhist skillful means, and another nonduality, and therefore something that the East knows far more about than Christians.

Abe will write elsewhere: "Sunyata can be better understood as ultimate reality, without form and content (substantiality), infinitely open and in that sense absolute no-thing-ness. No-thing-ness as the mother of all things, as a creative and dynamic nothingness, transcending the duality of something and nothing."[50] A statement like this could be the starting point for a deep metaphysical conversation that could interest both Buddhist thinkers and Christians ones. St. Thomas, for example, was a diligent commentator on the writings of Pseudo-Dionysius, and it would be possible to create, I think, a genuine existential Thomist metaphysical language, drawing in part on Pseudo-Dionysius, with the necessary correctives, and aimed at expressing metaphysical insights that would be congruent to what Abe is saying. In such a language it would be possible to say not only that God is, but that God "is not."[51] Or God "is no thing." This would not have to be a return to a neo-Platonism in which there is the one somehow beyond being. Even a Thomist could say God "does not possess *this* kind of existence and not *that*."[52] In this kind of language non-being is not mere nothingness, but "an excess of being."[53] But if we continue to accuse Abe and the Kyoto School of somehow substantializing emptiness, and turning it into an ultimate principle like God, or being, in the West, and evoking Nagarjuna in order to say that these deep metaphysical impulses cannot be pursued either in the East or West, then such a conversation is ruled out before it can even begin.

The biblical language, itself, for O'Leary becomes a form of upaya "to be deployed skillfully in order to do justice first to the phenomenality of the Christ-event."[54] But just how do we come in contact or know this event? The traditional answer was never by metaphysics, but rather, by faith. And faith, in turn, was never reduced to being only conceptual statements. It is certainly important to protect the mysteries of Christianity from being subjected and dominated by metaphysical categories, but in order to do this we don't need to dig a ditch between faith and reason, and have a fideism on one side, and a phenomenology that cannot really know things, themselves, in a conceptual way, on the other. If O'Leary means that the "phenomena of revelation" cannot be properly contacted or assented to by reason, still less by abstract metaphysical systems, he is certainly correct. But he appears to be saying a lot more than this. "Presuppositionless Buddhist *prajna*, penetrating discernment, should come before the investment of faith, clearing the ground for a demystified apprehension of the phenomenon of Jesus so that this phenomenon in its 'thusness' can draw forth the appropriate response of faith, which may no longer be that of biblical or classical Christian times, but something quieter, subtler, more open-ended."[55] Just how presuppositionless Buddhist categories are is, of course, questionable, as we have just seen. We are left with the impression that the whole Christian tradition somehow resists all genuine knowing. "Yet in the end the status of this entire tradition, with all its logical and phenomenological constraints, remains contingent. It is an interpretation whose relation to the truth of things in themselves eludes us, even if we say that in revelation the truth is no longer noumenal but is given as a phenomenon to be lived, that life takes a variety of forms, and is enacted as a series of finite occasions."[56]

O'Leary's tentative reflections on how we can remake traditional Christianity by appealing to Buddhist emptiness give scant comfort. First we must see that traditional Christology is "intrinsically "empty","[57] and is but a makeshift historical construct, then we can go on to see how Jesus is empty of his own-being and the "emptiness of the risen Christ is one with the emptiness of the eternal Logos, the emptiness of God himself."[58]

In the end, however, O'Leary wants to hold on to something of the distinctive nature of Christianity, and tells us "we must retain a sense of the irreducibility to Buddhist categories of the incarnational covenant between a transcendent God and human finitude."[59] But we can certainly wonder just what is left of traditional Christian doctrine when it has been surrounded in all directions by epistemological "no trespassing" signs.

In a review of *Mysticism Buddhist and Christian: Encounters with Jan van Ruusbroec* O'Leary sums up his program. "…certain of the categories governing the debate (e.g., immanence and transcendence, personal and impersonal God, Creator and creature) have reached the limits of their usefulness. For a breakthrough in interreligious thinking these categories must be historicized and deconstructed as Christianity opens itself to the critical impact of Buddhist epistemology and ontology at the level of its most basic self-understanding. Only slight beginnings have been made in this daunting task, but is sure to be a major project of Christian thought in the next century. A groundbreaking contribution is John P. Keenan's study of Buddhist and Christian mysticism."[60]

We will look at Keenan's work in a moment, but this kind of program of deconstruction is the equivalent of dynamiting a building into rubble, then constructing a new building out of the rubble, a building that has no real connection with what went before.

John Keenan

The Episcopal priest and Buddhist scholar John Keenan's *The Meaning of Christ* carries the subtitle *A Mahayana Theology,* and that is exactly what he gives us. This is not the use of Buddhist insights to stimulate and supplement Christian theology, but something much more radical in which the traditional understanding of God and Christ is replaced by Buddhist views. Emptiness and the no essence, or no-self, of Buddhism "entails the rejection of the metaphysical basis of Western theology."[61] Once again Nagarjuna is evoked to avoid reflecting on what might be the rich metaphysical dimensions of emptiness and no-self, and we are left with a theological instrument which tells us "all views are seen to be empty of essence and unable to sustain any claim to final validity."[62] This will function like the upaya or skillful means we have been seeing. All concepts are relativized, and therefore our traditional Christian understanding of Christ is no more privileged than whatever new understanding we might like to create. In this case we are left with emptiness and dependent co-arising as the fundamental Buddhist categories into which we must now force the Christian mysteries.

Traditional Christology is written off as non-binding because we are no longer Greeks, and therefore need not use Greek philosophy with its tendencies towards essentialism. This is a refrain that we have, of course, been seeing over and over again, but it is rather simplistic because it assumes that theology in the past was simply applying Greek philosophy to Christian themes, and it ignores the transformations that Greek ideas underwent in order to be used by theology to try to articulate something of the mystery of Christ, a mystery that was known primarily not by reason, but by faith.

Keenan tells us that the identity of Jesus as found in the Gospels centers on His perception of God as Abba, or Father, and on His dedication to establish the kingdom of God. But now we have to read them in the register of emptiness and no-self. But this kind of theologizing has already excused itself from what the theology of the past has had to say, and more importantly, from what the Christian community has always held by faith. Instead, Christian concepts are treated as if they can be turned into Buddhist ones, for whether they are Christian or Buddhist, they are simply upaya pointing to the same transcendental experience of enlightenment. Christian concepts no longer have any conceptual continuity with the Christian mysteries. Therefore, we can replace them easily enough without any real damage. In this case, our traditional understanding of Christ disappears and is replaced by a Mahayana one.

But what motivates this kind of project? Christians must stop indulging in "divine hero worship," and "illusory orthodoxy," but rather they must identify with Jesus "in conversion from me-consciousness to commitment to others, an awareness of Abba…"[63] which is going to be understood in terms of Jesus as empty of essence and dependently co-arisen. What is striking about all this is that while these central Buddhist ideas could, indeed, enter into a deep dialogue with Christianity, they are wielded here against basic Christian self-understanding. "There is no need to define the specific difference between Jesus and other human beings."[64] All are empty of essence. Jesus is not the mediator of divine nature to human nature, but announces "a preverbal mystic awareness,"[65] an awareness that is presumably no different than the awareness that Buddhists find in enlightenment.

Even the Abba experience of Jesus, which we were told was central to his identity, needs to be subjected to a merciless critique in the name of creating a Mahayana theology. "What on earth does it mean to say that God is Abba, when he obviously fails to perform expected fatherly deeds on behalf of his children in the world? It is quite all right to say that no sparrow falls without our Father's knowledge, but he does not in any manner break its fall or save it from crushing itself on the hard surface of the earth!"[66]

Even though the early Christian community, faced with the death of Jesus, affirmed Jesus as Lord, as well as the faithfulness of Abba: "Yet there is no empirical evidence that they were not simply mistaken and merely projecting their subconscious desires for happiness upon a silent universe. If one actually expects God to demonstrate his fatherhood in an observable manner by saving his children from suffering and dying, one might conclude, with Woody Allen, that, although God does exist, he is an underachiever."[67] "Yahweh does not save his people. He allowed them be consumed in the fires of the holocaust. Why bother calling him "Abba" at all then?"[68]

These are not the reflections of some interested Buddhist serenely meditating on the New Testament in a mountain cave trying to understand Christianity from his Buddhist perspective. There is something else going on here. It is a Mahayana theology that will come to our rescue by telling us there is no personal god, and therefore no loving providence, nor any resurrection of Jesus. Once having said all this, and adding "despite the insistence of manuals of Christian devotion, prayer is not a conversation with God,"[69] Keenan will attempt to retrieve some meaning for Christianity. Abba is "the support for a realization of meaning that conquers death by recognizing the dependently co-arisen emptiness of all self-affirmation. It is thus that one participates in the resurrection of Jesus."[70] Here we have rejoined in a theological way some of the attempts we saw in *Chapter 1* to reduce Christian life to a pursuit of Buddhist nonduality.

Jacques Dupuis

After these radical theological attempts to restructure Christianity in the light of, or even in the name of, interreligious dialogue, we might imagine that Jacques Dupuis, having been taken to task by the Congregation for the Doctrine of the Faith for his book *Toward a Christian Theology of Religious Pluralism,* would be equally radical to have merited such attention. But we have already seen his judicious remarks about Abhishiktananda, and when we look at his book we see that we are faced with a well-grounded theologian with a fine grasp of his subject who is presenting us with an inclusive Christology, yet one that he hopes will be truly open to other religions, and thus, could be said to be relational.

Dupuis starts by giving us an overview of the history and development of Catholic theology in regard to religious pluralism, starting with God's covenant with Israel, and then going on to the New Testament, the pluralism to be found in the Fathers, the axiom no salvation outside the Church, and he continues all the way to the Vatican Council and the modern debates about pluralism.

But the heart of the matter is his Christology. While Knitter, for example, had thought it necessary to alter classical Christology in order to advance the cause of dialogue, Dupuis does not. He sums up his perspective: "In agreement with the uninterrupted, mainline Christian tradition we have maintained the constitutive uniqueness and universality of Jesus Christ. This means that the person of Jesus Christ and the Christ-event are "constitutive" of salvation for the whole of humankind; in particular, the event of his death-resurrection opens access to God for all human beings, independently of their historical situation. Put in other words, the humanity of Jesus Christ, God's Son made flesh, is the sacrament of God's universal will to save. Such uniqueness must not, however, be construed as absolute: what is absolute is God's saving will. Neither absolute nor relative, Jesus' uniqueness is "constitutive"; in addition, we called it "relational"."[71]

The challenge is to articulate this in a way that satisfies both the demands of the classical Christology and the new Christian sense of how God wills all to be saved. This is not an easy task, and we will misunderstand what Dupuis is saying unless we realize that he is looking at the matter from the perspective of God's universal salvific will.

He will argue that the revelation of God in Jesus is limited because the human nature of Jesus cannot comprehend the totality of the mystery of God.[72] And he will write that the word absolute ought to be avoided in regard to Christ and Christianity, "The reason is that absoluteness is an attribute of the Ultimate Reality of Infinite Being which must not be predicated of any finite reality, even the human existence of the Son-of-God-made-man. That Jesus Christ is "universal" Savior does not make him the "Absolute Savior" – who is God himself."[73] At the same time, he tries to find his terminology that will safeguard the unique role of Jesus. "Jesus Christ, it will be suggested, is, among different saving figures in whom God is hiddenly present and operative, the one "human face" in whom God, while remaining unseen, is fully disclosed and revealed."[74]

Dupuis will make a distinction between the non-Incarnate Logos, or *Logos asarkos*, that is, the Word of God itself, and the *Logos ensarkos*, that is, the Incarnation of the Word in Jesus. In this way he hopes to find a way that will preserve the universal salvific role of the Word of God, and yet not limit this role to the action of the Incarnation of the Word in Jesus. But he realizes the difficulties in such a procedure.

"Admittedly, in the mystery of Jesus-the-Christ, the Word cannot be separated from the flesh it has assumed. But, inseparable as the divine Word and Jesus' human existence may be, they nevertheless remain distinct. While, then, the human action of the Logos *ensarkos* is the universal sacrament of God's saving action, it does not exhaust the action of the Logos."[75] In advancing in this direction, Dupuis finds support in the work of Claude Geffré, Edward Schillebeeckx and others. And all the while he is trying to honor the traditional understanding of the universal role that Jesus plays in the salvation of all people: "...salvation as revealed by God in Jesus Christ is the universal destiny devised by God for human beings, whichever situation they may find themselves in and whichever religious tradition they may belong to. The living Christian tradition implies no less."[76]

A final passage allows us to sense the real challenge that we face when we want to integrate our two fundamental principles. The "...Word's "humanization" marks the unsurpassed – and unsurpassable – depth of God's self-communication to human beings, the supreme mode of immanence of his being-with-them... However, the centrality of the incarnational dimension of God's economy of salvation must not be allowed to obscure the abiding presence and action of the divine Word. The enlightening and saving power of the Logos is not circumscribed by the particularity of the historical event. It transcends all boundaries of time and space. Through the transcendent power of the Logos, Trinitarian Christology is able to account for the mediatory function of religious traditions in the order of salvation, thus laying the foundation for the recognition of a pluralism in God's way of dealing with humankind."[77]

Dominus Iesus

Dupuis' struggles did not go unnoticed. He was questioned by the Congregation for the Doctrine of the Faith, and when it published its letter *Dominus Iesus: On the Unicity and Salvific Universality of Jesus Christ and the Church*, it was not hard to see that he had not been forgotten. *Dominus Iesus* wants to "recall to Bishops, theologians, and all the Catholic faithful certain indispensable elements of Christian doctrine,"[78] which could aid theological reflection in dealing with these kinds of issues. In the document's own words:

"The Church's constant missionary proclamation is endangered today by relativistic theories which seek to justify religious pluralism, not only de facto but also de iure (or in principle). As a consequence, it is held that certain truths have been superseded; for example, the definitive and complete character of the revelation of Jesus Christ, the nature of Christian faith as compared with that of belief in other religions, the inspired nature of the books of Sacred Scripture, the personal unity between the Eternal Word and Jesus of Nazareth, the unity of the economy of the Incarnate Word and the Holy Spirit, the unicity and salvific universality of the mystery of Jesus Christ, the universal salvific mediation of the Church, the inseparability – while recognizing the distinction – of the kingdom of God, the kingdom of Christ, and the Church, and the subsistence of the one Church of Christ in the Catholic Church."[79]

Dominus Iesus goes on to insist on this "fullness and definitiveness of the revelation of Jesus Christ," as opposed to theories that consider Jesus "a particular, finite, historical figure, who reveals the divine not in an exclusive way, but in a way complementary with the other revelatory and salvific figures... More concretely, for some, Jesus would be one of the many faces which the Logos has assumed in the course of time to communicate with humanity in a salvific way.

"Furthermore, to justify the universality of Christian salvation as well as the fact of religious pluralism, it has been proposed that there is an economy of the eternal Word that is valid also outside the Church and is unrelated to her, in addition to an economy of the Incarnate Word. The first would have a greater universal value than the second, which is limited to Christians, though God's presence would be more full in the second... In this regard, John Paul II has explicitly declared: "To introduce any sort of separation between the Word and Jesus Christ is contrary to the Christian faith..." "[80]

Just what is the relationship between what Dupuis is saying and *Dominus Iesus*? They are both addressing the same central questions, but from different directions. Dupuis, with his keen sense of the exigencies of the East-West dialogue, is advancing on the problem of the universal role of Jesus and the Church from the direction of the universal salvific will of God. *Dominus Iesus* is coming from the other direction. It wants to assert, against the threats it perceives, the universal role of Jesus and the Church, but it needs to take into account God's universal salvific will. It is this difference in direction that probably more than anything else stands in the way of a meeting of the minds.

Dominus Iesus insists on "certain indispensible elements," but it does so from the starting point of the universal role of Jesus, and in a language that makes it inevitable that it will be read against the background of the old "outside of the Church there is no salvation" theology, and reacted to accordingly. This is why it insists on things like a distinction between faith and belief, and that the inspired texts of the Bible differ from the inspired texts of other religions, and how the Church of Christ subsists in the Catholic Church. Let's look at the distinction it makes between faith and religious belief in order to see how it is proceeding. It insists that we have to distinguish between the theological faith by which Catholics assent to the truths of the faith as revealed by God, and religious belief in other religions "which is religious experience still in search of the absolute truth and still lacking assent to God who reveals Himself."[81] But in doing so, it is concentrating on the role of Jesus and the Church in making these truths present to us, and losing sight, for a moment, of the implications of the doctrine of the universal salvific will of God. If faith is necessary for salvation, and God calls all people to be saved, and all people do not know the role of Jesus in the Church, then we have to say that they still exercise faith, that they interiorly assent to God, without that knowledge. Explicit faith in Jesus and the Church is not essential in order to have this interior assent to God.

Not only are Jacques Dupuis and *Dominus Iesus* coming from different directions, but the principles they are advancing from have different characters. The principle of God's universal salvific will we called an existential principle, while the universal role of Jesus in the Church, an essentialistic one. The first deals with the concrete state we find ourselves in, while the second looks at the nature, or essence, of things. The first brings us face to face with an intimate mystery of love that is working itself out in all our hearts, while the second with the quest for truth. What we are seeing in Jacques Dupuis and *Dominus Iesus* is not a winner-take-all kind of battle where one or the other of these principles must gain ground at the price of the other. Instead, we are looking at two very different kinds of principles that operate at different levels while addressing the same problem.

When the Congregation finally issued its notification on Dupuis' book it stays within the perspective it took in *Dominus Iesus*: Jesus as the Word is the universal mediator of salvation, and revelation in Him is not limited, incomplete or imperfect; a separation cannot be made between the salvific action of the Word and that of Jesus, and so forth.

We are caught, as it were, between these two perspectives. On the one hand, I need to say that God wills everyone to be saved, and this will is efficacious in the sense that everyone has the opportunity. This means that God makes this offer of salvation to us both in our hearts and in the outer events of our lives, especially through our religious practices and sacred writings. Therefore, we can say that people can be saved without any conscious explicit knowledge of Jesus.

On the other hand, Christian faith proposes that God wills this salvation through Jesus, and theologians have attempted to understand how this takes place. If Jesus is the very Word of God, then His humanity, transformed by its union with the Word, undergoes a transformation, or we could even say a deification, but it is not, itself, divine, for it is a true human nature just like ours, and so in this sense it is not absolute, for it is not divine by nature. But neither is it a limited human nature in the way we possess ours. This transformed human nature takes up within itself the already existing unity of the human race and deepens it so that Jesus stands at the center and is the efficacious sacrament of the divinization of our humanity, which is the salvation that God wills for us. What Jesus is by nature we are called to by grace, and so grace, itself, has a Christological character.

This kind of Christology, rooted in the Scriptures and the Fathers, found one of its highest theological expressions in the work of Emile Mersch, to which I alluded earlier, and it is the kind of Christology being advanced in their own ways by Rahner and Dupuis. Dupuis, for example, will say: "Jesus lived his personal relationship to the Father in his human awareness. His human consciousness of being the Son entailed an immediate knowledge of his Father, whom he called *Abba*. Thus his revelation of God had its point of departure in a unique, unsurpassable human experience. This experience was actually none other than the transposition to the key of human awareness and cognition of the very life of God and of the Trinitarian relations among the persons."[82]

But this classical Christology has only begun to be brought into conscious contact with God's universal salvific will. This is what Dupuis and others like Michael Amaladoss in his *Making All Things New* are trying to do. Clearly, it is incompatible with a perspective that would make Jesus one savior among many, or with a view that the revelation that took place in Jesus is somehow limited and deficient, and needs to be supplemented by other revelations. But our sense of the fullness of revelation, and its definitive nature in Jesus, does not tell us how all this works out in the concrete. Our viewpoint is too limited. We see things in a linear historical fashion of before and after, and can scarcely imagine how God sees the same things. In short, there is a trans-historical dimension to Christology that must be honored because it is based on who Christians say Jesus is, but this does not reveal to us how Jesus' salvation takes place in history, and does not spell out for us God's salvific intentions and actions in all times and places. The fact that we believe that Jesus is the definitive Word of the Father, and thus the unsurpassable revelation of God, still leaves us struggling as Christians to embody this understanding in our lives, and wondering what gifts God has given to others in order that the salvation achieved in Jesus can take root in their minds and hearts, as well.

When Dupuis makes a distinction between the action of the Word and the action of the Word made flesh, he is perhaps using a language that is unnecessarily complicated. It might be enough to say that as Christians we believe in the definitive role that Jesus plays in the salvation of all people, but we realize that this salvific action plays itself out far beyond the visible boundaries of the Catholic Church, and beyond any conscious knowledge of Jesus. Once we see the different perspectives from which Dupuis and the Congregation of the Doctrine of the Faith are coming from, much of the tension between these two views disappears.

Why did the Congregation give Dupuis such a hard time, especially since his work represents a basically sound attempt to work out a theology of religious pluralism? Part of it has to do with the different perspectives we have just been seeing. But perhaps they wanted to send a message to the Catholic theological community, and criticizing Dupuis suited their purpose because then it would be a message heard not only in Europe and North America, but in Asia because of Dupuis' long sojourn in India, and by the Jesuit theological community, as well. Whatever the actual reason for the Congregation's action was, it should have realized that its words were going to be read against the background of the century-long struggle that began with modernism, and especially against the polarization that exists between the Vatican and a large part of the theological community since the time of the Vatican Council. It would have been much more effective, and fruitful, for the Church as a whole if they had sat down with Dupuis and had an open conversation about the issues that bothered them in his book. That would have been a step towards confronting the crisis that exists in Catholic theology, and trying to resolve it.

We have gone from looking at Catholic attempts to dialogue with Buddhism and Hinduism, to the theological background of these attempts, and now we need to return to the possibilities of East-West dialogue, itself.

Notes

1. Rahner, Karl. "Observations on the Problem of the 'Anonymous Christian'." p. 284.
2. Ibid., p. 286.
3. Rahner, Karl. "Observations on the Problem of the 'Anonymous Christian'." p. 293.
4. Rahner, Karl. *Faith in a Wintry Season.* p. 21.
5. Ibid., p. 48
6. Rahner, Karl. *The Dynamic Element of the Church.*
7. Maritain, Jacques. "The Immanent Dialectic of the First Act of Freedom," p. 218-235.
8. Ibid., p. 69.
9. Ibid., p. 69-70.
10. Ibid., p. 70.
11. Ibid., p. 73.
12. Ibid., p. 76.
13. Ibid., p. 77.
14. Ibid.
15. Ibid., p. 78.
16. Ibid., p. 83.
17. Knitter, Paul. *No Other Name?* P. 171-172.
18. Ibid., p. 173.
19. Ibid., p. 191.
20. Ibid.
21. Ibid., p. 217.
22. Ibid., p. 219.
23. Ibid., p. 218.
24. Ibid., p. 227.
25. Ibid., p. 227-228.
26. Ibid., p. 228.
27. Knitter, Paul. *The Myth of Christian Uniqueness*, p. 181.
28. Ibid., p. 184.
29. Ibid.
30. Ibid.
31. Knitter, Paul. *Jesus and the Other Names*, p. 73.
32. Ibid., p. 76.
33. Ibid., p. 80.
34. Ibid., p. 94.
35. O'Leary, Joseph. *Questioning Back*, p. 5.
36. Ibid., p. 9.
37. Ibid., p. 10.
38. Ibid.
39. Ibid., p. 12.
40. Ibid., p. 13.
41. Ibid., p. 18.
42. Ibid., p. 19-20.
43. Ibid., p. 20.
44. Gardet, Louis. *L'experience du soi*, p. 347.
45. O'Leary, Joseph. *Religious Pluralism and Christian Truth*, p. 159.
46. Ibid., p. 179.
47. Ibid., p. 191.
48. Ibid., p. 197.

49. Abe, Masao. As cited in *Buddhist-Christian Studies*, 1990, p. 260.
50. Abe, Masao. As cited in *Buddhist-Christian Studies*, 1991, p. 291.
51. Pseudo-Dionysius. P. 98.
52. Ibid., p. 101. 53. Ibid., p. 73.
54. O'Leary, Joseph. *Religious Pluralism and Christian Truth*, p. 213.
55. Ibid., p. 241-242. 57. Ibid., p. 251. 59. Ibid., p. 257.
56. Ibid., p. 240. 58. Ibid., p. 256.
60. *Japanese J. of Religious Studies* 23/1-2, p. 202.
61. Keenan, John. *The Meaning of Christ*, p. 224.
62. Ibid. 65. Ibid., p. 239. 68. Ibid., p. 244.
63. Ibid., p. 238. 66. Ibid., p. 243 69. Ibid., p. 250.
64. Ibid. 67. Ibid., p. 243-244. 70. Ibid., p. 251.
71. Dupuis, Jacques. *Toward a Christian Theology of Religious Pluralism.* p. 387-388.
72. Ibid., p. 249, 271. 74. Ibid., p. 283. 76. Ibid., p. 312.
73. Ibid., p. 282. 75. Ibid., p. 299. 77. Ibid., p. 320-321.
78. Congregation for the Doctrine of the Faith. *Dominus Iesus.* No. 3.
79. Ibid., No. 4. 80. Ibid., No. 9-10. 81. Ibid., No. 7.
82. Dupuis, Jacques. *Toward a Christian Theology of Religious Pluralism.* p. 249.

CHAPTER 5

WHAT KIND OF DIALOGUE?

Let me try to illustrate the problems that exist in contemporary East-West dialogue by looking at some of the ambiguities that exist in Buddhist-Catholic dialogue. Here I give myself leave to exaggerate a bit and poke a little fun.

Two Catholics and two Buddhists plan to have a dialogue. The first Catholic and the first Buddhist arrive early. The Catholic is a Western post-modernist who feels that the Church is a roadblock on the way to interreligious cooperation in confronting pressing world problems, and it has treated him poorly, to boot. He finds no justification for metaphysics, and considers Christian doctrine a mythological projection of the inner quest for enlightenment, and all philosophical and theological languages as skillful means pointing to that transcendent experience.

The Buddhist has grown up Catholic, and is a Western post-modernist who feels that the Church is a roadblock on the way to interreligious cooperation in confronting pressing world problems, and it has treated him poorly, to boot. He finds no justification for metaphysics, and considers Christian doctrine a mythological projection of the inner quest for enlightenment, and all philosophical and theological languages as skillful means pointing to this transcendent experience.

They get along famously. Dialogue, they feel, will be a piece of cake. Then the second Catholic arrives. He still believes in a personal God, and in all the doctrines enunciated in the Nicene Creed. And he also thinks that metaphysics is a way to gain deep insight into reality, and he happens to mention these things. There is a profound silence. The first Buddhist and the first Catholic are dumbfounded. Here they are faced with a throwback to the classical era that has been definitively destroyed by our new historical mentality. Here is a Catholic fundamentalist who actually expects to approach the table of dialogue encumbered by all these outmoded beliefs. They want to have a Buddhist-Christian dialogue, but not that kind. In fact, they really want to have a conversation between a certain kind of Buddhism and a certain kind of Christianity without really having to deal with things they outgrew long ago.

In the meantime, the second Buddhist, who is a Tibetan monk just off a three-year retreat in the mountains, has arrived and is struggling to figure out what is really going on. As soon as it is polite, the first Buddhist and the first Christian go off to continue their conversation. The second Catholic and the second Buddhist sit down, and discover they have all sorts of interesting things to say to each other ranging from metaphysics and scholastic-style debate, to the question of the existence of God.

Fun aside, it is important to be clear about what kind of dialogue we are having, and what its presuppositions are. First, we will look at some of these presuppositions from the Catholic side, and then at just what kind of dialogue we are aiming at here.

Catholic Pluralism

There is a de facto, or existential, pluralism that exists today in contemporary Catholic philosophy and theology. No one can become an expert in all the various specialties that make up these disciplines. No one has the time to keep up in all these fields. Thus, we could say that there is a pluralism that will not be overcome. But it is quite another matter to go from a recognition of this existential pluralism and embrace a de jure or a theoretical pluralism that says that not only do different philosophies and theologies have different starting points and different ways of expressing themselves, but they can never be brought into relationship with each other. It is hard to see how such a theoretical pluralism is compatible with Christian faith, and the oneness of God as truth.

There are certainly different conceptual pathways to express the same reality. For example, the Eastern and Western Christian churches have different theologies, liturgies and ecclesiologies, but we cannot say that these differences are irreducible in principle - which is quite a different question than asking whether they should be reduced in practice so that the entire Church, for example, would have the same liturgy.

Let me test your patience with a simple example. There are certain words or phrases in Spanish or French, for example, that do not translate readily into English. They have been born out of a particular history and culture, and a long process of linguistic formation, and so they do not readily find English equivalents. But this is not the same as saying that they are untranslatable in principle. The word untranslatable can have two distinct meanings. It can have an existential sense in which a line of Spanish poetry cannot be translated into a line of English poetry of equal size and equal beauty because of a variety of concrete circumstances such as the particular historical and emotional resonances of the words, their sound and length, the lack of poetic genius of the translator, and so forth.

But it is quite another matter to say that these Spanish words are intrinsically or essentially untranslatable, or mediate some reality inaccessible to English speakers, or don't mediate reality at all beyond the words, themselves, and so are unique and are unable to be rendered into any other language.

Another example will build on the first. A Biblical exegete is immersed in New Testament Greek, and discovers valuable things that we can all benefit from, but we don't need to be left with the impression that because we are not Greek scholars there are certain essential dimensions of the Scriptures that remain closed to us. There is a form of anti-conceptualism which fractures theology into a group of specialties that cannot in principle truly communicate with each other. Each scholar is locked in his or her own little world.

The transcendental Thomism of Rahner uses a very different vocabulary from the Thomism of Gilson, but in substance they can talk to each other. They each weave a distinctive web of concepts, but each web looks out upon a different aspect of the same reality. But there has to be something beyond these webs of concepts that allows us to tell when they are true and when they are false. Philosophy and theology cannot survive the attempt to embrace mutually contradictory positions. Catholic faith has always expressed itself in concepts with the assumption that they mediate some knowledge of the Christian mysteries themselves. We may, and should, have contextual theologies, theologies that grow out of a particular time and place and are preoccupied with pressing social issues. Thus, we have a liberation theology, or a black or Asian theology, or a feminist or ecological theology, and each weaves its distinctive web of concepts, and in this sense is unique. But again, the purpose of the concepts are to be windows on the Christian mysteries. There can be no masculine theology that in principle is inaccessible to women, or Asian theology that in principle is closed to South Americans. Here we come back to the basic theme of the relationship between concepts and things we have been seeing over and over again.

Christian Philosophy

This new era of Catholic pluralism has two faces. On the positive side there is a refreshing and vitalizing contact with the world in which we live. On the negative side there is a loss of a common conceptual language, and a synthetic or integrative view of theology as a whole. But with the collapse of the old philosophical and theological framework at the time of the Council we need to ask ourselves if we only gained in terms of a broader, more ecumenical and contemporary outlook, and didn't lose anything. Isn't it possible that the underlying assumption of the previous age that we somehow shared a common faith that we were trying to articulate has become overshadowed?

Let's see what that means from the point of view of philosophy. There has been a tremendous explosion in interest and expertise in philosophies and theologies from far beyond the borders of the Catholic Church. This interest is a valuable compensation for the narrow parochialism that so often marred Catholic life before the Council. But is every philosophy compatible with faith, or equally baptizable? Just because Plato and Aristotle made their way into the Church – with a great deal of trauma and deep structural changes – does that mean that all sorts of contemporary philosophies are capable of that journey? Can we, for example, take various forms of post-modern philosophies stemming from Heiddeger or Wittgenstein or Whitehead and create new theologies out of them? We can certainly make use of the insights they provide, but there will come a point when we need to make a judgment of whether these new postmodern inspired Catholic philosophies and theologies are compatible with the faith. Thomas Guarino, in a carefully crafted article, "Postmodernity and Five Fundamental Theological Issues" which reviewed this question, concluded: "Without a foundationalist ontology of some sort, there is no possibility for logically sustaining the stability of textual meaning or a referential sense of truth which appears to be an essential principle for a traditional understanding of doctrine."[1]

Even asking the question about the compatibility with faith of various modern philosophies and theologies can be read in certain circles as a reactionary desire to return to the safe but narrow and, indeed, even sterile confines of neo-scholasticism. It does not have to be. It can simply raise the larger question of whether we are proposing new ways to understand the Christian faith that stretches back through the centuries to the medieval theologians and the Fathers, and to the early Church and Jesus, Himself, or are we proposing a radical departure from this faith for various epistemological or metaphysical reasons that supposedly tell us that we cannot know the divine mysteries by faith, and therefore, hardly need to worry about the continuity of our faith with those who have gone before us? Actually, this issue extends far beyond the use of modern and post-modern philosophy, and can be seen in analogous ways in the dialogues with Eastern religions, depth psychology, the modern sciences, etc., as we have been seeing.

This raises the question of whether we can talk of a Christian philosophy. If we mean by this a philosophy that is particularly Christian because it receives its principles, method and conclusions from Christian faith, then the answer is no. Such a philosophy would no longer be a philosophy at all, for if philosophy is to be anything, it has to be the free creative exercise of the intellect which tackles the deepest questions that face all human beings regardless of their religious convictions. Thomas Aquinas, for example, never suggests that Aristotle or Avicenna were not philosophers because they were not Christians.

But our inquiry has to go beyond this necessary assertion. The real question is whether Christian faith, itself, implies certain philosophical positions. Again, it is not a question of it containing a ready-made philosophy which it dispenses to those who believe, but rather, whether believing in the central mysteries of Christianity like the Trinity and Incarnation imply certain philosophical positions. I think that it does, both in terms of a realist epistemology, however much we need to nuance our ability to know, and a certain view of God and God's relationship to the universe, and especially to us.

Therefore, whatever philosophy that during the course of the history of Christianity, was taken into the Church, was also modified and developed so that it would be in line with these implied positions. This was often a long and arduous process, as witnessed with Greek philosophy in the early centuries of the Church, and in the Middle Ages. If this appropriation and transformation of a philosophy was so difficult, why did the Church do it at all? It is simply because we need to think about our faith as deeply as possible, and this demands the best philosophy we can get. It might be objected that I am contradicting myself. On one hand, I propose philosophy as the free exercise of the mind, but on the other, I say that faith implies certain philosophical positions. Doesn't the latter make the former impossible? I don't think so. By faith we assent to the divine mysteries, which we would believe transcend what reason can fathom, but do not contradict it. Faith can be a nourishing context in which philosophy can grow, and even be guided without losing its essential nature or method. We need to distinguish between the essential nature of things – in this case philosophy – and the existential context in which they are lived out, which here is inside the Christian community of faith.

As thinking Christians we need to cultivate a radical openness to good philosophy wherever we find it, but we don't philosophize in a vacuum. We philosophize in the context of the faith, a faith that has a definite content, a content which is, in principle in some limited degree, knowable to us on the pain of there being no faith. However transcendent the mysteries of Christianity are, they are in principle revealable, for if they were not, there could be no Christianity at all. Both the content of the faith and its implicit epistemology sets up a dialectic with any philosophy. If we give philosophy the absolute right to judge faith, then our faith will change with the prevailing philosophical fashions and might disappear altogether. From a Christian perspective this is unacceptable. Faith has a definite content which creates its own philosophical context which, in turn, makes demands on any philosophy we may care to use.

The Nature of Theology

The rapid transition from the old narrow neo-scholasticism to a contemporary Catholic theology colored by its reactions to the past has left important issues unexamined. The old theology, for example, however much it asserted the supernatural character of faith, and repeated with St. Thomas that our theological knowledge did not end in concepts, but in the Christian mysteries, themselves, and even gave a nod to the piety of theologians, rarely came to grips with the nature of theology, itself. Instead, it accepted the truths of faith like the axioms of geometry, and then proceeded to act as if reason, alone, was adequate to develop the science of theology. Modern reaction theology, in contrast, rightly criticized the conceptualism of the past, but then it sometimes proceeds to act as if the renewal of theology is to come about solely through the better use of reason in the form of exegesis, history, more contemporary forms of philosophy, and so forth. But the underlying question of the nature of theology still remains unexamined. In some way theology must make living contact with the Christian mysteries, themselves. It has to be a way of Christian knowing that operates by faith and is guided by love. Contemporary Catholic theology has to rediscover how a certain kind of knowledge by connaturality is at the heart of both faith and theology.

Theology is meant to be a deep reflection on the Christian mysteries in order to understand them in themselves and in their relationships to each other. As such, it demands the forceful and disciplined use of the human mind through the use of philosophy, history, linguistics, psychology, etc. These disciplines provide different lights that can help us see into the meaning of Christian revelation. The deficiencies of the neo-scholasticism of the manuals vividly points to what happens when we fail to truly think and truly enrich and stimulate our thinking with the best of the sciences. But the reaction to this narrow conceptualism has been an openness that sometimes fails to recognize its legitimate limits and begins to lead to a loss of the faith, itself. Theology is not philosophy or history or psychology. The historical method, in and by itself, will not lead to the Christ of faith. Various forms of modern and post-modern philosophies, or even Eastern religions, cannot become the ultimate norms by which we interpret the Christian mysteries. There has to be more to theology than the various disciplines we make use of in it. It has to have something distinctive in itself, or otherwise it will simply be history or psychology applied to religious themes.

What makes theology different is that it is rooted in and ultimately sees by means of the light of faith. The lights of these other disciplines are taken up and employed in a new way by the light of faith in order to explore the Christian mysteries. We can sum up the question before us like this: what is the distinctive nature of theology? It has a distinctive nature, or else it is identical to philosophy, or history, etc., and then is no longer theology.

Someone once asked Karl Rahner what he thought his most important writings were. He responded that it was not this or that book, but certain ideas that were very important to him. Along with his transcendental theology, itself, he singled out what he called "the logic of the concrete individual knowledge in Ignatius Loyola," which we saw before, and which is an answer that one could hardly have anticipated. And he goes on to comment, "Such matters are important, I believe; they are new to a certain extent and really could have consequences for questions and groups of problems, even where people do not yet see this so clearly."[2] Even Jesuit theologians "propose some sort of essential and rational theory of knowledge as the only possible one and didn't realize that Ignatius had taught them something entirely different." They didn't "fertilize their theology" with this kind of knowledge.[3]

There is more to what he is saying than first meets the eye. I believe he is pointing to the issues that surround the question of what kind of knowledge faith is. In traditional theology it was accepted that the act of faith was a supernatural act that took place under the impetus of grace so that the assent of faith was not simply the result of affirming a conclusion made evident by human reason. But the implications of this for doing theology were rarely brought out. Again, it was as if it were simply enough to say this, and then act as if theology was a matter of the rational elaboration of the propositions accepted by faith. What was overlooked was that the light of faith that was seen to be operative in the initial act of faith had to remain operative throughout the entire process of doing theology. In short, as theologians theoretically asserted, the light of faith allowed us to make contact with the Christian mysteries, themselves, and elevates the disciplines of reason so that they could be employed by this light of faith to explore these mysteries. This was not a common topic of meditation in an era when theology wanted to show how rational and reasonable it was.

Rahner's concrete knowledge of the individual, or Maritain's first act of freedom, are particular instances of what could be called the kinds of knowing that operate by faith which embrace on the personal level the act of faith, itself, the doing of theology, and Christian mystical experience, and on the ecclesial level, biblical inspiration, canonicity and doctrinal development and the exercise of the magisterium. None of these forms of knowing can be truly or adequately understood as purely rational forms of knowing, and therefore, equivalent in their own way to the human disciplines of history or philosophy or psychology. These kinds of knowing by faith do not operate solely in a rational mode, but by a mysterious connaturality which involves the heart as well as the mind. It would take us too far afield to examine this issue. I have done that elsewhere in *The Inner Nature of Faith*. But we have to note that these kinds of supernatural knowing find natural analogues in the arts and poetry, and have interesting affinities with the kind of connatural knowing found in Eastern forms of meditation.

The old neo-scholasticism was cast in a narrow, rational mold. The propositions accepted by faith were accepted much like the postulates of geometry, and the real work of theology was seen in their logical development. Modern Catholic theology has broadened the base upon which it does theological work, but we can certainly wonder if it has truly broken with the old rationalistic forms. Does it not now appear to practice theology after the models and patterns of the human sciences that it is employing?

The exercise of human reason, as vital as it is in theological activity, is not ultimately adequate to explain faith and our reflections on our faith. Faith allows us to come into a living contact with the Christian mysteries which, after all is said and done, are persons, and love is essential for this. This contact is not broken so that we can begin the properly rational work of theological collaboration, but rather, it guides the process of theological reflection, itself. Even on a purely natural plane we cannot imagine the creative process taking place in an orderly consciousness where clear ideas are laid out in rows, and

CHRISTIANITY IN THE CRUCIBLE

their manipulation takes place by the rules of formal logic. Creativity emerges out of the depths of the soul, and ideas are born out of the rich fertile matrix of the unconscious. In an analogous way in theology, it must remain in intimate contact with the Christian mysteries, and it is faith animated by love that allows us to do so. There is, in this sense, a theological instinct that guides and inspires the theologian, not in the sense of supplying in some miraculous way for the necessary process of reflection, or for the effort that we need to master the human disciplines employed, but by directing theological activities to this or that aspect of the mystery we are considering, and helping us find a way to penetrate within that mystery.

Two Kinds of Mysticism

There are two kinds, or fundamental categories, of mystical experience. One is a relational mysticism of love, and the other, a nondual mysticism, or mysticism of the Self. Both are to be found in different ways and in different proportions in Hinduism, Buddhism, Islam and Christianity. In Christianity the mysticism of love predominates, but the mysticism of the Self is not unknown, as Meister Eckhart witnesses. In Sufism a case can be made that both currents strongly exist there. In Hinduism we are faced with different varieties of the mysticism of the Self like those found in the Uphanishads and the Yoga Sutras, but there is also a devotional mysticism of bhakti expressed by someone like Ramanuja. In Buddhism we are confronted not so much with a mysticism of the Self, but what could be called a mysticism of the No-Self, but still within the broader family of nondual mysticism. But here, too, there are also strong devotional currents.

Given this testimony of the world's religions we can wonder if there is not something in our very natures that leads us to express ourselves in these two ways. We might try to characterize these two forms of mysticism by saying that in the one love predominates, while in the other, wisdom. But this immediately calls for clarification. Christian love mysticism, for example, has a strong element of wisdom, while nondual mysticisms can have a strong element of love. We could call the one personal, and the other impersonal. But however we try to categorize them, they form a useful way in which to focus on the drama that we have seen played out in the previous chapters.

What, for example, is the source of the fascination that Catholics deeply involved in Eastern religions like the Catholic Sanbo Kyodan Zen teachers, or Abhishiktananda, have for nondual mystical experience? At first glance we might think that they would be attracted to the devotional side of Hindu and Buddhist mysticism. But this appears not to be the case. It is almost as if nondual mysticism, because it is mostly lacking in the Christian tradition, attracts them in order to supply that lack. Further, it is entirely possible that in their minds Christian love mysticism is looked upon as a mostly conceptual path, and therefore lacking the depth they find in nondual Hinduism or Buddhism. This would fit the historical situation from which they emerged, which was dominated by an over-conceptual theology and philosophy, and a loss of the Christian mystical and metaphysical traditions, as we saw.

Louis Gardet

Let's look at these two fundamental forms of mysticism more concretely. Louis Gardet, for example, in *L'experience de soi* contrasts what he calls two great lines of Islamic mysticism, the one a mysticism of love, and the other a mysticism of the Self. The first expresses itself under the heading of *tajalli*, or the irradiation of the divine in the heart of the faithful. It is a *wahdat-al-shuhud*, a "unity of the testimonial presence."[4] This is not a unity of substance, "but of the intentional order by an act of will, an act of love." This unity of love is found in Hasan Basri and Rabi'a al-'Adawiyya, and culminates in Hallaj.

But another later current appears under the heading of *wahdat al-wujud*, a unity of being, or more precisely, a unity of the act of existence. This is a union of substance in which the human subject disappears and, as Gardet remarks, such a *fana*, or disappearance, of the human subject, is how a mysticism of the Self would appear in a monotheistic climate.[5] It is this kind of mysticism that has become predominate among the Sufi schools and which seems to have originated with Abu Yazid al-Bistami, and with whom it took a form that was close to the Hindu Vedanta, a point we will return to in a moment: "Then I considered my essence. I was, me, He."[6]

Gardet feels that Hallaj had a sense of the difference between these two kinds of mysticism which was, to Gardet's mind, a rare occurrence, for those who are inclined to the mysticism of the Self see love mysticism as a preliminary stage of it, while those who are devoted to a love mysticism, even though they might experience touches of the mysticism of the Self, allow it to be lost in that love experience. If Hallaj recognized these two currents, Ibn 'Arabi was to reproach him for a certain duality in his mysticism, and Ibn 'Arabi, himself, pursued a mysticism of the Self most of all.[7]

R.C. Zaehner

R.C. Zaehner comes to similar conclusions about these two forms of mysticism in his *Hindu and Muslim Mysticism*, and does so following his own distinctive path. He will distinguish four kinds of mystical experience, that of the Upanishads, the Yogic, the Buddhist, and bhakti. But for our purposes we can see the first three as forms of the mysticism of the Self. He demonstrates in considerable detail that both these fundamental forms of mysticism exist in both Hindu mysticism and Sufism. In the Upanishads, for example, we find the strong nondual assertions: I am Brahman. I am That, which are to be taken up by Sankara in his advaita, or nondualism.[8] But we also begin to see certain theistic comments in the Upanishads that begin to develop into a love mysticism in the Bhagavad-gita. This beginning of bhakti will be taken up and developed by Ramanuja who, like Hallaj, will distinguish it from nondual mysticism and make it clear that the soul's realization of itself prepares it to enter into a personal relationship with God.[9] Hinduism, therefore, moves from a world where the mysticism of the Self predominates to one in which a love mysticism begins to emerge. And Zaehner traces an opposite course for Muslim mysticism which he characterizes as originally theistic but developing in the direction of nonduality. He puts forth a detailed argument in favor of Abu Yazid al-Bistami, having been influenced by the Vedanta through his teacher Abu Ali al-Sindi who Zaehner takes to be an Indian convert to Islam.[10]

So Zaehner outlines a position roughly equivalent to Gardet. For Hindu mysticism, for example, the eternity of the soul is a given, and its whole thrust is to liberate this soul from space and time. But in the actual experience of this liberation, the immortality of the soul comes to be equated with the immortality of the immortal Being, and its being is identified with that Being.[11] And Zaehner goes on to quote Martin Buber's *Between Man and Man* who, himself, experienced this undivided unity which seemed like a unity with the Godhead, but who later reflected and felt that it was the attainment of a "original pre-biographical unity," "an undifferentiable unity of myself without form or content,"[12] but in final analysis, still an individual soul and not the soul of the All.[13]

Jan van Ruusbroec

Jan van Ruusbroec (1293-1381) was an important Flemish Christian mystic, and it would make an interesting comparison to look at his writings and those of Meister Eckhart, and perhaps find in them concrete examples of the two fundamental forms of mysticism that we have been talking about. Eckhart's name pops up over and over again when it is a question of Buddhists or Christians deeply involved in Buddhist practice looking for parallels to Buddhism within Christianity. The fundamental reason for this is that there are strong elements of the mysticism of the Self in Meister Eckhart. Ruusbroec, on the other hand, represents what could be called the mainstream of Catholic mysticism, that is, a relational love mysticism. But our comparison can be even more pointed because Ruusbroec was familiar with the contemplative movements of his day, including those influenced by Marguerite Porete and Meister Eckhart and his disciples. And he was a severe critic of the natural contemplation, or mysticism of the Self that he felt they both embodied.

It is difficult, however, to uncover the essential nucleus of Ruusbroec's thought, for it is wrapped in the common intolerance of his times towards heretics and non-Christians. Two points, however, can be made, drawing on the study of Ruusbroec's natural mysticism by Paul Mommaers in the book he wrote with Jean van Bragt, *Mysticism Buddhist and Christian: Encounters with Jan van Ruusbroec*. On the one hand, Ruusbroec shows penetrating metaphysical insight into the nature of this natural mysticism, and yet on the other, he severely criticizes it as being incomplete, and therefore a danger to the Christian mystical life of love. Put in another way, this natural mysticism is good because it is a good of nature, but in itself it has limits, or as Ruusbroec says: "However high the eagle soars, it cannot fly above itself."[14] But the real problem he sees in it is that it can close off its practitioners from the currents of love and grace that are meant to carry them to God.

He describes this natural contemplation as a "sitting-still (*een stille sitten*) without any practice within or without in emptiness (*ledicheit*) ..."[15] And it leads to an experience of the soul's essence "as to its origin and its natural rest."[16] The essence of the soul is experienced as suspended in God. "It is immobile and is higher than the supreme heaven and deeper than the bottom of the sea and wider than the whole world... and it is a natural reign of God and the end of all the soul's activity."[17] In this way people given to this natural contemplation can have a genuine experience of God, and of creatures in God. "They feel nothing save the simplicity of their essence, hanging in the essence of God."[18]

Ruusbroec's characterization of this natural contemplation remarkably foreshadows the theory of natural mysticism, or mysticism of the Self that Jacques Maritain was to develop in the 20th century and which will capture our attention in a little while. But Ruusbroec vehemently criticizes it, not so much in itself, but as a practice for those whom he feels are called to a Christian mysticism of love. This natural contemplation leads, he believes, to an excessive sense of self-sufficiency, and a certain blindness on the part of the contemplative to the Christian contemplative path, and finally to incorrect formulations of the relationship between human nature and the divine. It is as if they are caught up in this natural mysticism and it blinds them to its limits and even makes them feel excused from the Christian devotional path. Ruusbroec feels that they have experienced their own essence and mistake that experience for God.[19] Perhaps a more nuanced way of looking at it would be to say they have experienced God in their own essence, and yet they have done it through emptiness, and there is no way to distinguish in that emptiness between God and the soul. Any statements that stem from this experience but are uttered in an ontological mode then appear erroneous because they identify the substance of the soul with the substance of God.

We are now ready to explore the possibility of a dialogue not between Christian mysticism and enlightenment, but Christian metaphysics and enlightenment.

What conclusion should we come to from the fact of these two quite different kinds of mysticism? First of all, it misses the point to try to extract some sort of common essence or use some sort of many paths, one summit, kind of approach. There is an underlying "pluralism" built into religions East and West that can't be eliminated. They naturally tend to roughly sort themselves according to a metaphysical, or cosmic, or impersonal mysticism of the self, or nonduality, or whatever terminology you might like to use, on the one hand, and a love, or interpersonal, or relational, or theistic mysticism on the other. But this kind of sorting takes place within each of them, as well. How many pure advaitans in the way the West imagines advaita are there actually in India compared to theistic Hindus?

To apply our distinction between the essential and the existential once again, it is an essentialistic analysis that distinguishes a metaphysical mysticism from a relational one. But from an existential point of view, it is hard to see how they can exist without each other. From a Christian perspective the very pursuit of enlightenment can be seen as a "sacrament" of the working of grace. If someone is leaving everything, even the most personal of interior goods, to try to reach the All, how could Christians imagine that this could not be a response to grace, and thus the very interior practices involved a means of reaching a deeper union with God? This is not, of course, to say that this nondual mysticism in itself in its structure and goal is a relational love mysticism. But God calls all people to divine union, and this calling can inspire these kinds of heroic quests which can be means of grace without minimizing or relativizing the differences between the two paths. What I want to do next is explore the contours of a metaphysical dialogue between East and West.

Notes

1. Guarino, Thomas. "Postmodernity and Five Fundamental Theological Issues," p. 660.
2. Rahner, Karl. *Karl Rahner in Dialogue*, p. 195.
3. Ibid., p. 196.
4. Gardet, Louis. *L'experience de soi.* p. 214.

5. Ibid., p. 216.   6. Ibid., p. 218.   7. Ibid., p. 223.
8. Zaenher, R.C. *Hindu and Muslim Mysticism.* p. 8.
9. Ibid, p. 15.   11. Ibid., p. 17.   13. Ibid.
10. Ibid., pp. 93ff.   12. Ibid., p. 18.
14. Mommaers, Paul. *Mysticism Buddhist and Christian: Encounters with Jan van Ruusbroec.* p. 219.
15. Ibid., p. 220.   17. Ibid., p. 225.   19. Ibid., p. 262.
16. Ibid., p. 224.   18. Ibid., p. 230.

PART III

A METAPHYSICAL DIALOGUE

CHAPTER 6

ISLAMIC METAPHYSICS

In *Parts I* and *II* we tried to see how our questions about the relationship between enlightenment and contemplation, and metaphysics emerged in the concrete in the midst of the East-West dialogue. We saw that they were at once pervasive and obscure, and pose serious challenges for Christianity.

Now we need to explore the nature of enlightenment, not as it expresses itself in the East – there is an enormous literature about that – but from a Christian philosophical perspective. What kind of dialogue can Christians have with Eastern religions if they have no idea what enlightenment is? This kind of exploration is quite different in perspective from that of Christians who have gone to the East, seriously practiced different forms of meditation, and then look at Christianity with Eastern eyes. Rather, what we want to do is to ask whether Christian metaphysics has anything to say about Eastern enlightenment.

Paradoxically we will begin our inquiry outside the borders of Christianity in order to avoid some of the baggage that accompanies the very idea of metaphysics, even metaphysics in a Christian context.

We have had the occasion to cross the trail briefly of the metaphysics of St. Thomas which I feel could play a major role between Christianity and Buddhism and Hinduism. Yet I am keenly aware at how far-fetched such a program might appear in the East. Nor do I think that the Catholic participants in either the Zen-Christian dialogue or the Hindu-Christian dialogue have, for the most part, a special place in their hearts for such an approach. Zen certainly and even advaitan Hinduism in its own way with their emphasis on transcending discursive thought makes such an approach seem quite unlikely. What we need is a bridge between East and West.

Hadi ibn Mahdi Sabzawari

To build such a bridge we will first go as far away as we can from the world of Thomism, and travel to the town of Sabsavar in Khurasan in Persia in the 19th century. There on a little farm, dressed in a ragged robe, and living simply and sharing the farm's fruits with the poor and his students, we find Haji Mulla Hadi ibn Mahdi Sabzawari (1797/8-1878), one of the greatest metaphysicians of his age who helped bring about a revival of interest in one of the most profound thinkers in the world of Islamic philosophy, Sadr al-Din Shirazi (1571/2-1640), known as Mulla Sadra.

Each day Sabzawari would go off and teach at the local madrasa, or religious school. His *Ghurar al-fara'id*, which was also called *Sharh-i manzumah* or *Commentary on a Philosophical Poem*, was to become one of the most popular metaphysical textbooks in Iran even in modern times.

Until fairly recently Western philosophy's awareness of Islamic metaphysics stopped at the Middle Ages with Avicenna and Averroes who had played an important role in Christian scholasticism. But this lack of Western awareness certainly didn't stop Islamic philosophy from continuing to develop, especially in Iran, in an unbroken tradition stretching down to our own days. Like any scholasticism, Eastern or Western, that has endured over the centuries, it will take a certain effort on our part to penetrate beyond its formulas and set expressions and discover its metaphysical heart.

Toshihiko Izutsu

Ironically, one of the best ways to gain some idea about the insights of the metaphysics of Mulla Sadra as expounded by his great commentator Sabzawari is to go even further afield to Japan where a child has been forced by his father to do zazen, and rebelling against this experience, decides to study linguistics. By the time he was eighteen Toshihiko Izutsu was teaching Russian at the university level and he went on to learn Arabic, Persian, Turkish, as well as other European and Indian languages, and became an Islamic scholar both at McGill University in Canada and in Teheran where he lectured on Ibn 'Arabi. His linguistic skills were to come together with his keen philosophical intellect to make him one of the great modern students of comparative Eastern religions. In his later years he gave himself over to the task of trying to bring into focus a metahistorical, or metaphilosophical view of the common metaphysical core that could be found in Buddhism, Hinduism, Taoism, as well as Islam, and he did this by putting his appreciation of language at the service of philosophy. Together with Mehdi Mohaghegh he translated Sabzawari's *Sharh-i manzumah* from Arabic into English, and he wrote a special introduction to it, printed separately, called *The Concept and Reality of Existence*, which is one of the most profound studies of the Islamic metaphysics of Mulla Sadra of whom Sabzawari was one of the leading 19th century exponents.

Historical Background

The metaphysics of Mulla Sadra and Sabzawari is rooted in Aristotle and Plato on the one hand, and Islam on the other. The philosophy of the Greeks, probably with some help with early Middle Eastern Christian thinkers, was taken into the Islamic world. There the theme of the relationship between essence and existence, which had remained implicit in Aristotle, began to receive a clearer formulation. Seyyed Hossein Nasr, one of the leading figures in the revival of traditional Iranian philosophy and its transmission to the West, puts it like this: "There is no issue more central to Islamic philosophy and especially metaphysics than *wujud* (at once Being and existence) in itself and in its relation to *mahiyyah* (quiddity or essence)... To understand the meaning of these basic concepts, their distinction and relationship, is, therefore, to grasp the very basis of Islamic philosophical thought."[1]

The development of this doctrine can be traced in the Islamic world first to al-Kindi and al-Farabi. Al-Farabi, for example, is thought to be one of the first of the Islamic philosophers to try to reconcile the Greek idea of a necessarily existing universe and the biblical idea of creation. He states in his *Gem of Wisdom* that essence and existence are distinct in existing things. Existence is not part of the constitutive character of a thing, that is, something that makes it what it is, but an accessory accident. Etienne Gilson, the great Christian historian of philosophy, comments, "This important text marked the moment when the logical distinction introduced by Aristotle between the conception of essence and the affirmation of existence became the sign of their metaphysical distinction."[2]

Al-Farabi's thought was taken up by Avicenna who was the last great common figure in the development of both Western and Eastern philosophy. During the course of the 20th century there has been considerable discussion among scholars about just what Avicenna meant by his doctrine on the relationship between essence and existence and how well he was understood both in the West and the East. According to some modern Islamic interpreters of Avicenna, for example, Thomas Aquinas, reading Avicenna through Averroes, misunderstood Avicenna's idea that existence was an accident of essence by understanding accident as the kind of accident that inheres in a substance. On the other hand, one of the modern commentators of Mulla Sadra, Fazlur Rahman, felt that Mulla Sadra, himself, misunderstood what Avicenna was saying. In any event, Avicenna was to play a pivotal role in posing the problem of the relationship between essence and existence.[3] Later, Suhrawardi, the great illuminationist philosopher gave primacy to essence, at least on the surface of his thought, but his doctrine of light was to become an important element in Mulla Sadra's thought.

Mulla Sadra

Muhammad ibn Ibrahim ibn Yahya Qawami Shirazi had been born in Shiraz in 979-980/1571-72 and had gone on to study in Isfahan with some of the great masters of his day. His life can be divided into three parts: first, his education in Shiraz and Isfahan, then a long period of withdrawal from the world in which he went to live in the little village of Kahak near the holy city of Qum, and devoted himself to spiritual practices, and finally, a return to a public life of teaching and writing in Shiraz.[4] He was a prolific writer with his and pride of place is given to his massive *al-Hikmat al-muta'aliyah fi'l-asfar al-'aqliyyat al-arba'ah* (*The Transcendent Theosophy concerning the Four Intellectual Journeys of the Soul*), commonly known as *Asfar*, or *Journeys*. He died in 1050/1640 at Basra, returning from his seventh pilgrimage to Mecca. Mulla Sadra created a new way of doing philosophy which combined the study of the Koran with what we understand in the West as philosophy, together with a deep intuitive perception of reality that transcended concepts.[5]

Our particular task here is to look at the possibility of a dialogue between this Islamic scholasticism and that of Thomas Aquinas, and in doing this to focus on two essential points: the relationship between essence and existence that stands at the heart of each tradition, and the intuition that each sees giving birth to this fundamental insight.

Izutsu, who had some knowledge of western scholasticism, rightly insisted that it was no longer acceptable to limit and terminate the study of Islamic philosophy to the role it played in medieval western philosophy, but rather it is necessary to realize that it continued not only to exist but to flourish into the 20th century. "A comparative study," he writes in his masterful study on Islamic metaphysics *The Concept and Reality of Existence*, "of these two different forms of scholasticism, Eastern and Western, would surely yield a number of important results which might even go beyond the horizon of comparative philosophy to affect the very *Problematik* of the significance of philosophical thinking in general."[6]

Now it is a striking fact that while in the history of western scholasticism Thomas Aquinas is credited with recognizing the primacy of the act of existing, Mulla Sadra played a similarly revolutionary role in Islamic metaphysics. This remarkable convergence did not go unnoticed by Izutsu and others, but it is worth pausing for a moment and reflecting on its significance. Both eastern and western scholasticism, working independently from the Middle Ages, have in the persons of Thomas Aquinas and Mulla Sadra and their schools distilled a partially common tradition rooted in Greek, and Islamic philosophy viewed in the context of biblical monotheism, and arrived at very similar insights into the primacy of the act of existing, and in the way this insight is achieved. It is as if two metaphysical experiments, which had run for centuries independently of each other, had turned up with almost identical conclusions.

But remarkably similar or convergent results do not mean complete identity, and we need to look more closely at how this primacy of existence expressed itself in each tradition.[7] In the East there arose two principal schools. One of them championed the principality of existence while the other the principality of essence. And in Mulla Sadra we have the first fully conscious and reflective articulation of the primacy of existence in the Islamic metaphysical tradition. And now we have arrived at our first question: how does his concept of existence relate to that of Thomas Aquinas?

The starting point for metaphysical activity is much the same. Here is how Izutsu sums it up: "It pertains to the most elementary and fundamental structure of our daily experience that we constantly encounter in our lives an infinity of things. We find ourselves surrounded by them and we cannot escape from the consciousness of the presence of various and variegated things. The actual presence of things is their "existence". They are there. They do exist, as we ourselves exist. On the other hand, they are not there in the form of pure "existences." They "exist" as various and variegated things: man, horse, stone, tree, table, etc. This latter aspect of their "existence" is called "quiddity."[8]

Jacques Maritain, one of the finest 20th century Thomist metaphysicians, will say virtually the same thing, and he insists that it takes more than a general sense of existence to become a metaphysician. Otherwise everybody would be one. Somehow we must see into the mystery that everyday things present to us as Izutsu has already begun to do in the passage we have just seen. How can things be truly different through and through, be a stone, for example, or a horse, and yet both be said to exist? We need a metaphysical insight, which Maritain called the intuition of being, and Izutsu asserts much the same thing: "For, in the view held by Mulla Sadra and Sabzawari, "quiddity" and "existence" do not stand on the same ontological level. Their view is based on a profound and extraordinary experiential intuition of "existence" which is of a Sufi origin."[9]

So here we have arrived at our second question about this insight into existence which is inextricably joined to what is seen in the doctrine of the primacy of existence. Izutsu also calls this insight a "personal mystical intuition,"[10] a certain "mystical or gnostic experience," or "superconsciousness,"[11] "a sudden illumative realization,"[12] and "a super-sensible intuition."[13]

These expressions also find their parallels in Maritain's writings, and so we are faced with a remarkable convergence of these two metaphysical traditions which both insist on the primacy of the act of existing and a metaphysical intuition in order to achieve it.

But let's probe the matter a little further and look at the content of this intuition, or the precise relationship between essence and existence. For Izutsu, quiddity is "that which is given in answer to the question: what is it?"[14] while existence is precisely that which neither has a quiddity nor is a quiddity.[15] And while conceptually "each concretely existing thing can be divided into "existence" and "quiddity," in reality they are both "completely unified with one another, there being no real distinction between them."[16] The world of reality "is diversified into an infinity of particular "existences" (*wujudat*), i.e., particular acts of existence."[17] For the principality of existence school, the world is not made up of existent quiddities, "it is rather the reality of "existence" which is determined and delimited quiddity-wise in the form of particular "existences" (*wujudat*) from which the abstract concept of existence is extracted."[18] In reality, existence precedes essence and they are not on the same ontological level, and it is a "profound and extraordinary experiential intuition of "existence" that allows us to realize this."[19] Through this perception we realize "all "quiddities" are found to be deprived of their seeming self-subsistence and turn out to be nothing other than so many partial determinations and delimitations of the unitary reality of "existence.""[20]

This whole analysis of the relationship between essence and existence could be reproduced almost word for word from the perspective and sources of Western scholasticism, and the last passage is particularly significant, for it expresses a radically existential point of view that in the West reached its high point in William Carlo's *The Ultimate Reducibility of Essence to Existence in Existential Metaphysics*. This work which has been rather completely ignored in the West is precisely what Izutsu goes on to cite to illustrate the kind of existential point of view he is taking, and he does so in the form of a quotation from the Jesuit metaphysician Norris Clarke's preface to Carlo's book.[21]

Quiddities that appear as independent existing things to us and strike us most forcefully because of their differences are, in reality, according to Izutsu, "modalities of existence," "intrinsic limitations or determinations of "existence"," "they are merely interior modifications of the all-pervading "existence."[22]

Izutsu insists on this point because it is central to his understanding of Mulla Sadra's metaphysics. "The reality of "existence" in its absoluteness is unlimited and undetermined. In itself it cannot be anything particular; it is in this sense "nothing," quiddity-wise."[23] Instead of understanding quiddities as extrinsic determinations of existence we must understand them, Izutsu tells us, as intrinsic determinations. And once again, Izutsu turns to William Carlo to explain what this idea of intrinsic modification means. This is what Izutsu feels that Mulla Sadra saw when he had his deep metaphysical insight. He quotes Mulla Sadra to the effect "all of a sudden my spiritual eyes were opened and I saw with the utmost clarity that the truth was just the contrary of what philosophers in general had held... As a result (I now hold that) the "existences" (*wujudat*) are primary "realities", while the "quiddities" are the "permanent archetypes" (*a'yan thabitah*) that have never smelt the fragrance of "existence." The "existences" are nothing but beams of light radiated by the true Light which is absolutely self-subsisting Existence except that each of them is characterized by a number of essential properties and intelligible qualities."[24]

What Izutsu has done without directly intending it is to set the stage for a dialogue between Islamic and Thomistic scholasticism, or more precisely, between Mulla Sadra and Thomas Aquinas and their schools. Izutsu, himself, had no desire to enter into the internal debates of Thomism. When it comes to a question of whether Carlo was giving an adequate reading of St. Thomas, he says rather pointedly that he is "not interested to discuss" it.[25] Izutsu, writing in 1969, may have been aware that there had been some negative comments about Carlo's book, which had appeared shortly before, and perhaps thought it best to side-step anything that might embroil him in needless controversy and was not directly relevant to the point he was making, which was that Carlo's interpretation of St. Thomas is the same as Mulla Sadra's central metaphysical insight.[26]

But let's return to our properly metaphysical inquiry. Particular existences are reflections of Absolute Light or Existence. Thus, they cannot be looked at as "independent and self-subsistent entities without any relation to their source..."[27] Thus, these existences are real, but not independent. Their reality comes from their relationship to the metaphysical sun, which is their source. This leads to a grasp of the analogical gradation of existence, for the one reality of existence exhibits "varying grades and stages in terms of intensity and weakness..."[28] The question of whether the relationship of the source and the particular existents is the same in both Mulla Sadra and Thomas Aquinas thus begins to emerge. Izutsu will ask, "Is there no essential difference between the Absolute, i.e., the necessary Existent and the possible "existents"?"[29] In the highest stage of existence in a state of pure and absolute transcendence, the Absolute is pure existence. In the next stage existence is a state of free indetermination. It is in potentia in relation to all possible existents, and at the lowest stage existence manifests itself as concrete individual existents.

Fazlur Rahman

Let's review some of the central points in the metaphysics of Mulla Sadra by looking at the reflections of Fazlur Rahman on Mulla Sadra's *Asfar* in his *Philosophy of Mulla Sadra*. For Mulla Sadra "Nothing is real except existence."[30] Essences do not exist in reality. Only existence does. The mind looks at things and abstracts essences. Through its normal conceptual working it knows essences, but not existence because existence is not a concept, and if it wants to know existence it needs a special intuition.

God is absolute existence, and for Mulla Sadra, the Platonic ideas are not separate or external to his essence. God is pure existence and manifests Himself in contingent beings, which are modes of existence (*anha al-wujud*). Creatures are, in fact, only modes of existence, but the mind in its normal conceptual working discovers essences in them. Essences only exist in the mind, and they exist there because of the attenuation of existence. God as pure existence has no essence, and essences are nothing in themselves. "Essences, therefore, constitute negation of and are dysfunctional to existence. Existence is positive, definite, determinate and real; essences are vague, dark, indeterminate, negative and unreal."[31]

For Mulla Sadra there is no real distinction in things between essence and existence. There is only existence in all its modes, and it is in these modes that the mind finds essences. "Far from essence being something positive which *acquires* existence, essence *per se* is nothing positive at all. Indeed, in external reality, essence is simply not there. What is there is a mode of existence. When this mode of existence is presented to the mind, it is the mind that abstracts an essence from it, while existence escapes it, unless it develops a proper intuition for it."[32] Existence is the sole reality, and it cannot be conceived, but only intuited directly.

Even when Mulla Sadra quotes Avicenna who believed there was a real composite of essence and existence in things, he understands him to say that the distinction exists only in the mind and not in things. For Sadra existence exists in various modes which are more or less perfect, and he goes on to develop a view of existence as *tashkik* by which he brings out its ambiguous or analogical nature. All things exist, so in a certain sense they are one. But existence, itself, creates fundamental differences among things, and so in another sense they are many.

Mulla Sadra had started out as an essentialist before he had his realization of the sole reality of existence, and he was also an existential monist, that is, inclined to the view that only God existed, but he changed his understanding of this, as well. Fazlur Rahman still finds a tension in this thought between his insistence that God, alone, is, and his assertion that contingent beings also exist. Sadra will say, "In the Abode of Existence, there is no other inhabitants save God."[33] But he will also say, following his principle of *tashkik*, "that it is impossible that God's being, itself, should form the existence of contingents."[34]

In short, Mulla Sadra experienced a powerful intuition in which he saw that existence alone was reality, and God was pure existence without essence. Creatures, in contrast, were manifestations of Existence. They were modes of existence, and in them there was nothing but existence, but the mind abstracted essences from them.

So far it would be difficult to find beyond certain hints anything in Izutsu's and Rahman's profound expositions of Islamic metaphysics that differ fundamentally from what can be found in the metaphysics of Aquinas. But our inquiry is not at an end. We need to look into the question of the relationship between pure existence and the concrete existents more fully, and we can do this by examining another of Izutsu's essays which he called "The Basic Structure of Metaphysical

Thinking in Islam."

Creator and Creation

As I have said before, many of the key notions of the metaphysics of Mulla Sadra finds strong parallels in that of St. Thomas, and while I am not claiming that the two are identical, in each existence plays the primary role and essence is in one manner or another reduced to it. In the case of Mulla Sadra, essences do not exist in things. There are only modes of existence, and in St. Thomas, especially in his more radical commentators like Carlo, essence is nothing existing in itself. It is a refraction or a contraction of existence.

But the question that faces us now is whether it is the same insight or intuition that produces this profound sense of the primacy of existence in both traditions. In the highest kind of knowledge, which is the knowledge of existence, Izutsu tells us that the human subject is completely identified with its object. The identity of the knower and the known in the act of knowledge, itself, by way of an intentional existence, or presence, is a well-known Thomistic principle. But is this what Izutsu is saying? It doesn't appear that it is, for he goes on to state that while ordinary knowledge works through concepts and objectifies things, and even turns existence into a concept, this intuition works "from the inside, by man's *becoming* or rather *being*, "existence" in itself, that is, by man's self-realization."[35] We have returned by a very different route to the question of nonduality.

By intuition, or illumination, or tasting, we can come to this sort of knowledge, but only if we transcend our egos. "For the subsistence of the individual ego places of necessity an epistemological distance between man and the reality of "existence" be it his own "existence." The reality of existence is immediately grasped only when the empirical selfhood is annihilated, when the ego-consciousness is completely dissolved into the consciousness of reality, or rather, consciousness which *is* Reality."[36]

This is where the Islamic idea of *fana*, or annihilation, enters, and we begin to depart from a Thomist view of the intuition of being. Indeed, fana can reach such a pitch that there is an annihilation of annihilation in which there is "the total disappearance of the consciousness of man's own disappearance."[37] For Izutsu this kind of annihilation finds its exact counterpart in the shunyata, or emptiness, of Buddhism. It is an annihilation which is not only a subjective state, but "the realization or actualization of absolute Reality in its absoluteness."[38]

In our ordinary consciousness we first look at the things around us as self-subsistent entities; we see the waves and do not pay attention to the sea from which they come. When we gain some intuitive insight, we become enamored with the oneness of things and tend to believe that the contingent things around us don't really exist; we see the ocean, but consider the waves illusory. But when our insight deepens and we can exercise both reason and intuition, we see both the waves and the ocean. "The one selfsame "existence" is seen at once to be God and the creature, or absolute Reality and the phenomenal world, unity and multiplicity."[39] We have reached "a fundamental intuition of the single reality of "existence" in everything without exception."[40] This is what is called the oneness of existence, or *wahdat al-wujud*.

In the West with St. Thomas the intuition of being is expressed in a philosophical way. However much it was born and nourished in the context of Christian mysticism and theology, it was distinguished from them. But in Mulla Sadra something different is going on. A remarkable existential metaphysics emerges, but this time under the powerful sun of nondual experience, and this is why his doctrine of creation is pulled in two directions.

The real issue centers on the question of nonduality, expressed in this case in the relationship between the Absolute and the contingent, or the Creator and the created. Many of the formulations that Izutsu has presented to us as basic to Islamic thought are acceptable from a Christian metaphysical point of view. The Absolute, for example, can be said to be that which alone exists in the full sense of the term, but when Izutsu writes, "that the Absolute, insofar as it is the Absolute, cannot really dispense with the phenomenal world,"[41] we have entered into a territory that is strange to Christianity and of questionable compatibility to it. He goes on to say, "in the realm of the extra-mental reality, the Absolute cannot even for a single moment remain without manifesting itself."[42] A little later he amplifies this thought: "Both in Vedanta and Islam, the Absolute at this supreme stage is not even God, for after all "God" is but a determination of the Absolute, insofar at least as it differentiates the Absolute from the world of creation."[43] The absolute principle that he is putting forward is a metaphysical vision of unity in multiplicity and multiplicity in unity that is neither monism nor dualism, and thus we could say is a non-dualism which he feels is shared "by many of the major philosophical schools of the East."[44] It is our task next to look more closely at this common nonduality.

The kind of Islamic metaphysics that culminates in Mulla Sadra and Sabzawari still attracts considerable interest in Iran,[45] and beyond, for example, in Syed Muhammad Naquib al-Attas' *Prolegomena to the Metaphysics of Islam*. Unfortunately, Christian philosophers for the most part have not made contact with that tradition, with some exceptions like David Burrell,[46] or Jason Escalante.[47]

Notes

1. Nasr, Seyyed Hossein. "Experience (*wujud*) and Quiddity (*mahiyyah*) in Islamic Philosophy." IPQ p. 409.
2. Gilson, Etienne. *History of Christian Philosophy in the Middle Ages*, p. 186
3. It would take us too far afield to explore the difficult historical question of how well Avicenna was understood in both East and West. It may very well be that Thomas Aquinas, following Averroes, did misunderstand Avicenna when Avicenna said that existence was an accident of essence, but this does not resolve the deeper issues involved. If Aquinas misunderstood Avicenna, then that only highlights Aquinas' originality in asserting the primacy of existence over essence. It is also interesting to note that Etienne Gilson, who played an important role in the rediscovery of the primacy of existence in Thomism, first believed that the distinction that St. Thomas made between essence and existence had already been found in Avicenna, not to mention other philosophers both East and West. (See John Noonan's article, "The Existentialism of Etienne Gilson," p. 418) Then as Gilson's understanding of St. Thomas' doctrine of existence grew deeper, his historical opinions changed. By 1931 he was on his way to seeing that the position of St. Thomas was quite different from that of Avicenna. (Ibid., p. 419) And when we look at his master work,

Being and Some Philosophers, where he treats extensively of the metaphysics of Avicenna, we find that he clearly distinguishes it from that of St. Thomas.
4. Nasr, *Sadr al-Din Shirazi and his Transcendent Theosophy*, p. 38.
5. Nasr, *History of Islamic Philosophy*, Part I, p. 645.
6. Izutsu, *The Concept and Reality of Existence*, p.68.
7. For Izutsu the question of the relationship between essence and existence is implicit in Aristotle as illustrated by a passage in his *Posterior Analytics*. (Izutsu, *The Concept and Reality of Existence*, p.88.) In the Islamic tradition it was al-Farabi (d.947/950) who began to make the issue more explicit, and it was Avicenna (980-1037) in particular who set the stage for the metaphysical revolutions that were to come in both the East and West.
8. Izutsu, *The Concept and Reality of Existence*, p.86-87.
9. Ibid., p. 87.
10. Ibid., p. 59.
11. Ibid., p. 61.
12. Ibid., p. 65.
13. Ibid., p. 67.
14. Ibid., p. 77, note 35.
15. Ibid., p. 75.
16. Ibid., p. 78.
17. Ibid.
18. Ibid., p. 84.
19. Ibid., p. 87.
20. Ibid., p. 87.
21. For an examination of Carlo's metaphysical work, see my *The Mystery of Matter*.
22. Izutsu, *The Concept and Reality of Existence*. p. 102.
23. Ibid., p. 127-128.
24. Ibid., p. 104.
25. Ibid., p. 129.
26. Given Izutsu's rather extensive use of Carlo, it is worth taking a small detour and looking at some of his other comments on Western scholasticism. He felt, for example, that the Eastern philosophical schools had a historical continuity that had been ruptured in the West by the rise of modern philosophy, and thus possessed a "degree of refinement not found in Western scholasticism." This break in the West, he felt, caused someone like Maritain not to fully appreciate modern existentialism when Maritain takes it to task in his *Existence and the Existent* for phenomenalizing the concrete existent. Izutsu cites in passing, but with approval, Gilson on Aristotle, but feels that Gilson's remarks on Avicenna miss the mark, and it is interesting that while he cites Sartre's *La nausée* where Sartre talks of his experience of the existence of the tree roots, he makes use of this passage much like

Maritain uses the very same passage in his *Existence and the Existent*. It appears that Izutsu had rather good taste in his reading of modern Thomism, but it was not his intention to actually open the door of dialogue between it and Islamic metaphysics. It was enough for him to indicate the possibility of such.

27. Izutsu, *The Concept and Reality of Existence,* p. 138.
28. Ibid.
29. Ibid., p. 145.
30. Rahman, Fazlur. *Philosophy of Mulla Sadra.* p. 28.
31. Ibid., p. 30.   33. Ibid., p. 38.
32. Ibid., p. 32.   34. Ibid., p. 39.
35. Izutsu, "The Basic Structure of Metaphysical Thinking in Islam." p. 8.
36. Ibid., p. 11.   39. Ibid., p. 25.   42. Ibid., p. 31.
37. Ibid., p. 12.   40. Ibid., p. 26.   43. Ibid., p. 33.
38. Ibid., p. 13.   41. Ibid., p. 31.   44. Ibid., p. 34.
45. www.mullasadra.org
46. Burrell, David. "Thomas Aquinas (1225-274) and Mulla Sadra Shirazi (980/1572-1050/1640) and The Primacy of Esse/Wujud in Philosophical Theology."
47. Escalante, Jason. http://www.innerexplorations.com/philtext/islamic.htm

CHAPTER 7

A DIALOGUE WITH NONDUALITY?

We have just seen how a dialogue between Islamic and Christian metaphysics could be a very fruitful one, but such a metaphysical dialogue could be extended to embrace Buddhism and Hinduism, as well. Here the initial difficulties would be more daunting given the lack of a common history and vocabulary, but if these obstacles could be overcome, the different traditions would have much to say to each other.

There is, however, one methodological issue that would have to be dealt with at the onset, and that is the difference between a speculative metaphysics and a practical one, or one that wishes most of all to contemplate the mystery of being and express it in concepts, and the other, that wants to go on an interior spiritual quest to realize the ultimate ground of things beyond all words. These two different kinds of metaphysics use words in different ways towards different ends. And if we keep in mind this fundamental difference, Christians can read Eastern "metaphysical" texts with profit and delight A fitting symbol of the treasures that exist in the East can be seen in the Dalai Lama's description of the libraries of the Portola Palace: "Here were rooms full of thousands of priceless scrolls, some a thousand years old... In the libraries were all the records of Tibetan culture and religion, 7,000 enormous volumes, some of which were said to weigh 80 pounds. Some were written on palm leaves imported from India a thousand years ago.[1]

Ippolito Desideri

Let's take the example of Tibetan Buddhism which has a wonderful scholastic tradition of study and debate that has many parallels with Western medieval Christian scholasticism. These two great scholastic traditions have yet to really engage each other, but they could, and the life of Ippolito Desideri is a good symbol of that promise. Desideri was a Jesuit priest who spent years in Tibet in the early 18th century, but he was no mere traveler. He immersed himself in the Tibetan language, and even its philosophical vocabulary, and studied some of the major Tibetan religious treatises at a Gelugpa monastery in order to engage the lamas in debate on the relative merits of Christianity and their own religion. In this way he became perhaps the first European to study Gelugpa philosophy.[2] In the course of this debate he touched on many of the topics that were to be taken up in later Buddhist-Christian dialogues, like the existence of God and the transmigration of souls. He tells us that, above all, he strove to understand the doctrine of emptiness which, in his mind, did away with the existence of an uncreated and independent God.[3] After much personal effort and prayer, and consultation with the learned lamas, he finally felt he understood emptiness. It would certainly be interesting to see the results of modern studies in progress on Desideri's works, especially his *Essence of Christian Doctrine*, written in Tibetan, where we find "the first historical engagement of the Summa with the Great Stages, the interaction of scholastic method of Thomas Aquinas with the scholastic method of Tsong Kha pa. Desideri opposes Thomas' philosophy of being (esse) against Tsong Kha pa's philosophy of emptiness (S: sunyata, T: stong pa nyid)."[4]

Desideri summarizes the Tibetan view of emptiness in his *Essence* as one in which "there is not even one substance established as inherently existent. They understand that all existing substances are viewed as empty, the emptiness of inherent existence itself."[5] Elsewhere he writes: "Nothing exists because nothing has any essence by itself, and therefore, nothing exists which is not dependently originated or unconnected, unfettered, and without correlativity."[6] As I said, it would be interesting to examine Desideri's *Essence* further, and later we will take a look at this question of the existence of a self in more detail. But for the moment it is enough to look briefly at this issue.

Geshe Rabten

"All things instinctively appear to us as though they did exist independently, as though they were endowed with their own autonomous self-existence," writes the Tibetan monk Geshe Rabten in his *Echoes of Voidness*. One night, for example, a violent storm partially destroyed his hut near Dharamsala, and he repaired the roof by using a tree trunk as a pillar to support it. This pillar then became the object of his meditations. There was the tree trunk before him, but his reasoning led him to question its existence. That reasoning went like this: every phenomenon has the quality of a dependently arising event; it depends on a whole web of causes and conditions. The tree trunk, for example, depends on the living tree, which in turn depends on the sun and rain and soil. Each of the apparently existing things in front of us is a dependently arising event, and thus does not have its own autonomous self-existence. Each existing thing could therefore be said to be void, and indeed, voidness could be called "the ultimate mode of being of every phenomenon."[7] With this kind of analysis, "not the slightest trace remains of anything being established autonomously, independent of its parts."[8]

From a Christian perspective, we accept the existence of the things around us as real. The pillar will still be supporting Geshe Rabten's hut after he leaves. What common sense tells us is not to be disregarded, but to be reflected upon in order to come to a deeper philosophical perspective. Nor would we think to deny the fact that the things around us depend on a variety of conditions and causes. The pillar is in some real way connected not only with the tree, but with a web of causes that spread out to embrace the whole universe. There is even a way in which we could say that things lack their own autonomous self-existence because if we mean by this an independence of conditions and causes, then this quality cannot be applied to any creatures, but only to God. Then to say that things are void, or that voidness is the ultimate mode of being of phenomena is to begin to develop a notion of emptiness which is close to what the followers of Thomas Aquinas would call existence. Existence is the ultimate mode of things, and things, while they truly exist, exist in a limited way without possessing autonomous self-existence, but receive existence from Existence Itself, which is the proper metaphysical name of God. Then emptiness is not really about the non-existence of things, but the absence of inherent existence in the sense of autonomous self-existence. Therefore, the nothingness of Buddhism is not nihilism. It is not simply the absence of *svabhava,* or "self-existence" in ourselves and the things around us.

The thrust of the metaphysics of St. Thomas is to go beyond essence – without denying it – and to see essence in relationship to existence. The transcendence of being (essence) is not only negative, that is, non-being, non-essence, but eminently positive, indeed, the most eminently positive reality in terms of no-thing-ness, which is what Thomas calls existence, and which in Buddhism is called emptiness. This is not to say that Thomas' existence and Buddhism's nothingness are identical. They are not. But they are much closer than one might first imagine.

Dzogchen

The nothingness of Buddhism has a long history of being expressed in positive terms, however illusive and mysterious these terms might be. The Dzogchen tradition in Tibetan Buddhism provides us with some wonderfully metaphysically rich texts and commentaries that the Christian metaphysician could enjoy pondering.

"The true nature or condition of all things is the great shunyata which is not just a vacuum, a void, an empty; but it is luminous emptiness. It has a quality of "isness," of suchness, the *tathagatagarbha*. It is the emptiness endowed with the heart of compassion or wisdom. It is called the natural Great Perfection, the innate Great Perfection, Dzogpa Chenpo; this great emptiness endowed with the core of luminosity, the inseparability of cognizance and emptiness, of awareness and compassion. Where truth and unconditional love are not different."[9]

This luminous emptiness, or isness, the followers of St. Thomas could easily apply to God as existence, itself, who is beyond all concepts, essences or forms. The same is true when Nyoshul Khenpo Rinpoche and Lama Surya Das write, "After his great awakening beneath the bodhi-tree in Bodhgaya, Lord Buddha said that the ultimate nature of the mind is perfectly pure, profound, quiescent, luminous, uncompounded, unconditioned, unborn and undying, and free since the beginningless beginning."[10] And Christians could say with them that this is "the very heart of our original existential being."[11] Here we are drawing close to our central question of the relationship between these kinds of experiences of emptiness and Christian metaphysics.

John Myrdhin Reynolds, commenting on *The Golden Letters of Garab Dorje* writes: "Shunyata, the state of emptiness itself, is the source of this primordial energy that brings all possible forms, even the universe itself, into manifestation... Thus, the Base, the Primordial State, is not just emptiness in the negative sense of void or nothingness, a mere absence of something. Rather, the state of shunyata, this vast empty space where emptiness and luminosity are inseparable (*gsal stong dbyer-med*), represents the state of pure potentiality. It is the space of dimension or matrix of all existence out of which all possible forms or manifestations (*snangba*) arise, like clouds appearing spontaneously in the empty open sky. It is not just that forms lack an inherent nature (*rang-bzhin med-pa*) or substance, but equally inherent in shunyata is the potentiality for the arising of forms; this is the meaning of luminosity (*gsal-ba*)... If shunyata were a mere nothing, then nothing would arise at all. But this pure nonexistence or nothingness contradicts our experience. Thoughts and appearances are arising all the time, arising continuously, and this is only natural. But equally, if forms were not empty, then there would exist no possibility for change because all things would be locked up in a static unchanging state of their own self-identical essence or inherent nature (*rang-bzhin*, Skt. *svabhava*)."[12]

This is an extremely powerful and moving statement of great metaphysical insight. Forms are empty of their own self-existence, and in some way are related to the matrix of all existence. Here it is called a pure potentiality, but it does not seem it would change the sense of the passage if it were to be called a pure actuality as long as this act were to transcend all essence, or as Christian metaphysicians would say, this act were existence, itself. Unfortunately, Christians have scarcely begun to explore the riches to be found in Tibetan Buddhism, with some exceptions like Bernard de Give.[13]

A Dialogue with Nonduality

In the last chapter we saw Toshihiko Izutsu suggesting the possibility of a dialogue between Islamic and Christian metaphysics. But he was convinced that the same core experience of nonduality could be found not only in Islam, but in Buddhism, Hinduism and Taoism.

If that is true, then despite their differences, they shares the possibility of creating a nondual philosophy, or philosophical reflection on this core experience. And if that is true, then the way opens up for this nondual philosophy, now strengthened by seeing itself emerge from its concrete eastern forms, to enter into dialogue with Christian metaphysics. It is worth exploring this possibility by looking at Izutsu's work further, and then at David Loy's, which later and independently, made a similar case for the existence of a common core experience of nonduality in various Eastern religions.

Toshihiko Izutsu

Toshihiko Izutsu's deep insight into Islamic metaphysics was part of a wider vision of what he called "a new type of Oriental philosophy," or following Henry Corbin, a meta-historical dialogue which would try to grasp not only what was at the heart of Islamic philosophy, but other major Eastern religions, as well, and allow them with a renewed sense of their own distinctive nature and energy to enter into dialogue with the West. His first attempt to do this was to become his masterful *Sufism and Taoism: A Comparative Survey of Key Philosophical Concepts*. There his description of what he is going to attempt to do in his analysis of the work of Ibn 'Arabi can be applied to his wider project. He wants to look at the central concepts of being and existence in Ibn 'Arabi "to penetrate the "life-breath" itself, the vivifying spirit and the very source of the existence of the philosophizing drive of this great thinker, and to pursue from that depth the formation of the whole ontological system step by step..."[14]

Then he will go on to do the same thing in regard to the Taoism of Lao-tsu and Chuang-tsu. Later he will complete the same process in regard to Zen Buddhism in his *Towards a Philosophy of Zen Buddhism* and the reader of these studies is led to the conclusion that Izutsu found at the heart of each tradition what could be called an existential metaphysics centered on the relationship between essence and existence which had, at its heart, an intuition into being that, for him, was no different from what we are calling Eastern enlightenment. Clearly, he was keenly aware of the very different ways in which this enlightenment expressed itself in each tradition. But he was convinced that they shared a central vision in common, and therefore it would be possible to have a dialogue between this experience of nonduality and Western philosophy. We could go further and say with a Western philosophy that was truly an existential metaphysics.

Ibn 'Arabi

It is worth looking briefly at Izutsu's *Sufism and Taoism* to gain a concrete sense of the being and existence that he is finding in these different traditions. He is going to focus his attention on Ibn 'Arabi's (1165-1240) *Fusus al-Hikam*, or *Bezels of Wisdom*, and the commentary on it by Abd al-Razzaq al-Qashani (d. 1330)

Being in its highest sense in Ibn 'Arabi means "Being *qua* Being", or "Something beyond all existents that exist in a limited way, Something lying at the very source of all such existents existentiating them. It is Existence as the ultimate ground of everything."[15] Al-Qashani comments that in such a Being *qua* Being, "its existence is its own essence."[16]

What we are faced with here is once again with a deep metaphysical insight that is close to the one that lies at the heart of the Christian metaphysical tradition. But we are immediately also confronted with an issue that surfaced before. What is the relationship between the Absolute and the things around us? The Absolute, according to Izutsu's reading of Ibn 'Arabi, would remain unknowable if it were impossible for it to express itself in forms. But the forms, as long as they are in the Absolute, are in potency, and only become actualized in creation. There are various stages of the manifestation of the Absolute. The first is the archetype. Ibn 'Arabi writes: "... the world is nothing but a self-manifestation of the Absolute in the forms of the permanent archetypes of the things of the world."[17]

The highest and most comprehensive name of God is *Rahman*, the merciful, to which Ibn 'Arabi gives an ontological meaning. It "is primarily the act of making things exist, giving existence to them."[18] "God is by essence 'overflowing with bounteousness' *(fayyad bi-al-jud)*, that is, God is giving out existence limitlessly and endlessly to everything. As al-Qashani says, 'existence *(wujud)* is the first overflowing of the Mercy which is said to extend to everything'."[19] For Ibn 'Arabi every archetype or essence asks for existence from God, and al-Qashani comments: "The permanent archetypes in their state of latency have only an intelligible existence (as objects of God's Knowledge); by themselves they have no actual existence. They are desirous of actual existence, and are asking for it from God. When the archetypes are in such a state, God's essential Mercy extends to every archetype by giving it a capacity to receive an ontological Divine self-manifestation. This receptivity, or the essential 'preparedness' for receiving existence, is exactly the archetype's desire for actual existence."[20]

The many in the plane of oneness are "pure intelligibles and not real concrete existents. They are nothing more than 'recipients' (*qawabil*) for existence."[21] They have, in Ibn 'Arabi's words, "not even smelt the fragrance of existence."[22] Yet the names hidden in the Absolute seek expression in the world of external existence. Bali Efendi likens the Absolute to a man holding his breath and feeling the torment of not being able to expel it. When the breath bursts forth, it "is the same as God uttering the word "Be!" (*kun*) to the world."[23] The notion of self-manifestation (*tajalli*) is central to Ibn 'Arabi's thought, and in its first and most intense stage the Absolute manifests itself to itself in self-consciousness, and this self-manifestation has occurred from eternity.

Izutsu has left us again with a keen appreciation of his depth of metaphysical insight, especially by signaling the importance of essence as "nothing more than recipients for existence," but he also leaves us with the same question we saw before of whether the Absolute is ontologically distinct from creation, or whether creation necessarily emanates from it.

Chuang-tzu

If Islamic metaphysics can serve as a bridge between the East and the West, and therefore a way that the experience of enlightenment can be brought into relationship with an existential metaphysics like that of Thomas Aquinas, so can other Eastern traditions, as well, like Taoism, that philosophically articulate the same enlightenment experience. Izutsu looks at Chuang-tzu to see how he embodies "metaphysical concepts designed to explain the very structure of Being."[24] Chuang-tzu wants us to see things in their essence-less state by means of an illumination (*ming*). This requires a loss of ego. "There no longer remains the consciousness of the inner 'ego' as the center and all-unifying principle of man's mental activity."[25] There is a certain oblivion we must achieve. In ordinary experience we are pushed and pulled by our pursuit of the things around us which constantly change. We reach a measure of freedom when we become like a mirror inside, which is still while the things outside continue to change. At a higher or deeper stage of oblivion things still exist, but they show themselves without limits or boundaries, and we become one with the ten thousand things. But at a still higher stage, we become united with " 'the Mystery of Mysteries,' the ultimate metaphysical state of the Absolute"[26] before it begins to differentiate. Our egos fall away, and as a result the world inside and out disappears. We become identified with the way, or absolute reality. This is the stage of the void, or nothingness.

But as we descend out of this nothingness we begin to see that the way potentially contains the ten thousand things, but without boundaries among them. Further into the descent we reach the stage of pure essences by which each thing marks its own boundaries, and the absolute reality has become graspable in them. But if we descend yet further, the essences lose their living contact with their source, and we fall into an essentialism. So for Izutsu, Chuang-tzu's metaphysics is an existentialism in the same sense that is to be found in Ibn 'Arabi. It is not that the level of essence is being denied, but rather, when it is separated from its source which is existence, itself, then essences "in the sense of hard and solid ontological cores of things" are set up against each other in a fashion that goes against the way, or ultimate ground of things.

But even if essences seduce us into seeing things incorrectly, that does not mean that essences are mere illusions, and here we return again to Izutsu's view of the relationship between essence and existence. Essences "are not ontologically groundless." They are not "sheer nothing."[27] And he finds that his view is confirmed in Chuang-tzu's beautiful description of the cosmic wind:

"Listen! Do you not hear the trailing sound of the wind as it comes blowing from afar? The trees in the mountain forests begin to rustle, stir, and sway, and then all the hollows and holes of huge trees measuring a hundred arms' lengths around begin to give forth different sounds.

"There are holes like noses, like mouths, like ears; some are (square) like crosspieces upon pillars; some are (round) as cups, some are like mortars. Some are like deep ponds; some are like shallow basins...

"However, once the raging gale has passed on, all these hollows and holes are empty and soundless. You see only the boughs swaying silently, and the tender twigs gentle moving."[28]

Izutsu comments that when the hollows imagine that they are independently existing, and therefore making those sounds, they are wrong. "Not that the "hollows" do not exist at all. They are surely there. But they are actualized only by the positive activity of the Wind."[29] Both for Chuang-tzu and Ibn 'Arabi, existence is moving. It is not a thing. It is an *actus*. "No one can see the Absolute itself as 'something' existent, but no one can deny, either, the presence of its *actus*. And that *actus* is philosophically nothing other than Existence."[30] For Chuang-tzu the Absolute has two faces. "In its cosmic aspect the Absolute is Nature, a vital energy of Being which pervades all and makes them exist, grow, decay, and ultimately brings them back to the original source, while in its personal aspect it is God, the Creator of Heaven and Earth, the Lord of all things and events."[31]

David Loy

David Loy is both a Buddhist practitioner and student of Yamada Roshi, as well as Buddhist philosopher and social critic, and we met him before with his informal survey of Yamada's Christian students. And it is from this perspective that he launches a vigorous criticism of the problems of our Western culture, a culture which is fast becoming a global one. He incisively analyses in "Trying to Become Real: a Buddhist critique of some secular heresies," our obsessive pursuit of meaning by way of money, fame, romantic love and technological power, and in "The Religion of the Market," he extends his analysis to capitalism and consumerism, or economics without a sense of the human values it is meant to serve. He fortifies this Buddhist critique by similar insights coming from psychoanalysis and existentialism, which themes he develops in his *Lack and Transcendence*.

What makes this a Buddhist critique is the solution he proposes for these ills. Our modern sense of ego-consciousness gives rise in us to a sense of lack which we try to fill by these various means like money, fame, etc. Why not strike at the root of the problem, which is the ego, itself? Why not bring to an end the duality between the ego and the things it pursues? "If a sense-of-*lack* is the inescapable "shadow" of our sense-of-self, then the only way *lack* can be ended is by ending the sense-of-self – that is, by transforming the sense of myself as a Cartesian-like, self-sufficient self-consciousness separate from the objective world, into a more relational awareness that is nondual with the world."[32]

Loy, in his masterful book *Nonduality*, shows that such a solution is solidly based not only on Mahayana Buddhism, but on the advaitan Vedanta and Taoism, as well. They all share a common nondual experience which they articulate in various ways which, on the surface might appear contradictory, but which, in fact, express different aspects of the same core experience. Therefore, Loy's social criticism and the solution that he proposes takes on a new depth when we see it against this panoramic exposition of Eastern thought. Modern Western philosophy, he argues, has been enmeshed in duality from the time of Descartes, so it can hardly be expected to heal our afflictions that come precisely from duality. Why not seriously consider the philosophy of nonduality as a genuine alternative to modern Western philosophy and the social ills of Western society?

But just what is this nondual philosophy? It is not a philosophy in the modern Western sense of the term, or a philosophy which proceeds by way of concepts. Rather, it demands that we travel the narrow road of practice to our own experience of nonduality, which is called in the East enlightenment or liberation, and which we arrive at by meditation:

"Since the sense-of-self is a process of consciousness attempting to reflect back upon itself in order to grasp/ground itself, such meditation practice is an exercise in de-reflection. Consciousness *un*learns trying to grasp itself, real-ize itself, objectify itself. Enlightenment or liberation occurs when the usually-automatized reflexivity of consciousness ceases, *which is experienced as a letting-go and falling into the void and being wiped out of existence.* "Men are afraid to forget their minds, fearing to fall through the Void with nothing to stay their fall. They do not know that the Void is not really void, but the realm of the real Dharma.""[33]

Philosophy can never grasp nonduality because its attempts will always be "inherently dualistic and thus self-defeating."[34] And thus, if the remedy of our ills demands transcending dualism, philosophy will remain impotent. Nondual experience, therefore, "must transcend philosophy, itself, and all its ontological claims."[35]

Let's summarize the major points so far. Western society is afflicted by a craving for meaning that it tries to assuage in ways that will never succeed. A solution is to be found in transforming the ego by way of an experience of nonduality, an experience that can be found in various ways in Buddhism, Hinduism and Taoism. This experience, while it gives rise to various philosophical articulations, is not in itself or in its expressions, a philosophy in the Western sense of the word, but rather, it is attained by means of meditation.

This is a powerful argument that Loy has developed in detail. But what does it look like from the point of view of Christian metaphysics and mysticism? The Western philosophy that he has in mind is modern post-Cartesian philosophy bedeviled by a subject-object dichotomy, but this dichotomy does not exist in the same way in the philosophy of Thomas Aquinas. Thomas would never imagine that the concept is known first, and then the thing itself. In the act of knowledge the knower and the known are one in an intentional existence, a super-existence in knowledge, and the concept is a purely formal means of reaching that new existence. In the same way, in mystical experience the human person becomes one with God through a gratuitous super-existence of love. Is this duality or nonduality? It certainly is not an ontological nonduality in the sense that the distinctions between things and between creatures and God is destroyed or discovered to have been faulty all along. But it is not the modern Western duality that Loy rightly takes to task.

It could be argued that philosophy, by the very fact that it uses concepts, will never be able to resolve the problem of the separation of the subject and object. But from a Thomist point of view there is nothing inherently wrong in the use of concepts or the use of reason, which is a genuine way of knowing despite its limitations. Further, the philosophy of St. Thomas is rooted in common-sense experience available to everyone. It is founded on experiences like the fact that trees exist and I exist, and I am not the tree, as we saw before. In short, it is a realism, and it looks at modern science as being implicitly realistic, as well. There are real things that we can know and which exercise causality on each other. While Thomism has to strive to be a truly "critical realism," it is a realism nonetheless, and while it can admit the existence and the importance of nondual experiences, it does not feel compelled by them to imagine that reality, itself, is nondual. It would be wrong to imagine that while Zen has a view of the intellect that transcends concepts and culminates in wisdom, or *prajna paramita*, Thomism rests on nothing but concepts. It, too, has a vision of wisdom, and understands that concepts must be vivified by *intellectus*, or intuitive insight.

Working from a nondual perspective, Christian mysticism, as well, will appear to Loy to be dualistic, and in need of going the final step to the realm of nonduality:

"...before we become completely enlightened, we shall experience the operation of the Absolute upon us as God. God is the Absolute seen from "outside," but that is the only way the Absolute can be seen, since in itself it is so devoid of characteristics that it is literally a nothing. God is God only in relation to me, but when there is no longer a "me" then the spiritual quest is over."[36]

"...theistic mystical experience might be understood as an "incomplete" nondual one. In it, there is the awareness of consciousness pervading everywhere, but insofar as the experience is an awareness *of*..., it is still tainted with some delusion; whereas complete union – as in Advaita's Nirguna and Eckhart's godhead – is to become that ground which is literally nothing in itself, but from which all issues forth."[37] Here we have rejoined themes we have seen before.

This fundamental outlook remains basically unchanged in Loy's "Comparing Zen Koan Practice with the *Cloud of Unknowing*." Here, too, from a Thomist point of view, Christian contemplation is not just a matter of love, while Buddhism uses the intellect. Rather it, too, is a form of wisdom, or a knowledge coming through love and not through conceptual means. It is understandable why Buddhists would focus on those aspects of the Christian mystical tradition that are most like Buddhism, for example, Meister Eckhart, or attach special importance to the Buddhist-sounding remarks of modern Christian practitioners of Buddhism, but in final analysis, it might be more fruitful for the Buddhist-Christian dialogue to concentrate on what appears most radically dissimilar between the two traditions, for example, the mysticism of John of the Cross.

When Loy writes in his article on *The Cloud of Unknowing*, "Can we then understand the difference in goals as due to the difference in paths..."[38] perhaps he has come closer to building a bridge between the two traditions than he realizes. Is it possible that nondual means or paths will give rise to nondual experiences or goals which, in turn, give birth to nondual "philosophies" while Christian metaphysics, which makes use of concepts, arrives at a similar insight but expressible in conceptual terms, and Christian mysticism which goes by way of unknowing, but not the unknowing of Buddhism, arrives at another goal? This is not to say that all these different goals are not somehow intimately related to each other, and perhaps this is the primary subject matter for a deep Buddhist-Christian dialogue.

What is the nature of the ego that undergoes this process of de-reflection? If it is a Cartesian-style ego that is identical to self-consciousness, then we could say that the ego ontologically disappears. If the ego was always a construct, then it would, indeed, evaporate in the sense that it ceases to recur.[39] But what if ego-consciousness is a reflection of the soul on its acts, as Thomas Aquinas would have it, or in more modern terms, the soul is much more than ego-consciousness and embraces the unconscious, as well? Then the experience of the loss of the ego is still a painful death-like experience, but it is not an ontological loss of the soul. Rather, it is a manifestation that the true nature of the soul is very different than we imagined it to be.

In final analysis, what we see emerging is the possibility of a metaphysical dialogue between nonduality, perhaps discovering itself in a new way, and Christian metaphysics. The real question is why hasn't it been taking place. Here we return to the reasons that we saw earlier. For the most part the Catholic participants in East-West dialogue find it difficult to imagine that Christian metaphysics really has anything to say. And we have rejoined the attempts brought forth by Christians in *Chapters 1* and *2* to explain Christianity in terms of nondual experience.

But it is one thing to point to the common core of nonduality that can be found in the East, and which we have just been seeing from a Buddhist perspective in the works of Izutsu and Loy, and which we could look at from an Islamic perspective in the work of Frithjof Schuon[40] and Seyyed Hossein Nasr,[41] or from the point of view of transpersonal psychology in the work of people like Ken Wilber,[42] or Michael Washburn,[43] but it is quite another thing, and a much more problematical one, to try to fit Christianity into this nondual pattern.[44]

Notes

1. Dalai Lama. *My Land, My People*, p. 54.
2. Goss, Robert E. "Catholic and Dge Lugs Pa Scholasticism" p. 76.
3. Desideri, Ippolito, SJ. *An Account of Tibet*. p. 105.
4. Goss, Robert. E. "Catholic and Dge Lugs Pa Scholasticism, p. 79.
5. Ibid., p. 80.   6. Ibid., p. 86, note 10.
7. Rabten, Geshé. *Echoes of Voidness*, p. 30.
8. Rabten, Geshé. *Song of the Profound View*, p. 62.
9. Khenpo Rinpoche, Nyoshul and Lama Surya Das. *Natural Great Perfection: Dzogchen Teachings and Vajra Songs*, p. 106-107.
10. Ibid., p. 78.   11. Ibid.
12. Reynolds, John Myrdhin, *Self-Liberation Through Seeing With Naked Awareness,* p. 281.
13. de Give, Bernard. http://www.scourmont.be/degive/non-dualite.htm
14. Izutsu, Toshihiko. *Sufism and Taoism*, p. 3.
15. Ibid., p. 25.   21. Ibid., p. 155.   27. Ibid., p. 367.
16. Ibid., p. 26.   22. Ibid., p. 161.   28. Ibid., p. 368-369.
17. Ibid., p. 42.   23. Ibid., p. 132.   29. Ibid., p. 369.
18. Ibid., p. 116.   24. Ibid., p. 301.   30. Ibid., p. 372.
19. Ibid.   25. Ibid., p. 340.   31. Ibid.
20. Ibid., p. 118.   26. Ibid., p. 346.
32. Loy, David. "Trying to Become Real," p. 424.
33. Ibid., p. 424-425.
34. Loy, David. *Nonduality*, p. 5.
35. Ibid., p. 4.   36. Ibid., p. 291.   37. Ibid., p. 295.
38. Loy, David. "A Zen Cloud?" p. 51.
39. Loy, David. *The Nonduality of Life and Death*, p. 166.
40. Schuon, Frithjof. *The Transcendent Unity of Religions*.
41. Nasr, Seyyed Hossein. *Knowledge and the Sacred*.
42. Wilber, Ken, Jack Engler, and Daniel P. Brown. *Transformations of Consciousness*.

43. Washburn, Michael. *The Ego and the Dynamic Ground*
44. For three examples of this kind of dialogue, see the dialogue I had with Judith Blackstone and Philip St. Romain at http://www.innerexplorations.com/ewtext/dialogue.htm, another with Dan Berkow at http://www.innerexplorations.com/ewtext/more.htm, and a third at the 2000 Tacoma meeting of the Society of Buddhist-Christian Studies with David Loy in the video: *Questions at the Heart of the Buddhist-Christian Dialogue: David Loy and James Arraj*. See also the video: *David Loy: Zen Philosopher & Social Critic*, and *A Zen-Christian Interior Dialogue* at http://www.innerexplorations.com/ewtext/Z-Cdialogue.htm.

CHAPTER 8

THE METAPHYSICS OF ST. THOMAS AND ENLIGHTENMENT

We have been seeing a core experience of nonduality that has been subjected to various kinds of deep philosophical reflection. Here the question is whether it is possible to have a Christian metaphysical explanation of enlightenment. In my earlier *God, Zen and the Intuition of Being*, following the path blazed by Jacques Maritain, I arrived at such an explanation from a different direction. There I started with the metaphysics of St. Thomas, and Maritain's intuition of being. Later, in *Mysticism, Metaphysics and Maritain*, I situated this explanation of enlightenment between philosophical contemplation on one hand, and mystical contemplation on the other. Since *God, Zen and the Intuition of Being* is included in this volume, and so can supply this kind of Thomist metaphysical background, I will simply summarize here this metaphysical view of enlightenment, and spend the rest of the chapter applying it to the difficult question of the existence of a self.

The heart of the metaphysics of St. Thomas is his revolutionary insight into the relationship between essence and existence, an insight which one of his great 20th century followers, Jacques Maritain, called the intuition of being. Thomas' path to this insight in the 13th century took a similar trajectory to the one we saw Mulla Sadra taking in the 17th century. Thomas had before him both Greek and Islamic metaphysical writers, and he pondered them within the context of Biblical monotheism, in this case, in the light of Christian theology and mysticism. He saw that, while for Aristotle essence had been in the foreground and existence in the background, existence was, in fact, primary, and ultimately essence could only be understood in relationship to existence. This was no abstract or theoretical conclusion on his part, but was born out of a fiery touch of the mystery of being.

The intuition of being is rooted in the most basic and undeniable facts. Things exist. We are surrounded by actually existing things. The oak tree stands in the garden. The sun is warming us. The child is laughing. Different things exist. My cat is not the same as the bird that he is chasing. But we take these experiences for granted and rarely ponder them. But if we did, we would be on the road to metaphysics. Things exist, yet different kinds of things exist. There are, therefore, two fundamental and distinct reports that our minds give us. They tell us that things are and what things are. The ultimate challenge of metaphysics is to reconcile these two reports. We need to see just how the *what* and the *that* relate to each other.

Thomas expressed it by saying that essences are certain capacities for existence. We are surrounded by different kinds of existence: tree-existence, if you will, cat-existence, stone-existence. What exists are actually existing things, not essences. Essences are not pre-existing containers waiting to be filled with existence. In our minds they are simply ideas abstracted from the different kinds of existences, or existing things, that we encounter.

But if different things exist, then existence cannot be limited to being a tree, or a bird. It overflows this or that kind of existence. It transcends the very order of the whats, or essences. Essences are certain capacities for existence. They limit and contract it so that it is this or that thing. They are intrinsic limitations of existence, as we heard Izutsu say, echoing William Carlo.

But existence as received and contracted demands existence as unreceived. This or that existence points to existence without essential limitation. If different things exist, then Existence, itself, must exist, and Existence, itself, is like the sun which gives birth to a whole rainbow of different colors.

St. Thomas' intuition of being is just one kind of the intuition of being in the larger sense of the term. It anchors one end of the spectrum of the intuition of being, the more properly philosophical and speculative end. At the other end of the spectrum we see things like Zen where nondual experience is primary, and philosophical reflection quite secondary. At various places in the middle of this spectrum we could place Tibetan Buddhism with its scholastic tradition, or Mulla Sadra's wisdom philosophy which develops a true existential philosophy, but one that is also illuminated by nondual experience.

Once we realize that there is a metaphysical continuity underlying all these positions, we are in a position to have an East-West dialogue on a deep metaphysical level. Many of the foundations for such a dialogue are already in place. We just saw how Izutsu and Loy arrived at very powerful philosophical understandings of the common core experience of enlightenment that underlies much of Eastern religions.

Maritain developed a Thomist metaphysical view of enlightenment which could provide us with another of the necessary foundations for an East-West metaphysical dialogue, which can be summed up as follows: If someone were to descend into the depths of his or her spirit, driven by the desire to embrace the deepest and richest and most ultimate reality he or she could find there, and was willing to abandon all concepts and the normal workings of ego-consciousness to attain that goal, what would that person discover? They could experience in those depths a living contact, although by night, with the mystery of existence. They could touch Existence, itself, in and through the experience of the very existence of the soul, itself, as it comes forth, moment by moment, from this very source of existence. It would be an experience of existence without essence, as it were, because all concepts had been left behind. But because it takes place in this night of concepts, it would be very difficult in post-experience reflection to distinguish the existence of the soul, the existence of all things, and Existence, itself. In order to make this more concrete, let's imagine a discussion between a Christian metaphysician and a Zen master.

Zen Enlightenment and the Intuition of Being

In the Christian metaphysical experience of a flower, it stands before us in all its beauty and radiance. It is! It floats on a pure and serene field of the emptiness of all essences, a field of pure existence. The flower is coming forth afresh in each instant from this field, and in itself is totally transparent to the ocean of existence from which it flows. The very existence of the flower is experienced and evokes with its whole being the source of existence, Existence, itself.

What would the Zen master say to his or her student who had experienced the mystery of being in this way? He or she would probably say: "Go back to your cushion. Become one with the flower. Don't let a hair's breadth of distance remain between you and the flower." And the master might think: "The experience of the flower is beautiful, but it does not go far enough. There is still the flower and the one who experiences it. The division into subject and object has not been overcome. This person must become one with the flower." And there is a certain view of the nature of things that underlies the master's thoughts. It is not that the flower and the student are one in the way the Western mind might understand that assertion. There is no flower in the flower, as the Dalai Lama once said. Nor is there any ego, or self, in the student, and therefore the unity of the student and the flower cannot exist on that level. The flower is an expression of the ground, or field of emptiness, or mind, or essential nature, and so is the student, and it is this that makes them one, and it is this the master wants the student to experience directly.

How would the Christian metaphysician reply? He or she could say that Zen does, indeed, come into living contact with the very ground of the flower, or the self, in and through a night of all concepts. And this ground is the very existence of the flower, or the mountain, or the river, or the student's self, and in and through them a contact with the ocean of existence from which they emerge moment by moment. This ocean is without essence in the sense that it transcends all essences, or specific natures. It can thus be called No-Thing, or empty, but it is an emptiness that is a plenitude beyond whatever concepts can grasp. The flower has no self-nature in the sense of independent existence. It is totally dependent on the ocean of existence for its own being. In this sense it is empty, and there is no flower in the flower, but it does have dependent and relational existence, an existence that is a limited and contracted reflection of Existence, itself, but which, nevertheless, is.

The experience of enlightenment and the philosophical intuition of being are both deeply metaphysical experiences of the same reality, but by different paths, and so they express themselves in different ways. Enlightenment touches the very ground of things, their very existence, and through them the source of that existence. The intuition of being does not. Rather, it uses concepts and explores them to their ultimate limit where it discovers that the very meaning of essence, or nature, is this or that capacity to exist. Essences cannot exist outside of their relationship to existence. The knowledge the intuition of being attains is certain but indirect. The very indubitable existence of the flower demands the existence of Existence, itself, but this ground is not touched. This working through concepts leads to an eidetic intuition of being, an insight into existence that remains in continuity with concepts as it peers beyond them, and asserts what it doesn't know by experience. The danger such an existential metaphysics perpetually faces is to lose its intuitive fire and settle for the concepts that were meant to ignite and lead to the insight, yet still believe itself alive when it has died and become a sterile conceptualism or essentialism, when it has ceased to see, and its concepts have become opaque.

Enlightenment avoids this danger for the most part by resolutely breaking with concepts and seeking the mystery of existence in a night of all concepts. But it is this very night which is the vital means by which the existence of things and through them the existence of the ground, itself, is touched, that poses its own danger for enlightenment. What is experienced is the existence of the flower, and in and through it the ocean of existence, but since this experience takes place in a night of all concepts, it becomes extremely difficult when the experience is over to articulate the relationship between the existence of a flower, the existence of the self, and the existence of the Self, or Existence, itself. Sometimes post-experience reflection tends to leave the impression that the flower in some way does not exist at all, or the flower is identical with the ocean of existence, and the ocean of existence is identical with the flower. The Zen master might object: "These things are not our concern. What we are trying to do is to lead the student to the experience because it will begin to transform and liberate him or her. All the words we use, or the gestures, are meant to point to the experience, itself, and help someone attain it. They are skillful means, and should not be given an ontological meaning."

But we might still wonder if there is a certain ontological thirst, or tendency, in all of us that leads to a double problem. On the one hand, Western ontological ears can be constantly trying to reshape Eastern words to give them an ontological meaning when they are not meant that way. But on the other, Eastern religions, after all is said and done, may sometimes be uttering statements that have strong ontological resonances no matter what the conscious intentions of their speakers are. There is a vital difference between speculative and practical language. The first tries to know things in themselves, and let itself be measured by them. The second shapes language to serve the goal to be achieved. Christian metaphysics uses a speculative language, and thus can misunderstand the Eastern practical, or liberative languages, and give them ontological meanings they did not intend. Did the Buddha, for example, really want to talk about the existence and nature of God or the soul? But Eastern liberative languages can act as if all languages must be formed as they are, and therefore, a metaphysics in continuity with concepts is impossible. Then, under the impact of the marvelous experience of existence, post-experience reflections using liberative languages can make ontological statements about the very ability of a philosophical metaphysics to exist. They can take the genuine devotion to the primacy of the experience of enlightenment, and use it to create a barrier that rules out other kinds of experiences of the same absolute. Any distinction between the flower and the ground of existence from which it comes is ruled out as the arising of the old conceptual dualism, and the question of the existence of God is decreed to be unaskable as well as unanswerable.

Despite these dangers from both sides, however, the core experience in both Christian metaphysics and Eastern enlightenment appears to be the same. The vastly different means they use to attain the experience accounts for the central differences in expressions that we have been seeing. They are like brothers who have been brought up far away from each other and have only begun to find each other. It seems possible, though extremely difficult, that they could learn to really talk to each other, and even find a common language they could both agree upon as a fitting expression of the wonderful mystery of existence they are both devoted to.

It would also be possible to extend this kind of Christian explanation of enlightenment to include kundalini yoga, as well. To do this we would have to see the deep relationship that exists between the human soul and the body, and the whole of creation, and to ponder the saying of St. Thomas that the body does not contain the soul, but the soul contains the body. The human soul is a spiritual being in potency that needs to be united with the body in order to activate itself. It contains within itself, as it were, the whole of the universe. Then kundalini appears as a fundamental energy of the soul that activates all its levels from the lowest to the highest, fitting it for enlightenment. Kundalini is that fundamental energy, or instinct of the soul, that is inscribed in its very being, which urges it to become fully alive and activated so that it can be and see its own existence and that of all things, and experience in them the radiant mystery of Existence, itself.

A Christian View of Enlightenment

Just what then is the mysticism of the Self seen from the Christian metaphysical point of view? It is a natural mystical experience of God in and through the existence of the soul, in a non-conceptual manner that makes it difficult to distinguish the human self from the divine Self. We can find a common mysticism of the Self in things as apparently diverse as the advaitan Vedanta, and those traditions that deny the existence of any self.

To call this a natural mysticism is an attempt to distinguish it from a relational love mysticism that comes about through grace in which the presence of God who is Existence, itself, is revealed as a loving Thou. This does not imply that those who pursue the mysticism of the Self are not in the context of this loving union that comes about by grace. They are. Further, their efforts to reach the goal of natural mystical experience can be means of growing in this loving union. But that, in turn, does not mean that these two kinds of mysticism aim at the same goal in the same way, and use the same means to arrive there.

The intuition of being in the wide sense of the term embraces both the philosophical intuition of being and the experience of nonduality, and it represents a foretaste of our ultimate natural human destiny which is a union with God by knowledge and love through our very existence. This is why people who experience it often characterize it as an ultimate experience, and then want to see relational love mysticism as a preliminary stage on the way to it. But relational love mysticism is not something that takes place outside the mysticism of the Self, but rather it is this Self, or Emptiness, making itself known to us in a loving and intimate way.

The deep metaphysical insights of the East are devoted to the pursuit of enlightenment. In the West, it has gone into metaphysics. So the first great conversation in East-West dialogue ought to be a metaphysical one. The obstacles to such a conversation are daunting. If Eastern religions insist that there can be no continuity between these metaphysical depths and conceptual expression, the conversation will fail. If Christianity does not rediscover a living contact with the best of its metaphysical traditions, this conversation will never happen. But I am optimistic. The core experience of nonduality that Izutsu and Loy have both so eloquently given philosophical testimony to could enter into dialogue with the metaphysics of St. Thomas once they both realize that they are talking about the same mysterious reality from very different perspectives. The other great conversation would be one between the Christian interpersonal mystical tradition, and similar traditions in the East.

The Loss of the Affective Ego

One of the greatest differences between Buddhism and Christianity concerns the question of the self, or soul. Christians believe that each person has an immortal soul, and God, in an analogous way, can be called a person, or self. Buddhists, on the other hand, at least some Buddhists, deny the existence of any self, whether divine or human. But we cannot accept this enormous apparent distance without careful examination.

From the Buddhist side, the denial of the self seems aimed at a self-subsisting self, that is, a self that is somehow independent and complete in itself so that its very selfness distinguishes it from other things and walls them out. This is a self that would somehow have complete existence in itself. Or if these kinds of comments have too many metaphysical overtones, we can say that the self that they deny is an ego-self that is always jealously defending itself and constantly striving to reinforce itself, and in place of this ego-self they put a dynamic network of relationships and insist that nothing can truly be understood or exist outside of this network.

Certainly it is true that Western thought has often been guilty of a reification of the self, of conceiving the self as an entity that is complete in itself and separate from other selves and things. But this is simply bad philosophy that is neither intrinsic to Christianity nor to the Christian philosophy of St. Thomas. It would be possible to show without a great deal of trouble that a Christian view of the soul is highly relational not only in regard to God, but to other people and even the entire universe. This human soul, or self, is not to be identified with the ego and it cannot be closed in upon itself, for it receives its very existence moment by moment from God and its inner growth depends on its relationship to other people and the whole of nature. But even if we show that a relational view of the self exists in both Buddhism and Christianity, the distance between the two positions has only partially diminished.

Philosophical Language vs. Liberative Language

It would be a mistake to take the Buddhist view of the self as a philosophical position in the classical Western sense of the term, which is a point we have considered before. It is not philosophy. Buddhists are aiming at liberation and enlightenment, and this overall direction shapes the very words they use. Another way of putting it is that they are engaged in a very concrete existential enterprise of attaining the goal of enlightenment and not in a philosophical analysis meant to describe the nature or essence of things. If this distinction were kept clear on both sides, then much confusion could be avoided, and I believe we would see that the Buddhist and Christian doctrines on the soul are much closer than we initially imagine.

This distinction between a philosophical mode of language and a liberative or salvific one is important in Christianity, itself. John of the Cross, for example, will say that all creatures in the sight of God are nothing. Does he mean that they don't exist? Not at all. He is not making a metaphysical statement, or contradicting the basic Christian doctrine that all things are good and have been created by God. He wants to lead us to union with God, and it is this intent that shapes his words. What he is saying is that all creatures, inasmuch as we cling to them inordinately, hinder our union with God and when they do this, they are like nothing, or worse than nothing.

The Buddha was not making ontological statements about God and creatures. He was teaching a way of liberation from suffering. And while he did this he was not inclined to philosophize, that is, to look at the nature of things in a speculative way, but such urges to speculative philosophy are an innate part of human nature. We therefore should not be surprised that these ontological tendencies would appear over and over again in Buddhism. But we really need to ask whether the result has been a Buddhist philosophy in the classical Western sense of metaphysics. I don't think that it has been. These Buddhist philosophical instincts are, for the most part, still exercised in the context of the quest for liberation, and in regard to experiences that have been generated in the course of that quest. It is a philosophy about the experience and practice of enlightenment. If this is true, then Buddhist statements about the non-existence of the self should not be read in a purely ontological register by either Christians or Buddhists. This doesn't mean that they don't have deep metaphysical resonances, but their translation into philosophical language in the Western sense of the term is more complex than we might first imagine. With this distinction in mind, let's look at spontaneous Western experiences of the loss of self to see if they can help us bring East and West closer together and situate enlightenment in a wider context.

Western No-Self Experiences

Modern Western accounts of the loss of self, or what I would rather call the loss of the affective ego, while infrequent and scattered, are not completely unknown. Michael Washburn in his *The Ego and the Dynamic Ground* talks of black holes in psychic space brought about by the eruption of the unconscious into the sphere of the ego, an eruption that interrupts the ego's internal dialogue. He quotes Wilson van Dusen who worked with psychotic patients: "In the hole one feels one has momentarily lost one's will. What one intended is forgotten. What would have been said is unremembered. One feels caught, drifting, out of control, weak... It is extremely important to know what people do when faced with encroaching blankness. Many talk to fill up space. Many must act to fill the empty space within themselves. In all cases it must be filled up or sealed off... The feared empty space is a fertile void. Exploring it is a turning point toward therapeutic change."[1]

This is not to suggest that the loss of the affective ego is necessarily pathological. It can be, of course, but even more fascinating are the more or less spontaneous modern experiences in the West of the loss of self that cannot be written off as pathological.

"All my thoughts, hopes and fears about the future have changed radically since I fell asleep one night in October 1985 and woke next morning without a self," writes Ann Faraday, an English psychologist. "I don't know what happened to it, but it never returned... I experience this Empty-ness as a boundless arena in which life continually manifests and plays, rising and falling, constantly changing, always transient and therefore ever-new."[2]

John Wren-Lewis had a similar experience when he was deliberately poisoned by a thief on a bus in Thailand in 1983, and went into a coma. "What *I* knew was that I'd emerged from something quite unlike any previous experience of sleep or dreaming. It was a kind of blackness, yet the absolute opposite of blankness, for it was the most alive state I've ever known – intensely happy, yet also absolutely peaceful, since it seemed to be utterly complete in itself, leaving nothing to be desired... For that dazzling darkness behind me did indeed transform my perception of the outside world, and here, too, I'm driven to religious or mystical language in trying to do the experience justice. The peeling paint on the hospital walls, the ancient sheets on the bed, the smell from the nearby toilet, the other patients chattering or coughing, the nurses and the indifferent curry they brought me for supper, my own somewhat traumatized middle-aged body, even my racing, bewildered mind – all were imbued with that sense of utter nothing-to-be-desired completeness, because *"not I, but the Shining Darkness within me," was perceiving them.*"[3]

"The best day of my life – my rebirthday, so to speak – was when I found I had no head....," is how D.E. Harding describes a similar experience. "It was when I was thirty-three that I made the discovery. Though it certainly came out of the blue, it did so in response to an urgent inquiry; I had for several months been absorbed in the question: what am I?... What actually happened was something absurdly simple and unspectacular: just for the moment I stopped thinking. Reason and imagination and all mental chatter died down. For once, words really failed me. I forgot my name, my humanness, my thingness, all that could be called me or mine. Past and future dropped away. It was as if I had been born that instant, brand new, mindless, innocent of all memories."[4]

One of the most fascinating accounts of this kind of loss of self was given by Suzanne Segal who was waiting for a bus in Paris when her self disappeared. "The personal self was gone, yet here was a body and a mind that still existed empty of anyone who occupied them. The experience of living without a personal identity, without an experience of being somebody, an "I" or a "me," is exceedingly difficult to describe, but it is absolutely unmistakable. It can't be confused with having a bad day or coming down with the flu or feeling upset or angry or spaced out... The mind, body, and emotions no longer referred to anyone – there was no one who thought, no one who felt, no one who perceived. Yet the mind, body, and emotions continued to function unimpaired; apparently they did not need an "I" to keep doing what they always did. Thinking, feeling, perceiving, speaking, all continued as before, functioning with a smoothness that gave no indication of the emptiness behind them."[5]

Unfortunately, this loss of self appeared to her when seen from the perspective of the ego as a terrible destruction, and she suffered enormously for many years. The suffering was all the more difficult to bear because she was without any way to place this experience in a positive context until she discovered Buddhism.

"One aspect of my experience that Buddhism was particularly helpful in explaining was that although individual identity had dropped away, all the personality functions remained completely intact. Now, however, those functions floated in a vastness that referred to no one. All the same experiences still happened, there just wasn't a "me" to whom they were happening. And the appropriate responses just happened as well, arising out of and then subsiding into themselves. Everything appeared and disappeared on the broad screen of the infinite – interactions, emotions, talk, actions of all kinds."[6]

Eventually she met Jean Klein who taught in the advaitan tradition of Ramana Maharshi, who told her, "You must stop the part of the mind that constantly keeps trying to look back at the experience."[7] She comments: "There was a part of the mind – perhaps what we call the self-reflective or introspective function – that kept turning to look and, finding emptiness, kept sending the message that something was wrong."[8]

Gradually she began to see "how the emptiness of a "me" was full of exquisite infinity."[9] Later she realized that "the infinite emptiness I knew myself to be was now apparent as the *infinite substance* of everything I saw."[10]

She began to meditate intensively, "just sitting in the vastness, as blossoms began appearing on the tree of emptiness."[11] This meditating culminated in an experience that sounds much like enlightenment. "The mountains, trees, rocks, birds, sky were all losing their differences. As I gazed about, what I saw first was how they were one; then, as a second wave of perception, I saw the distinctions."[12]

The Loss of the Affective Ego and Individuation

It is not surprising that Westerners like Suzanne Segal who experienced a loss of self would turn to the East for guidance, for the East knows more about it than the West, but this does not mean that any loss of the affective ego should be presumed to lead to an experience like enlightenment. Put in another way, we have to ask ourselves what are the positive purposes that the loss of the affective ego could serve. One possibility is that such a loss takes place in the psychological process of individuation.

Marie-Louise von Franz, a noted Jungian analyst, tried to describe a high level of individuation which she called the middle ground: "There is a complete standstill in a kind of inner centre, and the functions do not act automatically any more. You can bring them out at will, as for instance an airplane can let down the wheels in order to land and then draw them in again when it has to fly. At this stage the problem of the functions is no longer relevant; the functions have become instruments of a consciousness which is no longer rooted in them or driven by them... What does someone look like when he has detached his ego awareness, or his ego consciousness, from identification with certain functions? I think the nearest and most convincing example would be in some descriptions of the behaviour of Zen Buddhist Masters. It is said that the door of the inner house is closed, but the Master meets everybody and every situation and everything in the usual manner."[13] As far as I know, however, this interesting idea has not been developed within Jungian psychology.

The Loss of the Affective Ego and Christian Mystical Experience

What would happen if a Catholic deeply interested in the Christian mystical tradition experienced a loss of self? Then that person could be inclined to make this very real no-self experience a part of the Christian contemplative path. In doing so, he or she would run the same risk as the Catholic participants in East-West dialogue who at one point or another carried out this integration by reinterpreting Christianity in Buddhist or Hindu terms. Yet, there is nothing in the intrinsic nature of that no-self experience that demands that kind of outcome.

Philip St. Romain

The story of Philip St. Romain's spontaneous kundalini awakening that we saw in *Chapter 2,* had a dimension of the loss of the affective ego, as well. Early in this process he wrote, "I'm changing – much less ponderous and egotistical, much more self-assured, less passionately devoted to getting things my way, and less feeling, too, which is the strangest part… By May 1, however, I was beginning to experience a sense of emotionally fading in and out. "Sometimes I feel as though I do not know myself at all," I noted."[14]

As this kundalini experience deepened, he would become absorbed in its manifestations like shimmering mandalas of light. "Initially, I would be aware of myself as an "I" gazing into the mandala; then there would be no "I," only gazing; then there would be no gazing and no breathing – only the mandala. After a few seconds, however, I would return to myself, wondering where "I" had gone."[15] Later this process began to effect his life of prayer, making discursive meditation unproductive. He describes it as a spiritual black hole sucking him into itself, and drawing him into depths he did not know he possessed. In those depths there were "fewer lights, fewer thoughts, and no feelings at all."[16]

He began to experience spontaneous movements, or mudras, in the form of grimaces and gestures, and doubts surfaced about where all this was leading him:

"I lost my affective memory during this period; I no longer had a sense of emotional continuity about my life. For example, I would hear a song which, in the past, generally brought memories and feelings, but now the song brought only the memories and no feelings.

There were plenty of feelings about life here and now, but these no longer resonated with my past. Without an emotional memory, I lost all sense of identity and spent a great deal of time in my journal "looking for myself." But who was looking for whom? Which one was me: the one looking, or the one I was looking for?[17]

It was then that he discovered the writings of Bernadette Roberts on her experience of no-self, and her attempts to relate it to Christian mysticism. And he felt confirmed by the fact that what he was experiencing was not completely unchartered territory.

As the process continued he realized, "Once the body was freed from all emotional pain, it seemed that my Ego evaporated completely. There was an "I" of sorts, and I had all my memories – but no feelings attached to those memories. Furthermore, it seemed that my self awareness had become split from my self-concept."[18] And yet he could take care of his daily affairs without the ego that he had lost. He questioned himself, "Who was I? I realized that I was not my thoughts, not my feelings, not my memory, not my body, not even all of them together! What, then, was an "I"? While pondering this question one day while driving to New Orleans, I sensed a response coming from my intuitive higher self. "Philip St. Romain is dead!" came the word. "Quit trying to find him." Somehow I knew that this was true. Except for my body and my disaffected memory, there was nothing left to the person once called Philip St. Romain."[19]

This loss of the affective ego appears as a direct consequence of his kundalini awakening, which in turn seems to have the purpose of leading to an enlightenment that is no different in substance than what is found in the East. Once the process had done its work, he could say, "I am able, now, to use my senses without thinking. It is a wonderfully mysterious thing to just-look and to see with the eyes without thinking about what one sees."[20]

We have noted before the struggle that Philip St. Romain underwent to integrate this kundalini awakening harmoniously into his Christian life. But what would happen if a Christian were to receive some kind of powerful experience of the loss of the affective ego and come to the conclusion that it represented a higher stage of the Christian contemplative path, itself?

218 CHAPTER 8

Bernadette Roberts

Bernadette Roberts' *The Experience of No-Self* is an account of an inner journey she went on in the midst of trying to live out a Catholic contemplative life, a journey that ended in what she called the experience of no-self. But this very word no-self and an attentive reading of her description of her experiences reveal an inner structure and language that is much closer to Buddhist enlightenment than Christian mystical union, a fact made all the more interesting because the author was not trying to explain herself in Buddhist terminology.

She will say, for example, "Where there is no personal self, there is no personal God,"[21] or God "is all that exists... God is all that is."[22] The individuality of the object observed is overshadowed by "that into which it blends and ultimately disappears."[23] What is that which can neither be subject or object.[24] God is not self-conscious[25] and we must come to "terms with the nothingness and emptiness of existence,"[26] which seems equivalent to "living out my life without God." "I had to discover it was only when every single, subtle, experience and idea – conscious and unconscious – had come to an end, a complete end, that it is possible for the truth to reveal itself."[27]

But if there is no self, "What is this that walks, thinks and talks?"[28] The end of the journey is "absolute nothingness,"[29] but "out of nothingness arises the greatest of great realities."[30] It is the "one existent that is Pure Subjectivity" and "there is no multiplicity of existences; only what Is has existence that can expand itself into an infinite variety of forms..."[31] Our sense of self rests on our self-reflection and "when we can no longer verify or check back (reflect) on the subject of awareness, we lose consciousness of there being any subject of awareness at all."[32] This leads to the "silence of no-self."[33]

Bernadette Roberts as a Catholic and someone relatively unfamiliar with Buddhism has rendered an important testimony to the universality of this kind of mystical experience. But inevitably, she has had to face the question of its relationship to her own Christian contemplative heritage, and it is here that her conclusions need a careful examination. Since she had a life of prayer in the Christian contemplative tradition before she went on this journey that ended in the experience of no-self, it is understandable that she will see this experience as the next stage in the Christian contemplative journey, and a stage that the Christian mystics like John of the Cross know very little about. The one exception is, not surprisingly, Meister Eckhart, a predilection which is shared by many people in Buddhist-Christian dialogue, as we have seen. Thus she is forced to put the no-self experience at a level higher than the highest form of Christian mystical experience, the spiritual marriage described by John of the Cross and Teresa of Avila, and therefore place her own experience above that of the Church's mystical doctors.

I don't think this interpretation is correct. This mysticism of the no-self, as well as Zen enlightenment, is not a supernatural mysticism that comes from grace and leads to an experience of God's presence and of sharing in God's life. It is a very different kind of experience that attains to the absolute, to God, but through emptiness, as we saw. Just what Bernadette Roberts' experience of Christian mysticism was like is not a large part of this book, but it is striking that her no-self experiences began very young, and it is possible they colored her practice of the Christian contemplative life. While she recognizes the differences between these two journeys, she regards "the second movement as a continuation and completion of the first."[34] And she sees a possible progress of spiritual development starting "with the Christian experience of self's union with God... But when the self disappears forever into this Great Silence, we come upon the Buddhist discovery of no-self..."[35] "Then finally, we come upon the peak of Hindu discovery, namely: "that" which remains when there is no self is identical with "that" which Is, the one Existent that is all that Is."[36]

Once the no-self experience is seen as the same sort of experience as the Christian experience, or even a higher version of this same experience, then there is an almost irresistible movement towards reinterpreting Christian dogma in the light of this experience. This seems to be what is happening when Roberts says, "and when I finally saw 'that' which remains when there is no self, I thought of Christ and how he too had seen 'that' which remained – a seeing which is the resurrection itself."[37] Or "...even the seeing of the Trinitarian aspect of God is not the final step. The final step is where there is no Trinity at all, or when the aspects of God are seen as One and all that Is."[38]

Such an approach immediately runs into immense theological difficulty, and founders on the same misunderstanding that we saw before, which is the tendency to treat the Christian contemplative tradition as another path leading to enlightenment. But a real question that confronts us is whether the loss of the affective ego exists in the Christian mystical tradition, itself. Or put in another way, is there a loss of the affective ego that leads to contemplation?

St. John of the Cross and the Loss of the Affective Ego

The reading of St. John of the Cross (1542-1591), the great Carmelite mystic and poet, has always been a challenge for a variety of reasons: his profundity, the language he uses drawn from scholastic philosophy and theology, the misreadings of his writings that have accumulated over the centuries, and the many ways it is possible to read him, that is, as a poet or philosopher or a theologian, and so forth. But perhaps there is a new way in which we can read John of the Cross, and that is to see in him an example of how the loss of the affective ego plays a role in the beginning of Christian mystical experience.

Let's look at his book, *Dark Night of the Soul*. In the general schema of St. John's thought we must lose our normal way of functioning in order to go forward to deeper union with God. Thus, he describes a dark night of the senses, and an even more terrible dark night of the soul. But St. John meant these descriptions to serve an eminently positive purpose. The loss of self that he describes in great detail is meant to lead to a transformation of the soul by its union with God. But it is possible to read St. John's comments from our distinctive perspective of the loss of the affective ego. He is not talking about an ontological loss of the human soul. Such an idea never occurred to him. Nor, I believe, is he talking about a physical withdrawal from the world. What he is talking about is a loss of inordinate desires, and even perhaps a loss of the affective ego.

The soul, in order to go forth towards union with God, has to undergo a certain dying, St. John tells us, but it goes forth not from its physical life, but from its "affection,"[39] "its passions and desires with respect to their mischievous desires and motions."[40] We are confronted with an affective death, not a metaphysical one. In the time of our initial conversion the grace of God was like a loving mother. God makes the soul "find spiritual milk, sweet and delectable, in all the things of God, without any labor of its own and also great pleasure in spiritual exercises..."[41] The soul therefore is drawn to spiritual things by the consolation and pleasure it finds in them. And St. John, under the heading of the seven deadly sins, describes the great harm that this seeking after pleasure does.

But is there another way of looking at this? When John talks about the soul seeking pleasure and consolation, let's understand the soul as the affective ego. The death to all things and to itself that it must undergo is not in which things cease to exist, or even one in which the ego disappears. It is an affective death of the desires and attachments of the heart. The affective ego which formerly had been filling the mouth of its desires with the things of the world now, after conversion, fills it with spiritual things, but it does so driven by the pleasure and consolation it receives. It is drawn more by spiritual sweetness than by spiritual substance, more by consolation in the things of God than God, Himself. The soul weighs the things of the God in the scales of its own pleasure.

But the mouth of the affective ego is too small to truly swallow the things of God in themselves. The whole apparatus of the affective ego is destined to fail if spiritual progress is to be made. It must be weaned "from the breast of these sweetnesses and pleasures." This takes place by the advent of purgative contemplation, a dark fire which brings about the night of sense. Here there is a loss of the affective ego, and this is no trivial matter. It is the affect that glues the ego together and is intimately connected with a sense of self. This affective energy is the natural force of the faculties and sets them in motion more or less spontaneously in the hope of a reward of sweetness, consolation and gratification. It is this affective energy which drives the senses and imagination, and through them, the intellect and will. It is this affective energy that keeps the memory alive.

The night of sense, St. John tells us, is "the quenching of desire and affections with respect to all things."[42] "God has restrained its concupiscence and curbed its desires" so "it loses the strength of its passions and concupiscence and it becomes sterile."[43] "This aridity, too, quenches natural energy and concupiscence."[44] The natural affective energy of the ego leaves it, but in a very deep way, resulting from original sin, this natural affective energy is riddled with inordinate impulses, and so St. John writes: "natural energy and concupiscence."

The affective ego works through the faculties. It drives the faculties, and when the affective energy fails, the faculties are befuddled. They remain intact like the very things of the earth around us remain intact, and like the ego in the sense of a personal self remains intact. But they take on another character. They fail. They are no longer driven in their accustomed way. In relation to the life of prayer, the faculties were formerly employed by what John called meditation, by which he meant any exercise of the faculties in relationship to the things of God. When the faculties fail, meditation is no longer possible, but we have to understand this failure as an affective failure. Meditation has become dis-affected. It loses its flavor. We no longer have a taste for it. The affective energy has gone elsewhere. The sense impressions, images, thoughts and feelings, memories out of which we constructed our meditation are now flat. But the root of the faculties' failure is not the faculties, themselves. They work. Rather, it is the loss of the natural energy of the soul, the loss of the affective energy of the ego, that is at stake here.

This view of the affective ego allows us to approach John's description of the transition from meditation to mystical experience, or infused contemplation in a new way. If it is the natural affective energy that animates the ego and creates the concrete ego that we are so accustomed to, then the loss of this energy and that ego is deeply disorienting. We no longer have our normal way to judge our relationship with God, for our judgments were based, in large part, on the sweetness and consolation we experienced.

St. John's first sign of this transition from meditation to contemplation is that the lack of pleasure effects both the things of God and created things. The affective energy is lost in regard to everything. But since this loss might stem from "some disposition or melancholy humor," or we might say from depression that keeps us from any enjoyment, the second sign is important, which "is that the memory is ordinarily centered on God with painful care and solicitude..."[45]

This sign is equivalent to the third sign in St. John's *Ascent of Mount Carmel*. It is the actual dawning of the contemplative experience. The critical point is that while the faculties are suffering aridity, a deeper dimension of the soul is receiving contemplation. This contemplation is not always immediately conscious, in part because the affective ego, accustomed to the working of the faculties, is still searching and hoping that gratification will come through them, and a deeper dimension of the spirit is not yet "made ready or purged for such subtle pleasure" as comes from the contemplative experience, itself.

So at the beginning, this contemplation "is secret and hidden from the very person that experiences it." How could this be? How could there be an experience we don't experience? This paradox should not be resolved by imagining that contemplation is somehow not an experience – a matter of pure faith which should not be experienced. It is very definitely an experience, but not for the affective ego and the faculties. It is a new kind of experience that takes place in the depths of the spiritual unconscious. Contemplation is dark and secret from the perspective of the affective ego, but gives the soul an "inclination and desire to be alone and in quietness without being able to think of any particular thing or having the desire to do so."[46] In short, the experience of contemplation radiates from the depths of the soul and urges the ego to silence, and if the ego knows how to be quiet and not anxious about the exercise of its faculties in its old quest for gratification, it would "delicately experience this inward refreshment."

The soul can no longer meditate, "for God now begins to communicate Himself to it, no longer through sense, as He did aforetime, by means of reflections which joined and sundered its knowledge, but by pure spirit, into which consecutive reflections enter not; but He communicates Himself to it by an act of simple contemplation, to which neither the exterior nor the interior senses of the lower part of the soul can attain. From this time forward, therefore, imagination and fancy can find no support in any meditation, and can gain no foothold by means thereof."[47] Reflection which joined and sundered its knowledge describes the working of the discursive intellect with its apprehensions and judgments, but the simple act of contemplation cannot be grasped by this discursive activity. It takes place in a higher or deeper part of the soul and is another kind of knowledge. The pain and care described in the second sign arrived from the beginning of contemplation which darkens the faculties, and yet in a hidden way, preoccupies the soul with God whose presence is radiated from the spiritual unconscious and slowly rises to the point where it will, on occasion, enter the faculties from their roots and give them a conscious, yet not non-conceptual knowledge of the presence of God.

In the dark night of sense there is an inability to reflect, or work, or reason with the faculties. But this is an affective disability, not a general one, that is, one in which the faculties simply don't work. It is a disability in which the soul is unable to concentrate its "faculties with some degree of pleasure upon some object of meditation."[48] In this state "any operation and affection or attention wherein it may then seek to indulge will distract it and make it conscious of aridity and emptiness of self."[49] This is because, in trying to operate the faculties in their old mode, the soul becomes aware of their emptiness. If it leaves them alone, they function more or less, as circumstances demand, and it can rest in the new experience that is trying to make itself felt.

How, then, should the soul act at the time of contemplation? St. John gives us an explicit program. "What they must do is merely to leave the soul free and disencumbered and at rest from all knowledge and thought; troubling not themselves, in that state, about what they shall think or meditate upon, but contenting themselves with merely a peaceful and loving attentiveness toward God, and in being without anxiety, without the ability and without desire to have experience of Him or to perceive Him. For all these yearnings disquiet and distract the soul from the peaceful quiet and sweet ease of contemplation which is here granted to it."[50] The doing nothing is, of course, said in relationship to the faculties, and it would make no sense to say this if something else were not happening. The failure of the faculties is directly connected to the beginning of contemplation. Peaceful and loving attentiveness is not an activity of the faculties. It is not a way in which we actively do contemplation. The faculties can't do contemplation. They must "do nothing" and not be anxious about their ability to accomplish something. But I still think we need to read this in the affective order. They cannot feel or taste God in any way. Their limited and particular kinds of knowledge are ineffective. But this does not mean that the faculties fail in an absolute sense in their activities. If they did, a person would become completely non-functional. Peaceful and loving attentiveness is the loving receptivity of the contemplative experience welling up from the center of the soul. Therefore, John concludes: All these attempts to use the faculties in the old way of seeking pleasure and gratification distracts the soul "from the peaceful quiet and sweet ease of contemplation which is here granted

CHRISTIANITY IN THE CRUCIBLE

to it." Further, any operation, affection or attention with the faculties will distract the soul and "disquiet it and make it conscious of aridity and emptiness of self." The faculties will operate by themselves, as it were, and if we try to interrogate them as to the pleasure they are receiving, we see that the affective energy that once animated them is gone, and then we can be plunged into depression.

On the Nature of the Loss of the Affective Ego

Perhaps the most obvious feature to be found in the positive kinds of the loss of the affective ego is the way the functions behave. In their ordinary state, our functions of thinking and feeling, of sensation and intuition, the very working of the mind and imagination and senses, spontaneously and continually seek their goals, the objects which give them satisfaction. In doing so they generate a blanket of noise that tends to insulate us in our own cocoons of desires. We tend to see everything from the point of view of our ego desires.

But when the loss of the affective ego takes hold, the affective psychic energy that drove the functions begins to disappear. Now the functions stop acting spontaneously, and the level of the noise that they were generating falls off. This can be disconcerting, for we have spent our whole lives with their incessant activity and buffered by their humming. The ego begins to look around and try to figure out what has gone wrong. It looks to the loss of affective energy and tries to dream up ways to recapture it. As these attempts fail, the ego suffers from a general state of loss and depression.

In the midst of this loss of the affective ego, the functions still work normally when called upon. We think when we need to think, we feel when we need to feel. The problem is not the functions, themselves, but the failure of the energy that spontaneously activated them. Now the functions spring up when circumstances or the will demands, but they immediately withdraw when the job is done.

The loss of affective energy not only effects the functions, but our very sense of self, itself. The memory, for example, which in a certain way glues the ego together by joining the past with the present, also operates by affective energy. Our memories spontaneously remember because of the affective energy our memories contain. As the affective energy disappears, the memory remains functionally intact, but its spontaneous activity lessens dramatically. We can remember on command, but the past falls into a certain oblivion. New events do not reverberate in the memory in the same way. They happen. They even disturb the psyche, and then they fall away.

Ego consciousness, itself, which is at the very heart of our sense of ourselves, is effected, as well, because it is built on the activity of the functions. The spontaneous activity of the functions played a large role in the spontaneous generation of ego consciousness. Now with the loss of the affective energy ego-consciousness diminishes. This process leaves another kind of ego in its place. It is an ego that is not constantly driven by its desires. It is a quieter ego without the incessant worrying of the functions. In some ways, it might even be said to be a more vulnerable ego, for it is without its habitual protective wall of noise that kept out the noise of others. More positively, it seems to see more clearly the way things actually are. The old screens that surrounded the ego have become more transparent. Perhaps it suffers more from the impact of the world around it, and from the affects that still arise out of the unconscious. The ego is not fired up by its desires, but has to intend to go forward. From a psychological point of view there has been a decentering of the ego.

But underlying this general phenomenological description of what we are calling the loss of the affective ego is a deeper question. Even if we conclude that the loss of the affective ego can be a positive reality, we still have to ask ourselves just what it is in service of. It seems that there are three chief possibilities, or interior goals. The first is what Jung called wholeness, or psychological individuation. The second is enlightenment, and the third is Christian mystical experience.

The Spiritual Unconscious

On the negative side, the loss of the affective ego leads to various kinds of depression or affective disorders. On the positive side, it is an indication of the decentering of the ego that serves the goals we have just seen. The whole notion of such a loss of the affective ego implies, at least within the framework of Jungian psychology, that the energy has gone somewhere. If the ego is being decentered, it is because a new center is developing, and the dimension where these new centers are to be found could be called the spiritual unconscious. If there are

CHRISTIANITY IN THE CRUCIBLE

three major positive goals that the loss of the affective ego can serve, then this unconscious could be said to contain three dimensions. There will be a psychological unconscious, which is the realm explored by depth psychology, but there is also a metaphysical unconscious, and a mystical one.

It is in the realm of the metaphysical unconscious that we find the philosophical intuition of being, and the various forms of enlightenment, or nondual experience. They dwell side by side, and then can, and ought to, enter into deep conversation with each other. But it is wrong to imagine that one can swallow the other. It is even more mistaken to believe that the psychological unconscious, or the mystical unconscious, can be identified with the metaphysical unconscious. It is entirely possible to have metaphysical insights, or openings to enlightenment, without having arrived at the psychological maturity that comes with individuation, and neither are these insights equivalent to mystical experience. And the reverse is true, as well. We have to avoid collapsing these interior universes that make up the spiritual unconscious into each other. There is no doubt that these centers strongly interact, for they are all parts of the one psyche, but if we identify them, our interior world will become impoverished.

Enlightenment and the Experience of No-Self

When we looked at enlightenment from a metaphysical point of view, the central question was whether what was experience was, in reality, or in itself, nondual, or whether the nonduality resulted from the very means to attain this experience. We have reached a similar point in looking at the question of the existence of the self. There is no doubt that there are situations in which we dramatically experience the loss of our old selves. But does this mean that metaphyiscally there was no human self, or divine self, to begin with, or simply that we experience a loss of the affective ego? If we understand the experience of no-self as the loss of the affective ego, then I believe that the essential point of the East is safeguarded. The journey towards liberation demands a certain death of the ego, but this death should not be read in a univocal ontological register and put into opposition with a Christian view of God and the soul.

Notes

1. Washburn, Michael. *The Ego and the Dynamic Ground*, p. 171.
2. Ann Faraday in "Towards a No-Self Psychology." p. xx.
3. Wren-Lewis, John. "Aftereffects of Near-Death Experiences," p. 109.
4. Harding, D.E. in *On Having No Head*.
5. Segal, Suzanne. *Collision with the Infinite*, p. 54-55.
6. Ibid., p. 109.
7. Ibid., p. 114.
8. Ibid.
9. Ibid., p. 123.
10. Ibid., p. 130.
11. Ibid.
12. Ibid.
13. Von Franz, Marie-Louise. *The Inferior Function*, p. 63-64.
14. St. Romain, Philip. *Kundalini Energy and Christian Spirituality*, p. 19-20
15. Ibid., p. 21.
16. Ibid., p. 25.
17. Ibid., p. 26.
18. Ibid., p. 29.
19. Ibid., p. 30.
20. Ibid., p. 44.
21. Roberts, Bernadette. *The Experience of No-Self*, p. 24.
22. Ibid., p. 31.
23. Ibid., p. 34.
24. Ibid., p. 67.
25. Ibid., p. 75.
26. Ibid.
27. Ibid.
28. Ibid., p. 78.
29. Ibid., p. 81.
30. Ibid.
31. Ibid., p. 83.
32. Ibid., p. 86.
33. Ibid., p. 87.
34. Ibid., p. 106.
35. Ibid., p. 109.
36. Ibid.
37. Ibid., p. 131.
38. Ibid., p. 132.
39. John of the Cross. *The Dark Night of the Soul*, p. 36.
40. Ibid., p. 37.
41. Ibid., p. 38.
42. Ibid., p. 75.
43. Ibid., p. 83.
44. Ibid., p. 86.
45. Ibid., p. 64.
46. Ibid., p. 66.
47. Ibid., p. 67-68.
48. Ibid., p. 69.
49. Ibid., p. 71-72.
50. Ibid., p. 71.

SUMMARY AND CONCLUSIONS

CHRISTIANITY IN THE CRUCIBLE

Here is the story we have seen unfold. Catholics have gone to the East, and penetrated deeply into the inner spirit of enlightenment, as witnessed by the Catholic Zen teachers of the Sanbo Kyodan, and people like Abhishiktananda. But this exciting spiritual adventure has played itself out against the background of the problematical relationship that some of them have had with their own Christian metaphysical, theological and mystical traditions. This has led them to reinterpret Christianity in the light of the nondual experience of enlightenment that has dazzled them, and in this way, obscure Christianity's distinctive nature.

This East-West drama has not evolved in isolation. It is an integral part of the post-Vatican theological scene, and as such, it shares common traits with what I called a reaction theology, or a theology without a net. It is also allied with some of the theological currents that have emerged in the debate over religious pluralism.

Christian Mysticism and Metaphysics

All this has created an atmosphere in which the two great East-West dialogues, the metaphysical and the mystical, have become more difficult to pursue. The way to Christian metaphysics is barred for it is assumed that a philosophical metaphysics is invalid because it makes use of concepts. The mystical conversation is ruled out, as well, because its interpersonal character is denied. In each case, the experience of nonduality and its non-conceptual nature is held up as the supreme norm by which these other ways of knowing are judged.

The positive benefits for Christianity from the East-West dialogue are undeniable. The crucible of dialogue holds out the possibility of purifying Christianity from some of its institutional faults. There it can learn a certain humility in the face of the wisdom and goodness of its dialogue partners, and it can realize that the visible Catholic Church does not have a monopoly on how God's universal salvific will works itself out in the concrete. In that crucible the Catholic Church could learn to reach out to its brothers and sisters in other religions with an open heart, and cooperate with them in many important endeavors.

The experience of enlightenment, itself, is a beautiful multi-faceted jewel that has been appreciated in different ways by Hinduism, Buddhism, Taoism and Islam, and it could greatly enrich Christianity, as well. But unfortunately, some of the Catholics who have gone to the East and have come back to Christianity bearing this wonderful gift, have also wrapped it in various presuppositions that make it much more difficult for Christians to receive it. The chief of these presuppositions is what we have been seeing all along. It is assumed that all religions are paths to the one nondual summit, and thus, all their conceptualizations, including the central doctrines of Christianity, are but skillful means pointing to that ineffable experience.

Catholic Theology

At the root of the problems we have seen in the Catholic participation in East-West dialogue, as well as in a theology without a net and religious pluralism, is the question of faith. In the wake of the Second Vatican Council the glaring faults of the institutional Church became visible, and people who had entrusted themselves to the institution with the intent of trusting themselves to God and the life of faith, felt disillusioned and betrayed. They were told that the way to holiness was to be found in God's will and God's will was to be found in obeying those who stood above them in the ecclesiastical hierarchy. Unfortunately, in the name of God's will they suffered at the very human hands of men. Therefore they needed to liberate themselves from this paternalism that stunted their psychological and spiritual growth. The institution that they were rebelling against had confused Christian faith with its more fallible human presentations of it. Now those who reacted against it, struck out not only at the very real faults of the institution, but sometimes at the central message that it was proclaiming. It was as if they said if the Church in the persons of its leaders could act in a way that harmed those who had given themselves most intimately to it, then how could the message they proclaimed be trusted. In this way the delicate movement toward adult faith which takes place in the heart and demands that we reach out in love and entrust ourselves to God becomes more difficult. A loss of trust in the institution becomes a loss of trust in the Christian message, and the theology that emerges reflects this. This kind of painful drama played a part in the exodus from priestly and religious life, and may have even had a covert role in the sorry spectacle of priestly sexual dysfunction,[1] and it certainly seems to be active today in the theology without a net that we have looked at.

I am not saying that the challenge of faith today is not a serious one. It is. The Catholic faith we have received from the past and have grown up with has to become our faith and this means we have to examine it. Can we really believe in a personal God who surrounds us with love? Can we believe in Jesus as the only begotten Son of God Who, as one of us, lived and died and rose from the dead? But there is a difference between doing this with trepidation and prayer as we try to reach out to God, and doing it in an atmosphere tinged with emotional and intellectual bias against faith. But to adequately address this question of faith will not be easy. We need to admit the very real faults of the Church in which faith was, and sometimes still is, presented in an all too materialized and human form, even tinged, at times, with cult-like behavior.[2] At the same time, we should not imagine that a theology of reaction is an adequate response to this problem. The challenge is to distinguish faith, both in its essential content and how it operates from its counterfeits.

Faith is not simply the acceptance of what reason has told us. It is something much more mysterious and interior which addresses our hearts and makes demands on our ability to love. It is an invitation to reach out to God who is the mystery of love, and who is already warming our hearts. Nor is faith contentless, or opaque to the understanding by nature, for it tries to teach us something of what that mystery is. It is certainly time to transcend the polarizations that have locked up much of the Church's energy since the time of the Second Vatican Council so that that energy can be used for the contemplation of, and the entering into, this mystery of love.

Christian Enlightenment?

The very life of Christian prayer and contemplation grows out of our understanding of Christian faith, and in turn, nourishes that understanding. This interior life takes place in an atmosphere of interpersonal love, and expresses itself as a dialogue, whether in words or interior thoughts and feelings, or a wordless reaching out in love. What will happen to it if we imagine that any I-Thou relationship must be overcome, and Christian prayer is a somewhat childish misunderstanding of a higher and deeper nonduality?

What are we to say, then, about Christians practicing Eastern forms of meditation? In themselves, they can be extremely valuable because enlightenment can be understood as a deep metaphysical mysticism which has God as the author of being as its goal, and it can even be seen as the foretaste of our essential human destiny.

But in actual practice Catholics are often introduced to Eastern forms of meditation by Easterners, or Catholics who have gone East and brought back these kinds of meditation in the problematical ways we have been looking at. Given this state of affairs, Christians should consider creating what could be called a Christian enlightenment. In a way that is analogous to Christian philosophy this does not mean an enlightenment that is somehow Christian in content. That would make no sense. But rather, it is an enlightenment that is sought for and takes place in a Christian context, and so it remains open to Christian metaphysics, theology and mysticism. Then Christians would not have undertake over and over again the difficult and dangerous task of unwrapping Eastern forms of enlightenment from these presuppositions. Another way of saying this is that we cannot receive these treasures of the East as Christians without a firm grasp of our own deep spiritual traditions.

If such a journey to enlightenment could be carried out in a Christian atmosphere, then the light of the different wisdoms of the East and West, whether metaphysical, theological or mystical, could dwell harmoniously in the same depths of the spiritual unconscious, and strengthen and enrich each other. They would be distinguished from each other in order to be united.

Notes

1. Freburger, William. "A deeper clerical problem than sex," in *National Catholic Reporter*, April 16, 1993, p. 17.
2. "Diabolical Possession and Catholic Cults? The Lack of Psychological Awareness and the Materialization of Belief in the Catholic Church" at http://www.innerexplorations.com/chtheomortext/lack.htm

Bibliography

Abhishiktananda. (Henri Le Saux). 1986. *La montée au fond du coeur. Le journal intime du moine chrétien-sannyasi hindou*. Paris, France: O.E.I.L. English translation: (1998). *Ascent to the Depth of the Heart. The Spiritual Diary (1948-1973) of Swami Abhishiktananda (Dom H. Le Saux)*. I.S.P.C.K.

Aitken, Robert and David Steindl-Rast. (1994) *The Ground We Share: Everyday Practice, Buddhist and Christian*. Ligouri , MO: Triumph Books.

al-Attas, Syed Muhammad Naquib. (1995) *Prolegomena to the Metaphysics of Islam*. Kuala Lumpur: International Institute of Islamic Thought and Civilization (ISTAC).

Amaladoss, Michael. (1990) *Making All Things New: Dialogue, Pluralism, and Evangelization in Asia*. Maryknoll, NY: Orbis Books.

AMA Samy, Gen-Un-Ken. *Why did Bodhidharma Come to the West? On the Transmission of Zen to the West*. Bodhi Zendo, Kodaikanal, India. (unpublished manuscript in English)

Arraj, James. (1986) *St. John of the Cross and Dr. C.G. Jung*. Chiloquin, OR: Inner Growth Books.

_____ (1988) *The Inner Nature of Faith*. Chiloquin, OR: Inner Growth Books.

_____ (1993) *Mysticism, Metaphysics and Maritain*. Chiloquin, OR: Inner Growth Books.

_____ (1994) *Mind Aflame*. Chiloquin, OR: Inner Growth Books.

_____ (1996) *The Mystery of Matter*. Chiloquin, OR: Inner Growth Books.

Balasuriya, Tissa, OMI. (1997) *Mary and Human Liberation: The Story and the Text*. Harrisburg, PA: Trinity Press International.

Bäumer, Bettina. (1991) "A Journey with the Unknown" in *Spirituality in Interfaith Dialogue*, edited by Tosh Arai, and Wesley Ariarajah. Maryknoll, NY: Orbis Books.

_____ (May, 2000) "Abhishiktananda and the Challenge of Hindu-Christian Experience." *MID Bulletin*, Issue #64, p. 34-41.

Blackstone, Judith. (1997) *The Enlightenment Process: How It Deepens Your Experience of Self, Body and Community.* Rockport, MA: Element.

Buddhist-Christian Dialogue in Action: Boston 1992: Video. (1992) Chiloquin, OR: Inner Growth Videos.

Buddhist-Christian Dialogue in Action: Chicago 1996: Video. (1997) Chiloquin, OR: Inner Growth Videos.

Buddhist-Christian Dialogue in Action: Tacoma 2000: Video. (2000) Chiloquin, OR: Inner Growth Videos.

Burrell, David B. "Thomas Aquinas (1225-1274) and Mulla Sadra Shirazi (980/1572-1050/1640) and The Primacy of Esse/Wujud in Philosophical Theology." http://www.mullasadra.org/papers/david_b_burrell.htm.

Carey, Patrick W. and Earl C. Muller, S.J., editors. (1997) *Theological Education in the Catholic Tradition: Contemporary Challenges.* New York: A Crossroad Herder Book.

Ciolek, T. Matthew. Web pages on the Sanbokyodan School at http://www.ciolek.com/WWWVLPages/ZenPages/HaradaYasutani.html

Congregation for the Doctrine of the Faith. (2000) *Declaration "Dominus Iesus" on the Unicity and Salvific Universality of Jesus Christ and the Church.*

_____ (2001) "Notification relative to the book of Jacques Dupuis, *Toward a Christian Theology of Religious Pluralism.*

Corbin, Henry. (1981) *La Philosophie Iranienne Islamique aux XVIIe et XVIIIe siècles.* Paris, France: Éditions Buchet/Chastel.

Corless, Roger. (July 27 – August 3, 1996) "Dual Practice with Form and Without Form: The Doctrinal Consequences." Talk given at the Fifth International Buddhist-Christian Conference at De Paul University, Chicago.

_____ (1996) *Profiles in Buddhist-Christian Dialogue: Roger Corless: Video.* Chiloquin, OR: Inner Growth Videos.

Coward, Harold, editor. (1989) *Hindu-Christian Dialogue: Perspectives and Encounters.* Maryknoll, NY: Orbis.

Dalai Lama. (1962) *My Land, My People.* London: Weidenfels and Nicolson.

Dark Zen and The Zennists. (1994-1998) "Sanbo Kyodan Zen: The heritage of Western Zen" at http://www.darkzen.com

D'Costa, Gavin, Editor. (1990) *Christian Uniqueness Reconsidered: The Myth of a Pluralistic Theology of Religions.* Maryknoll, NY: Orbis Books.

De Mello, Anthony, S.J. (1978) *Sadhana: A Way to God: Christian Exercises in Eastern Form.* St. Louis, MO: The Institute of Jesuit Sources.

Desideri, Ippolito, SJ. (1937) *An Account of Tibet: The Travels of Ippolito Desideri of Pistoia, S.J., 1712-1727.* London: George Routledge & Sons, Ltd.

Dourley, John. (1984) *The Illness That We Are: A Jungian Critique of Christianity.* Inner City.

_____ (1987) *Love, Celibacy, and the Inner Marriage.* Inner City.

Dumoulin, Heinrich. (1963) A History of Zen Buddhism. Boston: Beacon Press.

_____ (1979) *Zen Enlightenment: Origins and Meaning.* NY and Tokyo: Weatherhill.

_____ (1990) *Zen Buddhism: A History. Volume 2.* NY: Macmillan Publishing Company.

Dupuis, Jacques, S.J. (1997*)* *Toward a Christian Theology of Religious Pluralism.* Maryknoll, NY: Orbis.

_____ (1991) *Jesus Christ at the Encounter of World Religions.* Maryknoll, NY: Orbis.

Escalante, Jason. "Islamic Metaphysics and Thomism: A Visit with Jason Escalante"
http://www.innerexplorations.com/philtext/islamic.htm

Evans-Wentz, W.Y., editor. (1958) *Tibetan Yoga and Secret Doctrines.* London, Oxford, NY: Oxford University Press.

_____ (1960) *The Tibetan Book of the Dead.* London, Oxford, NY: Oxford University Press.

Faraday, Ann. "Towards a No-Self Psychology." (this article will appear in *Voices on the Threshold of Tomorrow*, edited by Georg Feuerstein)

Franz, Marie Louise von. (1971) "The Inferior Function" in *Lectures on Jung's Typology.* NY: Spring Publications.

Fredericks, James L. (1999) *Faith among Faiths; Christian Theology and Non-Christian Religions.* NY/Mahawah, NJ: Paulist Press.

Gardet, Louis and Olivier Lacombe. (1981) *L'Experience du soi.* Paris: Desclée de Brouwer.

Gebara, Ivone. (1999*) Longing for Running Water: Ecofeminism and Liberation.* Minneapolis: Fortress Press.

Gilson, Etienne. (1955*) History of Christian Philosophy in the Middle Ages.* NY: Random House.

Give, Bernard de. (1999) "Colloque chrétiens-bouddhistes sur la Non-Dualité" at http://www.scourmont.be/degive/non-dualite.htm

Gleason, Philip. (1995) *Contending with Modernity: Catholic Higher Education in the Twentieth Century.* New York and Oxford: Oxford University Press.

Goss, Robert E. (1998) "Catholic and Dge Lugs Pa Scholasticism" in *Scholasticism*, edited by José Ignacio Cabezón. State University of New York Press.

Grant, Sara. (1991) *Towards an Alternative Theology: Confessions of a Non-Duality Christian.* Bangalore, India: Asian Trading Corporation.

Griffiths, Bede. (1992) *Exploring the Christian-Hindu Dialogue: Bede Griffiths & Russill Paul: Video.* Chiloquin, OR: Inner Growth Videos.

Grob, James. (1992) *Blossoms of Silence: Video.* Chiloquin, OR: Inner Growth Videos.

Guarino, Thomas. (1996) "Postmodernity and Five Fundamental Theological Issues" in *Theological Studies* No. 57 (1996), pp. 654-689.

Habito, Ruben. (1989) *Total Liberation: Zen Spirituality and the Social Dimension.* Maryknoll, NY: Orbis.

_____ (1990) "*In Memoriam*: A Tribute to Yamada Koun Roshi" in *Buddhist-Christian Studies*, Vol. 10, 1990, pp. 231-237.

_____ (1993) *Healing Breath: Zen Spirituality for a Wounded Earth.* Maryknoll, NY: Orbis.

_____ (1999) *Profiles in Buddhist-Christian Dialogue: Ruben Habito.* Chiloquin, OR: Inner Growth Videos.

Hackett, David. G. (1996) *The Silent Dialogue: Zen Letters to a Trappist Abbot.* New York: Continuum.

Haight, Roger. (1999) *Jesus: Symbol of God.* Maryknoll, NY: Orbis Books.

Hand, Thomas. (1999) *Profiles in Buddhist-Christian Dialogue:*

Thomas Hand. Chiloquin, OR: Inner Growth Videos.
Harding, D.E. (1986) *On Having No Head: Zen and the Rediscovery of the Obvious.* London: Arkana.
Hawk, Patrick, C.Ss.R. (May/June 1989) "The Pathless Path" *in The Catholic World,* pp. 129-131.
Hick, John and Paul F. Knitter, Editors. (1987) *The Myth of Christian Uniqueness: Toward a Pluralistic Theology of Religions.* Maryknoll, NY: Orbis Books.
Izutsu, Toshihiko. (1971) *The Concept and Reality of Existence.* Tokyo: The Keio Institute of Cultural and Linguistic Studies.
_____ (1982) *Toward a Philosophy of Zen Buddhism.* Boulder, CO: Prajna Press.
_____ (1983) *Sufism and Taoism: A Comparative Study of Key Philosophical Concepts.* Berkeley, Los Angeles, London: University of California Press.
_____ (1994) "The Basic Structure of Metaphysical Thinking in Islam" in *Creation and the Timeless Order of Things: Essays in Islamic Mystical Philosophy.* Ashland, OR: White Cloud Press.
Jäger, Willigis. (1987) *The Way to Contemplation.* NY: Paulist Press.
_____ (1994) *Contemplation: A Christian Path.* Liguori, MO: Triumph Books.
_____ (1995) *Search for the Meaning of Life: Essays and Reflections on the Mystical Experience.* Liguori, MO: Triumph Books.
John of the Cross, Saint. (1959) *Dark Night of the Soul.* Translated by E. Allison Peers. Garden City, NY: Image Books.
_____ (1960). *Poems.* Translated by Roy Campbell. Baltimore, MD: The Penguin Classics.
Johnston, William. (1989) "All and Nothing: St. John of the Cross and the Christian-Buddhist Dialogue" in *Areopagus Epiphany,* pp. 18-24.
_____ (1991) *Letters to Contemplatives.* NY: Orbis Books.
_____ (1995) *Mystical Theology: The Science of Love.* London: HarperCollins Publishers.
Jonas, Robert. (1996) *Profiles in Buddhist-Christian Dialogue: Robert Jonas.* Chiloquin, OR: Inner Growth Videos.
Kadowaki, Kakichi, S.J. (Dec. 1966) "Ways of Knowing: A Buddhist-Thomist Dialogue" in *International Philosophical Quarterly,* Vol. VI, No. 4, pp. 574-595.

_____ (1980) *Zen and the Bible: A Priest's Experience*. London, Boston and Hemley: Routledge & Kegan Paul.

Kapleau, Philip. (1965) *The Three Pillars of Zen: Teaching, Practice and Enlightenment*. Boston: Beacon Press.

Katz, Richard. *Education for Transcendence: !Kia-Healing with the Kalahari !Kung*. A revision of the chapter appearing in Katz's *Preludes to Growth*. Free Press, 1973.

Keenan, John. (1989) *The Meaning of Christ: A Mahayana Theology*. Maryknoll, NY: Orbis Books.

Kelsang Gyatso, Geshe. (1982) *Clear Light of Bliss: A Commentary to the Practice of Mahamudra in Vajrayana Buddhism*. London: Tharpa Publications.

Kennedy, Robert E. (1995) *Zen Spirit, Christian Spirit: The Place of Zen in Christian Life*. NY: Continuum.

_____(2000) *Zen Gifts to Christians*. NY, London: Continuum.

Khenpo Rinpoche, Nyoshul and Lama Surya Das. (1995) *Natural Great Perfection: Dzogchen Teachings and Vajra Songs*. Ithaca, NY: Snow Lion Publications.

Knitter, Paul. (1985) *No Other Name? A Critical Survey of Christian Attitudes Toward the World Religions*. Maryknoll, NY: Orbis Books.

_____ (1996) *Jesus and the Other Names: Christian Mission and Global Responsibility*. Maryknoll, NY: Orbis Books.

Krishna, Gopi. (1985) *Kundalini: The Evolutionary Energy in Man*. Boston & London: Shambhala Publications.

Küng, Hans. (1986) *Christianity and the World Religions: Paths of Dialogue with Islam, Hinduism and Buddhism*. NY, London: Doubleday.

_____ (1990) "God's Self-Renunciation and Buddhist Emptiness" in *Buddhist Emptiness and Christian Trinity: Essays and Explorations*. Edited by Roger Corless and Paul F. Knitter. NY and Mahwah, NJ: Paulist Press.

Lachs, Stuart. (1994) "Coming Down from the Zen Clouds: A Critique of the Current State of American Zen." at http://www.human.toyogakuenu.ac.jp/~acmuller/articles/USZEN3.htm

Lacombe, Olivier. (1979) *Indianité: Etudes historiques et comparatives sur la pensée indienne*. Parks: Société d'édition "Les Belles

Lettres".
Lassalle, Hugo Enomiya. (1974) *Zen Meditation for Christians*. LaSalle, IL: Open Court.
_____ (1988) *Living in the New Consciousness*. Boston & Shaftesbury: Shambhala.
Lee, Jiuan A. and Thomas G. Hand. (1990) *A Taste of Water: Christianity Through Taoist-Buddhist Eyes*. NY: Paulist Press.
Loy, David. (1988) *Nonduality: A Study in Comparative Philosophy*. New Haven and London: Yale University Press.
_____ (1990) "The Nonduality of Life and Death," in *Philosophy East and West*, 40, No. 2.
_____ (1990) "A Zen Cloud? Comparing Zen Koan Practice with *The Cloud of Unknowing*" in *Buddhist-Christian Studies* 9, University of Hawaii Press, January 1990.
_____ (1992) "Trying to Become Real: A Buddhist Critique of Some Secular Heresies" in *Internatioanl Philosophical Quarterly*, vol. 32, no. 4, December 1992.
_____ (1993) "Indra's Postmodern Net" *in Philosophy East and West*, vol. 43, no. 3, July, 1993.
_____ (1996) *Lack and Transcendence: Death and Life in Psychotherapy, Existentialism, and Buddhism*. Atlantic Highlands, NJ: Humanities Press.
_____ (1998) *David Loy: Zen Philosopher & Social Critic: Video*. Chiloquin, OR: Inner Growth Videos.
_____ (2000) *Questions at the Heart of the Buddhist-Christian Dialogue: David Loy and James Arraj: Video*. Chiloquin, OR: Inner Growth Videos.
MacInnes, Elaine. (1996) *Light Sitting in Light: A Christian's Experience in Zen*. Fount, An Imprint of Harper Collins Publishers.
Maguire, Daniel C. (1993) *The Moral Core of Judaism and Christianity: Reclaiming the Revolution*. Minneapolis: Fortress Press.
Maritain, Jacques. (1952) "The Immanent Dialectic of the First Act of Freedom" in *The Range of Reason*. NY: Charles Scribner's Sons.
Matus, Thomas. (1984) *Yoga and the Jesus Prayer Tradition: An Experiment in Faith*. Paulist Press.
Meadow, Mary Jo and Kevin Culligan. (1987) "Congruent Spiritual Paths: Christian Carmelite and Theravadan Buddhist Vipassana" in *The Journal of Transpersonal Psychology*, 1987, Vol. 19, No. 2,

pp. 181-196.

Merton, Thomas. (1968) *Zen and the Birds of Appetite*. A New Directions Book.

_____ (1983) "The Inner Experience. Notes on Contemplation" in three parts, in *Cistercian Studies*.

_____ (1985) *The Hidden Ground of Love*. Letters of Thomas Merton. NY: Farrar, Straus & Giroux.

_____ (1992) *The Springs of Contemplation: A Retreat at the Abbey of Gethsemani*. NY: Farrar, Straus, Giroux.

Mitchell, Donald W. (1991) *Spirituality and Emptiness: The Dynamics of Spiritual Life in Buddhism and Christianity*. NY: Paulist Press.

Mitchell, Donald. (1996) *Profiles in Buddhist-Christian Dialogue: Don Mitchell: Video*. Chiloquin, OR: Inner Growth Videos.

Mitchell, Donald W. and James A. Wiseman, OSB, editors. (1998) *The Gethsemani Encounter: A Dialogue on the Spiritual Life by Buddhist and Christian Monastics*. NY: Continuum.

Mommaers, Paul and Jan Van Bragt. (1995) *Mysticism Buddhist and Christian: Encounters with Jan van Ruusbroec*. NY: Crossroad.

Monastic Interreligious Dialogue in North America: An Evaluation by the North American Board for East-West Dialogue: Complete Summary. July 24, 1992.

Morewedge, Parviz. (1973) *The Metaphysical of Avicenna (ibn Sina)*. NY: Columbia University Press.

Morris, James Winston. (1981) *The Wisdom of the Throne: An Introduction to the Philosophy of Mulla Sadra*. Princeton, NJ: Princeton University Press.

Morwood, Michael. (1998) *Tomorrow's Catholic: Understanding God and Jesus in a New Millennium*. Mystic, CT: Twenty-Third Publications.

_____ (2001) *Is Jesus God? Finding Our Faith*. NY: A Crossroad Book.

Nasr, Seyyed Hossein. (1964) *Three Muslim Sages: Avicenna – Suhrawardi – Ibn 'Arabi*. Cambridge, MA: Harvard University Press.

_____ (1978) *Sadr al-Din Shirazi and his Transcendent Theosophy: Background, Life and Work*. Tehran, Iran: Imperial Iranian Academy of Philosophy.

_____ (1981) *Knowledge and the Sacred.* The Gifford Lectures, 1981. NY: Crossroad.

_____ (1989) "Existence (*wujud*) and Quiddity (*mahiyyah*) in Islamic Philosophy" in *International Philosophical Quarterly*, Vol. 29, pp. 409-428.

Nasr, Seyyed Hossein and Oliver Leaman, editors. (1996) "History of Islamic Philosophy, Part I " from *Routledge History of World Philosophies*, Vol. 1. London and NY: Routledge.

Nisargadatta Maharaj, Sri. (1973) *I Am That: Talks with Sri Nisargaddat Maharaj.* Durham, NC: The Acorn Press.

Nityananda Giri, Swami. (May, 2000) "Sadguru Sri Gnananda" in *MID Bulletin*, Issue #64, pp. 28-33.

Noonan, John. (1950) "The Existentialism of Etienne Gilson" in *New Scholasticism*, v. 24, No. 4, Oct. 1950.

Norbu, Namkhai. (1992) *Dream Yoga and the Practice of Natural Light.* Ithaca, NY: Snow Lion Publications.

Nugent, Christopher. (May 1993) "Satori in St. John of the Cross" in *Bulletin of Monastic Interreligious Dialogue.*

Okumura, Ichiro. (1994) *Awakening to Prayer.* Washington, DC: ICS Publications.

O'Leary, Joseph Stephen. (1985) *Questioning Back: The Overcoming of Metaphysics in Christian Tradition.* Minneapolis, Chicago, NY: A Seabury Book. Winston Press.

_____ (1996) *Religious Pluralism and Christian Truth.* Edinburgh University Press.

_____ Book review of Paul Mommaers and Jan Van Bragt's *Mysticism Buddhist and Christian. Japanese Journal of Religious Studies* 23/1-2, pp. 200-204.

O'Murchu, Diarmuid. (1997) *Quantum Theology.* NY: Crossroad.

Patchett, Joseph. (1991) *A Contemplative Journey: Video.* Chiloquin, OR: Inner Growth Videos.

Pelphrey, Brant. (1989) "A Journey Nowhere" (A review of Bernadetts Roberts' *The Experience of No-Self.*) in *Areopagus Epiphany* 1989, p. 42.

Pseudo-Dionysius. (1987) New York and Mahwah: Paulist Press.

Rabten, Geshé. (1983) *Echoes of Voidness.* London: Wisdom Pub.

_____ (1989) *Song of the Profound View.* London: Wisdom Pub.

Rahman, Fazlur. (1975) *The Philosophy of Mulla Sadra.* Albany, NY:

State University of New York Press.
Rahner, Karl. (1964) *The Dynamic Element in the Church*. Herder and Herder.
_____ (1976) *Theological Investigations*. Volume XIV: Ecclesiology, Questions in the Church, The Church in the World. NY: The Seabury Press.
_____ (1986) *Karl Rahner in Dialogue*. NY: Crossroad.
_____ (1989) *Faith in a Wintry Season*. NY: Crossroad.
Ralston, Helen. (1987) "Christian Ashrams: A New Religious Movement in Contemporary India" in *Studies in Religion and Society*, Vol. 20. Lewiston/Queenston: The Edwin Mellen Press.
Reynolds, John Myrdhin, translator with introduction and notes. (1989) *Self-Liberation Through Seeing With Naked Awareness: Being an Introduction to the Nature of One's Own Mind and ...* Station Hill Press.
_____ (1996) *The Golden Letters: The Three Statements of Garab Dorje, the first teacher of Dzogchen...* Ithaca, NY: Snow Lion Publications.
Roberts, Bernadette. (1982) *The Experience of No-Self: A Contemplative Journey*. Sunspot, NM: Iroquois House.
Ryan, Thomas. (2001) *Prayer of Heart & Body: Meditation and Yoga as Christian Spiritual Practice*. Mahwah, NJ: Paulist Press.
Sabzavari, Mulla Haji. (1977) Mohaghegh, Mehdi and Toshihijo Izutsu, translators. *The Metaphysics of Sabzavari*. Delmar, NY: Caravan Books.
Sadra Shirazi, Molla. Ed. Henry Corbin. (1964) *Le Livre des Pénétrations métaphysiques*. Teheran: Departement d'Iranologie de l'Institut Franco-Iranien and Paris: Librairie d'Amerique et d'Orient Adrien-Maisonneuve.
St. Romain, Philip. (1991) *Kundalini Energy and Christian Spirituality*. NY: Crossroad.
_____ (1991) *Christian Prayer & Kundalini: Video*. Chiloquin, OR: Inner Growth Videos.
_____ (1991) *Kundalini Energy and Christian Spirituality: Video*. Chiloquin, OR: Inner Growth Videos.
Schoof, Mark, OP. (1970) *A Survey of Catholic Theology (1800-1970)*. New York, NY: Paulist Newman Press.
Schuon, Frithjof. (1948/1975) *The Transcendent Unity of Religions*.

NY: Harper Torchbooks.
Segal, Suzanne. (1996) *Collision with the Infinite: A Life Beyond the Personal Self.* San Diego, CA: Blue Dove Press.
Sharif, M. M. (1966) *A History of Muslim Philosophy*, Vol. Two. Wiesbaden: Otto Harrassowitz.
Shark, Robert H. (1995) "Sanbokyodan: Zen and the Way of the New Religions" in *Japanese Journal of Religious Studies*, 22/3-4, pp. 417-458.
Siddheswarananda, Swami. (1998) *Hindu Thought & Carmelite Mysticism.* Translated by William Buchanan. Delhi, India: Motilal Banarsidass Publishers.
Sivananda, Swami. *Kundalini Yoga.* At www.sivanandalshq.org/download/kundalini.htm
Smith, Margaret. (1978) *The Way of the Mystics: The Early Christian Mystics and the Rise of the Sufis.* NY: Oxford University Press.
Stuart, James. (1995) *Swami Abhishiktananda: His life told through his letters.* ISPCK.
Sullivan, Francis A. (1992) *Salvation Outside the Church?: Tracing the History of the Catholic Response.* NY and Mahway, NJ: Paulist Press.
Takahashi, Shinkichi. (1970) *Afterimages: Zen Poems.* Selected and translated by Lucien Stryk and Takashi Ikemoto. Chicago, IL: The Swallow Press.
Teasdale, Wayne. (1985) *Essays in Mysticism: Explorations into Contemplative Experience.* Lake Worth, FL: Sunday Publications, Inc.
_____ (1987) *Toward a Christian Vedanta: The Encounter of Hinduism and Christianity according to Bede Griffiths.* Bangalore, India: Asian Trading Corporation.
_____ (1991) *The Heart of the Christian-Hindu Dialogue: Wayne Teasdale: Video.* Chiloquin, OR: Inner Growth Videos.
_____ (1996) "Christianity and the Eastern Religions" in Bruteau, Beatrice, compiler. *The Other Half of My Soul: Bede Griffiths and the Hindu-Christian Dialogue.* Wheaton, IL and Adyar, Madras, India: Quest Books, The Theosophical Publishing House.
_____ (1999) *The Mystic Heart: Discovering a Universal Spirituality in the World's Religions.* Novato, CA: New World Library.
Trapnell. Judson B. (1996) "Two Models of Christian Dialogue with

Hinduism: Bede Griffiths and Abhishiktananda" in *Vidyajyoti: Journal of Theological Reflection*. Vol. 60, pp. 101-110, 183-191, 243-254.

_____ (2001) *Bede Griffiths: A Life of Dialogue*. NY: State University of New York Press.

Waldenfels, Hans. (1988) *Absolute Nothingness: Foundations for a Buddhist-Christian Dialogue*. NY/Ramsey: Paulist Press.

Walker, Susan, editor. (1987) *Speaking of Silence: Christians and Buddhists on the Contemplative Way*. NY, Mahwah: Paulist Press.

Washburn, Michael. (1995) *The Ego and the Dynamic Ground*. State University of New York Press.

Wilber, Ken, Jack Engler, and Daniel P. Brown. (1986) *Transformations of Consciousness: Conventional and Contemplative Perspectives on Development*. Boston & London: New Science Library, Shambhala.

Wingling, Raymond. (1983) *Le théologie contemporaine (1945-1980)*. Le Centurion.

Wiseman, James. "Enveloped by Mystery" in *Église et Théologie*, 23 (1992), p. 241-260.

Woodroffe, John. (1974*)* *The Serpent Power: The Secrets of Tantric and Shaktic Yoga*. NY: Dover Publications.

Wren-Lewis, John. (1994) "Aftereffects of Near-Death Experiences: A Survival Mechanism Hypothesis" in *The Journal of Transpersonal Psychology*, Vol. 26, No. 2, pp. 107-115.

Yamada Roshi, Koun. *Zazen and Christianity*. At http://www.mkzc.org/zenand.html

Yü, Lu K'uan. (1973) *Taoist Yoga: Alchemy and Immortality*. NY: Samuel Weiser, Inc.

Zaehner, R.C. (1957) *Mysticism Sacred and Profane: An Inquiry into some Varieties of Praeternatural Experience*. Oxford at the Clarendon Press.

_____ (1960) *Hindu and Muslim Mysticism*. Jordan Lectures 1959. University of London: The Athlone Press.

Index

Abe, Masao 49, 141-3
Abhishiktananda, Henri Le Saux 17, 36, 69-86, 147, 166
Aelred, Dom 58
Aitken, Robert 42, 56-7
al-'Adawiyya, Rabi'a 166
al-Attas, Syed 184
al-Farabi 175
al-Kindi 175
al-Qashani, Abd al-Razzaq 193
al-Sindi, Abu Ali 167
Amaladoss, Michael 152
Amalorpavadass, D.S. 68
Animananda, Swami 67
Aquinas, Thomas 11, 13, 25, 77, 98-9, 102, 138-9, 141-2, 160, 162, 172, 175-7, 179-184, 188-9, 190, 194, 198, 200, 203-4, 208, 210
'Arabi, Ibn 167, 174, 192-6
Averroes 173, 175, 184
Avicenna 160, 173, 175, 181, 184

Balasuriya, Tissa 105-7
Bali Efendi 194
Basri, Hasan 166
Bäumer, Bettina 75-6
Berkow, Dan 202
Blackstone, Judith 202
Bragt, Jean van 168
Brantschen, Niklaus 20
Bromberg, Judith 118
Brunner, August 52
Buber, Martin 168
Burrell, David 184

Carlo, William 178-9, 182, 204
Cassian, John 60-1
Chaduc, Marc 70

Chuang-tsu 192
Clarke, Norris 178
Corbin, Henry 192
Corless, Roger 40-2
Culligan, Kevin 61-62
Cuttat, Jacques-Albert 67

Dalai Lama 38, 187, 206
Dandoy, C. 67
D'Costa, Gavin 44
Derrida 138
Desideri, Ippolito 187-8
Dogen Zenji 33
Dourley, John 113-16
Dumoulin, Heinrich 46, 51-2, 57
Dupuis, Jacques 73-5, 147-53

Eckhart, Meister 29-31, 33-4, 38, 48, 165, 168, 199, 219
Escalante, Jason 184
Evans-Wentz, W.Y. 88

Faraday, Ann 213
Finance, Joseph de 98
Franz, Marie-Louise von 215
Frederick, James 137
Fumon 14, 16, 92

Gardet, Louis 52, 140, 166-7
Gebara, Ivone 102-4
Geffré, Claude 148
Gilson, Etienne 98, 158, 175, 184-5
Giri, Swami Nityananda 78
Give, Bernard de 191
Glassman, Tetsugen 38
Gnananda, Sri 78
Grant, Sara 68, 77
Griffiths, Bede 68-9, 75, 80, 84-5, 87

Griffiths, Paul 137
Griggs, Philip 47
Grob, James 51
Guarino, Thomas 160
Gyger, Pia 20

Habito, Maria Reis 40-1
Habito, Ruben 20, 23, 25, 37
Hackett, David 57-9
Hallaj 166-7
Hand, Thomas 20, 35
Harada, Daiun Sogaku 20, 43
Harding, D.E. 213
Hawk, Patrick 20, 34-5, 38
Heidegger 138-141
Heinegg, Peter 30
Hick, John 131, 133
Hill, Edmund 105
Hirata Roshi 57-8
Huxley, Aldous 46, 56

Ignatius of Loyola 36, 54, 102, 124, 163
Izutsu, Toshihiko 173-4, 176-83, 191-6, 200, 204-5, 210

Jäger, Willigis 20, 29-32, 34
Johanns, P. 67
John of the Cross 13, 15-6, 30, 32-4, 39, 45-7, 53-4, 60-3, 68, 79, 91-3, 97, 200, 211, 219-20
John Paul II 150
Johnston, William 63
Jonas, Robert 51
Jung, C.G. 113-6, 131, 226

Kadowaki, Kakichi 54-5
Kapleau, Philip 42
Keating, Thomas 55-7, 59-60
Keenan, John 144-5, 147
Kelsang Gyatso, Geshe 88
Kennedy, Robert 20, 37-9
Kesshu 53
Khantipalo, Phra 58
King, Thomas 49
King, Winston 62

Klein, Jean 214
Knitter, Paul 130-7, 147
Krisna, Gopi 88
Kubota Akira 20
Küng, Hans 62

Lachs, Stuart 43
Lacombe, Olivier 67
Lao-tsu 192
Lassalle, Hugo 20, 23, 26-8, 41, 57
Lee, Chwen Jiuan Agnes 35
Leo XIII 98
Lotz, Johannes Baptist 139
Loy, David 21-2, 192, 196-200, 205, 210

MacInnes, Elaine 20, 32
Maezumi, Taizan 42
Mager 52
Maguire, Daniel 111-2
Maharshi, Ramana 69, 76, 84, 214
Mahieu, Francis 68
Main, John 38, 61, 97
Maritain, Jacques 48, 84, 98, 124-6, 130, 140, 164, 169, 177-8, 185-6, 203, 205
Maritain, Raissa 15, 84
Mataji, Vandana 68
Matus, Thomas 87
Meadow, Mary Jo 61-2
Mello, Anthony de 79-80
Mersch, Emile 129, 152
Merton, Thomas 22, 38, 45-9, 52, 58, 97
Messenger, William 60
Mitchell, Donald 49-50
Mohaghegh, Mehdi 174
Mommaers, Paul 168
Monchanin, Jules 68-9, 75, 82
Morwood, Michael 107-9, 118

Nagarjuna 143, 145
Nasr, Seyyed Hossein 174, 200
Nietzsche 115
Nishitani, Keiji 49

Nobili, Robert de 67, 80
Noonan, John 184
Nugent, Christopher 45
Nyoshul Khenpo Rinoche 190

Okumura, Ichiro 53
O'Leary, Joseph 137-41, 143-4
O'Murchu, Diarmuid 110
Oshida 58

Panikkar, Raimundo 131, 134
Pannenberg, Wolfhart 137
Pennington, Basil 60
Porete, Marguerite 168
Postal, Susan 22
Pseudo-Dionysius 53, 142

Rabten, Geshe 188-9
Rahman, Fazlur 175, 180-1
Rahner, Karl 102, 122-4, 126, 130-1, 152, 158, 163-4
Ramakrishna 68
Ramanuja 165, 167
Reiley, Kathleen 20, 37
Reynolds, John 191
Rikyu 53
Roberts, Bernadette 59, 217-9
Rogers, Murray 78
Ruusbroec, Jan van 144, 168-9
Ryan, Thomas 87

Sabzawari, Hadi ibn Mahdi 173-4, 177, 184
Sadra, Mulla 173-7, 179-84, 203-4
St. Romain, Philip 89-90, 216-7
Samy, AMA 20, 63
Sankara 77, 81, 83, 167
Sartre 185
Satyananda, Swami 61
Schillebeeckx, Edward 148
Schlütter, Ana Maria 20
Schuon, Frithjof 200
Segal, Suzanne 213, 215
Sharf, Robert 42-4
Siddheswarananda, Swami 67

Steele, Springs 62
Steindl-Rast, David 55-6
Stuart, James 84
Suhrawardi 175
Sullivan, Francis 121
Surya Das 190
Suzuki, D.T. 42, 46, 48

Takayama Ukon 53
Tauler 33-4
Taylor, Richard 69
Teasdale, Wayne 80, 82-7
Teresa of Avila 15, 28-9, 68, 97, 219
Toynbee 131
Trapnell, Judson 84
Troeltsch, Ernst 131
Trungpa Rinpoche 55-6
Tsong Kha pa 188

Upadhyaya, Brahmabandhab 67, 73, 75. 80

van Dusen, Wilson 212

Waldenfels, Hans 26, 53
Washburn, Michael 201, 212
Whitehead 159
Wilber, Ken 29-30, 36, 201
Wittgenstein 159
Woodroffe, John 88
Wren-Lewis, John 213
Wu, John 45

Yamada, Koun 13-4, 20-7, 29, 32-3, 35, 37-9, 43-5, 78, 196
Yamada, Masamichi 20
Yasutani, Hakuun Ryoko 14, 20, 23, 42-3, 56
Yazid al-Bistami, Abu 166-7
Yogananda, Paramahansa 15
Yü, Lu K'uan 88

Zaehner, R.C. 67, 167-8

To Jacques Maritain

God, Zen and the Intuition of Being

Table of Contents

SHORT ORIENTATION 255

PART 1: THE INTUITION OF BEING 257

CHAPTER 1: THE MYSTERY OF METAPHYSICS 257
  The Decline of Thomism 258
  Jacques Maritain (1882-1973) 259
  What is Metaphysics? 262
  Concrete Approaches to the Intuition of Being 263

CHAPTER 2: ESSENCE AND EXISTENCE 266
  The Existence of God 272
  Concrete Approaches to the Existence of God 273

CHAPTER 3: THE CULTIVATION OF THE INTUITION OF BEING 277
  Inner Dispositions for the Intuition of Being 279
  The Context of the Experience of Being 280

PART II: ZEN ENLIGHTENMENT 284

CHAPTER 4: ZEN AS METAPHYSICAL INSIGHT 284
  Keiji Nishitani 285
  Katsuki Sekida 287
  Reason, Intuition and Connaturality 289
  Connaturality 290

CHAPTER 5: ZEN ENLIGHTENMENT FROM A THOMISTIC VIEWPOINT 293
  Zen Language 296
  A Fanciful and Future Discussion 299
  Speculative and Practical Language 306

CHAPTER 6: METAPHYSICAL KOANS 309
  Zen Spirit 309
  Zen Techniques 312
  Metaphysical Koans 313
  The Way of Judgment 314
  The Way of Consciousness 316
  Cultivating the Intuition of Being 318
  A Zen-Thomist Dialogue? 318

PART III: ZEN BETWEEN METAPHYSICS AND MYSTICISM 321

CHAPTER 7: A MYSTICAL METAPHYSICS 321
  Christian Contemplation 324
  Acquired Contemplation and Zen 326

CHAPTER 8: ZEN CATHOLICISM? 334
  Zen and Western Catholics 334
  Zen and Oriental Catholics 335
  Zen Buddhism and Catholicism 335
  Distinguish In Order To Unite 336
  Epilogue 337

BIBLIOGRAPHY 339

INDEX 344

A Short Orientation

An encounter between Zen, the metaphysics of St. Thomas, and the mysticism of John of the Cross is inevitable. But the success of this meeting depends on how deeply we grasp their inner natures, and how much we thirst for the great gifts that each participant has to offer.

PART I explores the intuition of being, the metaphysical heart of Thomism, which it has neglected to its own great peril. It sees the metaphysics of St. Thomas through the eyes of one of his greatest 20th century followers, Jacques Maritain. It asks the questions, "Why does the Thomistic renewal seem to be over?" "And why did St. Thomas have to be rediscovered to begin with?" And it answers that Thomism has neglected its distinctive form of metaphysical insight, the intuition of being. Further, Thomism has yet to really ask how to cultivate this metaphysical seeing.

PART II examines how the spirit of Zen can reanimate Thomistic metaphysics, and in its turn understand its own nature better by seeing how the metaphysics of St. Thomas views it. It is the metaphysics of St. Thomas that is the least known and potentially one of the most powerful partners in any Zen-Christian or Buddhist-Christian dialogue.

PART III attempts to situate Zen between metaphysics and Christian mysticism, and describes Zen as a metaphysical mysticism, or even a mystical metaphysics.

A Note to the Second Edition

The text has remained the same, aside from some minor corrections. The Appendixes on essence and existence, and the mysticism of the self, have been removed, for the discussions they pointed to have been taken up at length in *Mysticism, Metaphysics and Maritain*, and *The Mystery of Matter*.

Two points of clarification. The phrase "stopping all conceptual thought" should not be taken principally as a description of actual Zen practice, but rather, as an attempt to point to the non-conceptual way in which enlightenment is experienced. The reflections in *Chapter 5* on the relationship between body and soul as the foundation for self-consciousness follows a typical Thomistic approach, which is developed and nuanced in *The Mystery of Matter*.

PART I

THE INTUITION OF BEING

CHAPTER 1

THE MYSTERY OF METAPHYSICS

The greatest obstacle that stands in the way of our appreciation of metaphysics is the difficulty we have in understanding that metaphysics is about something real. We are inclined to think of it as some abstruse theory that survives only in books on the history of philosophy. Instead, it is about the meaning and purpose of life, and when seen in this way, it is a subject that challenges our intellect to the utmost and can be exhilarating.

The doors that open onto the world of metaphysics are all around us. Someone I know well told me: "Early one morning when I was busy making breakfast the sun came over the horizon and its first rays streamed through a window and struck a red cup sitting on the kitchen table. I had seen that cup hundreds of times before. I had washed it, put it away, drunk from it, and let my fingers get warm around it, but until that morning I had never truly seen it. The sun seemed to illuminate the cup from within. It was no longer a simple kitchen utensil, but sat there in the middle of the table aglow with being. I felt, "This isn't just a cup. It is! And the radiance of this "is" took my breath away."

This is a taste of what metaphysics is about. It is one of a myriad of experiences that should form the warm living atmosphere in which genuine metaphysical thought unfolds. Unfortunately, all too often these experiences have been ignored, and metaphysics treated as if it were merely a matter of words.

The Decline of Thomism

The 700th anniversary of the death of Thomas Aquinas in 1974 also marked a century-long Thomistic revival.[1] Its work included an attempt to produce a critical edition of St. Thomas' writings, a historical analysis of his sources and major commentators, a systematic development of his thought, and finally, an encounter between Thomism and contemporary philosophy. But the greatest achievement of this Thomistic renaissance was the rediscovery of the true meaning of St. Thomas' metaphysics. In the years just preceding and following World War II, a number of scholars working independently and with different preoccupations came to fundamentally the same conclusions.[2] The central role of existence not only distinguished St. Thomas' metaphysics from his Aristotelian and Platonic sources, but was the very heart of his creation of a far-reaching and original synthesis.

Today, however, we are faced with what appears to be a widespread and pervasive loss of interest in this metaphysical work. How could such a prodigious effort to rediscover St. Thomas and place him in a contemporary setting fade so quickly? Even more to the point, why did St. Thomas have to be rediscovered in the first place?

Part of this eclipse can be traced to the inevitable rebellion of students subjected to the Thomism of the dehydrated and hyperlogical scholastic manuals.[3] But the roots of the problem go deeper than a question of textbooks. The philosophy of St. Thomas has rarely been presented in a living way. It had originally developed within his theology and when it was abstracted from it, it lost the sense of direction that theology had given to it and failed to find its own distinctive philosophical way of proceeding.

As Jacques Maritain, one of the foremost foes of this manual style of Thomism, put it:

"The *via inventionis*, or way of discovery, which is essential to philosophy, was ignored; so, too, was the procedure proper to philosophy which has its starting point in experience and a prolonged intercourse with the world and with sensible reality. The characteristic atmosphere in which philosophy takes shape, which is the atmosphere of curiosity where it dwells with its fellow sciences and from which it raises itself to the pure and more rarefied atmosphere of what comes *meta ta physica* was equally absent."[4]

But what was most lacking was the inner light from which genuine metaphysics originates and which guides its development. Another Thomism did exist in which this light was alive. It was a Thomism of a Fabro or a Gilson, a de Finance or a Maritain, but by and large the atmosphere of the manuals prevailed.[5] It is the neglect of this aspect of metaphysics that has brought Thomism to the brink of another decline, but its exploration could point the way to a genuine recovery. The best guide for such a journey is Jacques Maritain who first brought this light, which he called the intuition of being, to explicit awareness.

Jacques Maritain (1882-1973)

One summer afternoon at the turn of the century two young people in love wandered in the Jardin des Plantes in Paris. But their joy at having found each other was overshadowed by a deepening despair. Years of study had given them a miscellaneous collection of scientific and philosophical knowledge, but none of it could give them a reason for living. They decided that life in a world filled with injustice and sorrow could only be made bearable if they could find an answer to this question of meaning. They would exert all their energy in a search for a solution, and if they could not find one, they would kill themselves.[6]

Jacques Maritain and Raissa Oumansoff had met as students at the Sorbonne and had soon become inseparable. Raissa, sensitive and introspective, had looked forward with anticipation to her days at the university. There among the finest minds of France she hoped to find the answers to the meaning of life she was searching for. Filled with these unspoken questions, she attended the classes in natural science waiting for the day when these kinds of truths would be presented. But the sciences of the Sorbonne either stayed within the boundaries of their particular disciplines, or when they went further afield they embraced a variety of materialistic philosophical theories that left no room for questions about the ultimate meaning of life. Raissa wrote of these days, "we swam aimlessly in the waters of observation and experience like fish in the depths of the sea without seeing the sun whose dim rays filtered down to us."[7]

Raissa and Jacques did not fare any better in the faculty of philosophy. It was a philosophy that was taught but not lived. It hid itself in its own history while its practitioners "despaired of truth whose very name was unlovely to them and could be used only between the quotation marks of a disillusioned smile."[8]

This was a world dominated by the natural sciences which still retained much of the arrogance of the power they had achieved in the 19th century and produced an atmosphere which was corrosive to any way of knowing which was not their own. Philosophy had let itself be made over in the image and likeness of this science and parroted its methods and limitations. Yet Raissa and Jacques had unwittingly discovered the starting point of all genuine philosophical activity, which is an inner personal search for the meaning of life. Any philosophy divorced from pain and wonder and this burning thirst for understanding soon degenerates into the academic transmission of answers to listeners who have never experienced the questions.

Their search was first rewarded by finding Henri Bergson who was teaching at the Collège de France. Bergson drew large crowds, for he offered an alternative to the scientific materialism of the day with lucidity of thought and clarity of language. He defended the possibility of there being a genuine metaphysics by which the mind could know some sort of absolute. This bold program gave Jacques and Raissa hope, and the possibility of some sort of absolute knowledge excited them more than the details of Bergson's doctrine. They interpreted his knowledge of the absolute to mean "that we could truly, absolutely, know what is."[9] They married, and continued their search for what that absolute might actually be.

The second stage of their journey was something they had never anticipated. Jacques came from a liberal Protestant background and Raissa was Jewish, and neither one had any religious beliefs. Then they read a novel by Leon Bloy, *The Woman Who Was Poor*, that gave them a fleeting glimpse of the inner meaning of Christianity. Bloy had the reputation of being a literary brawler given to extravagant language, but the essence of his message strongly attracted them: "There is only one sadness and that is not to be among the saints." They were soon visiting him regularly, and they were impressed by the fact that he did not argue with them about the truth of his Catholic faith, but tried to live it out himself. He read to them from the saints and mystics who in some mysterious way seemed to be in possession of the kind of truth that they were longing for. Slowly they were drawn toward baptism and if, before, they had to struggle against the science of their day in order to find room for the possibility of philosophy, now they felt they were running the risk of losing the whole of the intellectual life if they embraced Catholicism. The externals of institutional religion put them off, yet finally they felt they had no choice. If the truth they sought was actually to be found there, they had to accept it despite the consequences.

After their baptism they were in the middle of a struggle to integrate the three basic elements of their lives: science, metaphysics and religion, and it was a very serious conflict because they refused to give up any one of them.

They moved to Heidelberg. Jacques had received a grant to study new developments in biology in Germany. Joined by Raissa's sister, Vera, their life became an apprenticeship in the practice of their newfound faith. And accompanying the scientific studies and spiritual exercises was a deepening awareness of the role metaphysics should play in their lives. Jacques wrote in his diary of the need for a "restitution of the Reason, of which metaphysics is the essential and highest operation... We now know what we want, and it is to philosophize truly."[10] But this was easier said than done. Such philosophizing demanded an intense effort at understanding science and religion. More than 25 years were to pass before the Maritains' fully mature solution appeared in Jacques' masterpiece, *The Degrees of Knowledge*.

The first crisis on this road was the conflict between the philosophy of Bergson and their faith. They reasoned that if faith can speak in words of its inner mysteries, how can Bergson claim that concepts must give way to intuition as the only true way to metaphysical knowledge? Implicit in this conflict was the question, "Is there a metaphysics that was open to both concepts and intuition, and to science and faith?"

The Maritains' Catholicism had not brought with it a ready-made philosophy like a convenient appendix. They were struggling to conceive of the kind of metaphysics which would be compatible with their faith, that would coalesce in a mind and heart enlightened by faith. When they discovered St. Thomas' *Summa Theologicae* several years later, they penetrated beyond the externals of his 13th century format into its metaphysical heart, for they were ready to receive what they later called its "luminous flood."[11]

What Is Metaphysics?

In ancient and medieval times metaphysics was the queen of the human sciences. It was the way men tried to come to grips with the ultimate nature of reality and the existence and attributes of God. Metaphysics does not depend upon any delicate instrumentation or an act of faith. It is the working of the human intelligence at its deepest level. But as profound as its subject matter is, it begins with the most basic facts of the world of common experience. It starts from the fact that things exist. Its natural and spontaneous beginning is not in some subtle and elusive form of introspection, but in seeing a flower or the flight of a bird, or a smile.

The basic facts that are at the beginning of metaphysics are so accessible that if there were not another vital ingredient necessary, then the disagreements in this field would be inexplicable. Simple facts are intimately familiar to us, but unfortunately, this alone does not make us metaphysicians. Metaphysics eludes us not because of its difficulty as if it were some kind of higher mathematics or nuclear physics, but because of its very simplicity. The fact of existence is all around us, but our intellectual sight is too weak to grasp what is right in front of our eyes. Our very familiarity with reality has rendered it banal. We are not attuned to hear the mystery of existence that all things are murmuring. Maritain compares the object of metaphysics to Edgar Allen Poe's purloined letter; it is perfectly hidden because it is brazenly put right out in front of us. "The little word "is", the commonest of all words, used every moment everywhere, offers us, though concealed and well concealed, the mystery of being..."[12]

Metaphysics starts with ordinary experience and common sense. This common sense is a pre-reflective and instinctive knowledge that can blossom into genuine philosophical understanding. With common sense we accept the fact that things exist, but unfortunately, existence is simply a predicate we give to each of the things around us, and then think no more about it.[13] What is lacking is an insight or intuition by which we glimpse the inner depths of this mystery of existence. And what is this intuition? "It is a very simple sight, superior to any discursive reasoning or demonstration, because it is the source of demonstration."[14] Intuition is not some spiritual vision that lifts us out of the human condition. It does not dispense us from the laborious construction of ideas and judgments. It goes hand-in-hand with these concepts and judgments, sometimes preceding them and sometimes following them, but always linked to them and vivifying them so they can rise to the mystery of knowledge in which we in some way become the things we know.[15] Intuition is the immaterial fire of the intellect. It glows and sputters and occasionally some breeze quickens it, and it flashes into flame. Then for a moment we see. These are the moments of intuition. They are not divorced from the normal ways of understanding, but permeate them and on occasion, lead them in unexpected directions. It is this intuition that according to Maritain makes the metaphysician. No intuition, no metaphysician.[16]

How do we arrive, then, at this indispensable metaphysical intuition? Maritain describes two pathways: one is by way of experience. Some concrete event triggers the intuition. The other, and probably much rarer, is by way of judgment. The strength of our reasoning leads us inexorably to a peak of tension that is resolved by a moment of insight.[17]

Concrete Approaches to the Intuition of Being

If our sight has been dulled by too long an exposure to the fact of existence, then something must come along to shake us loose and make us really see what is in front of our eyes. Our ordinary experience must be magnified so that existence appears before us with its original face. Maritain suggests that there are various paths that can lead to this intuition. He mentions Bergson's duration, Heidegger's experience of anguish, a "feeling at once keen and lacerating of all that is precarious and imperiled in our existence....,"[18] and Gabriel Marcel's sense of fidelity, but he stresses that all these approaches are insufficient in themselves. For though they are pregnant with ontological values, they do not deliver the intuition in all its naked intelligibility.

"The experience in question gives information only of itself." We must let "the veils - too heavy with matter and too opaque - of the concrete psychological or ethical fact fall away to discover in their purity the strictly metaphysical values which such experiences concealed."[19]

Here examples drawn from philosophy should not lead us to the conclusion that there must be something vaguely scholarly or theoretical about these concrete approaches. There is not. The propitious circumstances are woven into the fabric of our daily lives. A sudden manifestation of the beauty of nature can lead us in this direction, as can the discovery of human love, or simply an unexpected moment of insight with no obvious antecedents.

What are these experiences like? Raissa describes one that took place before their baptism, while she was in a car which was passing through a forest:

"I was looking out the window and thinking of nothing in particular. Suddenly a great change took place in me, as if from the perceptions of the senses I had passed over to an entirely inward perception. The passing trees had become much larger than themselves, they assumed a dimension prodigious for its depth. The whole forest seemed to speak of Another, became a forest of symbols, and seemed to have no other function than to *signify* the Creator."[20]

Maritain finds a similar experience described in the autobiography of Jean Richter. "One morning when I was still a child, I was standing on the threshold of the house and looking to my left in the direction of the wood pile when suddenly there came to me from heaven like a lightning flash the thought: *I am a self*, a thought which has never since left me. I perceived my self for the first time and for good."[21]

What distinguished the powerful experiences that could lead us to the intuition of being from those that, in fact, do so? Perhaps the inner questioning that permeated the life of someone like Raissa becomes focused and creates a fleeting pathway to being. Then the alluring palpability of the concrete gives way to another dimension, the inner world of metaphysics. What is this world like? It is the task of metaphysics as a science to attempt to conceptually articulate what is given in intuition.

NOTES

1. For the 19th century origins of the Thomistic revival: McCool, *Catholic Theology in the Nineteenth Century. One Hundred Years of Thomism.*
2. For a review of the work of most of the major figures: John, *The Thomist Spectrum.*
3. Unfortunately, these manuals continued in use long after better material was available. See p. 316.
4. Maritain, *The Peasant of the Garonne*, p. 136.
5. See note 2 and bibliography.
6. Raissa Maritain, *We Have Been Friends Together*, and *Adventures in Grace.*
7. Ibid., p. 57.
8. Ibid., p. 61.
9. Ibid., p. 72.
10. Ibid., p. 143.
11. Ibid., p. 157.
12. Maritain, *A Preface to Metaphysics*, p. 88.
13. Maritain, *Approches sans entraves*, p. 264ff.
14. Maritain, *A Preface to Metaphysics*, p. 50.
15. Maritain, *The Degrees of Knowledge*, Chapter III: Critical Realism, especially his summary on pages 112ff.
16. Maritain, *A Preface to Metaphysics*, p. 52.
17. Maritain, in any number of places, contrasts the *via inventionis* and the *via judicii*: the way of discovery and the way of confirmatory rational analysis. But the *via judicii* can itself become a path to the intuition of being as Maritain explains in a passage in *A Preface to Metaphysics*. This rational analysis "leads us by logical necessity, and in *via judicii*, to the threshold which an intuitive perception alone enables us to cross, the perception of being as such. When the mind once has this intuition it has it for good." (p. 59) Thus, there is a parallel we will note later between such a rational analysis leading to insight and intuition and Zen's koans.
18. Ibid., p. 54.
19. Ibid., p. 56.
20. Raissa Maritain, *We Have Been Friends Together*, p. 115-116.
21. Maritain, *A Preface to Metaphysics*, p. 52.

CHAPTER 2

ESSENCE AND EXISTENCE

There is an old pine tree I walk by almost every day. Often I am preoccupied and scarcely see it. Then it's a tree like any other tree. My subliminal naming it "tree" takes the place of any genuine awareness or contact. But some days as I go by it seems to be saying, "Wake up and listen to me. Really look at me, and don't just call me a tree and go on your way." And if I heed this silent message I become aware of this tree as a unique individual. I notice the power of its trunk, and the fissures in its bark. Each branch and needle reaches out. This pine is saying, in its own way, "I am. I am. I am." And if I listen closely to it, this one message has two distinct aspects. The "I" speaks of what it is. It is a tree and not a flower, or a blade of grass. This is what the ancients called essence. The second aspect, its "am," is the fact of its existence. It is. It exists. It stands outside of nothingness and at each moment defies it. The tree exerts and exercises the rich, silent, motionless energy that is existence.

These two words, essence and existence, are the best way to explore the content of the intuition of being. Their surface meanings are easy to grasp. Essence is what a thing is, and existence is that it is or that it exists, and what a thing is is not the same as that it is. There are two distinct attitudes of mind involved, one when we name something and the other when we assert that it exists. The "what" and the "that" form two basic ways in which our mind tries to make sense of the things around us, or put in another way, they are two distinct aspects of things that the mind grasps and tries to come to terms with.[1]

Yet, usually, essence is in the forefront. This is the face things present to us. We distinguish one thing from another and even oppose one thing to another. An elephant is not a carrot, and we don't expect anyone to confuse the two. But we rarely if ever stop and consider the ultimate nature of the whats we are constantly making use of.

What makes an elephant an elephant must be different from what makes a carrot a carrot, or else they would be the same. But what makes a what to be ultimately a what? What makes a what ultimately to be a what cannot be a particular what, or else all whats would be the same, and we know this is not true. In short, what if we asked an admittedly very strange question: what is the whatness of whats, the essence of essences? What makes a what to be a what? It cannot be a particular what, for no particular what or essence can be the foundation of many different essences.

If we seriously ask ourselves about the whatness of whats or the essence of essences we can travel to the brink of the intuition of being by upsetting our facile complacence that says we really know the things around us. And metaphysics is meant to instruct us in these kinds of things, and so we will look at the answer of St. Thomas as Maritain presents it, but just reading the words is no guarantee they will make sense. They are meant to be read in light of the intuition as an explanation of it.

If essences don't contain their own final meaning, the only place left to look for it is in that other fundamental stance towards reality by which we assert that something exists. But this time we have to go beyond the common sense notion of existence applied to each essence as a final boost that brings the pre-existing essence into actual existence.

If essences cannot explain each other, then the explanation must be rich enough to encompass all essences. If we are forced to look to existence for an explanation of essence, then the one thing that existence cannot be is an idea, concept, what, essence or form. In this sense, existence is no-thing. It must possess an ontological richness and density that goes beyond the whole order of essence.

But is it really possible to penetrate beyond the level of essences? If we leave the plateau of essence, don't we, indeed, fall off toward nothingness? Are we finally forced to admit "that existence is an unknowable upon which metaphysics builds without itself attaining to it?"[2] Maritain refuses to stop here. If anything, this kind of perception is but the tiniest taste, or better, the intellectual preparation for the intuition of being itself. Existence is not simply a limit that we asymptotically approach, but it is the most real of all reality. St. Thomas wrote in his *Summa Theologicae*: "Existence itself is the actuality of all things, even of the forms themselves."[3] The intuition of being is not only a realization of the non-essential nature of ultimate reality, it is a glimpse of the positive abundance and richness of this reality we call existence.

What, then, is the essence of essence? It is a certain capacity to exist. Maritain calls essences "positive capacities of existence"[4] and says: "the very intelligibility of essences is a certain kind of ability to exist."[5] The revolution inaugurated by St. Thomas was the transformation of essence which had been considered the ultimate principle of metaphysics because it indicated the central intelligibility of something. He brought this conception of essence into relationship with a higher principle, which was the act of existence: "...potency (essence, or intelligible structure already achieved in its own line of essence) is completed or actuated by another act of another order which adds absolutely nothing to essence as essence, intelligible structure, or quiddity, yet adds everything to it inasmuch as it posits it extra causas or extra nihil."[6] What is at stake here is a transformation of the whole essentialist perspective. Essence is displaced from the center of the metaphysical stage and the much more mysterious reality of existence takes its place. Essence is a certain capacity to exist. It stands in relationship to existence as potency to act, and essence is the potentiality for a certain degree of existence. Existence is what actualizes these different potentialities so that there are actually existing things. Existence is an act or energy whose richness exceeds the whole order of essence and founds it. It admits being realized in this and that way because it exceeds every particular manifestation. "Existence is perfection par excellence, and as it were the seal of every other perfection... Doubtless of itself it says only positing outside of nothing, but it is the positing outside of nothing of this or that."[7] The intuition of being is a perception of the transessential amplitude of existence in relationship to essence. What existence posits is not an accidental quality added to a somehow pre-existing essence. Essences do not exist in themselves. They do not have any actuality. They only exist in relationship to existence as potentialities for existence. The ultimate root of their intelligibility lies not in them-selves but in what Maritain called the superintelligibility of existence.

GOD, ZEN AND THE INTUITION OF BEING 269

Talk about essence and existence should not hide from us the fact that they are intellectual realities. We do not bump into an essence in the street, nor do we have some vision of existence. We are part of a world of existing things, existents, beings, and our minds find in these existents the two dimensions of essence and existence. Essence and existence are found there because they are actually there. They are not merely intellectual constructs. At the same time, the way they exist in the mind is not the same as the way they exist in things. This point becomes critical when we try to understand the nature of the intuition of being. There is a dynamism involved in this intuition that has its origin in the confrontation of the mind with existing things. The mind attempts to go beyond the level of essences. It sees that there is another dimension which it can provisionally label as existence and it tries to give a positive content to this dimension of existence and not simply to assert that it is beyond essence, and this positive content can best be called an insight into being as being. What is being? It is not simply essence, nor is it purely existence. It is that which exists. Because we can assert about each existent, that it is a being, then the notion of being cannot be univocal, that is, applied to everything in the same way, for then they would all be the same, which goes against our experience. At the same time, being is not attributed to things equivocally. Each thing is actually a being through and through.

Put in another way, what makes things similar must be being as well as what makes them different. Being is that which is. It comprises inseparably essence and existence. Our minds read in existing things the fact that being is more than this or that particular being. It discovers that essence, in short, is one particular capacity for the act of existence. This is an insight into the fundamentally analogical nature of being. When the mind turns towards the notion of existence as the source and plenitude against which all essences are measured, each essence is then seen as a refraction, a reflection, of this reality which is to be. The mind desires to grasp and disengage in its naked intelligibility this reality of existence. It wants to see this sun which contains all the colors of the spectrum of essences, but it cannot do it. Perhaps its very attempt to grasp existence is doomed to failure, for it is an attempt to turn existence into another essence, a super-essence, but existence is of a different order than this. The moment of the intuition of being is a moment where the mind is suspended between two worlds. It has overcome the diversity of essences and has seen how they converge towards the pinnacle which is the very act of existence in itself, disengaged from any limitation and reception by essence. But it cannot fully follow these converging paths. The unity it discovers is an imperfect and relative unity due to the spiritualizing power of the mind.[8] It rests on the foundation of the many whats we see that actually exist. It grasps in each existent the act of existence that actualizes and fills this capacity to exist. It moves from this limited act of existing to an intuition that the act of existing overflows all the possible modes of reception. We can grasp how existence is the actuality of all the forms, but we cannot grasp it in its deepest self where we would see that it is perfectly one and the source of all things. We grasp existence as transcending the limitations it has by being received as the existence of this or that particular capacity to exist, but we do not grasp it as totally unreceived and unlimited in itself.

No matter how we strive, our intuition is an intuition of both essence and existence, this time as disengaged from this or that particular existing thing and thus manifesting the transessential amplitude, of the act of existence, but only in an imperfect way, always turned toward the existent from which it has been born. The intuition of being touches the act of existence and releases its transcendence in relationship to all essences, but it cannot penetrate to the perfect unity of existence.

If essence finds its ultimate meaning in relationship to existence, why does Maritain insist on speaking of an intuition of being rather than an intuition of existence? Being is that which is. It is what is, essence existing. Why not simplify things and speak only of existence?

Imagine each existing thing as a bar magnet with essence as one pole and existence as the other, and imagine all the magnets being arranged in a circle with the existence pole of each pointing towards the center. What makes all these individual beings alike? It is not their essences, for that is what makes them different. Neither is it their individual acts of existing, for those acts, which are the actualization of various capacities, are different from each other. But each of these beings is made up of both essence and existence and each of them is oriented toward the same center.

We ordinarily look at the circle of beings from the outside and are confronted with the diversity of things. We see beings especially as being different from each other, as essences. But if we ponder the meaning of essence and ask what is the essence of essence, we begin to be led inside the circle. Each being points towards the center. The notion of being must in some way be richer than that of any individual being. It has to embrace essential differences. A stone and a flower are both beings. By the intuition of being we enter into the circle of beings and form a new concentric circle of being as being. We discover the common inner consistency of each being, that is, its relationship between its essence and its existence and the common orientation they all possess towards the center of the circle.

This discovery is an intellectual act of the highest intensity. Maritain called this intuition of being, a process of eidetic visualization by which we leave behind the empirical existence of the individual and grasp the intrinsic nature of being as being. In doing so we have reversed our perspective and look at things no longer from the point of view of essence, but rather from the point of view of existence. Or, more precisely, we see beings not as essences existing, but existing essences. We see beings with their face of existence turned towards us.

But despite the mind's supreme effort to reconcile the two basic facts of essence and existence, its success in the intuition of being is imperfect and relative. Being as being is an imperfect unity glimpsed by the mind but shattered when we leave the mind and look at concrete existing things. Beings do not have a secret kernel of being as being hidden within them. They are this or that being. But there is a deeper reason why our intuition of being is in need of completion. It has not reached the center of the circle. Existence has not been completely disengaged from essence and discovered in all its purity. We have glimpsed being as being, that inner relationship of essence to existence, that can be realized in each individual in essentially different ways, but the whole weight of this intuition is attracted towards the center of the circle, towards existence itself. The intuition of being is drawn towards becoming an intuition of existence, but it never attains this goal but is suspended in a sometimes painful tension towards it.

The Existence of God

It is within the context of the intuition of being that the question of the existence of God must be placed. Without this intuition, the conceptual statements that are framed to prove the existence of God will remain flat and unconvincing. Logic alone does not have the ability to make us see. St. Thomas could never have imagined a metaphysics without God at the center of it, and God was not superimposed on his metaphysics because of religious reasons, but was the very heart of the intelligibility of his metaphysics. We start with the most basic facts of everyday existence, and by means of the intuition of being we follow them inwardly and see that they point towards existence itself. Existence as received and contracted, this or that existing being, is not possible without there being existence unreceived. The intuition of being is the opening of our eyes to how every existing thing points to existence itself. St. Thomas gives his five ways leading to the existence of God, and Maritain adds a sixth, and there are others, but they must share the common essential ingredient of an intuition of being which vivifies them. Once the basic insight is in place, it is possible to grasp why St. Thomas gave God the attributes that he did.

There is no intellectual intuition of God Who is Himself existence. The limited and received existence of the beings of our experience demand there be a center to the circle on pain that there would be no beings. As soon as we disengage being as being from the empirical being of this or that existent, we must posit existence in itself. Essence must be finally understood as a certain capacity to exist, and essence-existence or being must be finally understood in relationship to unreceived existence.

Here we have reached the limits of conceptual or essentialistic understanding. God does not possess a capacity to exist. He is without essence in this sense. There is no reception or contraction of His existence by His essence. He is His existence. All essences are measured in relationship to Him. God is not a being among beings. He is not something among other things. It is possible to call Him no essence, no-thing, if we keep clearly in mind that this is not nothingness or no nature, but no potential or capacity.[9] He is not nothing, for existence is all actuality and reality. We cannot contain God within our concepts. We can say true things about Him basing ourselves on the very structure of the things that exist around us, but the way He exists in Himself is beyond our comprehension. Maritain writes that the concept of being:

"*is one in a certain respect*, insofar as it does make incomplete abstraction from its analogates, and is disengaged from them without being conceivable apart from them, as attracted towards, without attaining, a pure and simple unity, which could alone be present to the mind if it were able to see in itself - and without concept - a reality which would be at once itself and all things. (Let us say the concept of being demands to be replaced by God clearly seen, to disappear in the face of the beatific vision.)"[10]

In the intuition of being we glimpse the transessential nature of existence, but this is simply a weak reflection of what existence itself must be, of what God, esse subsistens, is like.

"The analogical infinitude of the act of existing is a created participation in the unflawed oneness of the infinity of the *Ipsum esse subsistens*; an analogical infinitude which is diversified according to the possibilities of existing. In relation to it, those very possibilities of existing, the essences, are knowable or intelligible."[11]

Concrete Approaches to the Existence of God

All this talk about essence and existence can sound very far removed from the concrete experiences that Maritain discusses which can give rise to the intuition of being. In fact, Maritain in trying to make clear the nature of this intuition is walking a tightrope. He is keenly aware of the glaring failing of scholasticism, of Thomistic philosophy institutionalized, which is its repetition of conceptual statements even when the intuitive fires and personal experiences that originally gave birth to them have ebbed away. On the other hand, his experience of Bergson and contemporary philosophy had sensitized him to the difficulties in developing an authentic metaphysics if the initial intuition were understood simply as a concrete grasping of empirical existence. No matter how powerful such an emotional and introspective grasping of the individual would be, it would not, itself, reach the intelligible level of being as being. In actual life, the relationship between concrete experience and metaphysical intuition can be natural and uncomplicated, as can the relationship between this intuition of being and the existence of God.

It can start with an awareness of the fact of existence:

"...I suddenly realized that a given entity, man, mountain, or tree, exists and exercises that sovereign act *to be* in its own way, in an independence from *me* which is total, totally self-assertive and totally implacable."[12]

But at the same time this implacable existence makes me aware of my own existence as riddled by "loneliness and frailty" which is "the death and nothingness to which my existence is liable."

Then this same intuition which had moved from "sheer objective existence" to "my existence spoiled with nothingness" inexorably arrives at "absolute existence" for "Being-with-nothingness as my own being is, implies in order to be, Being-without-nothingness."

Thus Maritain attempts to illustrate the diverse moments of the single intuition. And there are other concrete approaches that can bring us to this same intuition. Let me sketch another of these concrete approaches in more detail. The experience of human love with its emotional upheavals and intense joy and pain can become a pathway to the intuition of being. Love can change not only our behavior but our way of perceiving. If, for Maritain, the intuition of being can start with the perception of "the tremendous fact, sometimes exhilarating, sometimes disgusting and maddening, I exist ... ,"[13] it can also begin for the one who loves with an inner awareness: you, the one I love, you exist. You stand out with a richness, a density of being, that I have never experienced before. You are more real than all the things of the world. Somehow, someone is really real with a reality that rivals my own interior awareness of myself. Now the existence of things does not simply stand over against me with the implacable being of something that knows nothing about me, but I sense, for the first time, that being can be open to me and turn towards me, that being is not simply what makes me be myself and different from others, but somehow, in some obscure way, is the foundation of unity. In short, all the acts of the one I love, her gestures or smiles, are suffused with a mystery of being that I cannot fathom, still less express in conceptual terms, but which draws me towards her with an expectancy of hope mingled with fear, that this gateway into being will prove an illusion.

But this sense of heightened reality of the one I love, which

GOD, ZEN AND THE INTUITION OF BEING 275

removes her from my ordinary consciousness, brings with it another awareness. The one I love is lovable without her even knowing I love her. She is lovable independent of my thoughts and intentions about her, and what is more surprising she is, in some deep sense, lovable independent of her own consciousness and actions. She literally does not know how lovable she is. In some obscure way I sense that her lovableness is a quality of her very existence rather than simply her consciousness. She is lovable whether she knows it or not, intends it or not, and alas, whether she loves me or not, simply because she is.

Somewhere in the midst of this experience of love the possibility of the intuition of being can present itself. Certainly the concrete experience does not have to be illuminated by metaphysical insight, but the possibility is there. Perhaps it depends on that profound inner questioning that seizes the one who loves and makes him say over and over again: I know that I love and this is the most real experience that I have ever undergone, but why do I love? Why do I love you? Why are you lovable? I sense in some way, obscurely and in no way conceptually, the ultimate root of your lovability comes from somewhere else. The "why" becomes a search for the origin of this love. If the one I love possesses her lovability from another, what would this source be like? If the spark is so delectable, from what consuming fire does it originate? If you are lovable by being, what must Being be? If you are lovable, what must Love be? I have no experience of this source of lovableness, but I can sense how it stands like the sun in relationship to all the things that are illuminated by it. The one I love is a person suffused with loveliness, and thus the source of this beauty must be in some fashion a person who is the fullness of love.

The question of whether God's existence can be proved is surrounded by two difficult problems. The first is the difference between intuition and metaphysical statements that we have been examining. Repeating the careful logic of St. Thomas' ways for demonstrating God's existence has done little to convince people of their truth. The intuition of being in some degree is necessary to fire these concepts and let them become ways of seeing. Not even impeccable logic can make up for this lack of intuition.

The other difficulty is the fact that even a genuine certitude in the existence of God founded in metaphysical insight and carefully elaborated by metaphysical science is not identical to the kind of knowledge that we crave about God. Metaphysical understanding is one thing, and the desires of the heart often quite another. This second theme will recur more than once in *Parts II* and *III.* But for now we should continue exploring the implications of a metaphysics founded on intuition.

Notes

1. The what being what was called by the classical Thomists apprehension, and the that, the act of judgment itself.
2. Maritain, *Existence and the Existent*, p. 32.
3. *Summa Theologiae*, QIV, a. 1, ad 3um.
4. Maritain, *A Preface to Metaphysics*, p. 26.
5. Maritain, *Existence and the Existent*, p. 45.
6. Ibid.
7. Maritain, *The Degrees of Knowledge*, p. 217.
8. Maritain, *A Preface to Metaphysics*, p. 62.
9. This no-thing-ness which is a valid way to build a bridge to Zen language must be carefully understood not in the sense of some currents of modern philosophy as a nihilism, or lack of nature or essence, but only as a lack of potentiality. Maritain in his essay, "L'Aséitié Divine" in *Approches sans entraves* writes: "The notion of essence or of nature does not necessarily embrace potentiality. The latter is an absolutely necessary condition of every created essence to be in potency in regard to existence. It is not necessary that this fundamental thesis of St. Thomas, that the essence of all created things is in potency in regard to existence, impede us from another aspect of things, that is, that essence is act and perfection; it is an act. It is a perfection. It is the intelligible constitution of things; it is an act, it is a perfection, which is yet potency in relation to another act, in relation to the act of existence." (p. 98)
10. Maritain, *The Degrees of Knowledge*, p. 213-214.
11. Maritain, *Existence and the Existent*, p. 45.
12. Maritain, *The Range of Reason*, p. 88.
13. Ibid., p. 88.

CHAPTER 3:

THE CULTIVATION OF
THE INTUITION OF BEING

In an essay entitled, "Reflections on Wounded Nature," written near the end of his life, Maritain left hidden in a footnote, a clue to what the future might regard as one of his greatest metaphysical achievements. He said:

"The intuition of being has been lived and practiced by St. Thomas and the Thomists (the good Thomists), but I do not know (perhaps due to my ignorance) of a treatise or disquisitio where it has been explicitly studied by them."[1]

St. Thomas had this intuition. Throughout his writings from his early work, *On Being and Essence*, to his mature *Summa Theologicae*, a new metaphysical vision is presented centered on the act of existence. Unfortunately, we have no firm information about how St. Thomas arrived at this fundamental insight. The story is told of Thomas as a child wandering about asking, "What is God?", and this points to a temperamental inclination towards such an intuition, and Maritain suggests Thomas had the intuition as "the innate gift of an imperial intelligence serenely relying on its limpid strength."[2] But whether this intuition came as a natural endowment or a sudden revelation, whether it came from a religious meditation on the text of Exodus or pondering a metaphysical conundrum, Thomas never directly spoke of it.[3]

Maritain, on the other hand, never stopped speaking of it. In a career spanning more than 50 years, he returned again and again to the question of intuition, its nature and its interaction with reason. Unfortunately, what he hardly ever speaks about are the circumstances that surrounded his own arrival at this insight into being. The general context is clear enough. As an ardent Bergsonian, forced to break with his master, the central role of intuition in Bergson's metaphysics had to be in the forefront of his mind. Even more so would the vivid experiences of Raissa have affected him. He commented on her experience in the forest: "At the sight of something or other, a soul will know in an instant that these things do not exist through themselves and that God is." And perhaps Bergson's duration was his own concrete approach to being.

In an unpublished essay in 1906 he wrote of the intuition of duration:

"...in which the instants do not follow one upon the other, which does not at all admit of separated instants, but which completely conserves itself in the powerful simplicity and the expansion of its inconceivable unity... he is in the presence, not of an idea which seems true by its convenience, to be handled in discourse and explication, but of the real itself, which asserts itself royally, and makes itself known by its force, through which it enraptures the mind, and by its absolute nature, into which the most agile rapidities of thought hurl themselves in vain... Of this primary intuition he will retain, when he has returned to consciousness, only a primary truth, and he says: *I exist in an absolute manner*, that is to say, I perdure..."[4]

Much later he remarks about these lines that "under the mask of Bergsonian duration it was indeed the intuition of being which preoccupied me from that moment."[5]

If not in that moment, somehow, in some way, either while he trudged through the snow in Heidelberg pondering the demands of faith and the nature of Bergson's philosophy, or when he met the *Summa* with a mind hungry for metaphysics, he came to this intuition.

Maritain described it as a "natural revelation" or as "presenting the semblance of a mystical grace." He does this not because he was of the opinion that it was beyond human effort, for he explicitly rejects the position that it should be looked upon as a "mystical gift, a supernatural gift granted to a few privileged persons,"[6] but rather because of its gift-like quality. It is not simply the outcome of our normal ways of reasoning. It is not in easy continuity with our ordinary experiences. Its entrance into a consciousness conditioned to see everything by way of object or essence comes as a shock. The intuition of being is the natural crowning of the human intellect, but we live so far from it and so rarely arrive at it that we receive it with gratitude as a great unexpected gift.

Inner Dispositions for the Intuition of Being

Maritain indicates two basic dispositions that smooth the way for the reception of this intuition. The first is a sensitivity to the actual existing world around us. This means an immersion in the concrete world of things by means of our senses, for through them we have a "blind existential perception" of the mystery of existence. If we desire to be metaphysicians we must be "plunged into existence, steeped ever more deeply in it by a sensuous and aesthetic perception as acute as possible and by experiencing the suffering and struggles of real life."[7] This is the antithesis of a scholasticism which is purely academic, the simple transmission of concepts without a living sense of the reality they refer to.

The second necessary disposition for attaining this intuition is to be still enough to listen to the mystery of being that is whispered by all things. This intuition demands, not intricate intellectual technique, but rather an "active attentive silence" and a "degree of intellectual purification" by "which we become sufficiently disengaged, sufficiently empty to hear what all things whisper and to listen instead of composing answers."[8]

In short, Maritain made a decisive step and leaves us a well-developed exposition of the nature of the intuition of being, the concrete ways to approach it and even the interior dispositions that could help in attaining it. And all this implies the possibility of consciously cultivating it, and this Maritain hardly ever discusses. Perhaps it came to him and Raissa so much like a gift that such a possibility was thrown into deep shadows. Or since the explicit description of the intuition was such a dramatic departure from the normal Thomistic fare all his attention was on clarifying and expounding it. Yet, at least once Maritain did take the next step and formally recognized the possibility of cultivating this intuition. It came in the midst of an open letter to the authors *of Philosophy At The Time Of The Council*, which dealt in large part with how the teaching of Thomism could be improved. One of the passages in this work that caught Maritain's eye read as follows:

"Now there is with St. Thomas such philosophical intuitions - the initial intuitions of which Bergson spoke - that their vision of the real ought not to be lost sight of under the pain of a deviation from philosophy and all that depends on it in the Church and in the world."[9]

Maritain comments:

"The misfortune of ordinary scholastic teaching, especially that of the manuals, has been to neglect in a practical way this essential intuitive element and replace it from the beginning by a pseudo-dialectic of concepts and formulas. There is nothing to do as long as the intellect has not *seen* - as long as the philosopher or apprentice philosopher has not had the intellectual intuition of being. It could be noted from this point of view the great pedagogical interest of a year of initiation to philosophy entirely centered on the need to lead spirits to the intuition of being and to the other fundamental intuitions by which Thomistic philosophy lives."[10]

Thus, Maritain explicitly sets forth the possibility of the cultivation of the intuition of being and closely connects it with the success or failure of the whole philosophical endeavor. And as we have seen, his own metaphysical writings are pregnant with this possibility. You cannot talk about the indispensability of the intuition of being without preparing the ground for the inevitable question of how this intuition may be obtained. And so the possibility of its formal cultivation appears to Maritain. Regrettably, though, he does not leave us his ideas of how such a year of initiation would be structured and what methods it would use.

The Context of the Experience of Being

Yet there are potentially deeper reasons, which are less personal, that could have deflected him from the full consideration of such a possibility. There is something in the whole make-up of classical Thomistic metaphysics that militates against such a possibility. We saw at the beginning of Chapter 1 how the metaphysics of St. Thomas was at the service of his theology, and when it tried to leave that context it often failed to discover its proper way of proceeding. It could create syllogisms, but that is far from the lived logic of genuine philosophical activity.

But in practice, as Maritain points out, the intuition of being existed in St. Thomas, the good Thomists of the ages and, we could add, the fine minds that rediscovered St. Thomas for us. But even when this light exists it does not have to be distinguishable from other lights in the same person for it to do its work. The metaphysics of St. Thomas has been predominately exercised within a Christian context. As powerful as the metaphysical light may have been, it was always operative in a soul that relied on higher lights as well, and these lights would tend to make the light of metaphysics harder to see in itself, even while they strengthened it.

Even when Maritain discerned this light for itself, aided perhaps by the intuition of Raissa that predates their conversion, he was keenly aware that this intuition was but one moment in the ascent of the soul to God. He lived in the context of the gift of faith, whose ultimate earthly expression was mystical experience, and since the idea of technique was foreign to these realms, it would not have been easy to associate the idea of technique and the intuition of being.

The intuition of being constellates the question of God, but this question is not a purely metaphysical one. A metaphysical proof of God's existence does not satisfy the heart. We live in a world beset by pain and loneliness, and our search for meaning is the search for an answer to these sorrows. Given such a world, could a God of love actually exist? Now, the word existence has been transformed again, meaning neither essence nor existence in the philosophical sense, but whether God can exist for me. Even when I possess the intuition of being and know God exists, I am drawn toward the question of whether He truly exists for me so I can voyage in the darkness that surrounds Him and make contact with Him. Even a genuine experience of the intuition of being can be swallowed by these other deeper longings and not be examined for itself, still less in terms of whether it can be cultivated. Paradoxically, while the Christian context made possible in an existential sense the discovery and the development of the intuition of being, for it created the inner spiritual atmosphere where metaphysics could discover its deepest roots, it hindered the formal explication and cultivation of this intuition. For example, it would probably be possible to discern moments of the intuition of being in the experience of the mystics, for the higher experience created the condition of soul where it would flourish, but how could the mystics leave that living fire in order to pursue a reflection, even one as powerful as the intuition of being?

The question of the cultivation of the intuition of being becomes a specific instance of what Maritain described under the heading of Christian philosophy, which in its turn was a reflection of his own experience. If faith could not enter into the structure of philosophy without destroying it, it could provide its living context, the strengthening of soul, in which this philosophy could be best exercised. The metaphysics of St. Thomas is not Christian by nature. It is not a crypto-theology that demands revelation in order to discover its first principles or reach its conclusions. The intuition of being does not demand a Christian context in order to be discovered or elaborated, yet this is precisely the atmosphere in which it was born. And this is why the question of its cultivation has never become a real possibility.

Perhaps some student of history will attempt to piece together, before it is too late, how the leaders of the 20th century Thomistic renaissance arrived at the intuition of being. But could these men to whom the intuition came as a happy chance be attuned to the possibility of a cultivation which they never had to attempt for themselves?[11] Yet this is the critical problem facing Thomistic metaphysics. If without the intuition we cannot be metaphysicians, it is little wonder that Thomism, having neglected this issue, is sliding towards another period of oblivion. Can the intuition of being be cultivated? It can and it must be. But how can it be in a tradition that knows so little about such a venture? Imagine if in another time and place, men and women, suffering the same thirst for the meaning of life, discovered metaphysics, but this time it was not subjected to and lived out in relationship to revelation. Then all the longings that the West associates with mysticism would be directed to this metaphysics and to the intuition which is its heart, and the question of the cultivation of this insight would be in the forefront. Then it would be to such a tradition the metaphysics of St. Thomas could look for inspiration in how to resolve its own dilemma.

In summary, *Part I* asserts that the intuition of being is the soul of the metaphysics of St. Thomas. It is the living experience out of which metaphysical reflection and conceptualization has to emerge. Therefore, it is essential that we attain this intuition, and that we cultivate it. But we don't know where to look for an example of the methods that are geared to such a metaphysical cultivation. Enter Zen.

Notes

1. Maritain, *Approches sans entraves*, p. 267, note 31.
2. Maritain, *Existence and the Existent*, p. 30.
3. See Gilson on the theme, "Haec Sublimis Veritas" in *A Gilson Reader*, pp. 230ff.
4. Maritain, *Notebooks*, p. 28-29.
5. Ibid., p. 28.
6. Maritain, *The Degrees of Knowledge*, p. 2.
7. Maritain, *A Preface to Metaphysics*, p. 30.
8. Ibid., p. 53.
9. Kalinowski and Swiezawski, *La philosophie à l'heure du Concile*, p. 139.
10. Maritain, *Approches sans entraves*, p. 79.
11. Cornelio Fabro, for example, describes how a passage in the *Summa* (I. Q44, a. 1) "was the first that persuaded me of the central function that the notion of participation ought to have in Thomism." In *La Nozione...*, p. 230.

PART II

ZEN ENLIGHTENMENT

CHAPTER 4

ZEN AS METAPHYSICAL INSIGHT

It is Zen that provides a graphic example of the cultivation of metaphysical insight. Zen has been compared to Christian monasticism and mysticism, and to contemporary philosophy and psychotherapy. But it finds its closest Western parallel in an area that has received the least attention, the metaphysics of St. Thomas. The fact that Thomistic metaphysics is so rarely considered as a suitable partner in a dialogue with Zen is but another indication of the fundamental problem of Thomism that we have been reflecting upon in *Part I*. Thomistic metaphysics has failed to examine the role the intuition of being plays in it and the possibility of cultivating this intuition. It is only a Thomism without this intuitive dimension, and without the living, concrete experiences that give rise to it, that appears as a poor partner in any discussion with a dynamic Zen Buddhism.

Zen needs no introduction to the English-speaking world. A wealth of literature is available that ranges from simple introductions, translations of Zen classics, stories of modern Zen experiences, and attempts to bring Zen face to face with various facets of Western culture.[1]

The essential structure of Zen is simplicity itself. The goal is enlightenment, the experience of our true nature or Buddha nature, and the means is the stopping of all conceptual thought. Sitting in the lotus or half-lotus and regulating the breath stabilize the body, making the control of thought easier. The lectures of the master to his community, his private interviews with his students, and the intensive Zen retreats all provide the setting conducive to the stopping of the mind. The inner techniques of such an abolition of thought is the use of special Zen sayings or sitting with inner intent to stop all thought without any particular aid to focus the mind.

But if the end and means are simple, the actual accomplishment of this task can be exceedingly difficult. In this context, it becomes understandable why the Zen masters steer their students away from metaphysical studies. Any kind of conceptualization, no matter how noble, can become a hindrance by cluttering the mind with thought. Yet this general prohibition should not be taken as an impossibility of there being, not so much a Zen metaphysics, but a metaphysical reflection on Zen experience. A number of books that have appeared in recent years can introduce us to this kind of reflection, which in turn can lead to the possibility of the metaphysics of St. Thomas reflecting on the nature of Zen enlightenment. We have only to briefly look at some themes from Keiji Nishitani and Katsuki Sekida to see that this world of Zen metaphysics would not have been entirely strange to St. Thomas or Maritain.

Keiji Nishitani

Keiji Nishitani, a noted philosopher of the Kyoto School,[2] allows us a glimpse of some of the ideas of *Part I* from a Zen perspective. Philosophical thought has often equated being with substance: "Substance is used to point out the essence of a thing, the self-identity in which a thing is what it is in itself."[3] But this notion of being is incomplete and inadequate. Can the "selfness of a thing" really be grasped by the notion of substance, or is it beyond the level of concepts and essences? Nishitani's solution: "The emptiness of sunyata is not an emptiness represented as some "thing" outside of being and other than being. It is not simply an empty nothing but rather an absolute emptiness, emptied even of these representations of emptiness."[4] In contrast to nihility that would be a nothingness in opposition to being, on the field of absolute emptiness "all are returned to the possibility of existence. Each thing is restored anew to its own virtus - that individual capacity that each thing possesses as a display of its own possibility of existence."[5] Despite the initial strangeness of the language, the notion of absolute emptiness shows remarkable affinities to the esse of St. Thomas and Maritain, which is no-thing and in relation to which essence or substance finds its ultimate meaning. Thus, Nishitani goes on to say: "The "what" of a thing is a real "what" only when it is absolutely no "what" at all."[6] And he calls it "a completely different concept of existence, one that has not up to now become a question for people in their daily lives, one that even philosophers have yet to give consideration."[7] And he has especially in mind the philosophers of the West who have made the identification of substance and being. This same point has been made by the historians of the Thomistic renaissance when they contrasted the being of Aristotle as substance with the being of St. Thomas as esse, or existence. Further, Nishitani gives a role to nihility in showing the weakness of the equation of being with substance, while these same historians show how the doctrine of creation from nothing played a role in Thomas' metaphysical formulation of existence.

The way things appear to us by way of their form or shape are "like rays of light issuing from a common source," or "forms that appear on the perimeter" while the center "represents the point at which the being of things is constituted in unison with emptiness..."[8]

Nishitani clarifies this metaphysical conception by a diagram which contains two concentric circles. Reason is the outer one and sensation the inner. When a radius from the center crosses the two circles, these two points of intersection represent the objective forms under which the thing appears to sensation and reason, while the center of the circle represents the thing as it is in itself. Each radius coming from the center produces its distinctive objective forms, but all things as they are situated in the center "in their selfness are gathered into one."[9] Our normal way of viewing things is to look at the center from the circumference and see the One at the center as a result of mere non-differentiation. But this is not how Nishitani would have us view it. Not only should the One not be viewed with multiplicity and differentiation extracted from it, but it should not even be seen as a center within the circumference, but rather, "a center that is only a center and nothing else, a center on the field of emptiness... Each thing in its own selfness shows the mode of being of the center of all things."[10] And "even the tiniest thing, to the extent that it "is" is an absolute center situated at the center of all things."[11] Thus, while

Nishitani's diagram has many similarities with the metaphysical circle discussed in *Part I*, at the end it veers away from it by avoiding the notion of an absolute center.

Katsuki Sekida

Sekida, a modern Zen master, engagingly attempts in his *Zen Training* to postulate some physiological bases of Zen experience and some of the parallels that exist between Zen and contemporary Western philosophy. He, like Nishitani, leaves us a number of passages that resonate with Thomists:

"Man thinks and acts without noticing. When he thinks, "It is fine today," he is aware of the weather but not of his own thought. It is the reflecting act of consciousness that comes immediately after the thought that makes him aware of his own thinking."[12]

The discipline of Zen concentration eliminates this reflecting activity in order to come to what Sekida calls absolute samadhi or pure existence:

"ultimately the time comes when no reflection appears at all. One comes to notice nothing, feel nothing, hear nothing, see nothing. This state of mind is called "nothing." But it is not vacant emptiness. Rather is it the purest condition of our existence. It is not reflected, and nothing is known directly of it."[13]

It has been the reflecting activity of consciousness, the delusive pattern of thought, the ego as it is looking at everything as objects, that has prevented the awareness of this pure existence, "where you can vividly see existence in its nakedness,"[14] "a state in which absolute silence and stillness reign, bathed in a pure, serene light."[15] "In this stillness, or emptiness, the source of all kinds of activity is latent."[16] "Zen students train themselves earnestly in the first place only for the purpose of experiencing existence."[17]

Absolute samadhi eliminates all reflecting consciousness which has dominated and clouded our perception of the true nature of ourselves and of things. When we emerge from this absolute samadhi and before this consciousness wedded to essentialistic thinking and to the distinction between subject and object can assert itself, we encounter some existing thing, and its true nature can assert itself. The falling of a peach blossom or the sound of a pebble, coming through our purified senses, resounds with the whole mystery of existence. "At the moment of kensho intuitively activated sensation takes the initiative,"[18] and "One looks at the external world with unblinkered eyes. Then everything is found to be admitting a brilliant light."[19] This is close to what Maritain describes as the vital role of the senses in the primordial judgment of sense which gives to intuition the raw material to feed upon in order to come to the intuition of being. Zen and Thomism share a fundamentally realistic epistemological position. Sekida's "intuitively activated sensation"[20] is that which "directly (intuitively) penetrates the object and thereby achieves transcendental cognition."[21]

At the moment of enlightenment or kensho the true meaning of existence is revealed, or better, there is a direct experience of existence, even in the "bowl of rice, pail of water":

You must once have this experience and you will discover what a splendid thing the boiled rice in the bowl is. It shines like diamonds in the incandescent heat of a fire... It is the ultimate in spiritual revelation; you have looked into existence."[22]

It is not consciousness itself that is wrong, but consciousness that has lost sight of its roots. It is not the process of making distinctions that is wrong but is the essentialistic mode of thinking that has lost sight of its foundation of existence. There is another kind of consciousness given in ordinary experience besides the dualistic one. This is what Sekida calls the warm feeling of the eye which comes "from the mood that is latent in each nen,"[23] that is, in each thought impulse. This existential sense of the self can develop in the direction of the reflecting action of consciousness,[24] but it can also be pursued in the direction of pure existence. In the actual experience of enlightenment Sekida describes the expansion and extension of this feeling to all things; he emerged from absolute samadhi and looked at the bookshelves along the wall and they appeared to be coming into him. There was no spatial resistance:

"In a word, they and I were one. If I am you, you also are me. In the field of vision, they and I are distinct structures, each separately standing in its place. However, just as my own existence is intimate and warm to me, so now are they intimate and warm to me. We are not strangers; another me is standing there."[25]

This beautiful description of the direct experience of existence also

GOD, ZEN AND THE INTUITION OF BEING

indicates a difficulty in maintaining essential distinctions. The same lack of the sense of essence appears when Sekida discusses the relationship between the child and the man he has become. "Nothing is left of the child except one thing, your existence itself... there is nothing to be called a person."[26]

Neither is there any talk of God directly, yet Sekida will say: "Existence does not exist for others. It is of itself, for itself, by itself,"[27] giving it the very qualities that a Thomist metaphysician could attribute to God as existence.

These brief but suggestive metaphysical passages from Nishitani and Sekida could be augmented from the writings of others like Masao Abe.[28] Later we will look at powerful reflections of Toshihiko Izutsu.[29] But enough has been said to indicate that Zen has a rich metaphysical language which is at once tantalizingly familiar yet pursues goals strange to the metaphysics of St. Thomas. If Thomism is to avail itself of the gifts that Zen offers, an indispensable preliminary is a clear idea of the similarities and differences between Zen enlightenment and the intuition of being.

Reason, Intuition and Connaturality

It is clear that Maritain's intuition of being is going to be a valuable tool in developing a Thomistic appreciation of the nature of Zen enlightenment, which is the task of the next chapter. But he also provides another essential instrument for this work in his reflection on the relationship of reason to intuition, and their relationship, in turn, to a nonconceptual knowledge which he calls knowledge through connaturality.

We have already seen how Maritain had to struggle to reformulate the notions of intuition and concept that he had received from Bergson. And this reformulation under the light of St. Thomas was a task whose accomplishment can be traced from his first essay "Modern Science and Reason,"[30] to his first book *Bergsonian Philosophy and Thomism*,[31] all the way to one of his last essays, "No Knowledge Without Intuition",[32] written more than a half century later.

In Heidelberg, he finally had to admit to himself that Bergson's notion of the concept was wrong and he would have to begin his philosophical work anew. Later, St. Thomas showed him the way to do this. Certainly the concept could be and was abused. It was treated as a lifeless likeness of the thing to be known and subjected to mechanical manipulation. But our minds needed both intuition and concepts. To save intuition Maritain saw we cannot disconnect it from intellect and reason, and thus split the mind into an intuitive faculty and a separate and deficient conceptual one. It is intuition that is the heart of the intellect. We know. We see. Knowledge terminates not in ideas but in things. But we see through concepts. These concepts are not opaque to actually existing things. They are the very means, by which and through which, we see the thing. Our intellects are not angelic. We can't grasp something all at once. The intellect achieves its seeing, its intuition, this immaterial, intentional union with things, by bathing them in its own inner active light, thus raising them to the level of immateriality it enjoys and partially penetrating them with this light in order to carve and release from them a certain aspect of their intelligibility. Concepts are the thing brought into the mind, the thing existing in those conditions in which the mind can know it. And this creation of concepts, or intelligible aspects, by the mind finds its culmination in the affirmations we make that join these concepts together, and by which we assert that these diverse concepts are really united in the existing thing. In short, for Maritain following St. Thomas, the concept's entire being is subordinated and transparent to insight and intuition, for it is created in order that we might see.

If we understand concepts not as things to be known, but the conditions that the intellect needs in order to know and see, then we can steer a path between the various forms of idealism in which the idea is known first, and conceptualism in which intuition fades and concepts and their manipulation dominate. In both cases, knowledge of the existing things themselves is subordinated to our ideas.

Connaturality

Strange as it may seem, it was because Maritain championed the concept that he could become the champion of non-conceptual knowledge, as well. He could respect the validity of knowledge through the careful elaboration of concepts and judgments, while at the same time he recognized that the whole notion of a concept was much more flexible than the advocates of reason and logic would have it, and further, there could be genuine knowledge in which concepts played a minimal role.

Knowledge through connaturality is "produced in the intellect but not in virtue of conceptual connections and by way of demonstration."[33]

"In this knowledge through union or inclination, connaturality or congeniality, the intellect is at play not alone, but together with affective inclinations and the dispositions of the will, and is guided and directed by them. It is not rational knowledge, knowledge through the conceptual, logical and discursive exercise of Reason. But it is really and genuinely knowledge, though obscure and perhaps incapable of giving account of itself, or of being translated into words."[34]

In Maritain's hands knowledge by connaturality becomes a fluid notion that embraces art, poetry, morality and mystical experience. It extends to the hunches and image-laden primordial insights of the empirical scientist groping towards a new theory. It aids the artist whose dim perceptions do not reach the daylight of consciousness except in the work of art itself. Connatural knowledge is found in the conduct of the good man who consults his instinct rather than a text on moral theology in order to decide how to behave. It is intuition as divinatory, feeding not only on the input of the senses but of the imagination, emotions and heart. And it was this knowledge by connaturality that was to play a role in Maritain's understanding of the mysticism of the East.

Notes

1. An excellent introduction is Philip *Kapleau's The Three Pillars of Zen.*
2. See Notto Thelle, "The Flower Blooms On The Cliff's Edge; Profile of Nishitani Keiji, a Thinker between East and West," and James W. Heisig's *East-West Dialogue: Sunyata and Kenosis*, Part I. p. 142-145.
3. *Religion and Nothingness*, The Standpoint of Sunyata, p. 119.
4. Ibid., p. 123.
5. Ibid.
6. Ibid., p. 125.
7. Ibid., p. 128.

8. Ibid., p. 130.
9. Ibid., p. 143.
10. Ibid., p. 146.
11. Ibid., p. 147.
12. *Zen Training*, p. 108.
13. Ibid., p. 94.
14. Ibid., p. 161.
15. Ibid., p. 30.
16. Ibid., p. 34.
17. Ibid., p. 70.
18. Ibid., p. 194.
19. Ibid., p. 101.
20. Ibid., p. 194.
21. Ibid., p. 190.
22. Ibid., p. 135.
23. Ibid., p. 182.
24. Ibid., p. 183.
25. Ibid., p. 201.
26. Ibid., p. 122.
27. Ibid., p. 162.
28. Yamaguchi takes up the theme of connaturality in relationship to Bergson and Zen, and see especially Abe's remarks on the appropriateness of contrasting Buddhism's Mu with Christianity's U, that is, the Aristotelian concept of being: *Zen and Western Thought*, p. 98, note 8.
29. See p. 62ff.
30. This essay appeared in the *Revue de philosophie* in 1910 and was reprinted in *Antimoderne*.
31. *La Philosophie Bergsonienne*, 1914, 1930, 1948.
32. See, as well, some of the companion essays in *Approches sans entraves*.
33. On knowledge through connaturality: *The Range of Reason*, p. 22.
34. Ibid., p. 23.

CHAPTER 5

ZEN ENLIGHTENMENT FROM A THOMISTIC VIEWPOINT

In 1938 Jacques Maritain gave a paper at a Carmelite congress on religious psychology entitled, "Natural Mystical Experience and the Void."[1] This is one of the finest Thomistic contributions to a metaphysical understanding of Zen. It is somewhat ironic, therefore, that Maritain did not have Zen directly in mind, but rather the religious experience of India, and found his inspiration in a work by Ambrose Gardiel, *The Structure of the Soul and Mystical Experience*. Père Gardeil in turn found it a complete surprise that his ideas developed in relationship to Christian mysticism would be applied to the mysticism of India.[2]

Maritain's starting point is the structure of our self-awareness. This self-consciousness is a reflection of the spiritual nature of the soul which is by nature transparent to itself. But since the soul is profoundly united to the body it cannot realize, or actualize, this transparency. We have no inner vision of our spiritual nature. Instead, our self-consciousness is founded upon a reflection on the operations of the soul. We act and reflect on our acts and become aware that we are the ones that are acting, as Sekida noted. In Maritain's language there is not "even a partial actualization of the latent self-intellection of the soul reflecting upon itself."[3] This kind of auto-intellection is hindered by the union with the body, but it can still serve as the "metaphysical condition and the first foundation for the faculty of perfect reflection upon its own acts which the soul enjoys by title of its own spirituality..."[4]

The two basic orientations to reality, what something is and that it is, return here but now from the inside, manifesting themselves in the very nature of our consciousness. Our knowledge is oriented outward to the world of the things around us, and we come to understand both what they are and that they are. But when we reflect on these acts of knowledge and grasp from within ourselves as the subject of these acts, we have an intimate living experience of the fact that we exist and can assert "I am," but we have no direct grasp of our own essence, or of what we are. Our "experiential knowledge" of ourselves is "purely existential and implies no other quid (what) offered to my mind than my own operations grasped reflexively in the emanation of their principles."[5] I may reflect upon the nature of these acts that come forth from me, and by way of concepts attempt to reason about my nature, but I do not have a direct intuitive grasp of my essence.

This state of affairs surrounds self-consciousness with particular paradoxes and possibilities. My self-awareness has a deeply attractive immediacy by which I am myself. I am no longer knowing things from the outside, but I am present to myself within myself without the mediation of concepts. This is a deeper and richer way of knowing, but it is hedged about by all sorts of limits. To lose my consciousness can appear to be a loss of what is most precious in me, and yet, each day, I am subject to this loss many times over, whether it is in my sleep, or by inattention. Instead of my self-awareness being located in the center of my soul so that I would once and for all be and possess myself without fluctuation, it rides on the waves of my activity. I know that I am, but I really do not know who I am in all my amplitude. My consciousness, this very ego I call myself, is not at the center of my being. The very structure of my consciousness makes me realize the radical insufficiency of the possession I have of myself. I am faced with the tantalizing mystery of how to become fully myself. If I pursue myself in the direction of knowledge of things outside myself, and even within, it is their whatness that most confronts me. I become aware of their differentness and separateness from me, and no matter how much I know them and use them as a spring board by which to reflect and grasp my own self, I still remain a

"prisoner of mobility and multiplicity, of the fugitive luxuriance of phenomena and of operations which emerge in us from the darkness of the unconscious… The phenomenal content which occupies the stage and, indeed, is the only set of qualities to be grasped in the existential experience of ourselves."[6]

But there is another direction to explore, and this is the purely existential grasp I have of myself. It could be called the way of existence rather than the way of essence. The starting point is this experience we have of being present to ourselves, but now it is a question of a journey from this ego consciousness to our inner or absolute self. This happens, according to Maritain, by

"reversing the ordinary course of mental activity" so that "the soul empties itself absolutely of every specific operation and of all multiplicity, and knows negatively by means of the void and the annihilation of every act and of every object of thought coming from outside - the soul knows negatively - but nakedly, without veils - that metaphysical marvel, that absolute, that perfection of every act and of every perfection, which is to exist, which is the soul's own substantial existence."[7]

This stopping of all conceptual thought Maritain calls "an act of supreme silence," and the objection that has been posed to many Zen masters comes to his mind. If every image is removed, will not the result be pure and simple nothingness? And he answers in traditional Zen fashion, without realizing it, that this process of purification results "in a negation, a void, and an annihilation which are in no sense nothingness."[8] And these words "signify an act which continues to be intensely vital, the ultimate actuation whereby and wherein the void, abolition, negation, riddance, are consummated and silence is made perfect."[9] Even the principle that the soul knows itself by its own acts is maintained, in this extreme case where "the act in question is the act of abolition of all acts."[10]

The emptiness that results from the abolition of all essence becomes the formal means by which the substantial existence of the soul is known, but "negatively - transferred into the status of an object, not indeed of an object expressible in a concept and appearing before the mind, but an object entirely inexpressible and engulfed in the night wherein the mind engulfs itself in order to join it."[11]

The emptiness that is the elimination of essences or concepts becomes itself the means of knowing, not, of course, by concepts, but by connaturality. In this kind of connaturality, the void itself connatures the knower with that absolute which is the existence of the soul. And Maritain, paraphrasing the famous passage of John of St. Thomas on supernatural mysticism, *amor transit in conditionem objecti*, says, "vacuitas, abolitio, denudatio transit in conditionem objecti."[12] Emptiness is the proper and formal means of knowing the "to exist" of subjectivity.

But since this very experience requires as its indispensable prerequisite the elimination of any essence which would limit and contract the existence of the reality perceived, then this experience of the existence of the soul is at the same time an experience of the metaphysical amplitude of existence and God as the source of existence. The soul is experienced as an absolute which cannot be conceptually distinguished from that absolute given in the intuition of being and the absolute who is the author of being.

God, in this experience, is not the object of possession or union through love as He is in Christian mysticism, but He is attained through the negative experience of the existence of the soul so that it is legitimate to speak of a "contact with the absolute" and an "experience of God in quantum, infundens et profundens esse in rebus, indirectly attained in the mirror of the substantial esse of the soul," (as far as he is pouring and infusing existence in things).[13] But what is mirrored cannot be distinguished from the mirror. What springs up is a powerful metaphysical mysticism attained at the price of negating all essences.

But this essence-less-ness is a consequence, from the Thomistic point of view, not of the actual constitution of things but of the means by which they are known. It is the price that must be paid to arrive at this experience, but the consequence on the speculative level is the risk that the formal means of knowing will so color what is known that the absolute that is the existence of the soul will be identified with the absolute seen in the intuition of being and with the absolute which is God. Thus, a Zen master can say when one of his students achieved enlightenment, "Now you understand that seeing mu is seeing God."[14] Or Suzuki, in one of his later essays, could describe the discovery of the self in its "native nakedness" or "isness" by saying, "It yields a kind of metaphysical formula: self = zero and zero = Infinity; hence self = Infinity."[15]

Zen Language

Yet we should not make this lack of distinctions into a rigid principle. The Zen master is well aware of the differences of things as reflected in this traditional Zen saying:

"In the beginning mountains were mountains and rivers were rivers. Then all were one, and finally, mountains were really mountains and rivers were really rivers."[16]

This depicts, first of all, the state of unenlightenment, then the initial stage of enlightenment, and finally, a fuller development of that enlightenment. In some sense, distinctions do exist and it might be useful to comment upon this passage from the point of view of Thomistic metaphysics.

In the first stage, or what the metaphysician might call the stage of common sense, existing things are seen chiefly from the point of view of essence. What a thing is fills our whole vision and prevents us from seeing the rest of reality. We equate our idea of the thing with the thing itself. We look at the relationship between essence and existence and see only essence. We are looking from the circumference of the circle, and this circumference blocks our view of the center. Thus, mountains are mountains, rivers are rivers, flowers are flowers, all things are themselves and distinct from each other, and this sense of distinction fails to see the deeper ground of unity that exists between them all. Such essentialistic thinking is at the root of the opposition between myself and others. In actual fact, there is no me, no ego, that is purely essence without relationship to existence. In this sense the ego is a product of ignorance and a hindrance to genuine enlightenment. Zen language is moving on the practical and existential plane and not on the ontological one. Thus, when the ego stands in opposition to others in such a way as to deny the underlying unity of all things, it is a false ego. There is no ego in this sense.

In the second phase, where enlightenment has been attained in a certain degree, all appear as one. The unity of all things in existence has been revealed, the Thomist metaphysician might say. The view of existing things has been reversed. Now it is existence that is seen first and which blinds us with its splendor to the fact of essence. We see unity without diversity, where before we saw diversity without unity. Such a view is an important advance over the first, for it does not lead to opposition and strife, but it is still incomplete. Things are not simply existence without relationship to essence. Existence on the level of existing things is always the existence of something, and while the act of existence attains a relative unity in the mind, it is an analogical unity. Each existing thing has its own act of existence.

Balance is finally achieved in the third phase of full enlightenment. Mountains are again mountains and rivers are rivers, but there has been no return to the common sense notion of being. The everyday world is, indeed, the world of enlightenment, but the enlightened man does not see it the same way as the unenlightened man. Now existing things reveal themselves as transfigured by the mystery of existence. There is nothing in them that does not exist. Every fiber or fragment of everything exists. Essence is seen in its ultimate significance, which is its relationship to the act of existence, and existence is seen in those things which exist. In this sense there is no existence outside of the manifestation of existing things, and there are no essences outside of existence itself. In this sense form is emptiness, that is, essence is totally related to existence and emptiness is form.

Yet, the very real similarities between enlightenment and the intuition of being should not obscure the significant differences. The first and chief difference is the relationship between the insight and its elaboration in concepts or ideas. If both intuitions transcend the level of concepts, their transcendence is not the same kind. The intuition of being is radically open to concepts. It itself is an eidetic intuition. It is in continuity with the world of concepts even when it transcends them by pushing them to their limit.

With Zen the situation is very different precisely because the means to the intuition is the elimination of all conceptual thought. Zen looks at conceptual thought as a tyranny that it must overthrow. It avoids it, not simply because it has been overemphasized, but because the very nature of enlightenment demands that it be avoided. It asserts the absolute primacy of intuition not to restore the balance between intuition and concepts, but because the intuition it is striving for is antithetical to conceptual thinking.

This lack of conceptual continuity can be seen in the language of the Zen masters. They did not speak in cryptic sayings or koans out of a love of mystification, but firmly grounded in enlightenment they uttered or acted out some sign of this mystery, but always reluctantly, for they knew that words are a temptation to the beginner who will attempt to attain the insight through the concepts or by repeating the gesture. The words of the Zen master are an enigma and even a scan-

GOD, ZEN AND THE INTUITION OF BEING

dal to the beginner who is expecting him to reveal something and is constantly searching for their hidden meaning or someone who can interpret them and unveil their contents. These beginners miss the point, for they are looking for continuity between the concept and the insight. This is the pattern of knowing that they have grown up with and which appears much preferable to the work of stopping all conceptual thought, if, indeed, the latter even presents itself as a practical alternative. Only as the mind matures by means of Zen training does it become probable that the words and gestures that have originated from an experience of enlightenment in the master can trigger a stopping and a reversal of the mind in the student by which enlightenment can be attained.

Zen language, then, is highly distinctive. It communicates, but not conceptually. It is enigmatic without being a secret code. Even if we amass collections of koans, we cannot treat them as a cumulative collection of clues. There is no gradual dawning of understanding that results from our deeper and deeper penetration into the meaning of these Zen sayings. They are one-way realities: nonsense from the point of view of the discriminating ego but genuine expressions of enlightenment when seen from the point of view of enlightenment itself. By virtue of this unidirectionality they disconcert the mind's attempt to understand them, and they force it to exhaust its conceptual bag of tricks until finally, in the best of cases, conceptual thought dies out and enlightenment is born. The mind is forced out of its normal channels, and once satori is reached, then the koans yield their meaning. Thus, books that purport to give the answers to koans are not destructive because they can actually give away a genuine meaning, but they can be harmful inasmuch as they clutter up the mind with conceptual answers to something that cannot be answered conceptually.

A Fanciful and Future Discussion

In order to highlight both the similarities and differences between the metaphysics of St. Thomas and a metaphysical reflection on Zen, let us imagine a dialogue between Jacques Maritain and Toshihiko Izutsu, for as imaginary as it is, such a discussion can give us the flavor of what a Zen-Thomistic dialogue could be like in the future. Izutsu, in his collection of essays, *Toward a Philosophy of Zen Budd-*

hism, gives us one of the most penetrating modern accounts of metaphysics from a Zen perspective. I apologize to both men if I have put words in their mouths they would be unhappy saying.[17]

Izutsu: Each philosophy is based on a particular reality experience. Zen has its own noetic experience capable of giving rise to an ontology.[18]

Maritain: So does Thomism, and that was what I was driving at in describing the concrete experiences that give rise to the noetic experience of the intuition of being.

Izutsu: Yes, but in contrast to an Aristotelian perspective which asks, "What is man?", Zen asks, "Who am I?" It wants to intuit man in his most intimate subjectivity.[19] Western philosophy is primarily an essentialism. Zen would say it sees things as if in a dream and equates them with their essence. Zen devotes itself to breaking out of this ordinary consciousness split into subject and object, this thing and that, where the apple is the apple, A is A. Zen proposes to go beyond this level of essence, a solidly fixed ontological core which unalterably determines the essential limits of a thing.[20] In a certain way A is not A.

Maritain: And where does Zen want to go? What will it find beyond essence?

Izutsu: "At the ultimate limit of all negations, that is, the negation of all essences conceivable of the apple, all of a sudden the extraordinary reality flashes into our mind. This is what is known in Buddhism as the emergence of prajna, transcendental or non-discriminating consciousness. And in and through this experience, the apple again manifests itself as an apple in the fullest density of existence, in the 'original freshness of the first creation of heaven and earth'."[21]

Maritain: That is very interesting. It is easy to understand why you would look at Western philosophy as essentialistic. Many Westerners imagine St. Thomas as a simple follower of Aristotle and miss his originality. St. Thomas was as much concerned to take essence out of the center of the philosophical stage as Zen is. The ultimate principle of his philosophy was not essence, but existence. But he did not deny the reality of essence. Rather, he transformed it.

Izutsu: What did essence mean to him?

Maritain: It was simply this or that capacity to be. It was the contraction, reception or refraction of existence so as to bring about this

GOD, ZEN AND THE INTUITION OF BEING   301

or that existent thing. Existence holds the primacy. It is as act to potency, received to the receiver. There can be no meaning to essence outside of its relationship to existence. Essence is simply a certain capacity to exist. Thomists can say A is A, but we can also say A is not A if we understand this to mean the apple is not simply the apple in an identity of essence, but the apple exists, and to exist is itself not identical to the apple.

Izutsu: Let me put it another way. If something becomes itself, "thoroughgoingly and completely, to the utmost extent of possibility, it ends by breaking through its own limit and going beyond its determinations. At this stage, A is no longer A; A is non-A." And "it breaks through its own A-ness, and begins to disclose to him its formless, essenceless, and 'aspect'-less aspect."[22] Then it refinds the everyday world from the direction of essence-less-ness. A is A. Then A is not A. Therefore it is A. Can Thomism say this?

Maritain: Essence is the limit and determination of existence, of esse. And to see a tree or myself in the light of the intuition of being is no longer to see only its essence face. But, having seen how esse in itself is formless or essenceless, it is to see essence exercising the act of existing, transfigured, as it were, by this act of existence. A is A in that essence is essence. The tree is a tree and not something else. A is not A. The tree exists but it is not existence itself, rather one face or articulation of existence. Finally, A is A since this very tree is existing. Existence is actualized in this tree. In a certain way Thomism and Zen share an existential metaphysics, and this common ground should not be underestimated, but there are important differences, as well.

Izutsu: What are they?

Maritain: I believe we differ in the way we understand the realm beyond essence and its relationship to existing things.

Izutsu: Yes. I have the feeling that you believe in self-subsisting things, both the ego and the objects around us, while we do not. You believe in a metaphysical suprasensible substance governing the phenomenal world and we do not.

Maritain: Please elaborate your position further.

Izutsu: Let us say instead of subject or object actually existing, or a separate absolute being, there is an actus charging the entire field with its dynamic energy.[23] "Concrete individuals are actualizations of the limitless, aspectless aspect of an ever-active and ever-creative Act."[24]

What you take as the experience of an individual existing thing we see as the "total concretization or actualization of the entire field."[25] It is the absolute at this very moment in this very place.[26]

Maritain: It is interesting that you would use the word actus, which is a word we apply to God in the sense of pure act, act without potentiality. I think we are at the crux of the matter. We believe the ego in the sense of the human person to have its own act of existence, just as we believe the tree or the butterfly does. We believe God to be existence itself, and thus a subsisting being. Are you saying that concrete things are nil or the absolute is a mere nothingness?

Izutsu: There is no nihilism in Zen. When we speak of the absolute as Nothingness, it is not mere emptiness. When we speak of the non-subsisting character of the tree, we are not idealists. Nothingness is the "plenitude of being, for it is the urgrund of all existential forms."[27] In everyday awareness things are closed, seen essentialistically, if you will. Then in the process of enlightenment they are reduced to absolute undifferentiation or nothingness, and when they emerge from this nothingness they are ontologically transparent or open. Both subject and object are abstractions from the field of actus. "Nothing is to be regarded as self-subsistent and self-sufficient."[28] Zen wants to see the nonarticulated field articulating itself. Let me recount a famous koan in the Mu Mon Kan: "Listen! Once a monk asked Chao Chou, "Tell me, what is the significance of the first Patriarchs coming from the West?" Chao Chou replied, "The cypress tree in the courtyard!"

"This cypress tree is not simply or only a cypress tree. For it carries the whole weight of the Field… Out of the very depths of nothingness - Eternal - Present being actualized at this present moment…"[29] Don't look for nothingness by itself as a subsisting absolute. Don't look for the concrete subsisting individual. The cypress tree is the absolute and the absolute is the cypress tree. There is no transcendental absolute beyond the concrete thing. "The cypress tree in its concrete reality is the absolute at this very moment in this very place."[30]

Maritain: So when we speak of the enduring personality or existing thing or God, it appears as if we are locked in an essentialitic perspective and have not made contact with that nothingness which is beyond subject or object.

But you must understand that when we speak of God as substance or as esse subsistens we make no claim to capture Him in our concepts or to know His essence like we might know the essence of man. While He must have an essence in the sense that He is not mere nothingness, He has no essence we can grasp as a contraction of existence. He is no-thing. He is not this or that. There is no potentiality or capacity in Him. He is actus and the most intimate subjectivity if we purify these terms of all limitations. I am not you nor am I the tree, says our ordinary awareness. We do not reject this ordinary awareness, but go beyond it and transform it. I see that my root, my most formal and actual reality, is my existence, just as existence is what is most actual and formal in the tree. But existence in each is not absolute existence, though it comes from Existence itself and is sustained each moment by Existence. But the existence in myself and the tree are analogous. We are various capacities and reflections of what it means To Be. And these capacities find their ultimate meaning in relationship To Be, but as limitations of it, so they become a certain this or that. So that at the heart of my I, I find existence, that existence that allows me to affirm that I am, that existence which is directly issuing from the fountain of To Be. I am not an I without the relationship to Am. I Am. The Am is not a core or pith within the I. It is the very act and reality by which the I exists. The cypress tree Is. There is no inner part which is Is rather than tree, but the tree is as directly and always in the present moment issuing forth from the hand of God. On the philosophical plane we know that God exists by seeing His handiwork, these existing things, but they do not directly show Him to us. We are limited existents, in which existence is received by essence.

Izutsu: But why do you see separate existing things no matter how intimately connected, while we admit no separation?

Maritain: I don't believe that the differences reside in what could be called the metaphysical structure of reality. We are seeing the same things, but through the spectacles of different methods, and these different methods are what the differences in language reflect. We are both attaining metaphysical insight, but Thomists go by the way of ideas or essences, pushing them to their limits, to their ultimate foundation in esse, to an eidetic visualization or intuition of being. Thomists proceed by ideas in the very act of transforming them and seeing their trajectory swallowed up in the abyss of Esse beyond all ideas or essences. Zen, on the other hand, it appears to me, goes by the way of the negation of all essences. The void becomes the very means by which you know the absolute, and therefore you can discern no essences in it because you had to eliminate them in order to come to this intimate contact with existence. When you discover esse in the I or in the cypress tree, it is esse without essence or limitation, for all essence has been necessarily left behind. And so what we would call the existence of the tree you experience as existence in all its analogical amplitude. There is no way to distinguish the esse of the I from the esse of the tree or the Esse of the Absolute. Thus, whether you approach the I or the tree, you will arrive at the same place in which esse is articulating itself in either one, while at the same time it cannot be a self-subsisting esse. In short, Zen can make no distinction between the esse of the soul, the esse of things and the esse of God, but the critical point is why? Is it because in reality there is none, or because the very elimination of conceptual thought makes it impossible to make these distinctions?

Izutsu: This is a serious matter. You are saying that our method of stopping all conceptual thought is what eliminates the distinctions which are actually there and which you discover because you have not suppressed essences.

Maritain: I am saying both methods have their limitations. Since Thomists go by way of essences, they often end in essentialism. They don't have to end up there, but because human nature is what it is with its weakness of intuitive powers, the mind lets essences concretize and become opaque to all else. While we are aware of this problem, we have put very little energy into finding effective methods to overcome it.

Zen, on the other hand, has faired much better in maintaining the intuitive roots of metaphysics. It has done this by devoting itself to experience rather than to conceptual knowledge. But there is a price for Zen to pay just as we pay ours. While it may be true that in some very important lived fashion Zen has an awareness of the distinction between things, in the post-experience reflection there is no way to conceptualize these distinctions, or at least there has not yet been a way. Zen has not articulated a metaphysics which would account for what we feel to be actually existing distinctions, for their elimination has been the price that Zen has paid for attaining the experience in the first place.

GOD, ZEN AND THE INTUITION OF BEING

Izutsu: Isn't it asking a great deal of Zen to admit such a possibility?

Maritain: Here we come to the heart of the possibility of a real dialogue between Zen and Thomism. If Thomism cannot admit the possibility that Zen has outstripped it in metaphysical experience, it will remain with the ever-present problem of essentialism and the threat of the periodic oblivion of the insights of St. Thomas. But if Zen cannot admit the possibility that some of their post-experience formulas might reflect the very method of attaining the experience, as well as the experience itself, what room is there for genuine dialogue? If Zen has an actual experience of the esse of the soul, as we would put it, and through this esse the analogical infinitude of the act of existence, and God as the source of this esse, and thus an experience of God in and through this contact with the esse of the soul, this is all of the highest importance for Thomists as an inspiration to examine their own experiential roots. If St. Thomas has an articulated metaphysics of esse, could it not equally inspire Zen to clarify its own language, at least when it is aiming at metaphysical articulation?

Izutsu: Aren't you really asking more of Zen than of Thomism? Aren't you striking at the time-honored formulas of Zen which are intimately connected with Zen experience itself? When I say, "There is no longer I as a subjective reality, nor thou, or it, as an objective entity, there remains only Is..."[31] I do not think Thomists can follow me, for Zen "the undifferentiated cannot ex-ist in its original non-differentiation; that in order to ex-ist it must necessarily differentiate itself, i.e., concretely crystallize itself as something - whether subjective or objective."[32]

Maritain: This is precisely what the metaphysics of St. Thomas is trying to deal with. If ex-ist means not only to stand outside of causes and stand outside of mere nothingness, but to manifest or articulate a particular face of Is, then it belongs to the created existent in which Is is limited by essence. But we would say that in its most fundamental sense ex-ist is Is.

Izutsu: Yet we experience it otherwise and our words are a reflection of our experience, as I said, while yours are bound up with concepts.

Maritain: I admire your experience and the strength it takes to attain it, yet you must consider the possibility that the very way of attaining your experience will color what is experienced. To admit this, does it really effect Zen experience itself? The experience remains the same, but I wonder if some of your paradoxical language does not spring from attempting to articulate these distinctions. We agree that essence-less-ness is not mere nothingness.

Izutsu: Yes. In sunyata no fixed essence is established.[33]

Maritain: And the task at hand is to try to agree about the nature of this essence-less-ness, the positive meaning of No-thing-ness.

Izutsu: We are on the road, but it will be a long and difficult one.

Speculative and Practical Language

In such a discussion Maritain would, no doubt, soon have had recourse to one of his favorite themes, which was the difference between the speculative and the practical sciences. Even if two people are speaking about the same thing, the very noetic structure of their languages can be different. A speculative science desires, above all else, to know things as they are in themselves, while a practical science desires to know things in order that this knowledge will serve an action to be accomplished. And these differences are reflected in the very texture of the concepts they use. And if these deep structural differences are not recognized, the surface similarity of vocabulary can be misleading.

Maritain illustrated the meaning and the fecundity of this distinction between the practical and the speculative by discussing the work of St. John of the Cross. St. John was not a speculative theologian, but was most of all interested in leading people to the goal of divine union. Therefore, when he wrote, it was not in the style, in the structural language, of a St. Thomas who, above all, wanted to know, but it was by fashioning a practical language that would aid seekers to attain this goal of union. So when he spoke of how all creatures are nothing in relationship to God, or how desires blacken and darken the soul, he was not making an ontological statement, as if he were not aware that creatures are not nothing, or that it is an inordinate desire, not any desire whatsoever, that blackens the soul. If we read St. John in a speculative-ontological way we can misread him. But if we read him in the practical register, then we can appreciate his concern with how easily we are misled by our desires and blinded by them, so that we fail to come to divine union.

It is possible to imagine that Maritain honored St. Thomas as a speculative theologian, but put St. John in second place as being merely a spiritual director. But this would be to misunderstand both Maritain's appreciation of St. John, which was very great, and the true import of what he meant by a practical science. St. John has deep speculative gifts, both philosophical and theological, but they were in the service of a greater gift. He was enamored by the ultimate goal, which is union with God, and so he instinctively subordinated everything to this goal. We can find fascinating speculative, theological and philosophical vistas in St. John's work, but in order to do this with the greatest effect and least error we have to understand his overall perspective and make the necessary transformation of vocabulary lest we extract certain statements, read them in a different ontological register, and come to a conclusion at odds with St. John himself.[34]

What has this to do with Zen? Would it be fair to say that Zen speaks in a practical language just as St. John does? Everything is geared, not to divine union through love, but to that emptiness which is not mere nothingness. The Zen master is not directly interested in the speculative gifts of his students, but in aiding them to achieve this goal. He does not speak so that they can know, but he speaks so that they can not-know, and thus truly know. His language is one with the whole of Zen life which urges the student to achieve enlightenment. It is a practical language, not in the pejorative sense, but in the highest sense that it contains within itself beautiful and profound metaphysical vistas, but subordinates them to the supreme goal of enlightenment. Thus, Izutsu and other Zen philosophers are keenly aware that they are not simply philosophizing in a mode too often found in a facile way in the West, but they are reflecting on Zen experience. What does this mean but that they must enter into the particular structure of Zen and share its vital movement towards the goal that shapes all if they are to truly see Zen and interpret it properly? Zen metaphysics, then, has to make a delicate translation from one structural language to another, from the practical to the speculative, if you will. But here we are at the crux of the difficulty that arose in the dialogue between Izutsu and Maritain.

Is the Zen metaphysics that is emerging today written in the practical or the speculative register? Or is Zen itself so dominated by its practical intent and the supreme technique of stopping all thought that these metaphysical reflections still maintain a practical cast? If this is so, the clarification of the different kinds of languages used will be an indispensable prerequisite for a Zen-Thomist dialogue. As long as Thomists speak a speculative-ontological language, and their Zen partners speak a practical-ontological language, misunderstandings will abound.

Notes

1. It appeared in Maritain's *Quatre Essais* and in English translation in *Understanding Mysticism*, ed. R. Woods.
2. Ibid., p. 487.
3. Ibid., p. 485.
4. Ibid., p. 486.
5. Ibid.
6. Ibid., p. 487.
7. Ibid., p. 489.
8. Ibid.
9. Ibid.
10. Ibid., p. 490.
11. Ibid.
12. Ibid.
13. Ibid., p. 499, note 18.
14. *The Three Pillars of Zen*, p. 254.
15. *Self the Unattainable*, p. 16.
16. See the commentary in Abe's *Zen and Western Thought* and T. Izutsu's in *Toward a Philosophy of Zen Buddhism*, p. 28.
17. The essays were given at Eranos and elsewhere.
18. *Toward a Philosophy of Zen Buddhism*, p. ix.
19. Ibid., p. 4.
20. Ibid., p. 13.
21. Ibid., p. 14.
22. Ibid., p. 29.
23. Ibid., p. 25.
24. Ibid., p. 32.
25. Ibid., p. 46.
26. Ibid., p. 49.
27. Ibid., p. 127.
28. Ibid., p. 45.
29. Ibid., p. 48.
30. Ibid., p. 49.
31. Ibid., p. 159.
32. Ibid., p. 169.
33. Ibid., p. 109.
34. *The Degrees of Knowledge*, pp. 310ff.

CHAPTER 6

METAPHYSICAL KOANS

If Zen cannot give Thomistic metaphysics its supreme technique, which is the stopping of all thought, for they are both pursuing different goals, what can it offer? It can give two things of the greatest importance: an atmosphere of dedication to enlightenment, and the inspiration for Thomism to attempt to create its own metaphysical techniques and koans.

Zen Spirit

The spirit of Zen with its love of nature, the arts, and simplicity are vital ingredients for the cultivation of metaphysical insight, and would be a powerful antidote to the dangers of an over-academic Thomism. The things of nature have a vibrancy of existence that man-made objects rarely match. Nature can purify the senses and allow them to open and become attuned to the whole range of sensations. Listening to the falling rain or the wind sighing in the trees can be a step closer to the mystery of being. But we must listen to and exercise Maritain's active and attentive silence and avoid composing conceptual answers which separate us from the thing itself. This kind of listening or seeing lets things soak into us like a gentle rain and leads towards a deep union between the knower and the known. It is under these conditions that we can hope to meet being.

Zen's love of nature is not some vague nature mysticism or search for tranquillity. It is much more vigorous, and even metaphysical. Zen cultivates transparency of mind through which it attempts to fathom the ultimate secret not only of the mind, but of the flower or the pine tree. In ordinary perception, D.T. Suzuki writes:

"The one who beholds is separated from the object which is beheld; there is an impassable gap between the two; and it is impossible for the beholder to come in touch inwardly with his object. Here is no grasping of actual facts as we face them. If heaven and earth, with all the manifold objects between them, issue from the one root which you and I also come from, this root must be firmly seized upon so there is an actual experience of it."[1]

It is from the vantage point of this one root that the flower is beheld. Then nature is not something to be mastered or classified, or simply utilized. It is the face of this mystery of the one root, if we only have eyes to see. Ryokan, a Soto Zen monk, lets a bamboo shoot grow in his hut until it is scraping the ceiling. Then, while trying to make a hole in the roof for it with a candle he accidentally burns his hut to the ground. Is this foolishness and folly, or is true folly to confine our children in streets of asphalt surrounded by homes, cars, and all the objects of men's hands? Then what they see of nature is on television or in a zoo. But is this really nature? This nature is confined by men's ideas like the sterile landscaping of a shopping mall. Nature has been neutralized. It can no longer speak of its inner meaning. It is constantly being overwhelmed by man's conceptual mind and treated as part of his equipment. The poor animal in a cage loses the sense of mystery that its brother in the brush possesses as it flashes before our eyes, clothed in grace and freedom. This momentary sighting is a symbol, a tongue-tip taste of a world beyond consciousness and its grid of ideas. Not that nature has to be physically imposing. It can speak of its mystery in a butterfly fluttering over a field, or a tree simply standing in its native splendor, or the snow silently falling in the midst of a forest. As long as our minds are filled with our own ideas and preconceptions there is no room left for the message of nature to penetrate.

The transparency which Zen demands is the silencing of all this mental noise, and even of the concepts themselves. Though the intuition of being does not proceed by way of the elimination of all concepts, to lock philosophy in the lecture hall is to deal it a mortal wound. It is in nature that it finds its food by drinking of its infinite variety. We must soak ourselves in nature, listen to it and be carried by its gentle rhythms to its depths where metaphysics can be born. And it is the love of nature in this sense that Zen can teach to

GOD, ZEN AND THE INTUITION OF BEING

Thomistic metaphysics.

Another aspect of the love of nature is the love of simplicity. The simplification of life allows basic things to emerge from the shadows where they have been driven by the incessant clamor and din of the mind. The cup of water, the loaf of bread, is redolent with the mystery of being. The simple satisfaction of eating when we are hungry and drinking when our throat is parched can be done with a mindfulness in which we bite being and drink it down. How different all this is from a philosophy classroom filled with the discussion of the history of ideas. While history is of great importance in both metaphysics and Zen, it must be living history, living first because its students are actually becoming the heirs to the minds and hearts of their illustrious predecessors. It is not a dead system they are studying, but a living tradition that ought to resonate in their spirit. Thus, for a Thomist of today to read Augustine, Thomas or John of St. Thomas, or a student of Zen to hear the words of Huang Po, Dogen or Hakuin, there can be no complacency as if the mere passage of time has inexorably conferred on them some sort of superiority. These men ought to be our guides in our penetration of the metaphysical depths, and we cannot remain simply in the words of the great masters of the past, but have to attain in a burst of spiritual intensification and inner sight the very realities they perceived. And nature and simplicity are closer to these realities than an intellectualism that never goes beyond the study door.

A final aspect of nature and simplicity is found in the Japanese concepts of *wabi* and *sabi*, which Suzuki calls "an active aesthetic appreciation of poverty."[2] It is the sense that poverty does not have to crush the spirit but can liberate it. It is "an inexpressible quiet joy deeply hidden beneath sheer poverty."[3] If we are to look for such a thing in the West we have to look back to its monks, or to some of these modern descendants who have attempted to recapture the spirit of simple monasticism. In the true spirit of *wabi* a man learns "to be self-sufficient with the insufficiency of things"[4] and that very poverty helps pacify and purify the mind so that it can finally see that the golden leaves blown in the wind of autumn are finer than any jewelry, that the greatest riches reside not in material possessions but in simple things and a simple spirit to penetrate their ultimate meaning.

Zen's love of nature and simplicity and its cultivation of the transparency of mind permeates the Oriental arts, whether painting, the cult of tea, flower-arranging or calligraphy. All the training and techniques of these arts finally become swallowed in a deeper simplicity:

"Look! In the midst of the pure white paper, an instant touch of black ink is flashed and with the minimum possible number of strokes a persimmon is composed. There are no unnecessary strokes at all. The brush has caught a purest moment of change in which the beginningless, endless undifferentiation has cut into differentiation - persimmon! Do you understand?"[5]

With nature, art, and simplicity must come a sense of inner peacefulness so that things are not always being viewed in the context of equipment, as Sekida, following Heidegger, would have it. The mind has to stop its practical mode of operating, where each tree represents so many boards and each piece of ground a potential field, and simply let nature be, for it is this very sense of letting being be that brings us closer to our goal. It is the beauty of a spider's web caught in the rays of the rising sun, or a drop of water sparkling like a rainbow on the tip of a pine needle after a storm, that we have to see. These objects have no utilitarian value. They cannot be put to any human use, and as such, they can help inspire a sense of the mystery of existence that exceeds concepts and human consciousness. The senses become filled with the incredible variety of natural being, with the manifold faces of existence, and at the same time, each individual existent begins to loom up as actively exercising the extraordinary mystery of existence.

Zen Techniques

But the heart of Zen practice is zazen, and the most common form of zazen is wrestling with a koan. Can Thomistic metaphysics devise its own koans to help someone arrive at the intuition of being? Such a koan, if possible, would be essentially different from the koans of Zen. Zen's koans are aiming at stopping the mind and thus are not conceptually intelligible. A favorite koan for beginners is Joshu's Mu. A monk once asked Master Joshu if a dog had Buddha nature and Joshu replied, "Mu", literally, "No." But the Zen student cannot solve Mu by mentally debating whether the answer should be yes or no and what circumstances dictated Joshu's answer or what theoretical principle could be brought to bear to make Mu yield an answer. Instead, he learns to concentrate on Mu itself and to breathe in and out with it, to cling to it with all his strength, to become one with Mu. Mu becomes the way he stops the flow of conceptual thought, and when this happens he gains a realization of what Mu means. We might say that what draws him and gives him the strength to persevere is not something in Mu itself, which entices him, for Mu is likened to an iron wall. His motivation is the thirst for meaning that has come from the suffering and pain he has experienced in the world, and from his faith that the Buddha has found an answer to this suffering, an answer which is embodied in the community he lives in and, in a special way, in the Master, who by becoming enlightened, has become the Buddha in a very real sense. In this community of faith in the Buddha's achievement, he is urged, even pushed, to apply himself to Mu - to not to let go no matter how slippery Mu may be in itself. The lectures and dokusan, or interviews with the Master, help fasten him to the koan, while the striving of the whole community in sesshin, or retreat, helps enkindle his enthusiasm to stick with Mu until he arrives at enlightenment.

Metaphysical Koans

But things would be different in the cultivation of the intuition of being. Since the object is not to stop the conceptual mind, the same kind of pressure cannot be used. While a community geared to the attainment of this intuition is conceivable, the metaphysical koan must draw the student more than the community pushes him to apply himself, for it is out of the words of the metaphysical koan itself that the answer must emerge in order to maintain the conceptual continuity between essence and existence and safeguard the eidetic nature of the intuition of being. It is the metaphysical koan that must, in some fashion, function as the master. It must have intrinsic safeguards to steer the student in the right direction, and an internal structure that generates an increasing conceptual tension that will hopefully be resolved at the moment of insight.

Is it possible to frame such a "koan"? There are several preliminary difficulties that stand in the way. Who is to do this? If the framers of the koan have not had the intuition, how can they formulate a path to it? Yet, if they have it, it came by happy chance and not by technique, and so can they in actual fact personally experience the validity of such a technique and test its efficacy? Zen again provides a historical background to this kind of paradox. Somehow it made the transition from spontaneous enlightenment of its early masters to the cultivation of enlightenment. The antecedents of an intuition that comes by happy chance can be reflected upon and tentative techniques tested on new students, and slowly an effective method can emerge.

If the intuition of being is crucial, according to Maritain, why did it go virtually unmentioned by the other leading figures of the Thomistic renewal? Perhaps Zen can suggest an answer here, as well. There are two basic attitudes about coming to enlightenment: the Soto school of gradual enlightenment and the Rinzai school of sudden enlightenment. In the idiom of the intuition of being it is possible to conceive two ways, as well. There is the slow process of the scholar who ponders the texts and finds moments of joy in penetrating more deeply into them. He has flashes of insight in the course of his pursuit of understanding, but he does not pause to distinguish these insights from the context of conceptual elaboration that they are embedded in. He is content that he has arrived at the insight without reflecting on its gift-like qualities.

But Maritain is the first of the Rinzai school of the intuition of being. He stresses its discontinuity with ordinary experience, and ordinary philosophical thought. He calls our attention to the intuition of being embedded in personal experience. He refuses to accept any merely verbal substitutes. He urges us to mobilize our energies to break through the habits of ordinary consciousness, the common face of is, and see its true countenance. He expects this intuition to come in a decisive if not explosive moment.

The Way of Judgment

Maritain left us with a valuable approach to the formulation of such a metaphysical koan when he described the approaches to the intuition of being. In addition to the various concrete approaches, he indicated an approach by way of judgment. This way of judgment is intriguing, not as a confirmatory rational analysis which would explore the intellectual content of the already given intuition and show its rational necessity, but precisely as an approach to the intuition in

GOD, ZEN AND THE INTUITION OF BEING

the first place.

The pathway of judgment is much less tangible than the emotionally charged experience of the concrete approaches, but it has its own kind of advantages. We don't have to wait for it to happen, but can attempt to initiate it, and it brings with itself an understanding of the intellectual content of the intuition.

A lifetime of exposure to existing things has up until now made them safe from our metaphysical scrutiny. Who would think of meditating on a tree or a butterfly in order to unravel the mystery of existence? Our eyes have been conditioned to name and classify things, to discover their chemical makeup and to find ways of utilizing them. But now all this must be put aside in order for us to confront them at a deeper level. What, then, are the most fundamental facts that are waiting to be recognized?

The first fact is simply that things are. They exist. We are surrounded by existing things: birds, trees, sun, water, you and I. The existence of these things is not a figment of our imagination. They are there. They have tenacity and solidness and resist our purely mental manipulations. We stumble over a stone and hurt our toe. We bite into a juicy apple. Instead of nothing, amazingly, things actually exist. Even philosophers who like to call everything into doubt live and act on the basis of this certitude.

The second fact is equally obvious and undeniable: different kinds of things exist. Apples are not eggs and I am not you. These differences are not illusions that will be someday unmasked by the advances of nuclear physics. Existence does not belong to things like a pit inside a cherry. Things are different through and through, and they exist through and through.

These two facts, undeniable and apparently unremarkable, are the foundation for an entire metaphysics. There is more to them than our common sense finds. An apple is an apple. $A = A$. An orange is an orange. $B = B$. An apple is not an orange. A is not B, nor is B, A. But an apple exists. $A = C$. And an orange exists. $B = C$. Therefore, does not A, in fact, really $= B$? How can we reconcile these two reports of the mind? One focuses on diversity and shows us that there are many different things. The other focuses on the fact of existence and assures us that both the apple and orange exist. In this sense, they are one. How can they be one and many at the same time?

It would be a mistake to try to eliminate this tension too quickly. We should intensify it because it is in the genuine resolution of this tension that we could arrive at the intuition of being.

St. Thomas' proofs for the existence of God are like Zen's koans. We cannot simply repeat them verbally and expound them conceptually and expect to grasp them. But since they are in plain language, in simple Latin, they fare worse than Zen's mysterious sayings. The words delude teacher and student alike into believing that they truly know what they mean. We may scoff at Zen for spouting nonsense, but since we do not understand, there is always a latent uneasiness that we are missing the real point, and this uneasiness can draw us back for a more careful consideration. But with St. Thomas, since he spoke so simply, we are deluded into thinking we grasp what he says and find it inadequate. He is simple-minded and we are clever. He wants to talk of the existence of God and we know better. We hear the words and follow their logic but do not see into them. The words remain simply words instead of windows on the transcendent world of metaphysics. We fail to share St. Thomas' metaphysical vision. And this is the failure that explains how a multitude of students exposed to St. Thomas have come away indifferent or self-satisfied. Thomas must use words, but we have never considered what steps must be taken if we are to become capable of understanding them.

The weakness of Thomism is not a weakness of reasoning or careful scholarship. It is a pedagogical failure in the deepest sense of that word, and this failure has no greater dramatization than the fact that in decades following the publication of Maritain's works, especially his metaphysical studies, Thomism still clung to the manuals. Even when Thomism held undisputed sway in the days before the Second Vatican Council, these manuals were turning a whole generation against St. Thomas. Given the opportunity, they threw these books aside in a moment. Who can blame them? Yet, at the same time, too often they had the mistaken impression that it was Thomas himself they were rejecting.[6]

The Way of Consciousness

The same kind of tension can be generated when we look at the what and the that from the inside. If ego-consciousness is not the center of the soul, then the possibility exists for a radical shift and transformation of our awareness. From the perspective of ordinary consciousness there must be some sign or doorway to this deeper dimension of the human spirit. The Zen master says, "Show me your face before your parents were born." The Thomists might say, "In consciousness I grasp in an experimental fashion the fact that I exist." In either case there is an existential sense to human consciousness that can be pursued. We do not simply know what things are, but we know that we exist, and we can transcend the level of essence by attempting to pursue the isness of all things, particularly the isness of the self. We constantly say, "I am going to do this" or "I know that," but we do not reflect on the foundation of all these statements, which is simply, "I am." How simple this "I am" appears, but who really is this "I"? We are convinced we know, since we live with our "I" on such intimate terms, but the foundation for the true meaning of the "I" is not simply the "I" itself but it is the "am". The "I" is an expression, a contraction, of the "am", but do we know what this "am" is? All the attributes we can give to the "I" when we say, "I am wealthy" or "I am famous" or "I am powerful" or "I am intelligent" or "I am strong," all these attributes are secondary to the fact that "I am." If we do not know this "am" we do not really know this "I". If we question the "I" in the light of "am", it can lead us to an abyss where the very meaning of our "I" seems to crumble and we grow afraid that our "I" is dissolving and there is nothing beyond it. The Zen master would advise courage. The abyss is not the abyss of mere nothingness. Push on and discover the true nature of the "I", your own true nature.

The Thomist might frame his metaphysical koan: "I am, but is am I?" or "What is this am? Show me this am." Or he could say, "What is whatness?" and strive to reconcile the what and the that. And if he cultivates the tension involved in this question, he might finally arrive at the intuition of being.

Has anyone actually arrived at the intuition of being by means of pondering such metaphysical koans? Possibly not, intentionally. Just as the concrete ways of Maritain are potential ways, so are these ways of judgment or metaphysical koans. All of these things may have been used in a more or less spontaneous manner by individuals who arrived at the intuition, but the issue now is their conscious cultivation.

Cultivating the Intuition of Being

What would actual training in the cultivation of the intuition of being, patterned after Zen, look like? In it simplicity of life would join with love of nature. Quieting the mind, aided by posture and breathing, would provide the inner preparation for taking up the actual techniques that could lead to the intuition of being. These techniques could include wrestling with metaphysical koans, spirited interviews with an accomplished metaphysician, careful reflection on the writings of the great metaphysicians, the stimulation of living with people who share the same aspirations, etc.

But there is another factor that cannot be ignored. In actual fact, the metaphysics of St. Thomas has taken place within a Christian context, and the pursuit of Zen enlightenment has taken place within the context of Zen Buddhism. Is this simply a historical accident, or does this Christian or Buddhist religious context form an indispensable existential setting for the cultivation of metaphysical insight? If it does - and it will be the task of *Part III* to explore these religious settings - then any formal cultivation of the intuition of being would have to deal not only with the aspirations we have as metaphysicians, but the aspirations we have as men and women for the absolute.

A Zen-Thomist Dialogue?

The imaginary discussion between Maritain and Izutsu points out the difficulty that Zen practitioners and metaphysicians of the school of St. Thomas will have in coming to grips with basic issues. Zen stresses immediate experience, but because of the means it must employ to arrive at it, it cannot reflect on the essential differences between the existence of the self, the intuition of being and God. The gateless gate that prevents the conceptual mind from entering also prevents it from emerging and conceptually articulating what it has seen. The very efficacy of the Zen technique is a guarantee that a metaphysics in the ordinary conceptual sense will not easily emerge from it, no matter how much these basic distinctions might be lived out in the practical order.

GOD, ZEN AND THE INTUITION OF BEING

What are the implications of such non-conceptuality for a dialogue? From the Thomistic side, there must be men and women who actually possess the intuition of being and have a clear understanding of its implications. Yet, even if they met this requirement, would they not be hesitant to enter into a field of discussion in which the indispensable ground-rule is the cessation of conceptual thought and where concepts are not means to insight but hindrances to it? The Zen practitioners, on the other hand, who have learned through powerful inner experience the pitfalls of reasoning and the fruitfulness of the practice of no-mind, will be hard pressed not to immediately conclude that the words of the metaphysician are those very words that hinder real insight and thus, they are talking with someone who has no real insight into the nature of reality but only words about it. What will the medium of communication be? One will not trust words, the other cannot speak the nonconceptual "language" of the enlightened master. Is this an insuperable barrier? On the practical level this kind of dialogue has hardly begun, so it is impossible to say what can happen. Perhaps the genuine feel for metaphysical experience that both sides possess will go a long way in mitigating these difficulties.

But if such an interchange did take place, what could Thomism offer to Zen? The greatest gift Thomistic metaphysics could give to Zen is to help it advance and develop the kinds of reflections on Zen experience described in this *Part*. If Zen could articulate its nature in speculative metaphysical terms it would not become a metaphysical system, nor even a philosophy, but this process would create a bridge by which it could reflect on its relationship with the major aspects of Western culture.

In Japan, where the problem of the synthesis between East and West is particularly acute, Zen is called upon to establish a relationship to the sciences of nature, metaphysics, art and social philosophy, as well as theology and Christian mysticism. Thomism could help it in this task. It was one of Maritain's greatest achievements not only to clarify the subjective side of metaphysics, but to bring this revitalized metaphysics into relationship with modern science and art, as well as theology and mysticism.[7] A Thomism which, in fact, has certain remarkable affinities to Zen and rejects with Zen the subject-object dichotomy that was born with Descartes, could aid it in conceptually expressing its own nature. If Zen-inspired philosophers have virtually ignored Thomism up until now, it is a consequence of the recent date of the dialogue between Zen and the West, the poor external appearance of Thomism, and the small amount of work Thomists have expended on Zen. Thus, a Zen-Thomist dialogue could take place with great benefits for both sides, and it would prepare the way for understanding the relationship between Zen and Christian mysticism.

We have accomplished part of our task by beginning to situate Zen in relationship to the metaphysics of St. Thomas, and by suggesting the great benefits that Thomism could derive from drinking deep from the spirit of Zen. And we have looked briefly at what Thomistic metaphysics can offer to Zen. Now we must turn our attention to the other part of our work, which is Zen in relationship to Christian mysticism.

Notes

1. Suzuki, *Zen and Japanese Culture*, p. 353.
2. Ibid., p. 284.
3. Ibid., p. 286.
4. Ibid., p. 288.
5. Kobori Sohaku Nanrei, *A Dialogue*, p. 146. In *The Buddha Eye*, ed. Franck.
6. See Gilson's "Thomas Aquinas and Our Colleagues" in *A Gilson Reader*, pp. 278ff.
7. It was one of Maritain's lifelong dreams that a restoration of a genuine philosophy of nature would bridge the gap between metaphysics and the sciences of nature, and he devoted considerable effort to this project which is stated succinctly in *The Degrees of Knowledge*. Unfortunately, Thomism as a whole has failed to pursue this possibility.

PART III

ZEN BETWEEN METAPHYSICS AND MYSTICISM

CHAPTER 7

A MYSTICAL METAPHYSICS

Zen has come to the West to stay, and it brings the treasure it has amassed for more than a thousand years to a world in dire need of spiritual help. But it is a world with its own traditions of the interior life, and so a meeting becomes inevitable between Zen and Christian mysticism. And I have especially in mind that current of Christian mysticism that has been shaped and developed by Teresa of Avila and John of the Cross.

Yet such a meeting, inevitable though it may be, can take place at different levels. On the first level there is a sense of defensiveness and apprehension. On a higher level there is the recognition that we have much in common. Both sides realize they are talking to men and women like themselves, and they look for points of contact and convergence. On a still higher level the discussion focuses on differences, not in the defensive way of the first level, but with a genuine desire to see the truth. This is a difficult level to sustain, for it means a painful probing of ourselves and just what the other person is saying, but it holds the promise of yielding genuine mutual understanding and cooperation.

I have already discussed what Zen enlightenment looks like from the point of view of the metaphysics of St. Thomas. Let us say that this was a step towards describing the inner nature or essence of enlightenment. But the exploration of this inner nature must be completed by an examination of the actual existential state of Zen. Why does Zen pursue other goals than those of the metaphysics of St. Thomas? The intuition of being, and the whole metaphysics of St. Thomas, grew up within Christianity. In fact, while it remains a metaphysics in nature, could it ever have developed outside the embrace of Christianity, outside the existential context of Christianity? If we look at Maritain, it was faith that set the corner posts of his spirit within which his metaphysical understanding flourished. But one of the consequences of this is that metaphysics often remained under the sway of theology, and the intuition of being remained swallowed up in the higher lights of the spirit. The intuition of being was a stage on the road to faith, theology and mystical experience. The metaphysical perception that God exists immediately makes the question of the self-revelation more acute for anyone growing up in a Christian world. The impetus of the intuition of being is spent propelling the spirit into the realm of faith instead of being used to make the intuition itself more conscious. This seems the best explanation for the rarity of explicit testimony about it in the West.

But what of Zen? What would happen to men and women seized by the same thirst and desire for meaning and the Absolute that is in all people which Christians believe is a supernatural calling to divine sonship - but in a setting without explicit revelation? Is it not possible that these longings, both metaphysical and supernatural, would track the spoor of existence in all things, especially within the human subject, and pursue it with a preternatural strength, not to create a metaphysics in the conceptual sense, but to turn this metaphysics into a vehicle to assuage this mystical longing for the Absolute? Then all concepts would appear too weak and ineffectual and ought to be sacrificed for that one goal which is beyond all else, that emptiness which is fullness which they longed to embrace. Then we no longer have a metaphysics in the Thomistic sense, but a mystical metaphysics or a metaphysical mysticism. We have something that is metaphysical in nature but mystical in context.

What do we really mean when we say Zen is mystical in context? It means that all people live in the same world. God's invitation to the life of grace, to sharing in His own life, is extended to all. This grace is actually operative in every life whether the person knows about Christian revelation or not. In actual fact there is no simply natural

GOD, ZEN AND THE INTUITION OF BEING 323

destiny. No man is called to a purely natural end, and while it is certainly possible and important to distinguish the natural end of man from the supernatural one, in the very world we live in we are called to the life of grace. And this calling is not a simple word, a theory or doctrine. It enters our hearts to make us feel a longing and loneliness that goes beyond the simple exigencies of our nature. So, from a Christian point of view, the Buddhist experience of sickness, old age and death is not only a natural consequence of the nature of man, but it is a sign of the world in need of redemption, a sign of man called to union with the Absolute. Christians cannot look at Zen as a purely natural artifact. It is the creation of men destined to a supernatural end. It is the work of men and women thirsting for salvation and the Absolute. It is the creation of men suffering pain and anguish and the apparent meaninglessness of the world and striving with all their energy to find a solution. This impulse cannot be distinguished from the pain and suffering in the Christian heart. But without the explicit guidance of Christian faith, and therefore bereft of the means faith proposes, it had nowhere to turn but to turn in upon itself. It conceived the most radical act that human nature was capable of. It took hold of our very self, that reality with the highest ontological density in this world. It saw human consciousness as the doorway to the Ultimate, and being unsatisfied with all the words and concepts, all the elaboration of doctrines that could spring from the human spirit, it conceived in a moment of tremendous insight to leave all these words behind and to explore this spirit to its roots. Put in another way, it caught that scent of existence and pursued it at the cost of all particular things. And what was the driving force of such a radical effort but a thirst that went beyond the normal and natural desires of a spirit united with a body and knowing through ideas? Zen, penetrated by mystical desires, took up metaphysics and pushed it, not to its natural culmination, which would be the intuition of being, but beyond, to a preternatural union with *esse*. If it is natural in the sense that it remains within the boundaries of human reason and looks to human effort to attain to enlightenment, and thus is not the work of grace, this whole process is driven by a thirst identical to that which Christians assuage in mysticism. Thus Zen, in its own way, fulfills the demands of the Gospel in which a man has to lose his life in order to find it, to forsake all things in order to find the pearl of great price or the treasure in the field. In Zen there is a sacrifice of thoughts and ego awareness. The difficult road leading from normal self-awareness to its very sources is a thoroughgoing asceticism of the mind. The ordinary experience in which we experience that we are becomes the doorway in which we enter to discover what that *that* is.

Zen appears, then, as one of the most dramatic attempts to respond to the call of grace using the resources of human nature and a preternatural energy to leave behind all in order to find All. Out of the resources of human nature alone, it cannot break the barrier between nature and grace, but living in a world called to grace, and without any way to articulate this grace as grace, it goes beyond what human nature in itself would conceive. It turns human nature inside out and pursues the obscure experience of existence given in the heart of human awareness to its ultimate conclusion, to the very esse of the soul, which is receiving the divine creative influx. Therefore, it would be a mistake if we think it is possible to extract the Zen out of Zen Buddhism as if to be left with a Zen philosophy or a non-religious Zen. Zen is not religious by nature like Christianity; it is natural and metaphysical. But it is shot through by religious and mystical longings, and in this way becomes a symbol of grace.[1]

Viewing Zen as a mystical metaphysics helps understand some of the difficulties that Christians have in knowing what to compare it with in their own tradition. Unfortunately, for too many Christians metaphysics is something to be avoided. Therefore, discounting metaphysics, they try to compare Zen with Christian mysticism or contemplation. And this is difficult, for contemplation has several different meanings.

Christian Contemplation

From a Christian point of view we can distinguish three kinds of contemplation: a philosophical or metaphysical one, an infused or mystical or supernatural contemplation, and an active or acquired contemplation. If we briefly outline them, then we can compare them with Zen.

First, there is, however little noticed, a philosophical contemplation which is the result of metaphysical insights. If we imagine the intuition of being not only attained, but sustained and developed by conceptual elaboration and a long-term effort to deepen this central insight, then we have some idea of what a philosophical contemplation would be like, and its center will be a contemplation of God by negation, that is, a realization that God is beyond all the essences we can grasp. This kind of philosophical contemplation, allied with a natural love of God, can be a strong and beautiful experience.[2] In it the mind rises from created things and senses the darkness in which God dwells. We raise our minds to God as the source of all existence, for He is existence itself. But this contemplation does not grasp God directly. It is not spiritual vision. It knows by analogy, for it reasons from what exists in creatures to what must exist in God without delivering God to us. Philosophical contemplation is rooted in concepts even while pursuing their ultimate root. It tries to fathom their ultimate implications. If this philosophical contemplation were to be exercised within the context of Christian faith and the life of prayer, it would gain overtones of intimacy because by faith the Christian realizes that the God hidden in this darkness speaks through Jesus Christ. But in itself philosophical contemplation is a work of human reason and the culmination of metaphysics as a human science.

The second kind of contemplation is infused contemplation, or mystical experience. This is the contemplation that belongs properly to the life of faith itself. It is the fruition of the life of faith in this life, and is an actual experience of God dwelling in the soul. This experience takes place through love. This love or supernatural charity becomes the very means by which we experience God. Infused contemplation goes beyond concepts and discursive reasoning. They are swallowed up in the night, but this night is not simply a night of the absence of concepts. It is a night caused by the dawning of the contemplative experience itself which, like the sun, blots out the stars of human concepts with its excessive light. This kind of contemplation is the contemplation that the Christian saints speak about, especially John of the Cross.[3] In it they have the certitude of God's presence, at least when the experience grows sufficiently strong. They are aware that they are not exercising their faculties of intellect, memory and will, but are receiving this experience passively. And while infused contemplation can be accompanied by visions and revelations, it is distinct from them. In fact, John of the Cross is as adamant as any Zen master that these phenomena should be ignored lest they distract the soul. It is love that co-natures the spirit with God, unites it with God, and when the love is strong enough and the circumstances suitable, it overflows into a perceptible experience of God's presence.

We have scrutinized the relationship of a metaphysical contemplation founded on the intuition of being to Zen and seen, while it is a vital point of comparison, Zen goes beyond this kind of contemplation by actually achieving some kind of experience of the Absolute. But is it, then, a contemplation similar to the infused contemplation of John of the Cross? No. D.T. Suzuki in a number of places has pointed out how Zen differs from Christian mysticism. Zen does not deal consciously with God or union with Him or the experience of that union. It is not a knowledge through love, but a natural metaphysical knowledge working through a connaturality, to be sure, but a connaturality of emptiness, not union. For this reason it is much easier for a student of Zen to feel at home with the writings of Meister Eckhart than John of the Cross.

The third kind of contemplation that Christians sometimes speak about is called active or acquired contemplation.[4] The life of prayer has two main divisions: the first is active prayer or meditation. This is the use of the senses, imagination, intellect, will and memory to draw close to God. It takes various forms such as formal meditation where a scene is pictured, reasoned about, and leads to affective resolutions. Or simpler forms in which aspirations play a larger role and conceptual activity is diminished. The other main division of the life of prayer is infused contemplation, or the passive mystical experience we have just been discussing. Meditation in the wide sense is the use of the human intellect and will to understand and love God, and though the Christian believes that these activities are elevated by grace, they are also exercised whenever the person desires. They are under human control. Contemplation, on the other hand, is passively received, and the saints always emphasize its gift-like qualities and assert that no one can raise themselves up to contemplation by their own efforts.

Acquired Contemplation and Zen

It is clear that neither discursive meditation nor infused contemplation is Zen-like. The first makes use of concepts while the second

GOD, ZEN AND THE INTUITION OF BEING

is not something we can do on our own initiative. Both its object and mode of reception are gifts. But what if there were a Christian contemplation that was do-able, that is, neither discursive nor infused? Then such a contemplation would be a potential Christian counterpart to Zen. If we look at the history of Christian spirituality in the West, the most likely candidate for such a role is what is known as active or acquired contemplation.[5] It is an attempt to formulate a new stage in the life of prayer, a new contemplation that could be actively exercised by people moderately advanced in the spiritual life. The rationale behind it is straight-forward. The beginning of the life of prayer employs images and reasoning, and concludes with loving aspirations and affective resolutions. But as beginners become accustomed to employing the natural faculties of imagination, intellect, will and memory, they often reach a point where this kind of active praying brings less internal profit. Then a process of simplification sets in in which they concentrate on those aspects of their prayer which they feel have the greatest life in them. It may be a question of spending more time in making acts of love of God or in the realization that God surpasses all images and concepts, and thus dwells in a darkness we desire to enter to be with Him.

The creators of acquired contemplation turn this natural process of simplification into a contemplation in which a person would rest in God by faith without images and concepts. They would let all discursive activity fall into silence so that this union with God by faith might take over possession of the soul. In short, they wished to exercise as active not-doing so that the very emptiness and night they put themselves in would become filled with the plenitude of God Who is beyond all concepts.

At first glance it seems like we have remarkable parallels to many aspects of Zen, and thus acquired contemplation holds the promise of being a Christian Zen, or a Zen exercise for Christians. Unfortunately, this is not true. And why it is not true will become clear if we briefly look at the history of acquired contemplation. (I have examined this history more at length in *St. John of the Cross and Dr. C.G. Jung*).

Acquired contemplation was first developed directly in the aftermath of the writings of John of the Cross and Teresa of Avila, the two great Carmelite saints who raised mystical experience to a new plateau of self-awareness. St. John, in particular, took special care to describe the beginning of the life of contemplation, the transition between meditation and contemplation, and in doing so he laid down three signs by which a person could know whether it was time to leave the discursive prayer of meditation with its images, thoughts, and aspirations, and enter into infused contemplation. The first sign was an inability to meditate. The second was an evaluation that this inability did not come from distraction, dissipation, lukewarmness or psychological difficulties, and the third and most critical sign was that the beginning of the prayer of infused and passive contemplation was somehow making itself felt even though it could not be conceptualized or grasped discursively, and thus the soul would appear engaged in some strange sort of not-doing.[6]

After the writings of St. John and St. Teresa appeared, people seriously engaged in the life of prayer felt compelled to ask themselves: "Am I a contemplative?" And when they experienced a simplification of the discursive beginning of prayer it was natural for them to try to understand their predicament in the light of his teaching. They faced a real and serious problem. They were devoted to the life of prayer, and now their ability to pray was disappearing. What were they going to do? So when St. John said the first sign was the inability to pray, they took heart. Then they looked at the second sign which said this disability did not come from their own imperfections or from psychological causes. Here they examined their lives and could honestly say they could think of no obstacle that they had put in the way. They were devout and sincere. Nor could they see themselves as under the influence of any sort of psychological disease. Thus, they felt the second sign was confirmed. As for the third sign, which in St. John was the actual beginning of the experience of passive contemplation, this was not present. If it had been, then these formulators of acquired contemplation would have had no need to formulate it at all. They simply would have experienced a growing presence of infused contemplation, and that would have more than contented them. No. It was precisely because they did not experience the contemplation that St. Teresa and St. John talked about that they had the need to create another kind. They went back to St. John's writings and read them through the tinted glasses of their own needs. In the subtle and delicate descriptions of how contemplation tries to enter the spirit and is hindered because the person praying knows no other way to conduct

GOD, ZEN AND THE INTUITION OF BEING

himself except by the use of his faculties, in these descriptions the creators of acquired contemplation discovered something that was not there at all. St. John spoke in great detail of the need to leave behind all the products of discursive reason, for none of them could be the proximate means of union with God. He talked of the need of detachment from the senses, from the imagination, from the various kinds of understanding, as well as from the acts of the will and memory. But he always did so from the perspective that the new contemplative experience was dawning and would be hindered by the exercise of discursive activity. The creators of acquired contemplation took these descriptions and turned them into active means of attaining contemplation. They would stop all discursive activity and be left with naked faith. They would strip away all the human activity, and in doing so, attain to the contemplative experience.

Thus the scene is set for one of the more fascinating experiments in the history of the spiritual life. Would acquired contemplation actually serve as a proximate preparation for infused contemplation? And if we examine these attempts at creating a new stage in the life of prayer, is it possible to see a Christian counterpart to Zen experience?

Although acquired contemplation sprang up in the wake of St. John's writings and soon declared him as its father, St. John knew nothing of such a contemplation. It cannot be found in his writings. He knew of no middle way between meditation and infused contemplation. Its most notable practitioners appear not to have been successful in using it as a bridge to infused contemplation, but instead, gradually began to attach to this active contemplation the very qualities St. John attributed to the infused. They inadvertently made themselves into "contemplatives" by transforming, even deforming, the nature of contemplation. They imagined that intuition could be separate and free from all discursive activity and be maintained as a spiritual sight that could fix itself on God, and in the more extreme cases, could stay fixed on Him as long as the intent or desire for this union remained. Faith was no longer working in and through the natural faculties. Rather, in order to purify it, they stripped all this natural working away. But without the special activation of a supernatural mode of operating, this faith was deprived of both natural and supernatural ways of working. With an intuitive gaze of faith they lifted their minds and hearts to God, but failed to see how discursive and individual acts were necessary to nourish this intuition. The result was that the more they tried to live by naked faith without discursive activity, without concepts, images and aspirations, the more they entered a void. On the psychological level this interior attitude formed a vacuum that excited the unconscious which tried to fill it with images and affects. And the more purely "spiritual" this attitude was, the more it called forth counter-balancing sensual disturbances. Acquired contemplation through the course of the 17th century became more clearly delineated and more untenable psychologically, and was more intimately connected with the Quietism that culminated in the excesses of Miguel Molinos.

Acquired contemplation, then, failed to lead to the mystical life, and not only that, in its extreme form it led to a distrust of mysticism by way of reaction that we still experience. Even when it did not follow its interior logic to the end, it fostered a lack of psychological realism and created a smoke screen that has helped prevent a practical reevaluation of contemplation in the life of prayer. There is no doubt that the simplification of prayer represents a major milestone and problem in the life of prayer. But to imagine it can be met by a contemplative "activity" is to use the word contemplation in two vastly different ways. For St. John all the activity we can freely exercise belongs under the generic heading of meditation. Contemplation takes place in a passive way. Today we still maintain the ambiguous language of acquired contemplation, and this prevents us from seeing the real contemplative crisis that Christians face. Just how often does contemplation in the sense St. John describes it appear? We are certainly interested in contemplation, but how much do we really know about it by experience? If the life of prayer has an inner tendency to simplify itself, does this mean that this is a call to contemplation, or simply a call to simplified activity? In short, a renewal of the spiritual life will demand a careful scrutiny of the role contemplation should play and the prerequisite for this examination is a clarification of vocabulary.

But what has this to do with Zen? First of all, how can Christians compare contemplation with Zen if the word remains vague or even equivocal? And how can we compare the contemplative experience to Zen enlightenment if we have no experience?

The problem is somewhat mitigated by the fact that living the

Christian life does not depend on the experience of contemplation. It demands faith and love, and these can give us a sense of what their flowering in contemplation would be like, and how this experience would differ from Zen enlightenment. Nonetheless, we face a serious problem in recovering the sense of contemplation found in the Carmelite founders and understanding it adequately, and adding to it our own age's psychological resources.

But let's go on to the second part of the experiment of acquired contemplation. Did some of its creators in voiding all conceptual thought stumble on a Zen-like state? A fully adequate answer would demand a careful scrutiny of the works of men like Thomas of Jesus, Antonio Rojas, Juan Falconi and so forth, but my initial impression is that they did not. They might not have even stopped all discursive activity, for did they not maintain an attitude of interior expectancy, an inner turning of the mind and heart which reached in the darkness for the experience of contemplation? They had neither the guidance of a master nor the support of a community to fortify them. Instead, in the worst of cases, they suffered the onslaught from the unconscious, the feeling that the devil was in possession of the lower regions of the soul and made war on the life of prayer carried on in the soul's center. And in the best of cases, if this void had yielded for a moment its secret, would they have been able to understand it? Or would these flashes of Zen have been caught up in the framework of Christian theology and have left us a hybrid of the mysticism of the void in Christian dress?

But if acquired contemplation did not come to Zen - it would probably be easier to look to Meister Eckhart and the Rhineland mystics for traces, or *The Cloud of Unknowing* - can Zen come to our aid in the creation of a genuine acquired contemplation? Could the stopping of all discursive activity become an actual step beyond meditation and a preparation for contemplation? This is part of a broader issue about the use of Zen in the life of prayer.

There is no doubt that the spirit of Zen can strengthen the life of prayer much like it can aid the cultivation of the intuition of being. Its sense of quiet, nature, interior discipline and devoted communal effort are all valuable aids in the life of prayer. And if Zen could fortify our metaphysical sense, then this, too, would have favorable repercussions.

But what of Zen as Zen enlightenment? It is not the intuition of being, nor is it infused contemplation. Can it be a genuine acquired "contemplation", a more radical elimination of all conceptual thought? If this process of negation were directly aimed at infused contemplation, it would fall into the same errors that acquired contemplation did. The void of all concepts can be the connatural means to enlightenment, for the *esse* of the soul is present in the soul, for it is the soul. It can be uncovered, as it were, for it is the natural bedrock of the spirit. But God as an object of union in love is not present in the same way. This union is a gift that exceeds all the natural exigencies of the soul. The elimination of concepts will not inevitably bring it to light. There is no natural technique, however radical, that will bring us to divine union.

This still leaves the possibility that Zen could be used as part of the active ascetical preparation which helps fit the soul for the reception of divine union, or it could conceivably be employed to quiet the spirit when the faint beginnings of union come and the temptation remains to employ discursive activity.

St. John writes of the active preparation to enter the night of sense, that one should seek:

"not that which is a desire for anything, but that which is a desire for nothing."[7]

And

"In order to arrive at possessing everything,
Desire to possess nothing.
In order to arrive at being everything,
Desire to be nothing.
In order to arrive at knowing everything,
Desire to know nothing."[8]

And in a certain way Zen could be an aid in pursuing this nothing, despite the differences between the nothing of Zen and the nada or nothing of St. John. But such a use of Zen would transform Zen, for it would be animated by a desire for divine union which transcends the desire for enlightenment. This brings us to the larger question of the inner possibilities that exist as the meeting of Zen and Christianity proceeds.

Notes

1. The relationship between Zen and Christianity evokes the theological horizon of the distinctions between nature and grace in which the same distinctions between the essential and the existential can be applied.
2. See Maritain's "Pas de savoir sans intuitivité" in *Approches*, p. 413.
3. See a short summary of the beginning of the contemplative life in *St. John of the Cross and Dr. C.G. Jung*, Chapter 3.
4. Ibid., Chapter 5.
5. Ibid., Chapters 3, 4 and 5.
6. Ibid., p. 68ff.
7. St. John of the Cross, *Ascent of Mount Carmel*, p. 70.
8. Ibid., p. 72.

CHAPTER 8:

ZEN CATHOLICISM?

The two religious galaxies of Christianity and Buddhism begin, not to collide, but intersect and occupy the same space. This poses a challenge for Christianity that is comparable to its meeting with Greek thought or with the natural sciences.[1] How Zen might interact with Catholicism is one aspect of this larger encounter, and one we can look at under three different headings: Zen and western Catholics, Zen and oriental Catholics, and Zen Buddhism and Catholicism.

Zen and Western Catholics

A road has been opened up for a Catholic understanding of Zen by men like Heinrich Dumoulin, H.M. Enomiya Lassalle, William Johnston and Thomas Merton. Where does it lead? Where does it go once we see that Catholics can appreciate and practice Zen? What will happen when Catholics begin to attain enlightenment? It is then that it will be crucial for us to understand as clearly as possible the differences between Zen enlightenment and the ultimate goal of Christian life, and the different inner horizons that distinguish the Catholic from the Zen Buddhist.

For the Catholic, enlightenment is an absolute only in a particular order. It is not an absolute absolutely, which is reserved for union with God through love. But if Catholics begin to advance on the way of enlightenment under the guidance of Zen Buddhists, then it is possible that they will feel a tension between these two different ways of looking at enlightenment. Having gone through the gateless gate, how readily can they come forth and understand this experience, not in the traditional categories of Zen Buddhism, but within the perspectives of

GOD, ZEN AND THE INTUITION OF BEING 335

faith? How transparent will enlightenment be to divine union? How much will it capture the Catholic by its deep actuality and bedazzle him so he will have great difficulty in reflecting on this experience in a Christian way, especially since Christian reflection on Zen enlightenment has just begun?

The more a Catholic penetrates deeply in Zen the more will he have to ponder these questions, be aware of their potential dangers and strive to overcome them in order that the riches of Zen will flow into Catholic life.

Zen and Oriental Catholics

When will the day come when we have a distinctive Indian, Chinese or Japanese Catholicism? Catholicism is no more intrinsically Greek than Japanese. It is the task, immensely difficult and exciting, of oriental Catholics to create a Buddhist Catholicism or Zen Catholicism. This can take place if we can see the inner nature of enlightenment, and see that it not only does not conflict with faith, but is a beautiful creation of men and women who share an identical longing with Christians for the Absolute. Then Catholics could take up this age-old work of people called to grace and illuminate it with the treasures of their own faith while this very faith becomes enriched by a new understanding.

Zen Buddhism and Catholicism

If Catholics can turn to Zen, is it impossible to imagine Zen Buddhists becoming Catholics? This would demand that Catholics carefully articulate their own metaphysical and mystical traditions and show that they are not antithetical to the heart of Zen. But could a call to faith appear in the very midst of enlightenment? And could it not already be doing so in certain cases? John of the Cross describes how when a ray of light enters a dark room, if there is dust in the air the light becomes visible, and if the air is pure the light is not seen. He uses this example as a way of describing the rare contemplative state in which the light of contemplative union strikes an exceptionally purified spirit and plunges it into forgetfulness.[2] What of the inner mind and heart of those men and women who have forsaken all things and attained to this night luminous with existence? What hidden longings remain in the midst of enlightenment calling out to some unimaginable depth? And if contemplative union would begin to dawn, how could it be spoken of or known in the ordinary sense of the term? And if such a person could sense this calling, and in some cases its fruition, and then see that the Gospel was nothing else but the explicitation of this inner mystery, would becoming a Catholic be a betrayal of Zen or its crown? None of this implies that right now the Zen Buddhist is any less close to God than Catholics, for God calls all people to Himself and is the judge of how they respond. But if God has revealed Himself and calls out in the very midst of enlightenment, then imagine the Zen-Catholicism that would be born if this call were heard.

Distinguish in Order to Unite

The question of the cultivation of the intuition of being has led us far beyond the realm of metaphysics to Zen and Christian mysticism. This is as it should be, for such a question asks not only what the intuition of being is, but what subjective conditions will foster it. To paraphrase Maritain, we can and must distinguish between the intuition of being and Zen enlightenment and Christian mysticism, not to separate them, but to unite them by exploring the existential connections they have in us. We distinguish in order to unite. We draw clear lines between the intuition of being and Zen enlightenment, not to protect them from each other, but so they can enrich each other. We clarify the relationship between enlightenment and contemplation so they can dwell harmoniously and synergistically inside us.

Whatever has been said in the past chapters is but one step on this journey. The cultivation of the intuition of being becomes not just a metaphysical problem, but involves our whole self and its longing for the Absolute. It is only when we reach for the highest goal that we create the most ample interior space in which a genuine metaphysics can be born. This reaching, known to both Zen and Christian mysticism, provides the necessary complement to my remarks on the cultivation of the intuition of being.

We cultivate the intuition of being by pursuing our deepest inner

GOD, ZEN AND THE INTUITION OF BEING

aspirations that transcend metaphysics itself. The more we situate Zen in this ascent, the better able we will be to let it inspire both metaphysics and Christian mysticism, and be inspired by them in turn. Each is enamored by existence in its own way. The metaphysics of St. Thomas wants to understand it, and to do so, it uses concepts and pushes them to their ultimate limits where they display their innermost nature as reflections of existence. Zen wants to actively embrace existence so it resolutely puts aside all concepts, and in this emptiness finds the way to existence. Christian mysticism wants to be embraced by existence and see revealed in its depths its most intimate face, which is love. There is no reason except our own weakness that prevents all three from sharing with each other the riches they have found in the service of this one Existence, or Nothingness.

Epilogue

In the *Wan Ling Record*, Huang Po (d. 850) says:
"When your glance falls upon a grain of dust, what you see is identical with all the vast world-systems with their great rivers and mighty hills. To gaze upon a drop of water is to behold the nature of all the waters of the universe. Moreover, in thus contemplating the totality of phenomena, you are contemplating the totality of Mind. All these phenomena are intrinsically void and yet this Mind with which they are identical is no mere nothingness. By this I mean that it does exist, but in a way too marvellous for us to comprehend. It is an existence which is no existence, a non-existence which is nevertheless existence. So this true Void does in some marvellous way 'exist'."[3]

Huang Po's true Void that "does in some marvellous way exist," together allows us to drink from a deep spring of metaphysical insight which can become an inspiration to wake the metaphysics of St. Thomas from its slumber and rediscover a living sense of the intuition of being.

Zen relentlessly pursues that fundamental that, the very esse, or to be, or existence, of the cypress tree, or cherry blossom, or of ourselves. And when that existence finally manifests itself, in a night of all concepts, it is clothed with a God-like splendor. The very tree, or blossom, or self, IS.

If only a breath of this fresh mountain air would blow through the metaphysics of St. Thomas, then it would awake. It would renew its words in the living fire of metaphysical seeing. Then it could repay Zen's gift with its own. It could help Zen ask those questions that have been always waiting in the heart of its silence.

Notes

1. See note 6 in Chapter 6.
2. *Ascent of Mount Carmel*, Bk. II, Ch. XIV, p. 141.
3. *The Zen Teachings of Huang Po*, p. 108.

Bibliography

Abe, Masao. (1982) "Emptiness Is Suchness" *in The Buddha Eye*, edited by Frederick Franck. NY: Crossroad.

_____ (1985) "John Cobb's Beyond Dialogue" in *The Eastern Buddhist*, Vol. XVIII, No. 1, Spring 1985.

_____ (1985) *Zen and Western Thought*. Honolulu: University of Hawaii Press.

Aquinas, St. Thomas. (1949) *On Being and Essence*. Toronto, Canada: The Pontifical Institute of Mediaeval Studies.

Arraj, James. (1986) *St. John of the Cross and Dr. C.G. Jung*. Chiloquin, OR: Inner Growth Books.

Bañez, Dominic. (1966) *The Primacy of Existence in Thomas Aquinas*. Chicago: Henry Regnery Company.

Boyle, Leonard E. (1981) "A Remembrance of Pope Leo XIII: The Encyclical Aeterni Patris" in *One Hundred Years of Thomism*. Houston: TX: Center for Thomistic Studies.

Carlo, William E. (1957) "Commentary" in *Proceedings of the American Catholic Philosophical Asso.* p. 126.

_____(1966) *The Ultimate Reducibility of Essence to Existence in Existential Metaphysics*. The Hague: Nijhoff.

Clarke, W. Norris. (1957) "Commentary" in *Proceedings of the American Catholic Philosophical Asso.* p. 128.

_____(1974) "What Cannot Be Said in St. Thomas' Essence-Existence Doctrine" in *The New Scholasticism*. Baltimore: American Catholic Philosophical Association.

Cook, Francis H. (1986) "The Second Buddhist-Christian Theological Encounter: A Report" in *The Eastern Buddhist*, Vol. XIX, No. 1, Spring 1986.

Dumoulin, Heinrich. (1974) *Christianity Meets Buddhism*. La Salle, IL: Open Court.

Eusden, John Dykstra. (1981) *Zen and Christian: The Journey Between*. NY: Crossroad.

Fabro, Cornelio. (1950) *La Nozione Metafisica di Partecipazione.* Torino: Società editrice internationale.

Fields, Rick. (1981) *How the Swans Came to the Lake.* Boulder, CO: Shambhala.

de Finance, Joseph. (1945) *Etre et Agir.* Paris: Beauchesne et ses fils, éditeurs.

Gardeil, A. (1927) *La structure de l'ame et L'expérience mystique.* Paris: Librairie Victor Lecoffre.

Gardet, Louis. (1972) *Etudes de philosophie et de Mystique comparées.* Paris: Librairie philosophique J. Vrin.

Gardet, Louis and Olivier Lacombe. (1981) *L'expérience du soi.* Paris: Desclée de Brouwer.

Gilkey, Langdon. (1986) "Abe Masao's Zen and Western Thought" in *The Eastern Buddhist*, Vol. XIX, No. 2, Autumn 1986.

Gilson, Etienne. (1949) *Being and Some Philosophers.* Toronto, Canada: Pontifical Institute of Mediaeval Studies.

_____ (1955) *History of Christian Philosophy in the Middle Ages.* NY: Random House.

_____ (1957) *A Gilson Reader.* Garden City, NY: Image Books.

Graham, Dom Aelred. (1963) *Zen Catholicism.* HBJ

Heisig, James. (1987) "East-West Dialogue: Sunyata and Kenosis" in *Spirituality Today*, Vol. 39, No. 2, Summer 1987 and Vol. 39, No. 3, Autumn 1987.

Huang Po. (1958) *The Zen Teaching of Huang Po.* NY: Grove Press, Inc.

Izutsu, Toshihiko. (1982) *Toward a Philosophy of Zen Buddhism.* Boulder, CO: Prajna Press.

John, Helen James. (1966) *The Thomist Spectrum.* NY: Fordham University Press.

John of the Cross, St. (1958) *Ascent of Mount Carmel.* Translated and edited by E. Allison Peers. Garden City, NY: Image Books.

Johnston, William. (1970) *The Still Point. Reflections on Zen and Christian Mysticism.* NY: Fordham University Press.

_____ (1981) *Christian Zen: A Way of Meditation.* NY: Harper Row.

Kadowaki, Kakichi. (1966) "Ways of Knowing: A Buddhist-Thomist Dialogue" in *International Philosophical Quarterly*, Vol. VI, No. 4, Dec. 1966.

_____ (1980) *Zen and the Bible.* NY: Routledge & Kegan.

Kalinowski, Jerzy and Stefan Swiezawski. (1965) *La philosophie à l'heure du Concile*. Paris: Société d'Editions Internationales.
Kapleau, Philip. (1965) *The Three Pillars of Zen*. Boston: Beacon Press.
Kernan, Julie. (1975) *Our Friend, Jacques Maritain*. Garden City, NY: Doubleday & Co.
Kishi, Rev. Augustin Hideshi. (1966) *Spiritual Consciousness in Zen from a Thomistic Theological Point of View*. Nishinomiya-shi, Japan: Catholic Bishop's House of Osaka.
Kobori, Sohaku Nanrei. (1982) "A Dialogue" in *The Buddha Eye*, edited by Frederick Franck. NY: Crossroad.
Lassalle, H.M. Enomiya. (1974) *Zen Meditation for Christians*. LaSalle, IL: Open Court.
Maritain, Jacques. (1922) "La Science Moderne et la Raison" in *Antimoderne* by Jacques Maritain. Paris: Editions de la revue des jeunes.
_____(1930) *An Introduction to Philosophy*. NY: Sheed & Ward, Inc.
_____(1948) *Existence and the Existent*. Garden City, NY: Image Books.
_____(1952) "A New Approach to God" in *The Range of Reason* by Jacques Maritain. NY: Charles Scribner's Sons.
_____(1952) "On Knowledge Through Connaturality" in *The Range of Reason* by Jacques Maritain. NY: Charles Scribner's Sons.
_____(1955) *Bergsonian Philosophy and Thomism*. NY: New York Philosophical Library.
_____(1955) *An Essay in Christian Philosophy*. NY: New York Philosophical Library.
_____(1956) "L'expérience mystique naturelle et le vide" in *Quatre essais sur l'esprit*. Paris; Desclée de Brouwer. English translation (1980) "The Natural Mystical Experience and the Void" in *Understanding Mysticism*, edited by Richard Woods. Garden City, NY: Image Books.
_____(1959) *The Degrees of Knowledge*. NY: Charles Scribner's Sons.
_____(1962) *A Preface to Metaphysics*. NY: Mentor Omega Books.
_____(1964) *Moral Philosophy*. NY: Charles Scribner's Sons.
_____(1968) *The Peasant of the Garonne*. NY: Holt, Rinehart and Winston.

_____(1973) "L'aséité divine" in *Approches Sans Entraves*. Paris: Fayard.
_____(1973) "Lettre sur la philosophie a l'heure du concile" in *Approches Sans Entraves*. Paris: Fayard.
_____(1973) "Pas de savoir sans intuitivité" in *Approches Sans Entraves*. Paris: Fayard.
_____(1973) "Réflexions sur la nature blessée" in *Approches Sans Entraves*. Paris: Fayard.
_____(1984) *Notebooks*. Albany, NY: Magi Books, Inc.
Maritain, Raissa. (1961) *Adventures in Grace*. Garden City, NY: Image Books.
_____(1961) *We Have Been Friends Together*. Garden City, NY: Image Books.
McCool, Gerald A. (1979) *Catholic Theology in the Nineteenth Century*. NY: Seabury.
de Mello, Anthony. (1978) *Sadhana: A Way to God*. St. Louis, MO: The Institute of Jesuit Sources.
Merton, Thomas. (1968) *Zen and the Birds of Appetite*. NDP.
Miethe and Bourke. (1980) *Thomistic Bibliography*. Westport, CT: Greenwood Press.
Nishitani, Keiji. (1982) *Religion and Nothingness*. Berkeley, CA: University of California Press.
O'Hanlon, Daniel. (1978) "Zen and the Spiritual Exercises: A Dialogue Between Faiths" in *Theological Studies*, Vol. 39, No. 4, Dec. 1978.
Phelan, Gerald B. (1957) "The Being of Creatures" in *Proceedings of the American Catholic Philosophical Association*.
Raeymaeker, Louis De. (1954) *Philosophy of Being*. NY: Herder.
Sekida, Katsuki. (1977) *Zen Training*. NY: Weatherhill.
Senko, W. (1961) "Un traité inconnu "De esse et essentia"" in *Archives d'histoire doctrinale et litteraire du moyen âge*, 27. Paris: Libraire Philosophique J. Vrin.
Shizuteru, Ueda. (1982) ""Nothingness" in Meister Eckhart and Zen Buddhism" in *The Buddha Eye*, edited by Frederick Franck. NY: Crossroad.
Spae, Joseph J. (1980) *Buddhist-Christian Empathy*. Chicago: The Chicago Institute of Theology and Culture.

Suzuki, Daisetz Teitaro. (1959) *An Introduction to Zen Buddhism*. London: Arrow Books Ltd.

_____(1971) *Zen and Japanese Culture*. Princeton, NJ: Princeton University Press.

_____(1982) "The Buddhist Conception of Reality" in *The Buddha Eye*, edited by Frederick Franck. NY: Crossroad.

_____(1982) "Self the Unattainable" in *The Buddha Eye*, edited by Frederick Franck. NY: Crossroad.

_____(1982) "What Is the "I"?" in *The Buddha Eye*, edited by Frederick Franck. NY: Crossroad.

Waidenfels, Hans. (1980) *Absolute Nothingness*. Nanzan Studies in Religion and Culture.

Yamaguchi, Minoru. (1969) *The Intuition of Zen and Bergson*. Herder Agency. Enderle Bookstore.

Index

Abe, Masao 289
Aquinas, Thomas 255, 258, 261, 267-8, 272, 275, 277, 280-2, 284-6, 289-90, 299-300, 305-7, 311, 316, 318, 320-2, 337-8
Aristotle 286, 300
Augustine 311

Bergson, Henri 260-1, 263, 273, 278, 280, 289
Bergsonian Philosophy and Thomism 289
Bloy, Leon 260

Chao Chou (Joshu) 302
Cloud of Unknowing 331

Degrees of Knowledge, The 261, 320
Descartes 319
Dogen 311
Dumoulin, Heinrich 334

Eckhart, Meister 326, 331
Exodus 277

Fabro, C. 259
Falconi, Juan 331
de Finance, J. 259
Gardiel, Ambrose 293
Gilson, E. 259

Hakuin 311
Heidegger 263, 312
Huang Po 311, 337

Izutsu, Toshihiko 289, 299-307, 318
John of the Cross 255, 306, 321, 325-7, 335
John of St. Thomas 295, 311
Johnston, William 334
Joshu (Chao Chou) 312

Lassalle, H.M. Enomiya 334

Marcel, Gabriel 263
Maritain, Jacques 255, 258-9, 261-4, 267-8, 270-4, 277-82, 285-6, 288-91, 293, 295, 299-307, 309, 314, 316-9, 322, 336
Maritain, Raissa Oumansoff 259-60, 264, 278-9, 281
Merton, Thomas 334
"Modern Science and Reason" 289
Molinos, Miguel 3
Mu Mon Kan 302

"Natural Mysical Experience and the Void" 293
Nishitani, K. 285-7, 289
"No Knowledge Without Intuition" 289

"On Being and Essence" 277
Oumansoff, Vera 261

Plato 258
Poe, Edgar Allan 262

"Reflections on Wounded Nature" 277
Richter, Jean 264

Rojas, Antonio 331
Ryokan 310

St. John of the Cross and Dr. C.G. Jung 327
Sekida, K. 285, 287-9, 293, 312
Summa Theologicae 261, 268, 277-8
Suzuki, D.T. 296, 309, 311, 326

Teresa of Avila, St. 321, 327-8
Thomas of Jesus 331
Toward a Philosophy of Zen Buddhism 299

Wan Ling Record 337
The Woman Who Was Poor 260

Zen Training 287

INNER GROWTH BOOKS AND VIDEOS
See our complete catalog at www.innerexplorations.com

Inner Growth Books & Videos, LLC is dedicated to exploring the life-giving wisdom to be found in Christian mysticism and metaphysics, Eastern religions, Jungian psychology, and a new sense of the earth, and to bringing these areas into fruitful dialogue with each other. Every item in the catalog was created to give you the opportunity to meet experts in these fields, as well as pioneers in the dialogue between them.

Inner Explorations is an extensive web site which includes many discussion areas on the main subject areas in this catalog, **The Christian Prayer and Contemplation Forum**, photo galleries, audio and video clips and this whole catalog online. Visit us at: www.innerexplorations.com.

From St. John of the Cross to Us: The Story of a 400 Year Long Misunderstanding and what it means for the Future of Christian Mysticism by James Arraj. 272 pages, trade paperback, extensive bibliography, index, $18.00. ISBN 0-914073-10-9.

The Western Christian mystical tradition, so beautifully renewed by Teresa of Avila and John of the Cross 400 years ago, soon fell into crisis and a long, dark night from which it is still trying to recover. This is the story of that crisis which centered on a misunderstanding of the writings of John of the Cross, which has persisted until today and how it has shaped our understanding of Christian mysticism.

Meet the men and women, some famous, but most forgotten, who have shaped Christian mysticism as we know it today: Tomás de Jesús, a Carmelite prodigy of the early 17th century who almost single-handedly altered the course of Western mysticism, Antonio de Alvarado, Francisco Quiroga, Juan Breton, Miguel de Molinos, reviled as the chief of the Quietists, Augustín-François Poulain, Juan Arintero and many others, down to Thomas Merton, Ruth Burrows and Thomas Keating.

Mysticism, Metaphysics and Maritain: On the Road to the Spiritual Unconscious. By James Arraj. 182pp. $12. A vigorous and lucid look at the heart of the metaphysical and mystical thought of Jacques Maritain, one of the most creative and exciting Thomists to appear in the 700 years since the death of Thomas Aquinas. It examines in depth three kinds of contemplation: philosophical contemplation by which we are led from the very ontological structure of creatures to the abyss beyond all concepts where God dwells; supernatural contemplation, a knowledge that comes through love which is a taste of union with God; and mysticism of the Self, which Maritain felt could help Christianity understand Eastern mysticism. And it explores for the first time how Maritain discovered what he calls the spiritual unconscious, the very matrix in the depth of the human spirit where these contemplations dwell and interact.

Reviews: "**Mysticism, Metaphysics and Maritain** is a major contribution to Maritain scholarship... It offers a penetrating examination of the mystical experience, both natural and supernatural, not to mention a brilliant and original discussion of Maritain's thought on mysticism and contemplation. This is a "must-have" book for Maritain scholars and those interested in contemplative spirituality." *American Catholic Philosophical Quarterly*

The Inner Nature of Faith: A Mysterious Knowledge Coming Through the Heart. By James Arraj. 144pp, paper, $10. Faith is a highly distinctive kind of knowledge, a knowledge that works through love, through the heart, and because we misunderstand the nature of this knowledge we resist it, or fail to respond fully to its mysterious call.

Part I is a reflection on how I first heard this call of faith coming through an experience of human love, and struggled to respond to it and understand it.

Part II describes three ways in which this knowledge is in the process of being rediscovered in the 20th century: the debates of the theologians on the nature of faith, wisdom and gnosis in the Scriptures and Fathers, and Jacques Maritain on knowledge through connaturality.

Part III is an attempt to understand the inner nature of faith, after the pattern of human love.

Reviews: "The author narrates in a very simple way his own road to faith (part 1). He then cites Scripture, the Fathers, St. Thomas and some thinkers of our century, in order to highlight some of the more important points of the relationship between faith, love and knowledge (part 2). Lastly (part 3) he shares his own reflections, using a philosophy and theology of encounter." *Revista de Espiritualidad*

Five Profiles in Buddhist-Christian Dialogue: Buddhists and Christians around the world have entered into dialogue, and as this dialogue has deepened some of them have taken it within themselves. They have not only studied the beliefs of their dialogue partners, but have gone on voyages of discovery that embrace both Buddhist and Christian spiritual practices. In this series of profiles we are going to meet some of these inner explorers, hear their stories, and try to catch a glimpse of how they are bringing these spiritual practices into harmony within themselves.

1. Roger Corless. 47 Minute VHS Video, $15. Audiotape from video, $6.

In this video we visit Roger Corless who is both personally and professionally committed to Buddhism and Christianity. Professionally, he has academic degrees in Theology (B.D., King's College, University of London, 1961) and Buddhist Studies (Ph.D., University of Wisconsin at Madison, 1973). Personally, he has received baptism and confirmation as a Roman Catholic and is an Oblate of St. Benedict, and he has taken refuge in the Gelugpa tradition of Tibetan Buddhism. He attempts to live as a participant-observer in both traditions and to speak and write out of that experience.

2. Ruben Habito 54 Minute VHS Video, $15. Ruben Habito, a native of the Philippines, was one of the first Catholics to have kensho confirmed by a Japanese master, and he went on to complete koan training under Koun Yamada. He holds a doctorate in Buddhist philosophy from Tokyo University, teaches at

Southern Methodist University, directs the Maria Kannon Zen Center in Dallas, and is the author of *Total Liberation: Zen Spirituality and the Social Dimension*, and *Healing Breath: Zen Spirituality for a Wounded Earth*. Here he discusses his own Zen training and some of the questions at the heart of the Zen-Christian dialogue.

3. Thomas Hand, S.J. 34 Minute VHS Video, $15. Thomas Hand, S.J., spent 29 years in Japan and was one of the first Western Catholic religious to practice Zen meditation under the direction of Koun Yamada Roshi of the Sanbo Kyodon. He currently teaches Christian and Buddhist meditation at Mercy Center in Burlingame, CA. He is the author, together with Chwen Jiuan A. Lee, of *A Taste of Water: Christianity Through Taoist-Buddhist Eyes*. Here he talks about the origins of Zen-Christian dialogue in Japan and the impact it could have on Christianity.

4. Robert Jonas. 46 Minute VHS Video, $15. Audiotape from video, $6. In this video we visit Robert A. Jonas, who is a Christian in the Carmelite tradition and has received spiritual formation in Buddhist traditions. Currently a student of Sui-Zen, the Japanese bamboo flute, he is an active member of the Society for Buddhist-Christian Studies, a founding member of the Ruah Institute in Boston, and founder and director of The Empty Bell. He is the author of *Rebecca: A Father's Journey from Grief to Gratitude*. This video is the fascinating story of his own spiritual journey, and the insights he has gleaned from his encounter with both sides of the dialogue. It also includes a few minutes of Jonas playing the flute.

5. Donald Mitchell. 30 Minute VHS Video, $15. Audiotape from video, $6. In this video we visit Donald W. Mitchell, who is Professor of Comparative Philosophy of Religion at Purdue University. Originally raised as a Christian, he took up the practice of Zen Buddhism as a young man, and then returned to Christianity. This spiritual journey led him to become engaged in the Buddhist-Christian dialogue in the United States, Europe and Asia. He is married with four children, and is the author of *Spirituality and Emptiness: The Dynamics of Spiritual Life in Buddhism and Christianity*.

This video is the fascinating story of his spiritual journey, and the trials and joys he has experienced from his encounter with both sides of the dialogue.

David Loy: Zen Philosopher and Social Critic. 54 Minute VHS Video, $20. Audiotape from video, $6. A fascinating visit with David Loy in which he describes his own Zen journey that went from meditating in the beautiful and secluded valleys of Molokai in Hawaii to finishing Zen koan training with Koun Yamada Roshi in Kamakura, Japan. Intertwined with the story of David's growth as a philosopher conversant with both Buddhist and contemporary Western philosophy, and his incisive social criticisms in which he applies Buddhist insights to the ills of our modern world.

Questions at the Heart of the Buddhist-Christian Dialogue: A Dialogue Between David Loy and James Arraj. 83 minute VHS video, $20. Audiotape,

$6. The Buddhist-Christian dialogue may be the most wide-spread and intensive interreligious dialouge in the world today. But is it leading to any clear understanding of how these two great religious traditions relate at the deepest levels? Are they essentially the same? That seems presumptuous given their cultural, theological and mystical differences. Are they, then, quite different? That doesn't seem quite right, either. Those who practice both, or go from one to another, sense a deep relationship which has been difficult to articulate. In pursuit of this difficult goal David Loy, who teaches on the faculty of international studies at Bunkyo University, Chigasaki, Japan, and James Arraj, who is the director of Inner Explorations, both give short presentations, and then engage in dialogue with each other, a dialogue which is later opened to the audience.

Blossoms of Silence: A Visit with Jim Grob - Video. 66 Minute VHS Video, $20. Audiotape from video, $6. East meets West in the inner adventures of Jim Grob. Years of formal discursive Christian meditation had led him to an apparent dead-end in the life of prayer. Then much later he discovered the interior silence that is at the heart of Zen. Silent sitting led to a series of numinous dreams, awakening experiences, Christian contemplative experiences, and finally an understanding of the necessity of going by faith.

Here is one of the clearest explanations of the relationship of Zen enlightenment to Christian mystical experiences from a practitioner of both paths. Format: Straight interview punctuated by Jim Grob reading his haiku, which are like Blossoms of Silence.

Buddhist Dialogue in Action: Boston, 1992. 100 Minute VHS Video, $20. Audiotape from video, $6. Highlights of the Working Group "Zen Awakening and Christian Contemplation: Practice in Both Traditions" held at the 4th International Buddhist-Christian Dialogue Conference, Boston University July 30 - Aug. 3, 1992.

Buddhist-Christian Dialogue in Action: Chicago, 1996. 60 Minute VHS Video, $20. Audiotape from video, $6. Highlights from the Working Group "Practice Across Traditions" held at the 5th International Buddhist-Christian Dialogue Conference in Chicago July 28-Aug. 3, 1996.

Buddhist-Christian Dialogue in Action: Tacoma, WA 2000 3 1/2 hour VHS Video, $30. Audiotape, $12. Highlights from the Working Group "The Interior Dialogue" held at the 7th International Buddhist-Christian Dialogue Conference in Tacoma, Washington, August 6-11, 2000.

As the Buddhist-Christian dialogue spreads around the world, it is taking on a new intensity. Not only are many Christians practicing Buddhist forms of meditation, but some Western Buddhists are expressing a new interest in their Christian roots. At the International Conference of the Society for Buddhist-Christian Studies held in Tacoma, Washington in the summer of 2000, some of these Christians and Buddhists met as a working group on interior dialogue to share their own inner journeys. Included are presentations by Susan Postal, Ruben Habito, Mitra Bishop, Robert Jonas, Jane Shuman, Maria Reis Habito,

James Stewart, Myo Lahey, Ed Shirley, James Arraj and Tyra Arraj, and some responses.

Exploring the Christian-Hindu Dialogue: A Visit with Bede Griffiths and Russill Paul. 55 Minute VHS Video, $20. Audiotape from video, $6.
Bede Griffiths was a Benedictine monk, a pioneer of the Christian-Hindu dialogue, and the head of Shantivanam, a Christian ashram in India. Here he discusses his life in India, his attempts to enrich the Christian contemplative path through Hindu mysticism, and his hope for the formation of small lay contemplative communities in the West.

Russill Paul is a friend and disciple of Bede Griffiths, and is a professional musician. Born in the Anglo-Indian community of Madras in southern India, he has spent years living at Shantivanam. He is creating a new form of music whose goal is to aid the contemplative life. He is also exploring the possibility of creating lay contemplative communities in the United States. He briefly describes his life and work, and plays an example of his new form of music. Format: straight interviews with a musical selection by Russill Paul.

The Heart of the Christian-Hindu Dialogue: A Conversation with Wayne Teasdale. Wayne Teasdale is a Christian sannyasi, that is, someone who follows both the Christian and Hindu contemplative paths. He was a friend and disciple of the Benedictine monk Bede Griffiths who headed Shantivanam, a Christian-Hindu ashram in India. This wide-ranging interview, taped at Hundred Acres Monastery in New Hampshire, describes the history of the Christian-Hindu dialogue in India, the work of Bede Griffiths, and tackles the difficult question of the relationship between Hindu and Christian mystical experience. Format: straight interview with several insertions of photographs taken at Shantivanam. Reviews: "For those interested in the ground-breaking work of Bede Griffiths in India this is a very useful tape... and it would provide some helpful background material for discussion or reflection on the relationship between Hindu and Christian mystical experience." *Monos*

Christian Prayer and Kundalini:.A Visit with Philip St. Romain. 90 Minute VHS Video, $20. Audiotape from video, $6. After years devoted to the Christian life of prayer Philip St. Romain experienced an unanticipated awakening of an energy that in ancient India was called Kundalini or serpent power, and which played an important role in Hindu mystical experience. He unwittingly became a laboratory in which Christian spirituality meets the wisdom of the East. This is a detailed account of both his Christian life and his Kundalini awakening.

At the time of this interview Philip was the associate director for lay leadership and development at the Spiritual Life Center, Wichita, Kansas where he helped direct a wide variety of programs, as well as gave retreats and workshops. Format: Straight interview with some introductory shots of Philip at home, and later at the Spiritual Life Center.

ORDER FORM

For our catalog online go to www.innerexplorations.com

Name: _____

Organization: _____

Address: _____

City/State/Zip: _____

Title	Price	Qty.	Total
_____	___	___	___
_____	___	___	___
_____	___	___	___
_____	___	___	___
_____	___	___	___
_____	___	___	___
_____	___	___	___
_____	___	___	___
_____	___	___	___
_____	___	___	___
_____	___	___	___
_____	___	___	___

Shipping Charges: U.S. Orders: Book Rate: $2.50 for first item, and $.50 for each additional item. First Class: $4.00 for first item, and $1.00 for each additional item. Canada and other foreign orders: Surface Book Rate: $5.00 for first item, and $2.00 for each additional item.

Subtotal: _____

Shipping: _____

Total: _____

  Here is my check payable to: Inner Growth Books and Videos, Box 520, Chiloquin, OR 97624. Tel: 541-783-3126

(Videos are in the U.S. format only.)

About the Author

James Arraj and his wife Tyra are the directors of www.innerexplorations.com, an extensive website where Christian metaphysics and mysticism meet Eastern religions, Jungian psychology, and a new sense of the earth. James has a doctorate in theology specializing in Christian spirituality from the Gregorian University in Rome.

They live deep in a forest far from paved roads and power lines near Crater Lake, Oregon. There they raised their children, built their own house, grow salads in a solar greenhouse, and create books and videos with the electricity from their solar panels.

They invite your comments about this book.
Inner Growth Books
Box 520
Chiloquin, OR 97624

E-Mail: arraj@innerexplorations.com